A VANISHED VICTORIAN

PLATE I.—LORD CLARENDON IN MIDDLE LIFE

From a portrait by J. Sant, now in the Ambassadors' waiting-room at the Foreign Office.

A VANISHED VICTORIAN

Being the Life of George Villiers
Fourth Earl of Clarendon
1800-1870

BY HIS GRANDSON
GEORGE VILLIERS

1938
EYRE & SPOTTISWOODE
LONDON

Made and Printed in Great Britain for
Eyre and Spottiswoode (Publishers), London

To
MARJORIE
with love

AUTHOR'S NOTE

M Y thanks are due to His Majesty the King for permission to quote from the published letters and diaries of Queen Victoria and from unpublished letters to my grandfather; to the present Earl of Clarendon for placing the Clarendon papers and other matter unreservedly at my disposal; to Lord Newton for kindly allowing me to quote from his Life of Lord Lyons; to the Dowager Countess of Airlie for permission to quote from her books, *In Whig Society* and *Lady Palmerston and Her Times*; to Lord Mount Temple for permission to quote from letters of Lord Palmerston; and to Lord Verulam for access to the diaries and papers of the first Earl of Verulam. I have also to thank H.M. Foreign Office, and Office of Works, for permission to reproduce the portrait and the statue of my grandfather, both now at the Foreign Office.

I, of course, owe a great debt to the late Sir Herbert Maxwell, who cleared a path for any future biographers of Lord Clarendon. I have also made use of papers at the Public Record Office and at the British Museum.

GEORGE VILLIERS.

1938.

vii

CONTENTS

LIST OF ILLUSTRATIONS

A VANISHED VICTORIAN

CHAPTER I

EARLY YEARS, 1800-1823

§ 1

TO have been three times Foreign Secretary, to have handled several major crises in Europe with honour and distinction, to have served in the Cabinets of Russell, Palmerston and Gladstone, and to have been universally considered by contemporaries as almost above party in sincerity and integrity of political purpose—such qualifications, one would think, might fit a man for survival. And yet no statesman of the nineteenth century has so completely vanished from the body of contemporary recollection as the fourth Earl of Clarendon, of whom all this is true.

We know from contemporary accounts, from the letters and diaries of the time, that, apart from his political capacities and his high position in the Councils of the nation, he was, socially, one of the most charming and delightful of men. From these accounts, indeed, he emerges at times, a brilliant, an equivocal, a slightly mocking figure, moving as if by instinct in the heart of affairs, but in some undefined way, holding himself aloof from them, never quite descending into the arena of politics and of life. It is, perhaps, by reason of this detachment that his personality has more completely eluded the memory of posterity than that of many men far less able than himself. Certain it is that in the years that have elapsed since his death in 1870, the picture of him has lost outline, gradually, inevitably, until to-day it is enshrined only in the minds of very old persons who either remember the stir which his death made or who remember their parents discussing his merits in the old drawing-rooms of London sixty years ago.

Politically, there is also a reason for this extinction of fame. For in politics Clarendon was a specialist if ever there was one. Foreign Affairs were his province; and after his first apprenticeship in the Cabinets of Melbourne and Russell, he hardly ever accepted office which did not entail the conduct of our foreign relations. Domestic politics interested him not at all; and though he was a good Whig, the manœuvres of the party game, as such, were distasteful to him. And so, though his presence was a factor in nearly all the Whig Cabinets from 1839 to 1870, he was never to be seen by the fierce light which beat upon the problems of home politics, but withdrawn, rather, into the shadows which for most Englishmen (until the War) enshrouded the horizons of Foreign Affairs.

"Clarendon"—the very name has ceased to evoke to-day the features that smiled at our grandfathers from the pages of the *Illustrated London News* or the cartoons of *Punch*. To most of us, rather, it calls up the image of his ancestor, the Chancellor of Charles II's reign, Edward Hyde, Earl of Clarendon, statesman, legalist, and historian of the "Great Rebellion." And yet the Clarendon of the nineteenth century was a familiar enough figure in his time. As he threaded his way down Whitehall in the fifties of the last century, a tall, spare, aristocratic-looking man in a tight-fitting frock-coat and black stock, his greying hair and whiskers, curling out from beneath the flat-brimmed chimney-pot hat of the period, many would be the greetings that would cheer him on his way; many would be the nudges of passers-by as they recognised the well-known figure in public life.

Sometimes, but not often, for Palmerston had lectured him on not taking enough exercise, he would be seen in his carriage; and then the handsome pair would turn into Downing Street, and the coachman would salute with his whip as his master strode up the steps of the old Foreign Office and was lost to view in its labyrinthine interior. For this was Lord Clarendon, Secretary of State, in whose efficient hands the tangled threads of our foreign relations had rested for some years past. And the English world was proud of him, content to think that the English destiny was in his keeping. For his suave and capable handling of difficult foreign situations had already, more than once, saved the country from war, and his delicate touch on affairs was universally considered the chief factor for peace in the Europe of those days. Nor were the critics unmindful of his benign influence in regions nearer home; for it was said that Lord Clarendon insinuated the arts of diplomacy into the assemblies at No. 10, and on many occasions, it was whispered, the angry dissents of Ministers had been smoothed over and their rancour finally subdued by the graceful intervention of the Secretary of State. Charming, ubiquitous, gay, always there, always ready with a happy phrase, a pacific gesture, he was an essential figure in every Whig Government, and the nation had come to depend upon his presence. Such was Lord Clarendon, in middle life, Minister of Foreign Affairs, a man universally known, respected and liked.

If his name was one of honour to his English contemporaries, it was a "name of fear" in some parts of Europe. Indeed, Bismarck often stated that Clarendon alone could have prevented the Franco-Prussian War; and what the German statesman said was hardly exaggerated, for in his old age the British Foreign

Secretary saw what was coming, and the last years of his life were
devoted to a sustained attempt to avert the disaster of a breach
between Germany and France. From his early youth foreign
relations had fascinated him, and the shadow of things to come
had been apparent to him. When he was hardly more than a
boy, happening to be in Paris at the time when the Belgian kingdom was being formed, he prophesied a possible war that might
some day arise in Europe as an outcome of the circumstance.
" And what a war that will be, whenever it takes place," he
writes to his mother, " a war that will only end in the triumph of
the monarchical or democratic principle in Europe. And if the
means of resistance both possess be considered, who can predict
what the duration of such a conflict would be, and who would not
make any sacrifice to avert it?" Eighty-two years afterwards, in
the thunder of the guns at Mons, his prophecy was fulfilled.

Partly on account of this prescience, this positive genius for
realising what would probably result from given circumstances,
Clarendon was by middle life the " doyen," if not in years, at
least in spirit, of the Foreign Secretaries of Europe. " Send me
Clarendon," cried Napoleon III when a matter of great delicacy
was at stake between France and England. " Send me Clarendon," he cried; " we understand him and can do business with
him." " Send Clarendon," echoed Victoria when there was a
question of the Emperor's assuming, on his own authority, the
supreme command of the troops in the Crimea and someone had
politely to disabuse him of the feasibility of the scheme. " Send
Clarendon," said the Cabinet when, the war over, the business
of peace-making began. It was always the same cry. Whenever there was anything delicate or difficult to do or to say,
everyone's mind reverted naturally to Lord Clarendon. He
would know just how to say or to do it.

" It often happens," wrote the late Lord Rosebery, referring
to quite another politician, though his words are singularly
applicable to Clarendon, " that there is a member of a Government, who is no orator, who passes no great measures . . . and
yet, perhaps, his colleagues regard him as invaluable. He is
probably the peace-maker, the man who walks about dropping
oil into the machinery and preventing injurious friction."

And so we see the subject of this memoir as he passes across
the stage of nearly forty years of public life; at hand when
wanted, retiring gracefully and thankfully when he was not;
politically unambitious, standing a little apart, avoiding the lime-
light, yet accepting the highest responsibility when called upon
to do so; an elusive, intriguing and delightful figure.

The object of this book is to bring that figure to life: to re-
construct the man as he was, with his faults and his virtues, his

talents and his limitations: to place him again in the times in
which he lived and among the people with whom he consorted.
The late Sir Herbert Maxwell has written his authoritative biography.   In it he has entered very fully and ably into the
politics of the time.   But—perhaps for this very reason—the
picture of the man himself has suffered somewhat.   My aim is to
portray Lord Clarendon, not only as a statesman, but as a
human being and family man as well.   If politics obtrude they
do so only because Clarendon was so inseparably bound up with
the conduct of affairs that no account of his life would be possible
without some description of this, the element in which circumstances decreed that he should chiefly live and move and have
his being.   But here again it is no part of my task to revive and
discuss the political questions of the past in and for themselves,
but only in so far as they exhibit the personality of the men
who shaped them.   Cabinet Councils, Ministerial dissensions, the
vote on this, the vote on that—these may be dull enough
things *per se*.   But in so far as they show the interplay of
character between such men as Russell and Palmerston, as
Gladstone, and Clarendon and Lowe, they become alive and
electrical, exhibiting strange overtones of relevance and interest
far beyond themselves.   And for this they may be pardoned for
raising their heads into this narrative.

With the march of time political elements, even in England,
change their aspect.   But there is one phenomenon in English
public life which has resisted all change, being the very stuff out
of which all governance in this country arose in the past, namely,
the man of position, the aristocrat, whose birth-right is a life
naturally devoted to the service of the state.   Clarendon was born
to this destiny.   It is the key to his character and his life.

And now we must delay no longer; but set the piece and ring
in the players.

§ 2

George William Frederick Villiers, who was to succeed his
uncle as fourth Earl of Clarendon, was born a fortnight from
the eighteenth century; came into life in the same world as the
younger Pitt, as Charles James Fox and Richard Brindsley
Sheridan.   He was five years old when the coaches swung through
the land decorated for the victory of Trafalgar, and a boy of
fifteen when Waterloo put an end to the domination of Napoleon.
He grew to be a young man in Regency days; knew Lady
Holland; and first entered the Cabinet when Lord Melbourne
was Prime Minister.   He was acquainted with the London of
George III and lived to see Paris glittering under the Second
Empire.   He witnessed the rise of Disraeli, and died in office

serving Gladstone. He was, by birth, a scion of that younger branch of the old Villiers house, which his grandfather, Thomas Villiers, had raised to distinction by a remarkably successful diplomatic career abroad. This Thomas Villiers was a man of no mean parts. The second son of the second Earl of Jersey, he was not content to accept the portion of a younger son and to live and die in reflected glory of the family peerage. Independently minded, he travelled abroad, and was employed by the Government of his day as Ambassador successively in Dresden, Poland, Vienna and Berlin. So well did he do in these posts that the favourable eye of authority was drawn upon him and in 1756 he was offered a Barony. This he accepted and became Baron Hyde of Hindon (in Wiltshire). But twenty years later, after his term as Ambassador in Berlin, where he completely won the confidence and friendship of Frederick the Great (to the no little advantage of Great Britain), he was raised to the status of an Earl. Now he had married in 1752 the lady upon whom all the honours and most of the possessions of the Hyde family had devolved, and Villiers' choice of the title, Baron Hyde of Hindon, was a graceful compliment to his wife's maternal forbears, and an attempt on his part to resuscitate an honoured historical name which otherwise might have suffered extinction. For Lady Charlotte Capel was, through her mother, a Hyde, the descendant—the eldest surviving descendant—of that Edward Hyde, Earl of Clarendon, whom we have already mentioned, the "Chancellor" of Charles II's reign. Upon her grandfather's death, the line of Earls, founded by the old statesman three generations before, died out. So when Thomas Villiers was offered a further step in the peerage, he not unnaturally decided to sue for the recreation of the Earldom of Clarendon. If the accident of sex debarred his wife from being Earl of Clarendon in her own right, she should at least become Countess of Clarendon in his. And so it came about that a younger son of an Earl of Jersey—a Villiers—married a Hyde heiress: became, first, Baron Hyde of Hindon, and, finally, in 1776, 1st Earl of Clarendon of the second creation.

His wife brought Villiers land, pictures, plate, possessions of all kinds, including Kenilworth, that dream-like shell of Tudor beauty that stands near the town of Warwick. But Kenilworth was no longer habitable; and shortly before retiring from diplomacy Thomas Villiers, now a man of substance and position, looked round for a home for himself and his growing family. The Grove, near Watford, in Hertfordshire, seemed to offer most of what he required, and he purchased it from the impoverished heirs of the Earl of Doneraile.

Four generations of Villiers, as it proved, were to know and

love this place as their home. It is a delightful, but rather un-
characteristic, eighteenth-century building in sober red brick,
discreet but spacious, and mercifully lacking the inevitable
classic colonnade and pediment of the period. It stands in a
large, quiet, deer-haunted park of undulating grass merging in
woodland. In it were gathered together the bulk of the old Chancellor's possessions, his Van Dykes, his Cornelius Jensens, the
golden key of Hyde Park, the famous portrait of himself by
Sir Peter Lely. Here, amid these Stuart associations, the
Clarendons settled; and here their three boys—Thomas, John
Charles and George—grew to be men. The old Earl died in
1786, and was succeeded by Thomas, who died in 1824, unmarried. He, in turn, was succeeded by his brother, John
Charles, as third Earl. These two were the uncles of George
William Frederick; but we must leave them to be introduced, as
their avuncular rôles impinge upon his life, and turn for a
moment to the youngest of the three brothers, who was his father.

§ 3

The Hon. George Villiers is a somewhat pathetic figure.
Nothing, from the start, ever went quite right with him. The
accident of his birth precluded him from any likely share in the
family honours, for though Thomas was unmarried, John Charles
was married to the daughter of a certain Admiral Sir John
Forbes, a lady of clinging constancy, concerning the integrity of
whose wits there were grave doubts. She had, however, produced a daughter (Harriet), and might very well produce a son.
There was little likelihood, therefore, of George himself succeeding to the title, though his son might. With no talent or liking
for politics, and no desire for a military, diplomatic or ecclesiastical career, there seemed little for him to do save accept the
portion of a younger son and make the best of it. This, indeed,
he proceeded to do, acquiring land from his brother in Hertfordshire and settling down to farm on a large scale. But, except
for one reference to his " four hundred acres of hay," we hear
little of the success of his farming; and as, even early on, he was
perpetually in the state of moving from one house to another—
and generally to a smaller one—one can but surmise that land
for him was not an altogether profitable business. Moreover, in
his youth, he had acquired an unfortunate passion for the Turf
—a taste he shared with his brother John—and his frequent in-
cursions into the racing world at Newmarket were perhaps the
least profitable of his occupations. However, nothing daunted
by ill luck, he persevered and somehow managed not only to
watch other people's horses running, but to maintain a discreet

racing-stable of his own, and sport his own colours upon the
Turf. Of course, it must be remembered that there were ways
of supplementing one's income in those days. For instance, in
1798 he accepted the office of Deputy Paymaster of the Marines
under the Board of Admiralty, one of those pleasant little scraps
that privilege could always let fall from the rich banquet of
State. That year, too, he married the Hon. Theresa Parker,
daughter of the first Lord Boringdon. This was, perhaps, the
only really clever thing he ever did in life; for Theresa Parker,
" Mrs. George," as she immediately became to everyone, was a
remarkable woman.

With principles firmly rooted in the values of this world, she
possessed an unbounded vitality, coupled with an interest in
human affairs that was really surprising. With no looks to
speak of, and only the kind of charm that comes from complete
naïveté, she managed to laugh herself into the good graces of the
highest and most influential in the land, while her sound worldly
common sense turned every such contact to the highest advantage.
Not that she was discreet. Far from it. Imbued with warm
affections, a quick temper, and the habit of saying (and writing)
the first thing that came into her head, she must often enough
have been guilty of errors of tact. But her zest for life, her irresistible gaiety, and the inconsequence of the things she said,
gradually established for her the reputation of being a " character "; and it is to be observed with " characters " that nearly
everything is forgiven them; and that they generally manage to
get what they want in a world that will pay much to be amused.
But there was also another side to her—a family side. She was
genuinely fond of her husband, and devoted to her children—
and when the latter began to grow up there is no doubt that she
made for them a most affectionate and delightful home atmosphere, for, with all her worldliness (which was second nature to
her), she was at heart both simple and sincere. To her indolent
husband she was invaluable. Around him she created at all
seasons the stir and bustle of life, and when times were bad
she certainly seemed able to galvanise him into some show of
activity, and to coerce him into accepting positions which his
natural diffidence would otherwise have caused him to refuse.

We have in our possession two " pendant " prints of the Hon.
George Villiers and of his wife, the inimitable " Mrs. George."
And a perusal of them tells us much. He is shown as elegantly
dressed in the fashion of the day. A double-breasted tail coat
with wide lapels and gilt buttons is cut away to reveal a pair of
immaculately white nankin breeches. Below these again are
shapely Hessian riding boots with funny little gold tassels de-
pending from their tops. His head is uncovered, but he wears

the becoming grey periwig of the day, fastened at the shoulder with a broad black ribbon. Beneath a high sloping forehead, two brave but disillusioned eyes gaze out upon a world that, one feels, might have treated him better.

His bearing is proud and confident, his regard tentative. So he "stands for his portrait," a dignified, convincing enough figure, making a gallant show for the sake of posterity. But the truth was far different. For, despite the many sinecures that Mrs. George was able to procure for him, misfortune dogged his footsteps from the first and his life was a ceaseless struggle against adverse financial circumstances. With age came gout and ill-temper; and as his family grew up around him, he fell at last into the category of those who have to be humoured and teased and dealt with, but who are of no account in themselves as far as the values of this world are concerned. He was a kind and affectionate father, a dutiful husband. His family loved him, cajoled him, and called him, absurdly, "the Governor"; but they laughed at him and went their own way.

The companion print reveals a young woman dressed in the high-waisted white frock of the period, which shows off to great effect the poise and grace of her figure. Round a humorous face with strongly marked features, her hair is frizzed out in a dark aureole. Behind her in the distance are shown the roofs and chimneys of a famous house where legend reports her as having spent many happy hours.

In looking at her portrait, one finds it almost impossible not to answer with a faint smile the look of gaiety widely diffused over that alert and sprightly countenance, so different from the solemn gaze of her spouse in the accompanying print.

Indeed, it would be difficult to find two persons who exhibited greater contrasts of character and outlook than did these two. For if adversity was apt to sour the nature of George Villiers, it proved rather a stimulus to his wife. And if misfortune was liable to throw the Governor back into his shell, it served only to quicken Mrs. George's interest and perceptions and add a zest to the varied spectacle of human life as she saw it around her. And not much was to escape Mrs. Villiers in the course of a very long life. Her insatiable curiosity and interest in human affairs led her to take an almost passionate interest in the lives of all with whom she was remotely connected, and her indiscreet and voluminous correspondence makes good reading to this day. People she adored; and no candle was lighted in London to which, moth-like, she didn't flutter, her feathers bobbing in the draught of hall doorways, her laugh echoing indefatigably through the saloons and ante-chambers of Mayfair. Indeed she knew everyone, and everyone knew Mrs. George. Two

Royal Dukes were said to sigh for her; and though flirtation was
not very much in her line, their attentions must have flattered
that "hierarchic" sense to which all her life she was so passionately loyal.

And how she loved to share with others the sense of her own
enjoyment! With her head full of the excitement of the evening before, she would rush to her pen and pour out on paper next
day to whichever of her children were absent the minutest description of it all.

"The Esterhazy Ball was very splendid indeed, as far as
dress, foreigners, uniforms could make it. The King, the Duke
of York, the Duke of Wellington were all in Austrian uniform,
which, to say the truth, I did not think particularly becoming
to our worthy Sovereign, or his brother, in so much as from its
plainness, it shows shape so much. When we got there, the King
had been there about a quarter of an hour. I suppose it might
have been a quarter of an hour more before we got into the room,
and another quarter of an hour before the Duchess of Glo'ster
was dispatched to go tell Lady Conyngham to go into the other
room to meet him. He went in by another door, and never re-
appeared afterwards. I never got near him, nor do I believe that
he saw me; and when I reckoned he would return to the Ball-
Room I found that he had gone. York, Clarence and Cambridge
were there, as also old Augusta, Mrs. Kent, Mrs. Clarence, and
Miss Sophia of Glo'ster. Such loads, such waggon-loads of
foreigners, and such uniforms—no never! Such quizzes! Your
sister was very 'populous.' She danced with Clanronald, a
young Prince Metternich, son to the great Metternich; also
with Mr. Locke, Lord Henry Somerset, Simon Brodie, Bob
Grosvenor, Lord Cawdor (twice); and it all did very well till the
last, when everybody was going and Princess Esterhazy asked
us to stay on, and *ordered* all the men to stay. She then proposed dancing the 'Coquette.' Theresa, who, as you know,
hates that sort of thing, rather declined till she saw who *did*
dance; and when she found every girl in the room did (Mary
Ryder, Harriet Stewart, Lady G. Fane, Miss Seymour, etc.),
of course she had nothing to do but to dance it. The Harriet
Butler began it—and such an exhibition—no, never!—such romp-
ing, such laughing, such pulling—quite beyond! Theresa danced
it—and did it to perfection—with William de Roos, which was
lucky, as he is so gentleman-like; but such a horrid romp as the
dance was, I never saw. Only fancy, the Glo'sters were not
asked. . . . You never saw such monstrous, such ridiculous
plumes as the Fitz-Clarences had; and they put on lappets to
sham having been to Court. . . .

"The other night I went to an Old Music with the Governor,

and G. Metcalfe.   No, never was I so bored in all my life—not
that the music might have disturbed me much if I could have
talked. . . .   Well, I got through the bore of the second act,
then set G. Metcalfe home, and the Governor then set me down
at Almacks. . . .   Dickey Ball was there, and I saw him dance
with one of the Lennox's, so I suppose the pursuit is not quite
hopeless yet.   He looked as pretty as ever, and his moustachios
are in good preservation. . . .   Yesterday, your father and Hyde
went to a levée, and had ' How d'you do, George,' ' How d'you
do, Sir '—*et voilà tout*. . . .   Oh, who d'you think I saw—no
never!—at the old Music . . .?''

The pen runs interminably on, and was to do so for nearly
half a century more.   The torches and candles of the Regency
were to fade into the cruder, but more respectable illumination
of the Victorian age; candelabra to give place to the gasolier,
but still Mrs. George was to be observed crowding up the stairways of the great, pursuing the human scene with inexhaustible
fervour, and a gaiety that age could not wither nor custom stale.
Her children grew up; the poor Governor, racked with gout, and
crippled with debt, was gathered at last to rest.   She mourned,
and put on her weeds: but not for long.   The world was so
alluring, and people so kind.   In a year, she was rollicking about
town in the old way, dressed in a '' blue polka, trimmed with
white swans-down.''   Middle-age descended upon her; her
health began to trouble her.   She conquered her ailments and
went valiantly on.   More and more she became absorbed in her
children's affairs, following every detail of their careers with
passionate interest.   She was to live to see her eldest son hold
the highest offices of State: to be with him in Ireland, when, as
Viceroy, he entertained his Sovereign and the Consort.   It was
à propos this visit that Clarendon wrote to Lord Grey:

'' My mother as I need not say, has been in the highest state of
excitement and delight, and is not one bit the worse for it.   At no
period of her life do I remember her more fit for frolic, or more
indifferent to fatigue.   She is a marvellous old lady, and so everyone thinks her.   The Queen was very civil to her at Carton, and
I never saw anything better than her manner . . . and she looked
so well, and was so well got up.''

Six years later—September 22nd, 1855—Lady Clarendon was
writing in her journal:

'' Dear Mrs. George is 80 to-day—a wonderful, and admirable
woman she is—such a clear intellect, such warm affections, such
untiring energy of character, every sense unimpaired.   Then her
enjoyment and zest for everything surpass almost everyone's, old
or young.''

But, alas, the store of energy is limited, and even "zest" cannot last for ever; and within four months of this entry, Mrs. George was no more. She died, rather significantly, on the birthday of the son whose career she had watched over with such care. And so the laugh that had echoed through four reigns was silent for ever. For ever?—Not quite. Nearly three-quarters of a century later, in an attic at the top of a country house, a huge old box was found. It was covered with cobwebs, and so thick with dust that the label affixed to it was quite illegible. The lock was rickety, but tenacious, and no key would engage the rusty wards. A hammer was sent for; and, on the lid being prised open, there sprang to light quarto after quarto of closely packed sheets, bundle after bundle of letters, docketed and arranged in years, hundreds of them, all in the same forcible hand, as easy to read as print. "And now, my ever dearest dears, who d'you think I saw—no, never!—at——"

Mrs. George had outwitted even Death.

§ 4

Such, then, were the parents, and such the circumstances into which young George was born on January 12th, 1800. We suspect that the house in which he was born, a house in Upper Grosvenor Street, was lent for the occasion by the child's bachelor uncle, Thomas—or even by his other uncle, John Charles, for it is certain that George Villiers was still domiciled in the country at the time, and that he was still busy with his farming ventures.

The boy was duly christened George, after his father (and the reigning monarch), and William Frederick after a minor dignitary of the House of Hanover who consented to stand sponsor to the child.

Friends and relations, a score, had driven to Hanover Square to witness the christening of this first Villiers to be born in the new century; and as the shadows deepened on that February afternoon the steps of St. George's presented a gay little scene, the bright ribbons and flounces of the women fluttering between the sombre coats and tasselled canes of the men.

A pretty sight, it must have been, with Mrs. George all feathers and laces, bearing the favoured infant in her arms, with her husband, the tall and indolent George—the Governor, as he was to be affectionately named in the family from this hour— standing beside her at the font, a little vague, a little ineffectual for all his seventy inches, eclipsed perhaps by her more abounding personality. Royalty was present in the solemn persons of Frederick, Duke of Gloucester, and his Duchess, Mary, life-long

friend and intimate of Mrs. George. As has been said, the Duke
was standing sponsor, supported by the child's uncles, Thomas,
Earl of Clarendon, a sedate bachelor nearing fifty, and John
Charles Villiers, handsome, raffish, with his lackadaisical wife
clinging to his arm. Lord Boringdon, representing the Parkers,
must have gazed with affectionate amusement at his sister, to
whose animated figure the solemnity of the occasion imposed an
unwonted restraint.

And what a party afterwards in Upper Grosvenor Street, with
Frederick's loud Hanoverian laugh echoing through the dining-
room; the Duchess all tears and smiles, and Mrs. George bustling
round with a word for everyone, while the proud father sur-
veyed the scene with, who knows, a slight twinge of misgiving.
Children, yes, they were all very well in their way; and of course
he had wanted a boy. But children meant expense and a more
ample scale of life, and—well, he had been troubled lately . . . .

§ 5

Indeed, the years that followed were difficult ones for Villiers
and his family. A variety of circumstances combined to make
agriculture an extremely difficult proposition in those days. The
war with France, after a temporary lull, began once more and
dragged interminably on, year after year. At the same time an
unseen economic revolution was taking place; for the mechanical
means of production, so rapidly developing, were drawing
country hands to the towns. Agricultural labour was scarce,
and wages were high. As a consequence food became short, and
there was much distress. But Villiers battled on for a time; and
it was not till 1805 that a revolution took place in his affairs.

But in that year a staggering blow fell upon him, the precise
nature of which we have never been able to ascertain. Whether
it was a really portentous run of ill-luck on the Turf, or whether
the farms were mortgaged and the mortgages fell due, or the crops
failed on a prodigious scale, we do not know. But whatever it
was, these facts are certain: that, about this time, George Villiers
became liable for a very large sum of money; that his brother
Clarendon had to step in and help, and that thereafter a complete change took place in Villiers' circumstances and way of
life. No longer do we find him his own master, a gentleman
living on his lands. The farms are all sold up: the racing-stable
dispersed. A period of kaleidoscopic change ensues wherein the
family can never be pinned down to any fixed abode: there is
a flitting hither and thither as of birds in search of grain. One
house is changed for another in bewildering rapidity: fresh starts
are made and abandoned almost as soon as begun. The Princess

Amelia swoops down suddenly into the picture, and carries off
Mrs. George to be a member of her household, and thereafter
for a time the Villiers family are seen flung against the background of Royal Windsor.   Hardly have we become accustomed
to them in these novel surroundings than they are up and off
again, reappearing for a fitful flash at Kew, whither they have
gone in connection with some minor Court appointment which
the insatiable Mrs. George has been able to obtain for her
husband.

And was it not very much in the irony of things that during
the whole of this time Mrs. Villiers was hardly ever *not* in a condition of expectancy?   Indeed, the dear lady seemed as prolific
as her husband's troubles.   For, in quick succession, she presented him with four sons and a daughter, all born between the
disastrous years 1800 and 1806.   There was George William
Frederick, born in 1800; Thomas Hyde, the year after; Charles
Pelham, born in 1802; Maria Theresa, born in 1803; and
Edward Ernest, in 1806.   A discreet lull ensued; and then, as
the ends of history were converging upon Waterloo, she launched
Edward Montagu into the world; and while the allies were still
disputing the fate of Europe in Paris, the indomitable woman
sealed her efforts with the production of yet another boy,
Augustus Algernon.

So before the year 1820, George Villiers, a younger son,
harassed by debt and pursued by creditors, found himself the
father of seven hungry children.   But if, during these years,
there were times when Villiers was at his wits' end to know what
to do, his wife, though bravely producing, was visited with no
such doubts.   Privilege and Mrs. George could effect wonders.
The astonished Hertfordshire gentleman woke up one morning to
find himself " Registrar of Gibraltar," a fortress he had certainly
never visited in his life, and of the conditions of which he was
totally ignorant.   Hardly had he become accustomed to himself
in this new rôle than honours began falling thick upon him.   He
found himself successively (and concurrently) "Clerk of the
Council," "Registrar of the Duchy of Lancaster," and finally
and most grandiloquently of all, " Ranger of Cranbourne Chase."
How he bore the burden of these responsibilities we do not know,
but affectionate little references to the Governor's bursts of
ill-temper, " due solely to the gout," peep at this period, like
naughty cupids, through the leaves of Mrs. George's correspondence; so it is rather to be feared that, at moments, his irritability
got the better of his pride.

It is not really till 1812 that we get any coherent picture of the
Villiers family life.   But in that year a new arrangement was
made for them.   By then, be it said, the Governor was sub-

sisting almost entirely on an allowance from his brother Clarendon, for whatever money he could make on his own was immediately forfeit to someone else.   He was not, it appears, officially
declared a bankrupt; but terrified references to gentlemen alluded
to as " the Commissioners " seem to indicate that his affairs were
no longer in his own hands.   He had given up his Court appointments and was without occupation.   But in 1812 a suggestion
was made that the Villiers family should share the expenses with
the Boringdons (Mrs. George's brother and his wife) of Kent
House, a large rambling mansion in Knightsbridge, so arranged
that two families could well live within its capacious bosom without getting in each other's way.   Clarendon, it is evident, must
have made this arrangement possible.

So the family moved to London, and what was entered into as
a temporary arrangement proved as permanent as anything well
may be in a shifting world; for the children grew up there; and
the Governor died there; and Theresa was married from there,
and spent her widowhood and most of her second marriage there.
And as for Mrs. George, she spent the remainder of her life
there.   It was one of those old-fashioned, Georgian houses like
those still to be seen at Richmond and on the main roads out of
London, though they are now fast disappearing.   Large, spacious
and dignified, it stood back from the clamour of the streets in
a garden of its own, dear to the hearts of the Villiers children
and their many descendants who were to play there during the
first sixty years of the nineteenth century.

The house was completely divided and the two families had
separate establishments; but one communicating door remained
open; and through it would pass the brilliant and delightful Lady
Boringdon—Lady Morley as she was to become—an aunt as
nearly ideal as could be imagined to the young Villiers.

§ 6

There is a fashion in children as there is a fashion in most
things.   The modern child runs half naked in the garden, and
it is not till well past its sixth birthday that it is called in,
washed, and set down to learn its A B C.   The child of a
hundred and thirty years ago was burdened with clothes and
crammed with knowledge from the earliest age.   As is natural,
children react very differently to the two kinds of treatment.   In
judging the children of the past, it is difficult not to think of
them in comparison with the children of our own day, or of a
generation ago.   When Macaulay, aged five, and scalded at a
party by the upsetting of a cup of hot tea over his hand, replied
to an elderly sympathiser, " Madam, I thank you, the agony has

now somewhat abated," he was not saying anything that would have sounded odd to the children of his day. Children talked like that then. Indeed, they were expected to talk like that. But if a modern child gave vent to such an utterance, we should be inclined, and quite rightly, to box its ears. So when we strain back into the past to catch the first lisping accents of the Villiers children we must not be shocked to hear them giving vent to the most exalted sentiments in language the most high-flown. Nor must we think them prigs for so doing. They were simply talking (or writing) in the manner of the children of their day, not of ours. This, for instance, is the way in which young George, aged eleven, answered his mother, when she wrote to break to him a sad piece of news:

"DEAREST MAMMA,
    "You can't conceive how your dear letter made me sin-cerely feel the death of our beloved Friend and Protectress, Prin-cess Amelia, and I will try to explain to my brothers and dear sister to the best of my power. I have shewn them the letter, and they sincerely join with me in regretting the severe loss of the very best friend we ever had, or ever shall have in all our lives. Her affection for us all was truly maternal. Give my *very* best love and affection to dearest Papa. We are all *very* well—*happy* I cannot say. I will never, *never* lose the letter. The postman is waiting and I cannot write any more, so God Almighty bless you, and believe me to be at present, and always, Your very affec-tionate and dutiful son,
                              "G. W. F. VILLIERS."

But when some childish prank caused the two elder boys to be packed off to school in a hurry the next year, the tide of remorse for their past behaviour is too much even for George's English:

    "I do most heartily, on my knees, beg your pardon, indeed the paper on which I am now writing is wet with my tears, but alas you must indeed think them crocodile tears, after so many promises of good behaviour to have dared to offend the best of parents and of men, and then for our bad behaviour to have made Miss Atkinson behave in the manner she did to my darling sister (whom I love ten thousand times better than myself) speaks daggers to my afflicted mind, but the consciousness of having offended you, my ever dearest Papa, is more punishment to me than anything. But the greatest punishment that could be in-flicted . . ."

and so on for two and a half pages.
    From these effusions it would be difficult to form any concep-tion of the child as he was apart from what he was expected to

be. We can only hope that the exemplary sentiments expressed pleased his parents, which no doubt they did.

Two years later, however, when George was fourteen, we catch a more human and informative glimpse of him and his brothers when they were away on a holiday with their father. That they were so happened in this way. About eighteen months after the Villiers family settled in Kent House, the Governor was visited by a more than usually ferocious attack of gout, which caused Mrs. Villiers to wonder whether a course of the waters at Bath would not be of help to him. There was, it appears, no one adult to send with him just then, and Mrs. George herself could not spare the time away from Theresa. So she conceived the plan of packing him off to Somersetshire in charge of his three eldest boys. It would be good for them all: good for young George to feel that he was responsible for his father's well-being, good for Hyde and Charles to see the world, and especially good for the Governor to be away from home and alone with his boys for a while.

On all these counts it proved a huge success. As for George, he became a positive sick-nurse.

"To-day," he writes, "is our first visit to the Pump Room, where Papa was persuaded by me to take only the smallest glass." Thereafter he worked out a régime for his father, and writes a few days later:

"This morning he took a second sized glass at 8 o'clock, and at 9 o'clock took another of the same size, and at about 10 break-fasted. At half after twelve he took a small size, and does not dine till 3. So you see if we can keep on with this regular routine, we shall get on very well."

Not satisfied with the treatment and attendance of the first doctor they tried, George persuaded his father to dismiss him and engage another. The meek way in which the Governor fell in with the suggestion proves the extent to which he relied on the sound judgment of his son. And George changed his room to be nearer his father, "if," as he explains, "he should want any little thing in the night."

They had settled down in what would seem to us a lavish apartment; for, according to George, it comprised "a front and back drawing-room, two bedrooms and dressing-room, together with servant's room and servant's hall."

It is difficult to imagine how the poor Governor paid for all this, as Bath cannot have been cheap even in those days. But life was on a grander scale then, and certainly the pound went further. At any rate the boys were not stinted of work or play. They went on with their studies: fenced with a Mons. Roland,

whom they came to adore, and attended classes on various subjects. "Papa" occupied a good deal of their time, and writing
home to "dearest Mamma" a good deal more. But they had
ponies to ride, and most afternoons would see them cantering
over Claverton Downs, "whence," says George, with unction,
"the prospect is more beautiful than anything I ever saw in that
way in my life."

Indeed, Bath was an education in itself for the boys. It was
still the metropolis of the West, and to it, at one time or another,
came all that was great in music and drama and the arts. George
Villiers and his sons profited by this, though a musical festival,
one can see, somewhat appalled them.

"After breakfast, we went to the Oratorio," writes George,
"and in about an hour someone told Papa that it would not be
over till four. So we agreed (as the finer part was the latter part)
to run home and write our letters and then return. The music was
delightful, and we were very much entertained. Unfortunately,"
he adds, "Messrs. Shunke's wonderful performance on the
French Horn was just over when we returned."

But, above all, they loved going to the Play. Kemble was
then in the plenitude of his power; and almost every evening
(when it didn't interfere with dearest Papa's Pump-Room engagements) the father and his three sons set out for the theatre to see
the great old tragedian in all his most famous Shakespearian
parts: Coriolanus, Lear, etc.; and heartily they enjoyed themselves, becoming quite exacting critics of the various perform-
ances. Plays, indeed, were homely affairs in the early nineteenth
century, sketchily rehearsed, with much give and take between
actors and audience, and the following account of a performance
of *Henry VIII* sounds fantastic enough to modern play-goers:

"Somehow or other, I do not think Kemble acted half so well
as usual; and the Earl of Surrey, who, if you remember, is the
chief person when Wolsey has fallen from his 'exalted dignity'
was acted by Mr. Ley, who was so imperfect in his part that he
could not say a single word of it, and got so hissed that he came
forward with a great deal of grace, and made a *very* good
apology; upon which he was so clapped and applauded that I
thought the house would almost come down. He then took a
book and *read* the rest of his part. Miss Nash, who was adver-
tised in the Bill to sing 'Angels Ever Bright and Fair,' when
Queen Katharine was dying, was apologised for as having a bad
cold. She promised to do her best and hoped for the kind indul-
gence of the audience! (This was a great disappointment to
Papa, for you know how he *doats* on that song.) Well, she
began, but found herself so hoarse, that after many profound
curtsies, she was obliged to retire."

3

Nor did they wholly neglect the lighter side of the stage, for
they went to the *Beggar's Opera*, which they had seen before, as
George was able to note that "though a very good singer, Miss
Nash's Polly Peacham was very much inferior to Miss Stephens."
And on a famous occasion:

"We went to the Play where Mathews out-mathewed Mathews.
I do not know when I have laughed so much. I am sure not
since I have been at Bath. He acted 'Goldfinch' in the *Road to
Ruin*; and then his 'Somno' in the *Sleepwalker* was better than
ever. He gets new improvements every night; and his imitations
of Kemble drew down torrents of applause. He sang the 'Bang-
up Song': the 'Humours of the Playhouse,' and 'Manager Strutt
was Four Foot High,' and was encored in every *one*."

An uproarious evening. . . .

Meanwhile, in spite of these dissipations, the cure proceeded
apace; and after two months of assiduous Pump-Room attendance,
in which, among other things, a hose was "brought to bear
with considerable force on dear Papa's legs," an improvement
is duly noted, and the anxious young George breathes a sigh of
relief:

"I do hope now, thank God, that the waters have begun to
settle with him, if you understand what I mean, because at first,
I take it, they had a great deal to encounter . . ."

§ 7

The education of the boys was, of course, a great problem.
There was nothing in those days remotely corresponding to a
Preparatory School as we know it to-day, and the Public School
system (which made Preparatory Schools inevitable) did not exist.
Not that there were no Public Schools. Indeed, there were
plenty. But their inmates were of a mixed breed. Moreover,
the boarding system was not smiled upon by fathers who had
been born in the eighteenth century and brought up by tutors at
home. The education of gentlemen's sons was in a transitional
stage. Something more than tutors at home was needed for growing boys, it was felt. Yet nobody could quite see what it was.
It remained for Arnold at Rugby to lay the foundations of what
we have come to think of now as the "Public School system."
But Arnold was still to come.

As a half-way house between tutors at home and a boarding-
school, there was then in various localities day-schools run by
retired scholars or "Doctors" from the Universities. And there
were plenty of these. It was, in fact, lucky for the Villiers boys
that there were; for, brought up against an ever-changing back-

ground, they would have fared ill had there not been schools of this kind in most of the localities in which their parents settled.

To one such, the elder boys were sent after the escapade mentioned in the last chapter. Since George *wrote* to his father from there, it would seem that they actually boarded for a while at this one. This, however, was probably regarded as part of their punishment. In all likelihood they boarded with the headmaster for the middle of the week, returning home for Saturdays and Sundays.

When the family moved to London in 1812, George and Hyde, and later Charles, attended Dr. Thomas Hill's Academy in Kensington. This was a typical day-school of the period, run by an eccentric old gentleman, the father of Rowland Hill of Post Office fame. Dr. Thomas, as someone said of him, "possessed every sense, save common sense"; but he had a great gift for teaching and managed to inspire his pupils with a thirst for learning. For about eighteen months George attended his classes; but in 1814—the year he accompanied his father to Bath—he was entered at Christ's Hospital, the Bluecoat School. This was before the College moved to the country; and George would go backwards and forwards to his lessons from Knightsbridge to Westminster.

But if the *kind* of education to give his boys was a problem to George Villiers, the cost of it was a still greater one. He himself, harassed by gout and besieged by creditors, was immobilised alike by circumstance and health from earning sufficient for the needs of his growing family.

Sitting in the study at Kent House he must have wrung impotent hands over the situation, and have harped back in memory to the prosperous land-owning days of his early married life: to his four hundred acres of hay: to his beloved horses: to the times—only twelve years since—when he had been strong and fit and had commanded a Troop in the Yeomanry that was to repel the invasion of Buonaparte. And then, as like as not, in the midst of his meditations, Charles and Hyde would come rocketing in from school, shouting and banging doors, and his gout would flitch, and he would notice with annoyance that his sons' trousers were frayed at the edges and that the sleeves of their coats were too short. However, his wife's loud laugh, floating distantly down a corridor to him, would bring a certain measure of relief. Surely, he would reflect, if a body could laugh like that, things couldn't be as bad as they seemed. . . .

Indeed, Mrs. George's reaction to the situation was very different from her husband's. Sanguine by temperament, she was not the kind of woman to wring her hands over the decrees of fate. The past had brought its trials, but it was of no use dwelling upon them. The present was the important factor. Make good use of the present, and the future would take care of itself. And the present, so Mrs. George thought, demanded action. Somehow the boys should be educated, and Theresa launched in the society to which she had a right by birth; and this was not to be effected by sitting at home and remaining in genteel obscurity. Rather was it to be achieved by keeping the family well to the fore: by, so to speak, unfurling the family flag, and waving it on every possible occasion: by canvassing the great and being kind to the small: by going everywhere and being seen by everyone—in a word, by being natural and jolly, and enjoying oneself up to the hilt in the society to which one belonged. And since she was one of those people who by some obscure art seem able to grace the most exalted and expensive surroundings on apparently no income whatsoever, she achieved her end. In borrowed plumes and a hired carriage she was socially ubiquitous, always laughing, always gay, always the centre of an animated throng.

She eventually became a power at Almacks, sued to for tickets by the most exclusively elect; and twice a fortnight the poor old Governor was shaken into his evening clothes, whirled along in her chariot, and forced to point a gouty toe in the rooms off King Street, St. James's. So she schemed and plotted and prepared the ground for the future. Meanwhile the family helped. Lord Boringdon helped. He had influence and could pull strings, and was always a kind uncle to the boys. Lady Boringdon helped —with counsel, at least—for the two sisters-in-law were much attached to each other. But, best of all, Lord Clarendon helped.

From behind his park gates the old earl looked on not without amusement at the antics of his brother and sister-in-law. He was getting old now and had no children of his own; and as he sat, a solitary bachelor, in the green dining-room at the Grove sipping his port and surrounded by his Vandykes, his thoughts would recur not infrequently to the subject of George and his offspring. Certainly George had been very tiresome: had indeed achieved almost the limit of what a younger brother could do to one. Damn it! Hadn't it looked, on one occasion, as if the whole estate would have to be sold up, farms and all, to settle his wretched debts? Also, he had an insufferable wife, who talked too much; and as his mind lit on Mrs. George he chuckled sardonically. What a woman! And yet—flesh and blood, flesh and blood; after all, George was his brother, and a lovable fellow, though a fool, a damned fool, and weak. But since John's wife had produced nothing but the snivelling Harriet, one of George's boys would succeed to the earldom one day, he supposed. Fine boys, too. George, Hyde, Charles, Edward.

What was his brother going to do about their education? Young George, he had heard, had gone to Christ's, and Hyde was to follow him there in a term or so, so they were provided for. But what about Charles and Edward?—especially Edward? He liked Edward, what he had seen of him. What was going to happen to them, he wondered. Pity to let them grow up anyhow. Edward. . . . Well, he himself would have to see what could be done. . . .

Meanwhile both the elder boys took a hand in the education of their younger brothers, as a rather pathetic sentence in one of George's letters to his mother implies: "I am sorry about Charles's spelling. But it is the fault of those who undertook his English. If you remember I only undertook his mathematics and geography."

§ 8

While George was still at the Bluecoat School, the world at home and abroad was convulsed by the drama of the Hundred Days.

Waterloo came and went; and while a glittering throng of Kings and Emperors were re-making Europe in Paris, to the accompaniment of assemblies at which the bold and the fair of all nations were gathered together, George, a pale, lanky youth with pleasant features and a charming smile, was still conscientiously plodding on at his Latin Verses in the fogs and damps of Westminster. As peace descended upon a harassed Continent, and the terrible shadow of the Eagles departed for ever, George and his brother Hyde went quietly up to Cambridge together, and were entered at St. John's College for the autumn term of 1816. This was probably a more important step for them both than it sounds. It is unlikely that either of the two boys had ever before left the parental roof except for very short periods.

George had been a day-boarder at Christ's. Hyde, who was to have followed in his footsteps, was delicate and did not go. Sir Henry Taylor, who knew him intimately later, describes him as having been "educated at home." Neither of them had, therefore, taken that first step out into the world which is as salutary as it is unpleasant for most. They were very young; they were very eager; and they were completely naïve. And never having been disabused of the sense of their own value, the infant bloom of assurance was still intact upon them; and they advanced upon persons and events with a self-confidence that takes one's breath away. On their arrival at St. John's an avalanche of "exams" descended upon them. But "exams" had no terrors for them. Quite the contrary.

"I am just out of Hall," writes George, "and have only time to tell you that I have done *very* well in Locke the first time, and *beautifully* the second," while Hyde dithyrambically exclaims on the back of the same sheet of paper, "I did very well in Greek Testament to-day, and I believe George has done *quite beautifully* in Demosthenes." Thereafter for a week their letters home become pious chants of praise in honour of their own and of each other's prowess in the schools. However, this optimism seems to have been justified, since they passed their examinations with credit, and were well settled down to University life by the spring of 1817.

They rode: they fenced: they read conscientiously. And slowly and shyly they began to make friends and acquaintances. Charles Greville (of the *Journals*) is the first name that appears with any frequency in their letters, and with him they formed a friendship that was to last them their lives. Greville was older for his age than they, and of a sociable disposition. He made frequent excursions into a world that was as yet unknown to the solemn Villiers boys. They were immensely impressed, and bathed themselves deliciously in the reflected glory of his escapades.

"Greville arrived here time enough for Hall at 10 o'clock, which I think considering he was at Lady Castlereagh's supper last night was pretty well. I never saw any young gentleman more completely done up with his day and night's work than he was."

But George and Hyde, though they observed these high junketings with favour, confined themselves to the chaster diversion of driving over in a tandem to Newmarket, where they would have a "capital good dinner," and driving back again in "beautiful good time."

The proximity of the races, at set seasons, provided a thrill, and though they do not often seem to have attended them in person, they picked up whatever gossip was going about as to the doings on the course. Their letters home on these occasions become full of knowing racing terms, while the names of the famous animals involved—Lord Jersey's "Cannon-Ball," "Arena, who won the Oaks so easily last year"—became positive household words to them. Circumstances mercifully prevented the Governor from attending the races—a providence unfortunately not extended to his brother.

"I heard of my Uncle John to-day," writes Hyde. "He was standing thinking in the middle of the Course, sucking his thumbs."

PLATE 2.—THE GROVE, WATFORD

From a photograph by T. J. Stephenson, F.R.P.S.

§ 9

During the vacations, Mrs. George packed them off on a round
of visits. It was time for them to be seen and recognised as
cadets of a distinguished house: time for them to stand on their
own feet and establish contacts for themselves in a world to which
they would shortly be called to play a part. Accordingly,
nothing loath, and armed still with the assurance that had carried
them safely through their examinations, the brothers cheerfully
set out for Badminton, Petworth and Longleat.

From Badminton, after a ruminative silence of two days,
George writes: " The Duchess improves very much on acquaintance. She appears stupid sometimes; but that is from her
extreme deafness. But she is very religious." They danced
and made friends with the young Ladies Somerset, whom Hyde
found "excessively pretty," but whose looks, he sorrowfully
opined, would " go off just as the others did." The Duke lent
the boys horses, and they had "capital days' sport" with Lord
Decies' Harriers, the fox-hounds " being gone into Oxford-
shire."

The brothers met with the approval of their hosts, as they were
pressed to come again; and on other occasions, " the Duke and
Duchess and their fair daughters were very kind and pleased to
see us."

Longleat proved also a great success. There they "punished
Lord Bath's pheasants for him ": went out on the lake and
caught some " beautiful fine pike of 6 and 8 pounds ": flirted
with Lady Louisa Thynne, and made friends with Weymouth
and his younger brothers Henry and John. But it was chiefly
to Petworth that they returned again and again. Indeed, it
became almost a second home to them. Lord Egremont was an
old friend of the Governor's, and Charles and Henry Wyndham,
though older than the Villiers boys, became close friends with
them, and remained so always.

Sometimes, too, they spent a pleasant week at the Grove,
where they found old Clarendon charming and courteous as ever
—but vastly preferring Edward. And sometimes they went to
Saltram, where the clever, brilliant Lady Boringdon (or rather
Lady Morley as she had now become since her husband had been
raised to an earldom) behaved as a perfect aunt should—pro-
viding them with charming society and watching over their
manners.

Between visits they " took the air of town," learning to know
their fashionable London with its gay, outrageous figures, its
Dandies and its Beaux. A stroll down St. James's Street of a
morning would disclose to them " Poodle " Byng emerging from

White's in bottle-green coat and leather gaiters; and they would learn to penetrate his amusing disguise of country squire just up from the shires, and discover the Dandy and Exquisite beneath. Perhaps, even, they would be fortunate enough to encounter the great Brummel himself, picking his way delicately along the footway, his great ruffled fur cape humped about his shoulders. Or in Bond Street they would come upon Sir Lumley Skeffington "showing a leg" to the Town, with "Tea-pot" Crawford on his arm; or turn at a clatter behind them to spy Lord Alvanley caracolling on his horse en route for Rotten Row, and be just in time to see him bow—was he not famous for his bow?—to Lady Granville returning in her phaeton from Devonshire House. Sometimes they would grace the fashionable hour of five o'clock in Hyde Park, braving Count d'Orsay's stupendous waistcoats, and Mrs. Arbuthnot's unknowing stare as she passed by on the arm of "the Duke." They learned, too (but did not emulate), the ways of the "Bucks"—those incipient Dandies—and the modish pranks and pleasantries of "Oxford Jerry" and "Corinthian Tom" were not hid from them. They made their bow to Society, and were taken to Almacks, where they became members of that glittering throng that gyrated in the new-fangled waltz under the eagle eyes of Lady Jersey and Mrs. Burrell. Then off on another round of visits, after which back to Cambridge through the mild autumn weather. Tranquil leagues of English landscape passing the windows at six miles an hour; innyards, with ostlers standing in the sun; inn-parlours, and substantial meals washed down with ale, partaken in a hurry with the horses waiting outside. Frosty morning starts; "Coachey" with his innumerable capes; the ringing horn; the jokes—the laughter—the queer fellow-travellers—England in 1818.

"We arrived at Stamford just as they were putting the horses in. Our companions in the 'dedans' were a good-natured man who told us he had been *a great slave to hunting*, but that now he was turned broker and merchant at Liverpool—upon which we had a great talk to him about Canning whom he admires with all his soul. The other was a great, dram-drinking woman whom, by degrees, we found out to be the wife of Gillman, who keeps the largest travelling menagerie of Beasts in England. We found her out by her saying she had experienced the great curiosity of her tygress whelping at Brighton, and thereafter we got lots of "wild-beast" information out of her."

§ 10

The years passed; the boys became young men. Life grew to mean something more to them than a fashionable parade or a schoolboy lark. They evolved minds and personalities of their own. They read philosophy and developed ideas.

George in his twentieth year, we are told, was tall, slim and graceful, with very fair hair, blue eyes and a fair complexion. He was quick in conversation, brilliant, gay, with swift perceptions and a facile wit. He was of a sociable disposition, and popular with all classes of people. But though he was working hard for his final examinations at the University, reading, thinking and debating, the prospect of the brilliant career of public service that lay before him existed as yet not even in his imagination. His brother Hyde was of a more ambitious turn of mind, and was already consciously laying the foundations of a political future that only his early death in 1834 robbed of fulfilment. He, too, was handsome, his face being, we are told, "that of a fair, distinguished-looking child grown to the stature of manhood, with as little alteration as might be of its delicate features."

At Cambridge, during their last years there, the brothers formed part of a group of young men who were all, as it happened, destined to make their mark in the world. There was Charles Austin, a brilliant conversationalist, a keen debater, a charming companion, who, later, was to amass a huge fortune at the Parliamentary Bar; John Romily, a passionate Benthamite, sensitive and reserved—he, too, destined to make a name for himself at the Bar, rising in due course to be Master of the Rolls and a peer of the realm; Edward Strutt, a young man of sound knowledge and solid understanding, whose unpremeditated achievements in politics were in the end to raise him to the Upper House as Lord Belper; and last, but not least, there was Charles Villiers—Charles, fresh from Haileybury, where he had undergone education at Lord Clarendon's expense, but where he had imbibed an outlook on things very far removed from that which the old earl expected of him; Charles Pelham Villiers, perhaps the most brilliant of all the Villiers fraternity, a passionate radical, an ardent reformer, but cross-grained, malicious, with a sarcastic tongue that was to gain him many enemies in the course of his long parliamentary history. He joined his elder brothers during their last two years at Cambridge, and immediately became, through his wit and obvious abilities of mind, the youngest but not the least weighty of the charmed circle of young men with whom his brothers associated. Idle and slovenly in dress, he was good-looking in a feminine way. Hyde was in the habit of saying to his friends: "My brother's quite a good-looking fellow when he's picked and washed."

Liberalism was in the air, born of recent French history and the travail of the dawning century. A new political philosophy was emerging as the chaos of war and revolution subsided. That

eccentric and elegant pundit, Bentham, well on in the seventies,
was still basing his political sermons on a century-old text of
Hutcheson's; but the phrase "the greatest happiness of the
greatest number" was beginning to be looked upon by a rising
generation of politicians as something more than a pious ejacula-
tion of sentiment.

The young Cambridge circle were passionate Benthamites;
"Reform" was their catchword—reform of the electorate, reform
of jurisprudence and the conventions of law, reform of social conditions and the conditions of the poor, reform, reform, reform.
Endlessly they debated and discussed and read papers to each
other on the burning need for reform, and gradually they became,
as a group, associated as adherents of a new and advanced political
philosophy.

It is to this period and to these influences that we must attribute
the revolution in thought that caused George Villiers, when the
time came, to throw in his lot with the Whigs. The family
tradition was Tory. His father was the friend of Canning. His
uncle, the old earl, in so far as he was anything in politics, was
conservative, deploring new-fangled notions, and looking wistfully
back into the eighteenth century and pre-revolutionary days. His
other uncle, John, the friend and supporter of Pitt, had sat in the
House in the Tory interest. But George Villiers was essentially
the child of the nineteenth century; and, exposed to its intellectual
influences in the highly discursive atmosphere of a University, his
latent inclinations towards a liberal view of things took shape;
and, during his last two years at Cambridge, he discovered for life
the *nature* of his reactions to social and political questions.

Hyde and George took their degrees in the summer of 1819;
and although this event nominally ended their University career,
George, at any rate, kept a term or two after his final Honours
Examination, to continue the study of languages for which he had
discovered a decided bent, and to mark time till some post could
be found for him. He very well knew that, circumstances being
what they were, he must needs make his own way into the world.
Though heir-apparent to an earldom, the fashionable life of the
young aristocrat—the life of clubs, of coffee-houses, of gaming and
philandering—was not for him. It was essential, he knew, to
embark upon a career that would relieve his parents of the burden
of supporting him financially. His gift of languages, which
among all his other studies he had assiduously fostered, seemed
to point naturally towards diplomacy. That the Tories were in
office seemed no hindrance. Family influence was accordingly
brought to bear upon the situation. Words were dropped in high
places. Lord Palmerston was approached. George's uncle, Lord
Morley, turned assiduous canvasser for his good-looking nephew,

and slowly but surely the eye of Power was induced to focus itself for a moment upon this promising neophyte.

The omnipotent glance resulted in an offer from Lord Castlereagh to attach Villiers to the embassy of Sir Charles Bagot at St. Petersburg. But here was a hitch. The initial stages of diplomacy—the probationary attaché-ships—were unpaid. Indeed, there was even considerable expense involved in accepting them; and while George, disappointed and uncertain, was seen in London that spring at balls and parties, at the opera, the Governor negotiated over his future with the powers that be. A delay ensued, but luckily not a long one. In the early summer of 1820 George Villiers sailed for St. Petersburg to take up his first diplomatic appointment. We do not know how the difficulty was got over. It is probable that the *deus ex machina* on this, as on so many other occasions, was old Lord Clarendon. Soon after his arrival *en poste* George wrote to his uncle. The letter pleased the old earl.

"Nothing can be more grateful to one's feelings," he writes in answer, "than those little circumstances and pictures of the place of which you were writing; and it is the remembrance and notice, sometimes, of *little* things which brings hearts nearest together . . .

"Do not take from a pleasant hour or from one of business, *any* minutes for me. But if an idle one should ever occur, give me a little of *that*, and let me have the pleasure of hearing something of yourself, however little, however unimportant it may seem to yourself to be.

"And now my dear, amiable George, adieu! My love and every good wish attend you.

"C."

§ II

And in St. Petersburg we may leave him for a while. Indeed, the life of an unpaid attaché in times of peace is not very worthy of record.

To make himself useful on every possible occasion, both to the Ambassador and to the Chancery staff: to arrange interviews and deal with applications: to order the carriages and write the invitations: to be the smiling object upon which the wrath which pervades an embassy on "Bag-Day" vents itself, and not to mind: to be elegant in society, but to walk delicately there, pacifying compatriots and ingratiating foreigners—these are the perennial occupations of attachés all the world over; and Villiers seems to have performed them with average ability.

Needless to say, the loss of George's presence from the family circle was keenly felt, and by none more so than by Mrs. George, who rushed to her tablets and poured forth to him daily a never-ending stream of family news and social gossip. "As for telling you anything that your mother has omitted," writes the Governor rather testily in one of his rare epistles to his son, "it is a task too improbable to attempt."

Meanwhile two neophytes emerged from babyhood into the Villiers fraternity, and Mrs. George has much to say about them.

"I think I never knew anything so ridiculously like you as Montague and Algernon. Montague has all your prudence and discretion, tenderness, a little humbugging propensity upon occasion, such as my own dearest George used to have sometimes—and in a thousand little looks and ways he is *you—tout craché*—then Algy is Hyde *lui-même*, or even an *utter* Hyde, in wildness, giddiness, vivacity, *espièglerie*, fun—and so very like him in face. He has a perfect temper, and is very clever, though very idle, and therefore very backward in his book-learning."

Montague was destined to became a Bishop and Algernon to die a midshipman, but this was mercifully hid from the adoring mother as she watched their childish antics in the garden of Kent House.

About this time we catch an amusing glimpse of the rest of the family, struggling back to the old house in Knightsbridge after the completion there of some structural repairs which had necessitated the absence of the inmates. George had asked an acquaintance of his in St. Petersburg who was going home on leave to call upon his parents and give them news of himself. He found them in the middle of the move; but what did that matter if Mrs. George could have tidings of her beloved son?

"All Wednesday and Thursday we were employed in deménagé-ing, as our term of three months being up, we had to remove our goods, chattels, and persons to Kent House: and though it may sound as if the removal would be small; yet you know the ways of the family too well not to be aware of what *any* removal is; and being, at present, seven in family, all of whom have their own particular goods to remove, besides servants, etc., moreover, taking into consideration that the Governor's things were all to be moved, he being helpless from gout in the hand, and in such a state, being obliged to let everything be done for him, and thinking nothing done properly—well, you may pretty well guess our condition—in short we were all fagged and bored to death. Just fancy, *au beau mileu* of our work yesterday, first arrived your dearest of blessed letters—and then, within an hour, that dear old fellow Daniels himself. Now just fancy that, that's all!—No, it is really quite, quite impossible to say what a delight it was to us all. I could have kissed him with pleasure. Indeed, I was quite sorry not to have rewarded him when he said such pretty things of me. But that was a joke compared to the pretty

things he said about *you*. We questioned him about your looks,
and the Governor said to him, 'How *does* he look—as if he really
were in good health?' And he said 'Yes'; and then turning
round and looking at the three hopefuls, Hyde, Charles and
Edward, he said, "*He looks a great deal better than any of
these.*' I can't tell you how we enjoyed that! To be sure, at that
moment, it was perhaps not saying much, for three such horrors
as your brothers you never saw,—can't you fancy them all dirty
and dusty in old black coats, ditto neck-handkerchiefs, tied loose,
—Edward with his most cadaverous look—in short, I was quite
vexed that you should appear to have such a family! He said
he thought Charles the most like you, which I am sure could only
be from thinking him the least hideous. The Governor asked him
about your dress, whether you wore whiskers or moustachios, etc.
He said, 'Oh, no, none of that nonsense! He's only a little
fashionable about his Hair,' and put his fingers through his own
Hair behind, implying yours was something *à la* Crow's-nest.
(Just do me a bit of a drawing of it, dear George. Is it as much
of a Crow's-nest as Esterhazy's, or Bold Devon's?*) Then this
dear man told us how very much you were beloved and respected
by everybody, and that Mr. Cathcart was the nicest man that
ever was, and Sir Charles was such a nice man to . . ."

But it was not always that she wrote in this rollicking mood.
Financial affairs were no better than they had been, and the three
elder boys were very difficult to manage. There were times when
she desponded; and then, with an equal fervour, she would pour
out all her troubles to her beloved son in his distant post and
ask him for his comfort and counsel.

'So many things to think of, dearest George . . . Now for
instance Charles and Hyde. They were grown-up now. Of course
it was hard to think of them as young men, but after all they
were, were they not? And what she could do about them she
didn't know, for they seemed indifferent alike to the family situation and their own careers. Hyde lounged about London all day;
rushed back to dress and go out to dinner, and often didn't return
till two in the morning. And where he went and whom he saw
she didn't know, for he certainly never told her. He never
seemed to do any work; and surely he ought to for his nomina-
tion to the Colonial Office? Then there was Charles. Really, she
didn't know what to do about Charles. He was so cross and
taciturn—so "touch-me-not." Really his manner to herself was
sometimes *quite beyond*. She had had to ask the Governor to
speak to him—and of course, the Governor had said the wrong
thing, and there'd been a scene. Only Theresa could make him
civil. And even Theresa couldn't tell what was going on in his
head—they none of them could. He would mope about the house

* Nickname for the Duke of Devonshire.

in slippers all day long, apparently doing nothing; at least, no one dared to ask him what he was doing. When the Queen's trial had been on, Hyde and Charles had spent their whole time in the gallery of the House of Lords; and had come back holding, of course, quite the wrong views, praising Brougham to the skies, and swearing to the Queen's innocence, when everyone else— everyone one knew, George,—was thinking the King had been cruelly wronged. Most provoking it had been. Then as for Edward . . . well, of course, it was all very dear and kind of Uncle Clarendon to be supporting his education at the Charter-house and to have him so much at the Grove during the holidays, but the long and the short of it was the old gentleman was spoiling the boy. They hardly ever saw anything of him nowadays, and when he did put in an appearance he was so grand and con-descending, so "hoity-toity." It seemed life at home wasn't grand enough for him these days. It wasn't right, George. After all *he* wasn't going to succeed to the title. He wasn't going to live at the Grove with masses of servants to look after him, and every-thing just as he liked it. He had to make his own way in the world just as the others had. Her only comfort at home was Theresa, dearest Angel, than whom nobody on earth could be more perfect, more understanding, more helpful in every possible way. It was a pity, though, that she would still persist in regard-ing all young men—well, dearest George,—just as young men without distinction of fortune, rank and position. It didn't seem to matter to her whom she danced with at Almacks, or whom she rode with "at company-time" in the Park. After all, these things did count,—did they not?—and if only the blessed angel could make a really successful marriage . . .'

George tried his best to comfort his mother and, in a measure, to control the family destinies from his distant post. He wrote to his brothers about their behaviour and their prospects, urging the necessity of their making their own way in the world. To Edward he addressed an almost avuncular homily on the subject of family affection, but to Theresa he wrote more private epistles imploring her not to be guided into an untimely marriage by any thoughts of the family situation.

Theresa was going out that year under Mrs. George's maternal wing (having made her début the year before with the beautiful Lady Morley to give her the proper *ton*). Night after night they went to Almack's—a party of young people, Theresa, the Copley girls, Bob Grosvenor, the Wyndhams, "Boy Elliot," etc., chaperoned by the vigilant Mrs. George, who records in detail to her son the smallest inflection of Theresa's manner towards the swains that sued for her favours. All had gone well with her the year before. Her first vision of society had dazzled her. Devon-

shire House, Almack's, the excitement of the Coronation, with
the great Embassy balls that succeeded it, were sufficient to delight
any girl making her first bow to the world.

But it was not long before she wearied of the endless round,
or before she discovered the emptiness of the young men who
fell to her lot as companions at these festivities—admirable youths
in their way, but their very youthfulness bored her, and as for
their conversation, it was non-existent. In thought she had
matured early, and though she was not ambitious, Theresa
Villiers was interested in affairs, and felt competent to fill a more
or less responsible rôle in life.

And now, in her second season, she met and fell in love with
Lord Francis Leveson-Gower, and in a flash the world became
a changed place for her. That he treated her badly there can
be no doubt. But that he was the unprincipled villain that the
Villiers family proclaimed him to be is manifestly absurd. He
was very young and uncertain of himself, and he was hardly
aware of the position he had got himself into. If he escaped
from it by taking the line of least resistance, it must be remembered that he had very little idea of the damage he was doing or
had actually done.

Francis Leveson-Gower was a nephew of Lord Granville, and
it was probably beneath his roof and under the benign auspices
of Lady Granville herself that Theresa first became acquainted
with him. Though only a second son (his father was Lord Staf-
ford, who became the first Duke of Sutherland), he was heir to
an immense fortune, since the estates of his maternal grandfather,
the Duke of Bridgewater, were entailed upon him, though he had
not as yet inherited them. Later he was raised to the peerage as
Lord Ellesmere. He was, therefore, a highly eligible young man.
But, apart from this, he was, personally, an arresting and a somewhat uncommon type of youth. Good-looking and intelligent,
beneath a reserved and moody exterior he hid considerable sensi-
tiveness, a first-class brain, and a good deal of political ambition.
He was intellectual and he was shy; and at the time at which he
met Theresa it is safe to assume that he was in the throes of a
more than usually difficult adolescence. It is probable that in
Theresa he found a confidante, sympathetic and interested, a
personality steadier and maturer than his own, but with tastes
and ideas not unlike. More and more he felt himself drawn to
this clever, rather unusual girl, who could offer him something
more than the flippant coin of friendship current between young
people in the society of the day. Theresa, on her part, found in
him a boy of her own age and position in the world whose conversation was worth listening to and whose personality had possi-
bilities. She was attracted; she was interested; and, before she

knew it, she was in love. An attachment formed between them,
which on his side was far more a thing of the mind than of the
heart. He sought her out in society as companion, counsellor
and friend; and from the perfect openness of his behaviour towards her, it is doubtful whether it ever occurred to him that
there was an emotional content in the relationship on either side.
Meanwhile, of course, his conduct was giving rise to the highest
speculation. Night after night, that season, at Devonshire House,
at the Opera, he was at her side, gloomy, silent, but persistent.
That there was something between them, an understanding, a
sympathy, became obvious to all, and it was not long before
tongues began to wag. The Villiers family, breathless with
expectation, grew gradually demented. To George in distant
St. Petersburg his mother wrote daily, almost hourly, bulletins
of the course events were taking, while the brothers at home
awaited the *dénouement* with speechless anxiety. Would he
propose? When would he propose? *Where* would he propose?

The season wore on and nothing happened. Theresa was calm,
but the situation was beginning to tell on her. Great hopes were
entertained of Lady Jersey's ball. It was an end-of-the-season
affair—one of the last great festivities of a brilliant season.

After it, people would begin to disperse and go off into the
country. A certain emphasis had been marked lately in the
young man's manner to Theresa, as if his feelings were mounting to a climax. It was the last opportunity. Surely he would
speak at Lady Jersey's ball.

The night came and went. He was there, apathetic, silent,
very much himself. Two days later, without a word of explanation, without a word of regret, without a word of adieu, he
departed for Ireland with his cousin Bob Grosvenor, gliding
out of Theresa's life as silently and mysteriously as he had
entered it.

The Villiers were furious, outraged. Heaven resounded with
the maledictions with which they pursued the retreating form of
Theresa's lover. An incensed Mrs. George mounted her carriage
and drove round daily to Lady Granville, into whose patient and
sympathetic ear she poured the whole pitiful story, crying for
vengeance on the peccant nephew. The brothers stalked London,
muttering darkly of horse-whippings and thrashings to come.
Theresa alone behaved with dignity and composure. She calmed
the family and put a stop to all talk. After a few days she pulled
herself together and faced the world, being seen everywhere at
the end of that season, more than usually brilliant, more than
usually herself. But, in reality, she was deeply wounded and
unhappy. That summer in the country her health broke down;
she became subject to fainting-fits and to a curious paralysis of

the limbs that could not be accounted for medically. Mrs. George was in an agony of doubt and fear for their "beloved angel." But the nervous reaction wore itself out, and she was on her feet again by the winter.

But life had changed for her: impulse had gone out of it. And though in the years that followed she played the part that was expected of her, though she shone and sparkled and made her puns as she used, it was observed that the brilliance was a little hard, the gaiety a little forced: that, in fact, she was a slightly over-emphasised edition of her former self.

§ 12

As might be expected, the almost hourly recital his mother gave him of how matters stood at home did nothing to make George Villiers more in love with his post abroad. The distance from all that he held most dear in the world; the fact, obvious to him from the first, that this was in no sense a beginning of his true career, but only a temporary expediency, accepted because the opening had presented itself and there had been nothing else for him at the moment; but, above all, the knowledge that so far from relieving his parents of his financial support he was still, at twenty-three, a drain upon them in this respect—all these reflections caused him to become restless and dissatisfied with his post in St. Petersburg. He talked over his difficulties very frankly with his chief, and the Ambassador could only agree with him when he pointed out that in the state of promotion, as it existed then, it would certainly be another three years before he could hope to be raised to the position of even third Secretary. Villiers was due for leave in the spring of 1823. Sir Charles Bagot sent him home with the Bag and his blessing, well knowing that they would not see him again in St. Petersburg.

It was still the high summer of Tory ascendancy when he returned. Lord Liverpool, with the undisputed assurance of Jove, ruled contentedly over a Tory Olympus, ably supported by such luminaries as Eldon, Wellington and Peel. Castlereagh had died by his own hand the year before, but the waters had closed over his head without fuss or commotion; and Canning, no less supreme an abitrator in European affairs, reigned at the Foreign Office in his stead. It was difficult to believe that this Administration—or some variant of it—would ever cease to exist; and since it had brought the country with honour and safety through the latter half of the Napoleonic wars and the appalling consequences of the peace, there did not seem any reason why it ever should. Its sheer efficiency had to be recognised by the Whigs themselves.

4

Only Brougham was a menace on that side. His brilliant defence of the Queen had shaken the firmament with a thunder other than Jove's; and there had been a great commotion. The outraged gods had retired in good order; but they knew that their rivals could do nothing against them. This was true: for the Whigs were incapable of agreeing to a policy, far less of forming an Administration. Olympus was strengthened and re-shuffled, and the gods trooped back. Lord Liverpool, a now undisputed Jove, resumed once more his placid sway over the entire political scene.

If this field was dominated by the Tory element, no less a Tory flavour was given to society by the extraordinary glamour which, at this period, surrounded the person of the Duke of Wellington. That intrepid commander was rapidly passing into a British in-stitution; and though some years were still to elapse before a trusting monarch placed the supreme political office in his hands, his reputation for bluff honesty in public affairs was already firmly established, aided, no doubt, by his own simple convic-tion that he could serve his King as well in the Senate as on the field of battle. But if politically his career still lacked the con-summation of the premiership, socially he was already supreme. Of the right birth by origin, and advanced to a dukedom for his own great services to the country, his honours sat lightly upon him. He moved with grace and a certain courtly charm across the stage of English social life, welcomed to their houses by Whigs and Tories alike. His conversation was dull but typical; and there was about him something so invincibly English, at once so stupid and so shrewd, that subconsciously he was accepted by both sides as a symbol. In these few years before he succeded to the premiership, the Duke—"Beau Wellington," as he is affectionately termed in contemporary letters—was con-sidered as above party, almost as above the standards by which an ordinary human being is habitually judged. He *was* England; its quaint formal aspect, its flowering nooks, its stubborn un-yielding clay; and as he passed from country-house to country-house, unalterably himself, drinking his port, and blurting out to awe-stricken Whigs his brief, soldierly comments on current events, one comes to realise that a more than earthly halo, at this juncture, surrounded the victor of Waterloo.

It was, therefore, to very much of a Tory world that George Villiers returned in search of a post. Not that his politics would count for much at this juncture, for he had never had occasion to declare himself one way or the other, and he was not con-sciously heading for a Parliamentary career. Only being a Whig by sympathy, and determined to be associated in the future with the Whig side in politics, it was a little difficult, even a little irksome, to sue for a paid post in the Civil Administration when all such posts were in the gift of the other side. However, luckily for him, the family was Tory by tradition, and had a certain amount of Tory influence. Nor had his father been inactive on his behalf while he had been away. Indeed the Governor had even gone so far as to have a passage of arms with his brother on his account. For, about three months before George returned from Russia, it happened that Uncle John, going about his ways, became acquainted with the fact that a Commissioner-ship of Customs was going a-begging. The post in those days was considered rather a plum because, although the work was un-inspiring, the emolument was good. Uncle John, never in the best of conditions financially, gazed thoughtfully at the prize, and had just determined to go for it himself, when the fact that he was about to do so came to the ears of the Governor. Now the post was just such a one as he was in search of for his son; the pay would be such as to make him financially independent of the family, to set him up on his own, and give him a start in life. That John should have thought of it for himself, know-ing that his nephew was looking for just such a job, was more than he could bear. The Governor was furious, and, if we are to believe Mrs. George, he did not mince matters with his brother, but accused him to his face of trying to take the bread out of young George's mouth, and added a few home truths as to the relative age and fitness for the post of uncle and nephew. Uncle John, thus shamed and brought to a proper frame of mind, relinquished his claim, leaving the way clear for his nephew.

Meanwhile the Governor acted with decision. He called upon Canning, whom he knew personally, drew his attention to the vacant post, and mentioned the fact that his son, a promising youth, was coming home from Russia in search of a job. Matters stood thus when George reached England. He had had some correspondence with his father on the subject before he left St. Petersburg, but had no idea that the ground had been so far prepared. He was in great heart about it, and after the first transports of family reunion had subsided he went to see Uncle John to canvas his help in the matter. Under the circumstances the interview must have been a curious one. Thereafter he betook himself to the Grove to discuss the pros-pect with Uncle Clarendon. Him he found charming as ever, but unavailing in the present instance. The old Earl lived very much out of the world these days, and his influence in politics was negligible. However, he promised to do what he could, and George came away pleased with the visit. He was now very keen on getting the job. It would suit him to a nicety. The

work would entail living in London, where he could keep a
watchful eye on the family, and the pay would relieve his
parents of his financial support.

But the season advanced, people dispersed to the country, and
still nothing had been achieved.   George hung about London
waiting to hear, anxious and out of sorts, till the Bathursts had
pity on him and carried him off to Gloucestershire.   They were
old friends of the family, and Lady Bathurst was much in
George's confidence.   Moreover, she had influence in high
circles, and it was through her good offices that George's name
was finally brought to the notice of the Prime Minister.   There
came a day that autumn when George was called precipitately
up to London.   There were interviews and appointments, difficulties and delays.   The suspense was breathless, but the result
satisfactory.   Lady Granville, back in Paris again and survey-
ing the world from her Embassy window, wrote to her sister in
November, 1823, " George Villiers has got a post worth £800
a year, as Auditor of Customs."

CHAPTER II

THE CUSTOMS I—LONDON AND IRELAND

§ I

VILLIERS' life for the next four years was uneventful. He disappeared into the Thames Street offices and worked unobtrusively at the deadening routine of excise. At first he was contented; he had achieved his purpose. He had freed his father from the necessity of supporting him, and his stipend was even sufficient, on occasions, to overflow in the direction of his needier brothers. He had made a beginning. He was well-satisfied with himself. But in 1824 an event occurred which was a sadness to him and to all the members of his family. The old Earl died. He had been slightly ailing for some time, and, although George had found his mind and senses perfectly unimpaired when he went down to the Grove to see him the summer before, from his account of the interview one gets the impression that the old man had smiled and shaken his head at his nephew in the manner of one whose work is over and to whom it was useless to apply for anything that entailed action in the world.

"I go coughing on, and working on," he had written to Edward some years before, "just like one of Wallis' post-horses. No one thinks whether they are sound or not provided that they are going."

And a sentence at the end of the same letter sounds almost like a valediction to the nephew whom he had treated as his own son: "Adieu, my dear Edward. No one will love you better than I do till Mrs. Edward mixes love of a higher quality." But he had lived on for five years after writing these words. Now he was dead, and Uncle John succeeded to the title.

The old Earl had been marvellously kind to the Villiers family, supporting the Governor, and educating two of his boys. But he was a bachelor. Uncle John had a wife and a daughter. Things would be different at the Grove, and perhaps that bounty which had overflowered so generously towards Kent House would be somewhat curtailed. But since no change can be detected in the family mode of living, it seems that Uncle John must have continued the allowance to his brother on more or less the same scale as before. As it happened, he was to prove always kind and helpful to his brother's family. But they never trusted him, and when he came to die, his will was to prove a curious one. As Lady Clarendon was now well into middle-life without having borne a son, the Governor became heir to the Earldom.

This event was as a pebble thrown into the uneventful waters of Villiers' work on the Customs Board. But the commotion it created soon died down, and he turned again to his affairs.

§ 2

Residence in London fostered a keener interest in politics. George observed their ebb and flow with increasing attention; and since this new interest ended by governing his life, we too must take stock of the political situation.

The year eighteen-twenty-four dawned prosperously over England. The disorders, civil and economic, of the nine years since the war had at last been allayed. Riot and Revolution— grim shadows that had hung intermittently over the landscape for much of that time—had finally succumbed to a very English mixture of wise legislation and *laisser-faire*: Cato Street and Peterloo were forgotten; and the country settled down to take stock of its resources after a long period of social unrest.

That these resources were unexpectedly large and had extricated themselves from the entanglements which had encumbered them at the start, came as a shock of surprise to a people whose energies had been chiefly absorbed in civil disputes. The effect was miraculous. Confidence returned: trade began to boom; and, with the rapidly developing industries of the North, investment in British Companies showed quick and surprising returns.

Such a rush of speculation followed as had hardly been witnessed since the days of the South Sea Bubble. Thousands of companies were floated, and capital poured like wine into the capacious vats of British enterprise—much to be spilled and lost for ever—but more to ferment and increase, and be turned into the headiest and most dangerous vintage that was ever contrived. For in all this trafficking a new element had entered. With the greater accretion of wealth that the liberal conditions of the new century had made possible, money had come to be regarded as a thing having value in itself apart from the commodity it represented in Nature. All sense of barter—of value for value—was lost sight of in the welter of exchanges, and ''money'' as an arithmetical abstraction, divorced of its implications, came to signify a blind unit of power, to the handling of which no moral responsibility whatsoever was attached. And with this new conception of wealth as a thing to be juggled with, transformed and expanded at will irrespective of the consequences, eighteenth-century England, traditional England, the England of King and courtier, of peer and peasant—a feudal system, the members of which, for all their troubles, had been held together by ties of mutual respect and obligation—finally expired, and something new and astonishingly vital and ugly took its place. In disruption and competition and the loosening of bonds the Modern Age was brought to birth.

Over this changing scene a Tory oligarchy presided with continued self-assurance. And although most of its members stood essentially for the things that were so rapidly passing away, the superficial glamour of the times blinded them to the reality beneath; and they were far too occupied with the results of their beneficent legislation to understand what was actually taking place. There are certain words in the English language which, if repeated often enough and without exact definition, come to exert a hypnotic influence over the English mind, till their proper meaning is lost in manifold association, and a single word comes to stand for a state of society, a political cause and a religion all rolled into one. Such a word, in the years of which we are writing, was the word "Prosperity." It was a most useful noun. It seemed to purify and ennoble in one long polysyllabic sound, borrowed from Latin, that astonishing rush to "get rich quick" which was so marked a feature of the times, and which, surely, was so healthy a symptom for members of the body politic to exhibit. It seemed, for instance, to explain, even to beatify, the astonishing transformation that was taking place in the Northern Midlands, where rows and rows of little grey houses were beginning to stretch out into the country-side in deadening uniformity from Manchester and Liverpool, from Preston, Wigan and Crewe: where men and women in their thousands were crowding in to the great centres, abandoning the dignity of labour in the fields for cramped and straining team-work in the shadow of the machines. It seemed to vindicate the need for children working fourteen hours a day, and for families sleeping fourteen in a cottage. The word "Prosperity" explained it all. So when a member moving the Address in the House of Lords in 1825 exclaimed portentously, "Our present prosperity is a prosperity that extends to all orders, and all professions, and all districts," we are not surprised to find that nobody enquired what he meant—still less dared to contradict him. The hypnosis was complete. And from an age that could wax sentimental over the prospect of the landscape rapidly disappearing beneath the fogs and filths of industry, and describe it (as Cobbett described the valley of Todmorden) as a spectacle "the most curious and romantic that was ever seen, where the water and the coal seem to be engaged in a struggle for getting the foremost in point of utility to men," anything, indeed, but true foresight might be expected.

So " Prosperity " was the slogan of the hour.   Behind this doctrinal rampart the Tory Government entrenched itself with no small measure of satisfaction, for was not this very prosperity due to its own sage counsels?

Yet all was not well with Olympus.   The god-like slumbers of such enormous personages as Liverpool, Wellington and Peel were perpetually being disturbed by the watchfulness, within the party, of an advanced group whose programme was one of Reform. Canning himself led this group, and his lieutenants were political personalities of no less weight than Palmerston, Huskisson and William Lamb.   Supported by the Whigs, on account of their liberal principles, the Canningites were thus the determining factor in the party game, and their programme was highly distasteful to the more conservative members of the Cabinet.   The High Tory element was disgruntled and aggrieved.   It was one thing to approve, with the smile of patronage, the growing prosperity of the country, but quite another thing to embark upon a series of measures with a view to giving bent to the " liberal " and uncon- stitutional opinions that seemed—surprisingly—always to be arising out of that prosperity.   There was the question of Parlia- mentary Reform, for instance.   Certainly there were abuses and anomalies attached to parliamentary representation; but they were traditional, and a sweeping reform, such as was suggested, would mean tampering with the Constitution itself, a positive sacrilege, and not to be thought of.   As for Catholic Emancipation, Pro- testant England would hardly stand for *that*.   Could England be governed and her affairs administered by persons who refused spiritual allegiance to the King?   And yet there seemed a growing pressure from beneath, a concentration of interest in the public mind on both these questions.   It was very tiresome.   All the more so since the continued existence of the Government depended, in large measure, on the presence in its midst of the group who stood for these things, and who could avert by the mere hope they inspired of reform any very serious onslaught on the part of the Opposition.

Indeed, like so many other things in life at this time, the old Tory party was breaking up.   Its uses were outworn, its ideals obsolescent.   The political creed that had enabled Pitt to build up an Empire, and Wellington to save a continent, that had found England a mere appanage of Europe, and had placed her for ever in the forefront of its counsels, was ill-fitted to embody the social doctrines that the past fifty years had let loose upon the world. From its very nature the party, as it stood, was doomed; and in the end, after a series of grudging concessions, the Old Guard closed its ranks and smashed itself to pieces against the bayonets of Reform.   In the reconstruction that took place under Sir Robert

Peel a new Tory party was virtually brought to birth.   But the future was to the Whigs.

Meanwhile the two burning questions of the day were making themselves increasingly felt.   Session after session measures for Catholic relief were loudly advocated by one section of the Ministry in Cabinet, only to be denounced and rejected by another, while the Whigs, at the instigation of Russell, pressed on for Parliamentary Reform.   Harassed and divided within, the Government still managed to present an unbroken front.

As long as Lord Liverpool was at the head of affairs he was able, by sheer force of personality, to keep in abeyance the sharp differences of principle and opinion that in reality rent the Government into two distinct groups.   But Liverpool was old and tired. The yoke of perpetual office had sat heavily on his shoulders for some time past, and early in 1827 he had an apoplectic stroke which, though it did not immediately prove fatal, was sufficient to remove him at once and for ever from the field of politics.   With Liverpool gone the dissensions and animosities that had smouldered for so long beneath the complacent façade of Government unanimity burst into flames, and thereafter followed a period of political chaos, which, for chicanery and bad faith on all sides, is hard to parallel in the whole history of the British Parliament. Out of the clouds of intrigue there emerges the lonely figure of Canning bereft of support and dispossessed of the power which should have rightly been his—Canning whom a perverse Destiny lifts suddenly into the light at this juncture to fulfil the brief and bitter consummation of his long career.   Deserted by his late High Tory colleagues, mistrusted and hated by the rank and file of the party he was supposed to be leading, supported only by a handful of devoted followers who were powerless to carry him with honour through the ordeal of office, for four months he grappled with the forces against him, to sink at the end to a premature grave, literally hounded to death by the hatred and vindictiveness of his political inferiors.

He was succeeded by the lachrymose and incompetent Goodrich, who flaps ineffectually across the stage, like a ghost, wringing impotent hands over angry Cabinet meetings where his authority as Prime Minister was set at naught by colleagues who had their own quarrels to attend to.   Indeed, he had been raised to the supreme power and his position thrust upon him by the consent of both scheming factions of the party, who thought it convenient, until their difficulties were settled, to have a cipher at the head of affairs.   Treated with a lack of consideration that is hardly believable, harassed by the party situation and insulted by his inferiors, he crept ignominiously out of office after five months, tendering a tearful resignation to the King, who dismissed him with a word of contemptuous solicitude, and sent immediately for the Duke of Wellington. "My dear Arthur, the Ministry is defunct." The royal words, uttered from the depths of a touselled bed at Windsor, mark the opening of the last phase in the drama of Tory dissolution. With the accession of the Duke to power, invincible conservatism met to do battle for the first time with the liberal forces of the age. And though the Duke was far too wise a commander not to realise the necessity of giving ground on occasion, though he retreated, indeed, with honour, from positions which, at the start, he had fully intended to hold, on the Constitutional question he was adamant. On this ground he and his followers took up their last stand, and the Government went down, vanquished by the overwhelming odds in favour of Reform.

After a preliminary skirmish on the subject of corn, the campaign proper opened on the question of the Catholic disabilities. Pressure from Ireland was hourly becoming more acute, and Lord Anglesea—no alarmist—wrote disquieting despatches on the relative strength and growing tension of the Catholic Association and the "Brunswickers," both of which institutions were highly organised and arming rapidly.

Public opinion in England was still divided. The liberalism of the times demanded a sweeping abolition of ancient injustices. This view was reflected in Parliament by the attitude of the Canningites, who pressed eagerly for reform with the clamorous approbation of the Whigs. But a large section of conservative Protestant opinion saw in any loosening of the bonds that held Rome in check a weakening of the props that supported their own faith; and this view was shared by most of the High Tories, who were obdurate on the subject, and by the King, who was most obdurate of all.

His Majesty, indeed, held distinct views on the religious issue. He had envisaged Canning's accession to power with feelings of profoundest misgiving. His kingly position seemed threatened, his authority set at naught. Was he not "Defender of the Faith"? Undoubtedly he was. Was not this high stewardship a sacred trust handed down to him by his father (of pious memory) and confirmed by his own Coronation Oath? Undoubtedly it was. And yet he was invited—nay, compelled—to take into his service the very man whose chief policy seemed to be to weaken the defences that had immemorially protected English public life from the insidious advances of Rome. It was too much. How could he countenance such a man as his first Minister? How square it with that tender thing, his conscience? How, indeed. . . .

The royal scruples were mercifully relieved by Providence, which decreed that the hated Emancipation Bill, when it first

appeared, should be defeated in both Houses despite the passionate
advocacy of Canning. This was good. But it was followed up by
a further dispensation which removed the dangerous Minister for
ever from the field of his labours here below. This was better still.
His Majesty breathed again. Surely Heaven itself was on the
side of the Protestants?

But the royal breast was not wholly free from anxiety during
the interregnum of Lord Goodrich. Goodrich was unbelievably
weak, and his policy would be dictated by whichever section of
his scheming Cabinet got the upper hand. It soon became
evident, however, that the Canningites, with their leader gone,
were powerless to withstand the heavy artillery of the High Tories.
Goodrich disappeared into the mists from which he had come, and
Wellington loomed large as the Man of Destiny.

It was a blessed consummation. With "my dear Arthur" at
the head of affairs, supported by the implacable Peel, the royal
conscience could afford to relax. As soon suspect two English
Cathedrals of a desire to ring the Angelus, as two such paladins
of the old régime of harbouring Romish sympathies. All was
now well. The preferential treatment to Protestants would continue: agitation would die down beneath the firm hand of the
victor of Waterloo: the crisis was over. His Majesty dismissed
the subject from his anxious mind, and turned to the distractions
of Windsor, where the contemplation of Lady Conyngham's ageing charms could still stir a memory or two in the breast of the
Defender of Faiths.

But, in all this, it is evident that the King imperfectly understood the mind of the Duke of Wellington. The Prime Minister
was by no means as immovable on most articles of the party
faith as was generally supposed. The truth is, politics presented
themselves to the old Commander in terms of the field of battle:
party credences as a series of positions to be held as long as
possible, but to be abandoned with perfect decorum when the
tactical situation involved in holding them became impossible.
To him, expedience governed the game; and it was better to
retreat, when circumstances warranted, and hold on to the next
position, than to resign and let the other side in. Resignation was
the only ultimate defeat; and this was to be avoided at all costs
—or nearly all costs. So long as the Catholic question remained
an open one, he was entirely in sympathy with the King on the
subject and adamant against reform. But quite suddenly there
appeared on the Irish horizon a marvel and a portent of considerable magnitude; and in the fantastic light that it threw on current
events, it was not long before His Majesty became aware that
"dear Arthur" was talking and behaving in a manner wholly
strange and unfamiliar.

The news from Ireland was a bombshell. In the re-shuffle that took place on the secession of the Canningites from the Tory party, Vesey Fitzgerald had been appointed to the Board of Trade. He was an Irish landowner, personally and politically popular in Ireland, but, of course, a Protestant. He had stood for County Clare; and no particular interest was evinced when he offered himself for re-election. But, with dramatic sudden-ness, Daniel O'Connell himself stood forward and, backed by the whole Catholic Association, determined to contest the seat. The excitement in Ireland was indescribable. Fitzgerald hurried over to investigate the situation. But realising, after a few days' stay in the constituency, that he had not the remotest chance of success and that his presence in the district only aggravated the situation and would probably lead to bloodshed, he retired and left the field open to O'Connell, who was triumphantly elected to the Imperial Parliament by an overwhelming Catholic majority. His election created an uproar throughout the length and breadth of Ireland, and Wellington and Peel found them-selves standing on the edge of an abyss at the bottom of which was something that looked unpleasantly like Civil War.

Peel, at once alive to the situation, resigned, but patriotically withdrew his resignation on realising the immense support he could be to his chief at such a crisis. The Duke himself was imperturbable. Not an eyelid quivered, not a muscle twitched on the face of the intrepid old Commander. Who could have told that beneath the impassive exterior, the trim smiling figure that passed on horseback in the Row, or stooped to a lady's hand in an archway at Devonshire House, a complete change of front had, in fact, taken place? Not the King, at first. Not even his own associates in the Cabinet. But his mind was made up; and that summer (1828) he repaired to Cheltenham to consider the bitter draught he was about to swallow—almost as unpalatable, he reflected as he tossed off his glass, as the waters of Cheltenham themselves. . . . His own views were perfectly clear to himself. He hated not so much the principle of Catholic concession as the withdrawal of the preferential treatment in favour of Protestant subjects. Church and State—the two were indissoluble in his mind, and in this faith he had walked all his life. But the ways of Providence were strange; and it was not for him to question its inscrutable workings. Common sense—certainly an attribute of any Deity who could possibly be conceived of as national—pointed with no uncertain finger to concession. And the Duke was no fool. The enemy had carried the earthworks and were half-way up the slope. The time had come to retreat or be over-whelmed. He chose the wiser course. In July he wrote to Peel that he would be prepared to discuss the situation in the month of September. But he well knew the outcome. With a grim smile—for the Duke enjoyed irony—he set himself to the curious task of converting the King to the principle of Catholic Emancipation.

§ 3

Now it happened that, nine months before the Clare election, George Villiers was sent to Dublin on a mission connected with Customs and Excise. So not only was he actually in Ireland during all the excitement that led up to and accompanied the granting of Catholic Emancipation, but he arrived in Ireland long enough before it to go about the country and to form his own opinion on the burning question of the day.

Not much of importance had happened to him during the years of which we have spoken. He had worked on unobtrusively at his desk in Thames Street watching with interest the march of political events and keeping a vigilant eye on the family. Hyde and Charles were both heading for political careers. Charles, a fiery radical with startling views, was taking his law work very lightly and turning his face more and more towards Westminster. Hyde, calculating and collected, was already there, making a name for himself among the Whig back-benchers.

But there were not sufficient funds to establish these two in the independent careers they had chosen for themselves, and the family was still on the look-out for jobs. A forlorn hope presented itself when Lord Goodrich became Prime Minister, for he was Mrs. George's first cousin. George was sent to interview him; but he proved a broken reed, for all that he could offer was a seat on the Lunacy Board for Charles at a salary of £170 a year and no pension. Villiers was beginning to wonder whether he had not better bring his own job into the market and try to get something more lucrative, whereby he might help support the family, when he became aware that he had been chosen to assist in arranging the fusion of the English and Irish Excise Boards the following year. He was to go to Dublin in the autumn of 1827. This was not exactly promotion, but it was a proof that his work had been approved of in higher circles than he knew. And it was an opportunity; for, if he did well, it might lead to his being employed in a yet wider field. For private reasons he was reluctant to go: for public reasons and for the sake of his career he felt it his duty to go. But just before he left England an event occurred which not only caused him great personal sorrow but placed him in a new relation to his family. The Governor, after many years of ill-health, slipped quietly and gently out of life, died indeed so discreetly that it was hardly possible for his turbulent young family to realise that

he had gone.   To George it meant the assumption of the nominal
as well as the actual direction of the family's affairs.   More than
ever, he desired to remain in England; but, no power intervening
on his behalf, he sailed for Dublin in October, 1827.

And now a perfectly new life opened out before him.   As far
as work was concerned, never had he been so much his own
master or given so much scope in the handling of situations.
Chairman of the Board which was deputed to examine the state
of the Irish Customs, his colleagues were both tractable and unassuming; and it was not long before they realised that in George
they had someone to whom they could very well look for guidance and initiative.   Indeed, his talent for organisation and procedure was now for the first time given full play; the sense of
frustration under which he had laboured so long was removed,
and we see his whole nature, for the moment, coming to fruition
in the larger sphere of work and responsibility that had been
allotted to him.   The very tone of his letters changes.   He becomes more assured of himself, of his powers and of the future.
Thereafter, he plunged eagerly into work.   He went all over the
country on tours of inspection in order to look into things for
himself.   He developed an eye for detail and a mind to grasp
its significance.   He collated returns and considered individual
cases: he weighed evidence, delivered judgment and impressed
his findings on the Board with a suavity of manner which made
the most unpalatable decisions acceptable.   It was not long before
he became something of a personage in Dublin.   The unbiassed
judgment of the young Customs official became a by-word, and
his opinion was canvassed on more than one occasion, with
amused tolerance, in very high circles indeed.

But far more important than the work he was actually engaged
on was the vision of Ireland that was beginning to take shape in
his mind.   He had not journeyed through its fastnesses, penetrated
its small, sullen towns, descended from heights upon its noisy
ports for nothing.   The cool, appraising eye of a statesman was
watching and taking notes.   And something in all that he saw
appealed to his sense of justice, and through that to his sympathies.   His heart went out to the "seven millions of the finest
people in the world" whose affections were being perennially
estranged from the Mother Country by almost wilful misrepre-
sentation and misrule.

§ 4

He had arrived in the country almost a year before the Clare
election brought the Catholic situation to a head.   But already
the rival associations—Catholic and Brunswickers—were arming,
and the excitement, though suppressed, was intense.   Convinced

on purely liberal and political grounds of the need for Emancipation, George was all the more established in this belief by the language and demeanour of the anti-Catholic party. One of his early tours of inspection took him to Limerick, and during his stay in the district the Clancartys put him up. They were kind and pleasant hosts, but their conversation was a shock to him. It was the first time he had come in contact with the full blast of the Orange point of view. "More despotic, bloodthirsty and revolting principles," he writes, "it was never my misfortune to listen to." He adds: "I am convinced that many respectable, right-minded (as they think) men conceive it impossible that any Catholic priest *can* be honest, or that any Catholic acts but under the guidance of his priest. The disturbances of the country have *invariable* reference to that subject."

By the beginning of 1828 the situation was becoming acute. "The fact is," says Hyde, who was travelling in Ireland at the time with George, "they have agitated and increased the passions of the people—both Catholic and Protestant—and Catholic emancipation *must* be granted, or a convulsion ensue. The 'Brunswickers' think that if they can get up a row the Government must side with them. Then the Catholic question would be thrown out for years and years. The 'Brunswickers' are collecting money in large sums and arming the Protestants of the North. If there is any casual affray, and the latter were to put to death one or two Catholics, there can scarcely be a doubt that a massacre of the Protestants in the South would at least be the probable consequence. Yet the Government stands still, looking on, and doing nothing. It is truly marvellous."

So matters marched on to the Clare election. This bomb dropped into the quivering mass of conflicting opinion rent the country from end to end. The interest was intense, and now all focused on England and what the Government would do.

"O'Connell goes to England on Friday," writes Villiers to his mother. "You would be as surprised as I was at what a good case he is able to make out. He has done it most ably and ingeniously, and has made it, in my opinion, more than a debatable question. He clearly shows that the law is so confused in the matter of the oath that it is questionable whether they have a right to require it of a member at the time he takes his seat. He sent me his case, and (if he hasn't omitted any essentials of the law), I conceive it to be a pretty good one."

By this it will be seen that Villiers was for Catholic emancipation. Indeed, such was the state of excitement in Ireland that it would have been impossible to live there at that time without taking sides.

"I never entered so long, or so earnestly, I may say, so enthusiastically into any subject in my life. I feel quite wrapped up in it, and I really believe few people here have worked harder in different ways for it than I have. Ten years, aye, three years hence, we shan't bring ourselves to believe the excitement there was over this."

But if he felt strongly in the matter his sense of justice never deserted him, and he was able to look at the question from other points of view than his own:

"You ask me my opinion on the settlement of the eternal question, and I scarcely know what to answer, for under different circumstances, my opinion would vary. If you ask my opinion as an individual, it would be different to what I should give as a Minister. In the one case I should tell you what I thought *ought*, and in the other what I thought *could* be done. As an individual, I should say give full and unqualified emancipation. You would at once bind this country to you by the strongest ties. It would be the only real union of the two countries and consolidation of their energies . . . But, on the other hand, if I was a Minister, I should probably feel that unqualified emancipation was impossible; that the strong prejudices of many Protestants were to be respected because they are sincere. I would not, therefore, attempt, or even broach unqualified emancipation; but my *tendency* would be towards it; and I should deem that measure best that approached it nearest."

With regard to the Relief Bill, the Duke was not to be rushed. Though his mind was made up by the autumn of 1828, though he had discussed the matter fully with Peel and Lord Lyndhurst, and had decided, even, on the points of the Bill that was to be brought in, he continued to mask his guns till he judged the time fully ripe for disclosure. For over three months the strictest secrecy was preserved as to the intentions of the Government. Nor would he have it appear that any compulsion from without was being brought to bear upon himself or his colleagues. Lord Anglesea, the Lord Lieutenant, who had, upon occasion, expressed himself too openly and shown too plainly where his sympathies lay, was recalled and replaced by the Duke of Northumberland, who had systematically voted against Catholic Emancipation. This was a dramatic step, for Lord Anglesea was popular, and his removal at this juncture only accentuated the feeling in the country. Something of the intense excitement is borne down to us over more than a hundred years by Villiers' description of the final scene in Lord Anglesea's departure from Ireland:

"After the Levée," he writes in a letter dated January 21st, "he got upon his horse and roade down to Kingston where he embarked. The streets were lined with soldiers, and there was an immense, enthusiastic mob. He was escorted by a huge body of horsemen, who accompanied him down to the sea. There were many thousands of people assembled, and I never saw a more beautiful *coup d'œil*. The locality lends itself to this sort of spectacle prodigiously. It is nearly the largest artificial harbour in the world, in a sort of horse-shoe shape; and not being yet finished, blocks of granite and half-completed piers come down to the water's edge. And around and between, and a-top of these were clustered no small portion of the 'seven millions.' He took a row in the ship's barge round the harbour to afford fair bent to their enthusiastic acclamations, every ship saluting, and all their yards manned. The day was one of the loveliest I have ever seen since I have been in Ireland—just the Italian winter day you describe; and I never saw that splendid bay look so clear, or to such advantage. Can't you fancy its having been a satisfactory sight?"

By the end of the year the excitement in England was intense. In January, 1829, it became known in London that the Government proposed to bring in a Bill, and speculation was rife as to its nature and extent. The Duke of Cumberland, home in England again, alternately railed in the Lords, and endeavoured to stiffen the King to resist to the last. The King was in a fever. He alternately stormed at his ministers and kissed them on both cheeks. The Bishops were in a flutter, alarmed by the violence of the anti-Catholic press. Lord Eldon was formidable among his peers. But the Duke was confident. Peel was now safe to pilot the measure through the Commons; he himself would look after it in the Lords; and, for the rest, common sense would win the day.

The Bill was brought before the Commons in the early days of March. In its comprehensiveness it far exceeded expectations, and Villiers was in high fettle with the Government.

" . . . nobody, not the most sanguine," he exclaims, " ever hoped for the boon to be made so great, or that it would be so graciously and *willingly* conferred. . . . It is nearly unqualified Emancipation." True, the forty-shilling franchise was raised to £10. But since it was the forty-shilling freeholders, organised by the Catholic Association, who had elected Daniel O'Connell for County Clare and were responsible for the organised resistance of the whole of the South, their disenfranchisement was perhaps a sop to the principle of Law and Order. Brougham, member of the Opposition, but speaking in favour of the Bill in the Lords, referred to this part of it " as the price, as the high price, as the all but extravagant price of this inestimable good. That price, to obtain that good, he, for one, would most willingly pay."

5

After a stormy debate in the Commons the first reading was carried by 348 votes to 160. On March 31st it came before the Lords. A three days' debate ensued, in which Lord Eldon and the Archbishop of Canterbury led a heated opposition. But the voting proved how well the Duke had prepared the ground for it. The reading was carried by a majority of 105. On April 10th the Bill passed the Lords, and on the 11th it was taken down to Windsor for the Royal Assent. It was just before Easter, and Parliament adjourned for the recess. It re-assembled on April 28th, and on that date, for the first time since the Test Act of 1678, Catholic peers assumed their seats in the House of Lords.

CHAPTER III

THE CUSTOMS II—LONDON AND PARIS

§ I

VILLIERS' time in Ireland ended with the passing of the Emancipation Bill. Not that there was any connection between the work that the Customs Board was doing in Ireland at that time and the political situation which was rending the country from end to end. But it so happened that that work terminated and the Board was dispersed in the early months of 1829, just at the moment when the excitement over the Bill was reaching a climax. A good deal, however, remained to be done in the way of the winding up of affairs, and Villiers was considered on all sides to be the person to do it. He remained in Ireland, therefore, for some months after the other members of the Board had gone home, and was not himself back in England that year till the summer was well advanced.

The actual work in which he had been employed during all this time is highly technical, and since it is not relevant to the wider aspects of his career, it is unnecessary to examine it here. Suffice it to say that he accomplished the difficult task entrusted to the Board, of which he was chairman, with tact and adroitness; and, at a time when political and social animosities were never more inflamed, he had found it possible to move in all circles, to make friends with all sorts and conditions of men and, by a power of conciliation, to do much in an unseen way to further a cause he had taken to heart.

"Mr. Villiers," wrote a great London daily, commenting on George's return, "has been two years in Dublin, and unfettered by political situations or connexions, he mixed indiscriminately in the best society of that lively and intelligent capital; and to such a degree had he acquired the esteem and regard of the most eminent men of all parties, that he was invited (previous to his return to England) to a farewell dinner, which if it had taken place, would have displayed a social union of the most illustrious names in Ireland, without distinction of party or religion. Mr. Villiers, however, with much discretion and good taste, declined the proffered offer, on the ground that such a public mark of respect was due only to a political character, with which he was not invested, or political services, which he had never been in a

position to render; and he, therefore, shrunk from an exhibition
which, however gratifying and honourable to him, might be mis-
represented or misunderstood on this side of the water. When we
add that the Duke of Leinster was to have taken the chair, and
that among the party would have been the Lords Plunkett,
Prudhoe and F. Leveson-Gower, Archdeacon Singleton, the Commander-in-Chief (Sir J. Byng), the Solicitor-General, Messrs. R.
Gregory, Sheil, Curran, N. Sneyd, Crampton, Latouch, etc., the
value of the intended compliment to Mr. Villiers will be duly
appreciated, and (what is more important) the complete banishment of all political animosities from society be very forcibly
illustrated.''

There is no doubt that Villiers was henceforth a man marked
for promotion.

Meanwhile he was glad to be back in England after his time
away. He immediately busied himself in picking up the threads
he had begun to form in society on the eve of his departure, and
he was much seen that autumn and winter in the country houses.
He stayed with the Baths at Longleat, with the Bathursts at
Cirencester and with the Verulams at Gorhambury. He hunted
a little, shot a little, and talked a great deal, and so re-created
himself in the lives of his friends after his two years' exile in
Ireland.

He was now more assured of his future. It was only a question
of time, he knew, before he would be picked out for some more
spectacular post in which his abilities would be given full scope.
Meanwhile he set up on his own in rooms in Cleveland Court and
continued his work at the Customs. At home all was well. Mrs.
George, her period of mourning behind her, was taking to life with
her accustomed zest. Hyde and Charles were both now in Parliament; and Edward was still the same Edward, delicate, ironical,
aloof, a stranger in that robust family of budding politicians.
Good looking, fragile, difficult, his health would not permit him
to take up any definite work. The old Earl had left him a little
money, which enabled him to travel abroad with friends for most
of the year.

§ 2

In 1830, Theresa became engaged to be married to Thomas
Henry Lister, a Staffordshire squire with a taste for literature and
the arts. The mere statement of fact can give no idea of the
bombshell that this was to the Villiers family. In the eyes of her
mother, of George, of all the brothers, she was the expression on
earth of all they hoped to meet in heaven; and that a mere '' Mr.
Lister '' should have captivated this celestial being to the point of
being about to marry her seemed somehow all wrong and contrary

to the laws of nature.   For years they had surrounded her with a
slavish adoration.   Her beauty, her charm, her *espièglerie*, were
eagerly appraised, while her *mots* and her puns—for it was a
punning age—went the round of the family, and were received
with shouts of mirthful appreciation.   She was, for them, the
ultimate expression of the Villiers family; and since, it is useless
to deny, they had a pretty good conceit of themselves, they one
and all considered the best that the world had to offer was not
good enough for her, and believed that some special dispensation
of fortune would surely be reserved for her simply because she *was*
Theresa Villiers, and there was nobody else like her in the world.

This attitude was all very touching in its way, but it had its
disadvantages, especially for the person who called it into being.
Each new young man who swam into their orbit in society was
regarded simply as a target for Theresa's battery of charms.   It
was inferred that he must be madly in love with her, and thereafter he was subjected to the most rigid scrutiny on the part of a
distracted family.   Indeed the path to Theresa was strewn with
thorns for the unwary.   If a young man was too free and easy in
his manner towards her, he was considered a villain, a scoundrel,
a thing hardly fit for human society.   Equally if he failed at once
to succumb to her beauty, he was dubbed a person of no taste, no
discrimination, of hardly any breeding whatsoever.   And more
than one delightful young man who might at least have proved a
distraction to Theresa fell thus between Scylla and Charybdis of
family disapproval and sheered off lest a worse thing befall him.

And what of Theresa herself?   Life had not treated her kindly.
Beneath the sparkle and conscious brilliance of her personality
she was unhappy, and she was apathetic.   Above all, she was
bored.   *How* she was bored!   Life had made her a woman and
circumstances compelled her still to act the girl.   Her limbs moved
mechanically through the mazes of the social round.   She smiled
at Bob Grosvenor and waltzed with young Wilton.   She allowed
Charles Wyndham to sit at her feet and "Boy" Elliot to be her
cavaliere servente.   But her mind was abstracted, her thoughts
elsewhere.

Time passed without much incident.   A young peer proved
troublesome, and even went so far in his efforts to curry favour as
to offer Hyde a safe borough seat.   Theresa allowed George to
write and put an end to the nonsense.   Charles Wyndham—
rather touchingly—proposed.   Theresa was very gentle with him,
and they remained friends.

She was twenty-seven when, at Saltram, she met Thomas Henry
Lister.   He was considerably older than she was—a *litterateur*
with some pretensions to fame as novelist, playwright and writer
of articles.   He was set in his ways, rather pedantic and wholly

devoted to his work. He soon became attracted to a girl who could take an intelligent interest in his conversation. And Theresa gradually came to find in him a companion whose mind and personality had a certain charm for her. Also she felt safe with him. Here was no unformed boy whose character and career were still in the making, but a man of the world, established and assured, with tastes and occupations not unlike her own. And, above all, he would demand very little of her.

It was a curious courtship, protracted over six months. As usual, it drove the family nearly demented. To begin with, Thomas Lister was hardly the suitor they wished for Theresa. However, as she seemed drawn to him, they accepted him for her sake. Also, of course, he could give her a home and a background. Two or three thousand a year and a place in Staffordshire were not wholly to be despised. But, then, why this hanging about? Why did he not instantly propose? Why this hesitation and show of reluctance? George and his mother couldn't make it out at all; and they had just decided that he was a scoundrel, and had written very plainly to each other to that effect, rejoicing together that now there was no need to take such a viper into the bosom of the family, when, as a matter of fact, he *did* propose, and Theresa wrote from Saltram blazing with her news. It was very awkward, and they were hard put to it to explain to each other that what they had actually *said* was not at all what they meant, and that now that their darling was happy, etc., etc.

So Theresa was married in November, 1830, and departed out of the family on the arm of her Staffordshire squire. That she had gained peace and contentment at last is unquestionable. Villiers was devoted to his sister, and now that happiness had come to her he was delighted at the match. He wrote enthusiastically to her while she was on her honeymoon, and his obvious sincerity touched her deeply. " I should like to be married myself," he adds, and there is a ring to the remark which augurs rather sadly that he never will be. In this he was wrong, for he was to be married, and very happily married. But it is doubtful whether he was ever to be in love. Not much of romance had come his way. Passion he had known, and he was neither more nor less moral than the men of his age. Women attracted him; but he was, by nature, aloof. Only those who attempted to come close realised the height and depth of detachment which was masked by the smiling exterior. Emily Eden, Lord Auckland's sister—perhaps the most fascinating letter-writer of the nineteenth century in England—came as close as any. And sometimes from the tone of her letters one gets the impression that she would have come closer still. Certainly she had a deep attachment for Villiers, and understood him better than any other woman in his life. She was his contemporary; they had made their début in the world at the same time, and gone about to the same parties, so there were many ties of association between them. Moreover, she was keenly interested in politics, and the wit that she brought to bear upon the persons and events of that age make good reading to this day. She watched George's career with the keenest interest, became a great friend of his wife's and kept in touch with them both till her death in the late sixties of the century. She never married, but established a sort of salon to which the great Whig leaders came to imbibe wisdom, tolerance and common sense, for she had all these. George could have married her, but he never saw this; and there is sometimes in her letters to him a veiled amusement at his obtuseness which is very entertaining to those who read them after more than half a century.

§ 3

A year after Theresa's marriage, in December, 1831, George Villiers was again chosen by those in power to represent Great Britain on a Customs Commission abroad. A change had taken place in the political landscape since last he was so employed. The old Tory party, with the Duke at its head, had smashed itself to pieces the year before upon the question of Parliamentary Reform. The Whigs were now in power, and Lord Grey Prime Minister. Meanwhile a Whig Chancellor of the Exchequer, Lord Althorpe, wishing to take advantage of the friendly relations then existing between France and Great Britain, appointed an Excise Commission (at France's invitation) to revise the Customs treaties between the two countries, and to draw up a report which should form the basis of more liberal and up-to-date legislation on the subject. France proposed that Great Britain should appoint two Commissioners to meet two of their own, and that the discussions should take place in Paris. Lord Althorpe immediately appointed Dr. John Bowrigg, a public servant of some standing, a brilliant linguist, but a man of peculiar characteristics; and then, looking round for someone more diplomatic to counteract Bowrigg's oddities of manner, he lit upon Villiers, whose work in Dublin had not passed unnoticed.

He was plodding on at his desk in Thames Street, and this new work came as a welcome surprise. His instructions were short and to the point. "I have consulted with Palmerston," wrote Lord Althorpe, "and we agree that it is not desirable that you should have any formal appointment as Commissioner to Paris, or any written instructions. You will, therefore, not have to maintain any official correspondence with this country, but will naturally put yourself on a friendly footing of confidential

communication with Lord Granville (the British Ambassador),
and let us know how you are going on by private letters either
to Palmerston, Auckland, Thomson or myself. With respect to
money matters, the Treasury will pay all your expenses. This,
I think, is all that it is necessary for me to say, and it now only
remains that you should set off for Paris as soon as you possibly
can.''

George was in high good humour over his appointment—the
more so since here again, as in Ireland, his instructions were of
the most general order, and the success of the mission would
depend largely upon his own power (and that of his fellow-commissioner) to handle situations as they arose. The one fly in
the ointment, one gathers, was Bowrigg.

''Oh, Mr. Villiers,'' writes Emily Eden, who had no illusions
about George's fellow-commissioner after once having seen him,
''Bowrigg—your own dear Bowrigg—I think you will allow that
the first beginning—*le premier abord*—the rudiments of an
acquaintance with Bowrigg are hard to get over. He began by
flinging himself at full length on my sofa, saying, ' Well, what
have you been doing lately in the sketching line?' I was actually
awed by his audacity into giving him my sketch-book. 'Ah,
very good, very good. Well, now, this is the result of travelling.
I like a result. Always look for a result.' I really believe I
must be a fierce *aristocrate* by nature however, I behaved no
worse to Bowrigg than by contradicting every assertion that he
made—on subjects on which I knew nothing. . . . I do not
think our acquaintance was long enough for him to detect my
ignorance, because he argued to the last as if I were a reasonable
creature, and, thank Heaven, after two days' wrangling I had
the last word. However, barring his detestable manner, there
is a great deal to like in him. He is so intelligent, and quick;
and then, with such a fund of vanity that it must be mortified
ten times a day, he never let the mortification call on his temper,
but is always good-humoured and obliging. They say the first
time he dined with Leopold (of Belgium), he tripped lightly across
the circle of ladies up to the Queen, and hanging negligently over
her chair, asked her how she liked the thought of leaving her little
boy. . . .''

With this singular personality as his fellow-commissioner,
Villiers set out for France at the beginning of December, 1831.

He arrived in Paris to find France rising like a Phœnix from
the ashes of a fresh revolution. Two expiring causes lay pros-
trate at her feet—Legitimism, the cause of the Bourbons, and
Socialism, the cause of the People. Political power was in the
hands of the middle-classes, who were engaged in making a new
heaven and a new earth. The attempt of Louis XVIII and later

of Charles X and their ministers to re-create the past—the pre-revolutionary past—suffered final defeat in the stormy days of July, 1830, while the old revolutionary cause was as discredited and out-of-date as legitimism itself.   Its fiery pronouncements through the "Society of Friends of the People" fell flatly on unresponsive ears, and smelt, as Heine said, "like an old, greasy, much-thumbed number of the *Moniteur* for 1793."   A middle way had been found by the doctrinaire liberals of the time; and the new régime was a tragic medley of debased loyal-ism and democratic idealism.   Louis Philippe, the Citizen-King —King, not of France by right divine, but of the French by charter from the people—was firmly established on a constitu-tional throne, spouting liberalism through the mouthpiece of his ministers, men drawn chiefly from the professorial classes, and backed by the victorious bourgeoisie.

A weird aristocracy, composed of detached fragments of Napoleonic nobility, ennobled middle-class statesmen, and rem-nants of the old régime, glittered fitfully round the throne; while in the Chamber, Thiers, Guizot and Casimir-Périer happily evolved the science of the new way of life.   It was all very odd. And polite Paris, with its tongue in its cheek, watched the antics of the reformed monarchy with cynical detachment—never quite sure whether it was being governed by a President in a crown or a King in the top hat of a President.

But—marvellous to relate—it seemed to be going to work, this strange new régime.   The sun shone, and a mixed cosmo-politan society prepared to make hay in its genial warmth.   The Granvilles were at the British Embassy, and from the pages of Lady Granville's delightful letters to her sister we get a glimpse of the Paris of those days.   It was a strange meeting-place: there is a touch of phantasy, almost, in the startling incongruity of the contacts.   Balzac at the Opera—"a red, fat man whose locks flow"—staring from the pit at Lady Jersey aloft in her box and deciding her to be "*le vrai type de l'aristocratie anglaise*"; Sir Robert Peel sitting uncomfortably next the Queen at Neuilly, while she sought to penetrate the depth of his ignorance of the French language by bawling out every sentence to him syllable by syllable to the no small consternation of the company; Mme. de Lieven, divested of glory, and fallen at last for poor, plain Monsieur Guizot—surely there is a dreamlike improbability in these associations and encounters.

Indeed, it was a world of new orientations, social and political, of new personalities and new influences.   "Why are the funds so low everywhere to-day?" asks Louis Philippe of the British Ambassador.   "Because of the news from England, perhaps, Sire."   "News from England?   What do you mean?   I have

seen Rothschild. There *is* no news from England to-day." The
nineteenth century had set in in good earnest! But in the medley
of new types and personalities, society began to revive. Never
since the Revolution of '89 had Paris been so gay, so light-
hearted, so sure of itself. In the promise of peace and plenty
that the future seemed to hold even Ministers disported themselves.

"I dread a ball at Casimir Périer's on Monday," writes Lady
Granville, "an immense temporary room: two or three thousand
invited. I hear the roof is to be covered with *pompiers*, who are
to inundate us at a moment's notice, and that there are eighteen
doors to go out at, which last is my comfort."*

In the brilliant spectacle of Paris in the 'thirties, the new and
old touch hands. Ghost-like, they float across the vanished
stage: old Talleyrand, fresh from Whitehall, revisiting on the
arm of his niece, the Duchess de Dino, the scenes of his past
labours and allowing his eyes to rest in cynical amusement on a
Paris unbelievably changed; Talleyrand, who had served many
masters and deceived many men, of whom Lady Granville could
write: "It is very difficult to believe that he is not the best
man in the world, so gentle, so kind, so simple, and so grand."
Then the King, Louis Philippe, stolid, virtuous and dull,
but hiding beneath the enormous impassivity of his countenance
a keen grasp of European affairs, and a wit at least as pointed
as his Ministers'. "Sire, I am very subtle," said Thiers to him
with a smile, on one occasion. "I am more so than you,"
replied the Monarch, "for I do not say so." Thiers, Guizot,
Montalivet, makers of the new heaven and the new earth, pro-
fessor-politicians, a novel class of being altogether—they, too,
pass and are fêted and received. The new and the old—Flahault,
who had been the Emperor's aide-de-camp, and Morny, who was
to bring a later Napoleon to power—they meet, and touch hands
and make their bows in the candlelight of that vanished decade,
and history is in the melting-pot on polished floors where Madame
d'Aponyi, "looking divine in a salmon-coloured gown cut extremely high," beams a welcome to groups of bewildered Deputies, who blench to find themselves for the first time on the
stairways of the great. It was the *monde où l'on s'amuse*, not
only socially, but politically, too; and into its gay and varied
life at this juncture came George Villiers and Dr. Bowrigg, intent
upon Customs' concessions.

Villiers found the *milieu* very much to his taste, and began
immediately to execute a kind of Rake's Progress through the

* Letters of Harriet Countess of Granville, edited by Hon. F. Leveson-
Gower.

orders of society there. We first hear of him at a dinner at the Embassy. Lady Granville writes: " Susy (Lady Susan Leveson-Gower, her daughter) sat next George Villiers at dinner on Friday, and talked mostly to him. His agreeableness is *entrainant* to the greatest degree." A month later she writes: "We have now only George Villiers, who charming as he is does not dance or talk with anyone but married ladies of distinction, and therefore is no lark for us." Finally—a month later still—she writes with quite a touch of asperity: "Tell Lord Morley it would gratify him to see George Villiers executing admirable steps *en avant* between two princesses, of whom he is the favourite partner." So George became smarter and smarter, and savoured the rose with perfect polish and discretion. He writes home charmingly to his family upon all subjects, but is reticent about his own affairs. Theresa had been in Paris not long before on a visit to the Granvilles, and he delights to quizz her on the effect that she has had on all and sundry.

"Lady Granville asked instantly after you in detail," he writes, "and said 'Ka-a-lnt we have her here?' and the girls just the same. I saw Mme. Graham two days after my arrival, and she asked after you. Princess Bagration came in, and Mrs. G. said, 'C'est le frère de Miss Villiers que nous avons tous admirée ici,' upon which the Bagration closed her eyes and said softly, 'Ah, la delicieuse creature; comme je m'en ressouviens bien.' Then Morny gave us a dinner the other day at which there was a most good-looking young Frenchman—a Monsieur Alfred de Voisin—who instantly asked after you. He and his companion, a little Prince Galitzin, it appears, had both fallen head-over-ears in love with you. *En-as-tu assez? . . .*"

Paris was politely interested in English politics, and George spent much time answering questions about the great Reform Bill, which was passing through the House of Commons at the time. Everywhere he went he was bombarded with the same questions: "Eh bien, le Bill, comment va-t-il?" "La reforme passerait-elle? Ces nouveaux paires, ou sont-ils?—ils se font joliment attendu, ces messieurs."

Meanwhile Villiers and "the Doctor" made a beginning of the work they had come to accomplish.

"The Government are inclined to do one's bidding," he writes, "upon political grounds, and a little, too, upon sound principles, which begin to glimmer on their night. But the Chambers are ignorant and slow, and without them nothing can be effected." In March, 1832, Casimir Périer died of cholera; there was a reshuffle in the Ministry, and the Duc de Broglie, with little alteration in the personnel of his Cabinet, formed "a Ministry of all the Talents."

"The new Government," writes George, "particularly the
Duc de Broglie—is anxious that the Commission should proceed
as last year. The Doctor also is most eager for it; but I object
to going on with even enquiry and investigation till some effect
is given to the labours of last year, which, though promised, is
not yet performed."

In November, George's brother Edward turned up in Paris
for a few days, having wandered back from Constantinople,
where he had been for his health. Lady Granville was enchanted with him. "Edward Villiers is here," she writes. "He
is the image of George, only handsomer and graver." And
some few days later: "Edward Villiers is my love. He is delightful, excellent and interesting—a Villiers without any of the
shades," she adds rather snappishly, thinking of George and his
princesses.*

During that autumn all Paris was electrified by the news of
the capture of the Duchesse de Berri. Her attempt to raise the
South was the last flicker of life in the expiring Legitimist cause.
And with her put out of harm's way, and the death of the Napoleonic heir, the Roi de Rome, which had occurred in July, all
dynastic perils were removed from the path of the Orleans
monarchy. "Insurrection is dead," said Guizot at this time;
"the Socialists are dead; revolutionary propaganda is dead, and
the revolutionary spirit." The stars in their courses seemed to
be favouring the Orleans monarchy. Even the solitary pistol
shot that rang out through the autumn weather was a blessing
in disguise. For the bullet missed the bulky personage of the
King, and in the revulsion of feeling towards him after the
event, many doubtful voters hurried into the loyalist lobbies.
The attempt also served the purpose of revealing anarchist
elements in the underworld of Paris which it was desirable for
the police to investigate.

"The young gentleman who missed the King of the French
the other day," writes George to his mother, "is still in prison,
undergoing the questions which the Ministers go in person to
poke at him through the bars. The man appears to be of a
select few who consider it indispensable that Louis Philippe
should die for the people; and this information won't heighten
the pleasure of the Citizen-King's walks on horse-back in the
bosom of his subjects!"

However, the assassin was duly sentenced, excitement died
down, and the King, who, for all his solid, unromantic aspect,
was by no means lacking in personal courage, continued to ride
abroad in the bosom of his subjects.

* Letters of Harriet Countess of Granville, edited by Hon. F. Leveson-
Gower.

§ 4

All was now quiet on the home front, but a shadow still loomed large on the Northern horizon, where the troubles of the new Belgian kingdom (to which France was deeply pledged) looked as if they might involve the whole of Europe in a lurid conflagration. It would be too long to discuss here the complicated diplomatic threads that spun themselves round the birth of the Belgian kingdom. It was one of those cases where the principles involved are racial, and the means adopted to cope with them are purely political and cut straight across the principles themselves, producing a highly menacing state of affairs, which is (curiously) always a surprise to the politicians. The bare lines of the case are as follows:

The statesmen of the Holy Alliance who drew up the new settlement of Europe in 1814, and whose words and actions strangely resemble those of the League of Nations, constructed a barrier state between France and Germany which consisted of the Austro-Spanish Netherlands and the United Provinces. This state they placed, by a stroke of the pen, under the sovereignty of the House of Orange. It looked very well on paper, and theoretically it should have worked. Unfortunately—and we have heard of such cases in our own day—they omitted to ascertain the wishes of the nations concerned. It so happened that the people of the United Provinces, French by sympathy and tradition, had no desire whatever to be governed by the House of Orange. In the course of about fifteen years their resentment rose to the point of rebellion; but it was not until the July revolution of 1830 had placed Louis Philippe safely on the throne of France that they dared to act. Then they rose. Brussels was captured, and the insurrection spread swiftly through the Provinces. The King of Holland, alarmed and taken unawares, offered decentralisation and a measure of self-government. The Provinces demanded complete independence. Here were racial tendencies daring to assert themselves in defiance of the tidy plans which the Holy Alliance had made. The nations were shocked. Intervention became a duty. Summoned by Palmerston, the representatives hurried to London. An endless series of negotiations ensued, which had at least the merit of imposing an armistice on the two hostile parties. Eventually out of the fogs of deliberation a new barrier-kingdom emerged—Belgium—born under certain conditions of cleavage from Holland which were called *bases de separation*. But the new kingdom, French by sympathy and relying on France for support, now blandly offered the crown to the Duc de Nemours, Louis Philippe's second son. Had it been accepted, Belgium would have become a mere appanage of France. Whatever principles were involved, England was not going to stand for that, and Palmerston told Talleyrand bluntly in London that he had better call his master off. Talleyrand was realist enough to see that it would not work, and Louis Philippe was persuaded to refuse the throne on his son's behalf.

Prince Leopold of Saxe-Coburg-Gotha now rose upon the horizon as a possible candidate, and as his candidature would, seemingly, involve no dynastic complications, the distracted Powers clutched at him as a way out of their difficulty. As a sop to France and an inducement to himself, an Orleanist princess was dangled before his eyes. He succumbed, and was proclaimed King in June, 1831. His acceptance of the crown, however, had been made subject to certain modifications in the *bases de separation*. At the last moment Holland refused to accept these, and, immediately declaring war, marched into Belgium with fifty thousand men. Belgium, stricken and defenceless, appealed simultaneously for support to England and France. It was a ticklish moment. Louis Philippe could scarcely stand by and witness the destruction of the French-speaking provinces, and before a month was out France was in military occupation of Belgium. It now looked as if war between France and Holland were inevitable; indeed, as if a European conflict on a large scale were inevitable. Palmerston told France she could only remain in occupation of Belgian territory on pain of war with England. Yet how could she withdraw without endangering the new-won independence of Belgium? Happily the will for peace was present in the deliberations between France and Great Britain, and Palmerston and Talleyrand, both realists, conducted negotiations with reference to the facts of the case, completely undisturbed by the feeling in any of the countries concerned. After prolonged delay the London Conference proposed yet another scheme for the solution of the Belgian difficulty. In this they were ultimately successful—not, however, before the French had besieged Antwerp and the English fleet had blockaded the Scheldt. But by the end of 1832 the Powers had unanimously recognised Belgian independence, and in May, 1833, Holland herself had acquiesced. Thus came into being the Belgian kingdom under a constitutional monarchy and a European guarantee. Only by vigorous intervention of the Powers had war been averted.

A bewildered Mrs. George, looking out upon these high matters, had evidently not been able to make them out at all, and was greatly concerned at England being dragged into the quarrel. And George explains:

"I don't believe I answered your question last time about our interference in the Belgian affair. Conscientiously, then (without one atom of party feeling in writing to you) I believe it to have been unavoidable. It was deplored by none more than by those who undertook it, and who undertook it for no other object than to avoid worse things. When the Belgian *émeute* was fairly developed—Brussels taken, etc., etc., etc., it was evident the rent between the two countries was too wide to bridge. The Duke of Wellington who was in office at the time regretted, but admitted it. He went out and the Whigs who were against intervention came in, and, in pursuance of their pledges, refused to meddle at first. If they could have built a wall of glass round Holland and Belgium, and let the two nations fight it out they would have been overjoyed to do so. But common humanity in the first place could not tolerate the atrocities that were committed, and, secondly, the neighbouring powers for their own preservation could scarcely permit the continuance of such desperate anarchy. Nor could we, in justice to Europe or to ourselves, quietly submit to the growing feeling for France which ended in the offer of the crown to the Duc de Nemours, which was only refused in compliance with the wishes of England. There really were ample enough grounds for a departure from the policy of non-intervention. And, by-the-bye, this word is sometimes most unfairly interpreted. It never meant that we were to stand by and look at our neighbours thrashing and robbing each other without lifting a hand. If the two countries had had a mind to negotiate or settle their differences in any way that didn't disturb the whole neighbourhood, our interference would have been unpardonable. But since they didn't seem able to, I think European intervention was justified, nay, a necessity. In this case it was most important to have *all* the Powers in the same boat. What was the course open to the negotiating Powers? Either to abandon the whole thing to chance—*i.e.*, to the *status quo* of two years ago with all the *acharnement* and enlistment of new interests and passions during that time, which upon my honour, I believe would have entailed a general war (and what a war that will be, too, whenever it takes place—a war that can only end with the triumph of either the monarchical or democratic principle in Europe; and if the means of resistance both possess be considered, who can predict what the duration of such a conflict would be, and who would not make any sacrifice to avert it?)—either, as I say, a general war, or, by a timely coercion to carry into effect that which all the Powers had agreed was desirable, and which the conflicting parties themselves as good as admitted was a fair termination of their quarrel."

It is curious that it was in writing of Belgium that he should predict a war that he saw even then to be the inevitable result of the conflicting political ideas of the century. The war has come and gone. But whether the monarchic or democratic principle has ultimately prevailed in Europe who shall say?

§ 5

The leaves in the Tuilleries gardens deepened and fell that autumn of 1832, and Villiers still picked his way delicately through Paris. He was very well satisfied with the progress of the Commission and not a little with his part in it. Dr. Bowrigg had been tamed and his brilliant talents put to their proper use. Villiers had got the direction of affairs into his own hands and was pleased with the way things were going. He was *aux mieux* with the Ministers who counted, and even went so far as to have "a long and most interesting conversation with the King."

Meanwhile Paris was delightful. Society moved ceaselessly over the polished floors to the sound of laughter and violins. One danced, one flirted, one was gay. And there were other distractions, too. Grisi, reconciled to her husband, was singing divinely at the opera; and the polite world was strangely stirred that winter by an ugly girl who recited passages from Racine at a party at Monsieur de Delmar's. Her name was Mlle. Rachel. Moreover, George met an old friend, and renewed a personal contact that interested him not a little. The fascinating Madame de Montijo had settled in Paris and was establishing quite a salon. Political troubles had banished her husband temporarily from his native land, and the French capital, he thought, was as good a spot as any from which to conduct the intrigues necessary to getting back again. But Montijo, never on the best of terms with his wife, was absent a good deal, while Madame was very much present. She was beautiful, intelligent and gay, and in her apartment gathered at that time all that was smart and amusing in the social, political and artistic worlds. Some years earlier George had made her acquaintance by chance. The acquaintanceship had ripened into something deeper, and now he often frequented her society on occasions when the smart, the gay, the artistic worlds were definitely *not* present. How much he was personally affected it is impossible to say. But that she was a decided interest in his life at this time is certain. Twenty-five years later, when both of them, for very different reasons, had established considerable positions in the world, a scandal was put about concerning the relationship which had existed between them in their youth. Eyebrows were raised significantly and heads came together in whispers as Madame's beautiful daughter swept by in the royal equipage. But whether what rumour had to say of them was either plausible or probable remains a mystery to this day—even though the principals talked the matter over frankly together at that later date, and even though Clarendon, as he then was, went so far as to give an account of the conversation to his wife, who duly recorded it in her diary. . . .

By the beginning of December, 1832, the work of the Commission was drawing to a close, and Villiers was pleased with what had been accomplished. "My affairs have gone really well," he writes; "the modifications we have been contending for have already been introduced to the Chamber by the Minister of Commerce. . . . I am in high good humour with the people here about it all, for I think they have acted in good faith . . . and when I consider that just this time last year we were told by everybody both here and at home that French prejudices and French interests would be utterly insurmountable, it is very gratifying to think upon the progress which has been made in the time. I don't mean to say that our Commission has done this, but I don't think it would have been done without it. For instance, we demanded the right to have French raw silk, the exportation of which was prohibited—it being of a peculiarly fine quality, and constituting, as our manufacturers think, the ground of the French superiority in the silk trade over the English. We were told last year that if the Government were to moot such a question at Lyons there would be an *émeute* next day. And so I believe there would have been. We have worked with the Deputies, the Press and others: threatened retaliation, etc., etc. (and here I must say that Bowrigg's visit to Lyons did signal service), and the law permitting this export is now before the Chamber, and supported by a Minister *on the strength of a petition from Lyons demanding it*. Is not all this pleasantly progressive?"

But even as he wrote these words a blow was preparing to strike at him from without which was to put everything else out of his head for the time being. Many months afterwards he came upon the sheets in a drawer and scrawled across the bulk of them in pencil:

"I have found this not-worth sending letter, but I do not burn it, as I know you would wish to have it. I was in the act of folding it, when Lady Granville came in my room on that sad day."

The intelligence that Lady Granville came to break to him was the sudden death of his brother Hyde. It took him completely by surprise, as he had no idea that he was even dangerously ill. And now came the news of his death. Hyde, it appeared, had been electioneering in his Falmouth constituency, and staying at the house of friends. He had been far from well for some time past, and had suffered much from his old malady—ear trouble. But this had cleared, and he was going about his ways again when, quite suddenly, he was taken very seriously ill with an acute mastoid abscess, and he was dead in forty-eight hours. Mrs. George and Theresa were with him at the end, having rushed over from Saltram, where they happened to be staying. He died

6

peacefully and without pain, having been in a coma for twenty-four hours previously. The loss was a great blow to the whole family.

Hyde was, perhaps, the most brilliant of all the brothers—certainly the most ambitious. Already he had made an impression on the House of Commons, and, with a Whig Ministry in power, it would not have been long before an under-secretaryship had fallen to his lot. What he would have made of life and politics, had he survived, it is, of course, impossible to say. His life was dominated by a single purpose—the dream of a big political career—and he was prepared to sacrifice most things in his life to achieve it. Less scrupulous than George, he would have played the party game for its own sake. More astute and less dogged than Charles, he would have made fewer enemies and perhaps, also, fewer friends. But he was cut short almost before his career had begun, and it is idle to speculate what the future might have held for him.

George felt the blow keenly. Nearer to him in age than any of the others, Hyde had been closely associated with him at the University and after. The best of friends and companions, politically, too, they held the same views, and together had undergone that change of outlook which had thrown them when hardly more than boys into the junior ranks of the Whig party. George had been much abroad of late years, but he had kept always in sympathetic touch with Hyde's affairs, and on many occasions had even given him a helping hand financially. He believed in Hyde and was proud of him, and the shock of his death made a profound impression on him.

He rushed straight over to England, leaving Bowrigg to wind up the last details of the mission. He was in time to be with his mother at Saltram for the funeral. A fortnight later he was in London going through Hyde's papers with Edward. Hyde left debts—and other inconvenient legacies. Uncle John Clarendon appeared on the scene and was helpful even to the extent of a thousand pounds, which placed him high in the family estimation.

CHAPTER IV

MINISTER IN MADRID

§ 1

AFTER this sad event Villiers disappeared into the Thames Street offices and took up again the deadening routine of the Customs and Excise. But it was not to be for long. His work in Paris had put him in touch with the Government; and the correspondence he had conducted with Ministers at home during that period had not only proved to them his ability for affairs, but had shown them very clearly in which direction his political sympathies lay. Here was a neophyte to Whig politics who might be used to great effect by the party: a civil servant whose brilliant talents should be put to better use than had hitherto been the case. George Villiers was being wasted in the Customs and Excise. He was worthy of better things. So, at any rate, thought Lord Palmerston, who was Minister of Foreign Affairs at the time.

Now Palmerston, just then, was troubled over the affairs of the Iberian Peninsula. In accordance with the grandiose Whig vision of Europe he had at the time, he was anxious to establish an alliance of constitutional and liberal-minded nations of middle and southern Europe to act as a counter-weight to Russia and the autocratic governments of the North. Great Britain and France were to hand for his purpose; for though they were deeply suspicious, the one of the other, at least they were allied in deploring the influence of Russia and Austria, and all that they stood for in the politics of Europe. But new recruits to the scheme were needed, and he now sought to bring into line with his idea the Kingdoms of Spain and Portugal. Why he should have lighted on these two palpably backward countries to further his scheme it is difficult to imagine. Nor, as a matter of fact, was either country, at the moment, in an auspicious state for the "act of conversion" that he planned for them; for Portugal was in the throes of a disputed succession, while the politics of Spain were dominated by Zea Bermudez, a statesman who was the prototype throughout Europe of all that was retrograde and reactionary. But such considerations hardly deterred the Foreign Secretary from pushing forward his plans when once he had made up his mind to them. Geographically the countries in question served his purpose very well, and he was busy at the moment supporting what elements of liberalism he could find in both. But up to date he had met with little success. He had entangled Great Britain in the affairs of the Portuguese succession even to the extent of arms and bitterly against the wishes of his colleagues in office. At present very little to his purpose had accrued from that; while in Spain a situation of a very similar nature seemed likely to arise at any moment. Addington, the British Minister, had proved a broken reed, while Stratford Canning, who had been sent out on a mission extraordinary to emphasise the views of the British Government, had effected nothing. Both these gentlemen for one reason or another had been recalled. The Legation at Madrid was vacant. Why not George Villiers for the post?

Palmerston sent for George and explained matters to him: indicated his policy with regard to Spain, and offered him the appointment forthwith. Villiers was momentarily stunned, for although he had arrived at a time of life and experience when he knew that he might expect some kind of responsible position to be offered him—especially now that the Whigs were in power—it is doubtful whether he was prepared for the entirely new road he was asked to travel. That his feet had been itching to venture upon that road for ten years past there can be no doubt, for diplomacy was his gift; and his job at the Customs and Excise a mere expedient. So, though surprised, he accepted it without much hesitation, as it was exactly what he had been waiting for all these years.

It was the turning point in his career. Not that his future was destined to be wholly devoted to diplomacy. Far from it. But the years in Madrid served as the necessary apprenticeship to the political posts that were to fall to his lot later on, and were, moreover, to exert an immense influence on his whole character and outlook on things. He arrived there a rather opinionated and ambitious young man with all the theories which he had formulated at Cambridge still intact in his mind. When he left in 1839 he was a mature statesman, no longer avidly seeking occasions to distinguish himself, but willing to serve his country in any post in which he might help to bring justice and common sense to bear upon the confused issues of international politics. In this first post of responsibility, he was to see all his Whig theories set at naught, and having from the outset sincerely associated himself with the ultimate good of the people to whom he was accredited, he was big enough to realise that theory must give way to reality, and humble-minded enough to escape the imminent danger in which he had stood of becoming nothing more than a doctrinaire politician. In Spain, too, he learned to feel affection for a people that stood for almost everything of which he disapproved. Experience taught him humanity; and, appalled by the cruelty and corruption which he saw all around him, he no longer sought to impose the teaching of a particular political creed upon affairs, but was satisfied to devote his energies to solving whatever section of the intricate problem came before him, content to have made some part of the way straighter. And, thus, if he lost something in ambition, he gained by the acquisition of saner principles and sounder values.

§ 2

It is significant, perhaps, in view of all this, that Villiers' very entry into Spanish affairs was marked by an event which had the instant effect of severing the ropes that bound him to Whitehall, and of placing him at once in a position which demanded all his resourcefulness. The circumstance was dramatic enough. He arrived in Madrid on September 29th, 1833, and on the following day sought an interview with Zea Bermudez, the Prime Minister, to arrange an early date upon which he might present his credentials to King Ferdinand VII. At the Ministry, they told him that the Prime Minister was closeted with the King and couldn't be seen. After hours of waiting, Villiers was greeted by a staggering piece of news, when Zea, at last, white-faced and exhausted, stumbled into the room with the laconic, 'The King is dead' upon his lips. The event shattered the whole state of affairs in the Peninsula. At a blow George Villiers was faced with a political situation of international importance, with nothing but his own political vision upon which to rely. But now in order to understand the circumstances in which he found himself, we must turn for a moment to the complicated state of affairs that existed in Spain and Portugal just previous to his arrival at Madrid.

§ 3

The trouble in both countries centred round the succession to the throne. Portugal was already in the throes of civil war. A Pretender was now to darken the sunshine of Spain. King Ferdinand VII had married four times. Three of his marriages had proved childless; but his fourth consort, Maria Christina (who happened also to be his niece) bore him thus late in his life a daughter. According to the law in Spain as it had stood till then, collateral males were preferred to females in direct descent, and the King's brother, Don Carlos was heir-apparent. Ferdinand, however, unearthed a secret document signed by Charles IV in

1789—but never made public—which ensured the rights of females in the direct line. This he published shortly before the birth of his daughter to the great annoyance of Don Carlos, and the powerful reactionary interests—mostly noble and clerical— that as heir-apparent he had gathered about him. A few months later, Ferdinand became ill, and, imagining himself to be dying, was induced by Don Carlos' wife, and the pressure of palace intrigue, to rescind this law, and revert to the male succession. His Majesty, however, having rallied, judged this decision to have been wrung from him against his will, and, once more changing his policy, reinstated his daughter as heir to the throne. This time death caught him—and the Carlist party—unawares, and when he expired on September 30th, 1833, his infant daughter, Donna Isabella, became rightful Queen of Spain.

Now, by a turn of Fate, the situation in Spain was very closely paralleled, at this juncture, by what was happening in Portugal. Dom Pedro, Emperor of Brazil, had, in 1828, abdicated the throne of Portugal in favour of his daughter, a child of seven. He had appointed his brother, Dom Miguel, Regent during the Queen's minority. But Dom Miguel, on his appointment, tore up the Constitution and proclaimed himself King. Almost simultaneously a revolution in Brazil drove Dom Pedro into exile; and he and his daughter, Queen Maria, arrived in England as refugees. Encouraged by Lord Grey's Government, and materially aided by France, he collected a fleet, and was so far successful as to capture the town of Oporto from the Miguelites. Here matters remained for some time, as Dom Pedro imagined himself too weak in material resources to push the campaign any further. However, in July, 1833, his fleet, commanded by a British Admiral, achieved the totally unexpected success of beating and destroying Dom Miguel's squadrons in a battle off Cape Saint Vincent. Whereupon, fortified and encouraged by this change of fortune, Terceira, commander of the legitimist land forces, took heart to continue the war, and finally to capture Lisbon, routing Dom Miguel, and driving him from the Kingdom.

Now, most of this had taken place in Portugal before the death of King Ferdinand of Spain. And considering, in the matter of succession, how closely allied Ferdinand's own situation was to that of Dom Pedro, his natural policy would have been to uphold and support Dom Pedro and the legitimist cause. He saw, in fact, played out before him on the stage of Portugal, what his intelligence must have told him would inevitably repeat itself in Spain upon his own demise. The infant Queen—the wicked uncle—a disputed succession, and civil war; the ingredients were all there. It is impossible that he should not have realised their implication. But King Ferdinand's mind was a curious receptacle, and what was active in one half of it was as often as not contradicted by what was going on in the other. It was so in this case; for having settled the succession of Spain upon his own daughter, he proceeded to uphold and support the anti-legitimist cause in Portugal, and to lend his support both diplomatically and materially to the very forces that were so exactly and dangerously paralleled in Spain by his own brother and the Carlist party.

Truth to tell, Ferdinand was, by nature, a Carlist; and although a sense of justice to his own paternal pride caused him to favour his daughter in the matter of the succession, politically his sympathies were all the other way. For the Pretenders in both countries stood for the conservative and reactionary principles so necessary to the preservation of absolute monarchy, while round the persons of the two Infante, he observed with alarm, gathered all those subversive elements of democracy and liberalism that were so dangerous a characteristic of the age. So while he upheld his daughter and the legitimist cause in Spain with his right hand, with his left in Portugal he slyly supported the Pretender, Dom Miguel.

Now it had been the object of British diplomacy to induce King Ferdinand to reverse his policy in Portugal; and Stratford Canning had spent four fruitless months in Madrid, prior to Villiers' arrival, in an attempt to get him to do so. This was all in accordance with Palmerston's view of the Peninsula turned liberal, and ready to act in concert with France and Great Britain to counterbalance the autocratic nations of the Holy Alliance. Palmerston's colleagues in the Government, pledged to non-intervention, were strongly against his machinations in Madrid, but he was confident of being able to convince them when the time came for more decided action that the Pretenders stood for all those principles that it was the very breath of their political creed to see banished from the world. But as yet he had to walk delicately. Above all, he had to counter French diplomacy in that quarter. France was all for prompt and active intervention in Portuguese affairs from the first; and Louis Philippe tried to persuade Great Britain to join in an expedition to drive Dom Miguel out of Portugal and set Queen Maria on the throne. But it was clear that at the root of this enthusiasm lay a desire to marry his son to the little Queen. This did not suit Palmerston at all, as he had no desire to see France predominant in the affairs of the Peninsula. Better—far better—he thought, to induce Ferdinand himself to take a hand in settling the situation in Portugal. Hence his policy in Madrid, and the Stratford Canning mission.

§ 4

Villiers was instructed to take up the negotiations where Stratford Canning had laid them down, and "to second any inclination on the part of Spain to take joint action with Great Britain in settling the disorders of Portugal." But the death of the King of Spain at this juncture changed the face of everything. Within a fortnight of the proclamation of the young Queen Isabella, that which everyone expected to happen, punctually happened. Don Carlos raised his standard at Vittoria, and Spain passed into a state of open Civil War.

Villiers, fresh from conversations with Palmerston on the whole question of affairs in the Peninsula, knew very well how to act. It was obvious that Great Britain was prepared to support the Queen's cause, and he allowed no time to elapse before making personal contacts with the two people in Madrid upon whom that cause chiefly depended—the Queen-Mother, now proclaimed Regent, and Zea Bermudez, the Prime Minister.

Significantly enough the first Spanish politician with whom he was to make acquaintance was to prove untrue to all Villiers' preconceived ideas of him. The late King's first Minister, the formidable Zea Bermudez was held throughout Europe to be the very incarnation of reactionary conservatism. But the Zea of Ferdinand's reign and the Zea of the Regency were two very different men. Unsupported by an autocrat, Zea professed himself more favourable to constitutional government. And Villiers' own views as he gained more insight into Spanish affairs underwent a considerable change. While two months of the Regency convinced Zea that he must moderate his absolutist methods, two months' observation of Spanish character convinced Villiers that the country was not ready for anything like the degree of constitutional reform that he or Palmerston had hoped for. So from opposite angles the statesman and the diplomat converged upon points of view that were by no means dissimilar, and, by December, the British Minister was to find himself defending Zea's policy in despatches home, and even taking upon himself to explain to his chiefs at Westminster that any reforms in the nature of the Spanish Constitution must grow slowly out of the demand of the people, and not be imposed, ready-made, at the instigation of a foreign power.

The other person of note that emerged out of the crisis was Maria-Christina, the Queen-Regent. That she was a remarkable woman with a remarkable destiny is evidenced by her career. That with everything seemingly against her she managed to steer a course over a number of years which resulted in establishing her daughter on the throne of Spain for thirty-five years is a matter of history. But that she was able to effect this in spite of her violent and unruly nature, in spite of her impulsiveness, her passion, and her temper is something of a miracle. But whatever faults she might possess, she was a personality—a commanding personality. Ministries might crash about her ears and revolutions break out at her palace doors, still she was to be found dominating the scene, commanding and cajoling, or bowing before the inevitable, always courageous, always rising to the dignity of the occasion. She was a Queen, and she let everybody about her know it. Temperamental in the extreme, she lived openly with her lover Muños, a person of low origin, by whom she had one if not more children. In spite of this she was popular; and certainly she was the dominating figure in the Spanish situation. Villiers had a great admiration for her political capacities.

"There is in the Señora," he writes, "the elements for making one of the greatest sovereigns of our times. She is capable of taking large views. She is ambitious of glory, and has, at heart, the prosperity of Spain. She is, moreover, acute, docile, and absolutely without fear. . . ."

§ 5

The proclamation of the young Queen Isabella passed off quietly enough as far as the capital was concerned. The Madrilenos were staunch to a man. But ten days later, when Don Carlos came out into the open, the whole of the Basque country, Biscay and Navarre went over to his side, and a ragged army of banditti, gypsies and muleteers, fierce and undisciplined, but versed by instinct in the tortuous art of guerilla warfare, began to gather round the standard of the Pretender. By October 11th the courier system from the North became dislocated, and the capital began to feel the realities of Civil War. Nor at first did the Royalist troops achieve much success against the insurgents.

"The tract of mountainous country is so enormous," writes Villiers despondingly, "and the rebels so delight in their mode of warfare, and understand it so thoroughly, that I scarcely see what is to put it down. For the people are all armed: they assemble in vast numbers. The royalist troops there have information of them; are harassed by forced marches in pursuit, and when they arrive, find them dispersed; and only hear sometime afterwards of villages that they have plundered, cattle they have driven off, and of their being again assembled at some distant spot."

Rodil, the Royalist general, was sent to deal with them and the war dragged on through the autumn of 1833.

In the winter of that year a political crisis drove Zea out of office. His fall was in the main due to personal unpopularity, and to a deep mistrust on the part of the liberals of his newly acquired constitutionalism. They felt at heart that the old lion of "absolutism" could hardly change his pelt at this stage, and beneath what was a sincere realisation on his part that the old methods of governance could no longer deal with the situation, they suspected a deeper motive. The rising tide of opinion brought Count Martinez de la Rosa into office as his successor. He was an intellectual, fashionably imbued with liberal opinions, and something of a dilettante. Artist, playwright, gallant and poet, he was a politician more by accident than inclination. However, he was a *moderado*, a liberal, and consequently more sympathetic to the Whigs at home than his predecessor had been. Palmerston could offer him support without fear of criticism from his colleagues, and Villiers was instructed to pledge the Government to give effective aid to the Legitimist causes in Spain and Portugal. In a series of conversations with him Villiers developed the ideas of his Government and watched their effect upon the new Prime Minister. "I never advise, I merely throw out my ideas," he writes confidentially to his sister, "and you would laugh as I have done, over and over again, if I told you how often he has given me, three or four days later, my ideas as his own, adding: '*Que c'était une idée qui lui a passer par la tête.*'"

However, Villiers was not to have it all his own way with Martinez de la Rosa. For Martinez had strong French sympathies, and, while engaging in non-committal conversations with the British Minister, he was at the same time secretly treating with the Quai d'Orsay, who had also offered him terms of assistance. Villiers got wind of this and informed Palmerston, who realised he must act at once and act strongly. Villiers was instructed to prepare and draw up a Treaty as between Great Britain, Spain and Portugal for the support of the Legitimist causes in both countries of the Peninsula. This document, as will be seen, coolly disregarded France and her right of intervention. Villiers dangled it for several months before the harassed Martinez, and it proved too much for him. After all, the support of Great Britain, embodied in an actual Treaty, was not to be disregarded, and in the present state of the country he was hardly in a position to refuse. He fell. And now the fat was in the fire. Louis Philippe was furious, and there were ugly repercussions in Paris and Madrid, while in London old Talleyrand sat for hours in the antechambers of the Foreign Office waiting a chance to remonstrate with the Secretary of State. Palmerston felt trapped. He realised he had gone too far and that, as so often in the pursuit of his own vision of things, he had got himself into a scrape. But if this scapegrace of the Whigs was prone to bring trouble upon himself, he was sometimes visited by almost divine flashes of insight as to how to extricate himself. And so it was on this occasion. Instead of withdrawing, instead of calling the Treaty off and trying to effect the substance of it by some other means, he boldly invited France to co-operate, to join in the Treaty, and to undertake with Great Britain the task of establishing the two young Queens on their thrones. It may seem to us an obvious thing to have done, but at the time it was certainly a brilliant stroke. It must be remembered that French and British diplomacy in the Peninsula was divergent on many questions; that both countries were attempting to become paramount in the councils of Madrid; that, though both wished to see the Legitimist causes triumphant, it was for very different reasons. By inviting France to be a party to the Treaty, Palmerston disregarded these differences of motive, and assumed before the world the identity of French and British interests in Spain and Portugal. It was a bold stroke, and it succeeded. France, flattered and taken unawares, readily complied. So came to birth in April, 1834, the Quadruple Alliance, which pledged the Governments of Great Britain, France, Spain and Portugal to support with effectual aid the Legitimist causes in both countries of the Peninsula. Palmerston was jubilant.

"I carried it through the Cabinet by a *coup de main*," he writes to his brother, "taking them by surprise, and not leaving them time to make objections. . . . I reckon this to be a great stroke. I should like to see Metternich's face when he reads our Treaty."

Villiers was well pleased with the way things had gone, but he was also a little nervous for the future. Spain was becoming to him something more than a geographical abstraction. He was beginning to understand, if he could not condone, the unruly methods of the South, where government was conducted by passion and personality rather than by precedent and procedure; where fraud was age-old and ineradicable, and justice little more than a farce; where politics were objective and life natural; where the State proceeded upon its way by means of a hearty rough-and-tumble with events. The heat and the dirt; the bright sun-lit patches and the violent shade; the sharp extremes of temperature—all these elements of climate and environment which determined the destiny of this strange people—were beginning to have their weight with the British Minister, who, gazing out upon the varied scene from the windows of the Legation, wondered a little anxiously how much of all this the Government at home could realise.

Now Don Carlos stood for the *status quo* in Spain—for the maintenance of the whole untidy, happy-go-lucky scene as it was. But round the standards of the Queen gathered all the elements of modernity, every hope of social and political improvement. These elements looked to England, looked to France for support. If any amelioration was to take place, if Spain were to be lifted into the comity of constitutional nations, then the Queen's cause must be maintained *vi et armis*. The moral support of a mere promise of help had already worked marvels. Would Great Britain and France be prepared to redeem their pledges, and to redeem them honestly and generously? That was the question. So thought the British Minister as he looked into the future.

§ 6

In the autumn of 1834—a few months after the signing of the Quadruple Alliance—an event occurred in England which, a year before, Villiers would have deplored, but which now he contemplated with equanimity, almost—dare it be said?—with relief. The Whig Government fell; and in the Tory Administration which took its place the Foreign Office fell to the lot of the Duke of Wellington. Villiers was fully alive to the delicacy of his own position in this crisis. He was not of the regular service; he had owed his selection entirely to Palmerston, who had indeed picked him out of quite another job and placed him at Madrid as the person best fitted to understand and further his policy in the Peninsula. But in the fourteen months that had elapsed since he reached Madrid, Villiers had seen the folly of making international politics into a party game. From the first he had struck out an independent and personal line; and feeling that only the " man-on-the-spot " could judge of the expediency of the attitude to be adopted he had had frequently to disagree with his chiefs at Westminster. Believing, therefore, that he had given proofs sufficient to justify any Government in regarding his conduct in Spain as free from political prejudice, he decided to stay on at his post if the new Government thought fit to confirm him in it.

To His Grace, the Duke of Wellington, K.G.

(Private.)   " Madrid,
                                      " *December 7th*, 1834.

" My dear Lord Duke,
    " I have received from Lord Palmerston the official intimation that His Majesty has been pleased to confer upon you the seals of the Foreign Department, and that my official correspondence is henceforth to be addressed to your Grace.

"It is unwillingly that I obtrude myself upon you at a moment when the most important avocations must engage your whole attention; but I feel that I am justified in so doing upon public grounds, as the policy which your Grace may adopt towards Spain, under her present circumstances, is not only of vital interest to Spain herself, but will in some measure be looked upon as decisive of that which England will observe towards other countries.

"If during the last year of Ferdinand's life measures of common precaution had been taken for the crisis which all must have foreseen, the accession of his daughter to the Spanish throne would have met with little opposition. At the moment of the King's death, however, Don Carlos was still in Portugal; high offices of state were filled by disaffected persons; upwards of two hundred thousand royalist volunteers were in arms; the army itself was nearly disbanded, and the Treasury exhausted.

"It is manifest, therefore, that if the general sense of the country had been favourable to Don Carlos (and countless hosts of churchmen and employers left nothing untried to excite the people in his favour), there existed in the heads of the Government no efficient means of controlling the national will; but the conduct of the people sufficiently disproved the predictions of the representatives of the Northern Powers, that upon the death of the King, the country from one end to another would be found Carlist.

"Your Grace is too well acquainted with this country to make it necessary for me to expatiate upon the manner in which foreign influence is looked for and leaned upon, even by those who are most loud in their assertions of national independence. The recognition of the Queen by England and France at once turned the scale in her favour. The geographical position of France rendered her recognition, materially speaking, of vital importance; but it was upon the moral support of England that the dependence of the Queen's Party was placed; and the time and manner in which His Majesty's Government took that step, (second only in importance to the recognition of Louis Philippe under the Government of your Grace) saved Spain from a general Civil War. The partial insurrection in the Northern Provinces was at first commenced under the apprehension that the privileges peculiar to these Provinces, which had always been respected by the despotic Kings of Spain, would, as on a former occasion, be abolished under a more liberal form of Government. A word of promise on this subject, or an army well-commanded, would, at any moment during the first six months, have sufficed to restore tranquillity; but it is difficult to say whether the war has been more wretchedly mismanaged under a political, or a military point of view. It became one of savage retaliation, and the original objects, whether of ancient privileges, or succession to the Crown were lost sight of in the appetite acquired by each side for conquest.

"The arrival of Don Carlos in Navarre was wholly without result, save that of embarrassing his adherents: his presence can

scarcely have said to have added a recruit to the insurgent ranks:
and not a demonstration in his favour has taken place in any
other part of Spain. The War has never extruded itself out of
the mountainous districts, or much beyond the area of twenty
square leagues. Mina, who is now engaged in the only service
for which he is adapted, has been pursuing a system, the good
results of which are already visible in the improving spirit of the
population since his arrival.

"In the progress of the revolution, I have had abundant opportunities of observing the effect produced by the *moral support of
England*, and I feel certain that it is to the confidence which that
support has inspired that the Queen is indebted for the comparative security in which her cause is now placed. The enemies of
her cause are comprised of that numerous class in Spain who,
living by abuses, are interested in their maintenance, together
with the great majority of the monastic orders, as well as a portion of the secular Church, who feel that only such a Government
as that which Don Carlos would establish could venture any
longer to postpone the ecclesiastical reform for which the country
is desirous. On the side of the Queen are ranged the whole of the
grandees (with the single exception, I believe, of the Duke of
Granada, who is a religious fanatic) and of the wealthy, the intelligent, and the commercial and manufacturing classes of Spain—all
as hostile to revolution as they are to Don Carlos; but who, if
their enemies unexpectedly acquire force, would all be prepared,
literally, to die sword in hand, rather than submit to those in
whose hands Don Carlos would be but a blind and devoted
instrument.

"Such a state of things would perhaps be the most fearful
which this unfortunate country has yet witnessed. These numerous
classes are now too deeply compromised to hope for mercy from
the Prince they have opposed, and who during the last four
months has done little else than fulminate edicts of death and confiscation against them. They would, if rendered desperate, excite
a spirit of revolution, as the lesser evil of the moment; and a war
of opinions would commence, which it must be in vain to hope
would not extend itself beyond the Peninsula.

"If improvement be possible in Spain, it is through the instrumentality of the classes to whom I now refer that it must be
effected. They are all themselves aware of this; they are daily
becoming more united in opinion; and they feel that so fair an
opportunity for the regeneration of their country has not yet presented itself. They think, most justly, that the circumstances of
the present revolution differ from those of any other; that the
amelioration which is in progress has commenced from above,
and not, as hitherto, from below; that it is given, not taken; and
there appears to be a determination nearly general to profit by
experience, and avoid errors which in former political crises rendered the progress of rational liberty dangerous and difficult.

"I hope I have not been an inattentive observer of all that has
been passing around me during the last fourteen months; and I

have given your Grace as succinct a summary as I can of the reports which I have made, and the opinions which I have at different times developed to His Majesty's Government.

"Your Grace will now, perhaps, permit me to say a few words respecting my own position in this country; for, without presuming to erect myself or the post which I occupy into great political importance, there are circumstances connected with my appointment to this mission which make it imperative upon me to guard against the slightest misconstruction of my conduct.

"Lord Palmerston recalled my predecessor (Mr. Addington) because he felt no confidence in his desire to give effect to the policy of His Majesty's Government; and he selected me, who had no claim upon him, and was not in the diplomatic service, because he knew my opinions were in unison with his own, and as an act of friendship for which I shall be lastingly grateful to him.

"Under these circumstances, then, when Lord Palmerston quitted office, my inclination, and, I conceive, my duty to myself, would have dictated to me to lose no time in resigning this mission into your Grace's hands. Your Grace may, perhaps, be surprised at any hesitation on my part having taken place. I have, however, refrained from doing so purely upon public grounds, and because, during the last ten days, I have had ample evidence of the triumph it would be to that party whose success I, in my conscience, believe would be disastrous to this country. That party entertains the most exaggerated notions of the advantage which they shall derive from your Grace's accession to power; and my resignation upon the first receipt of the intelligence would, I know, both from the Spanish Minister and my own observations, have been hailed as a confirmation of their hopes.

"I shall therefore respectfully beg of your Grace to consider that I continue in the exercise of my functions so long as you may deem that I can be useful in the furtherance of that policy of which I have been the organ since my arrival at Madrid.

"It only remains for me to apologise to your Grace for the length of this letter. I have thought it my duty not to conceal from you the opinions which I have had so favourable an opportunity for forming upon a country to the well-being of which your Grace's future policy is of vital importance; and in the expression of those opinions I hope your Grace will not consider that I have used an unbecoming frankness.

"I have the honour to be, with great truth and respect, my dear Lord Duke,

"Your Grace's most faithful servant,
"GEORGE VILLIERS."*

The tone of this letter pleased the old Duke, and was later to please Palmerston when he returned to the Foreign Office and

* Foreign Office Despatch, quoted in Bulwer Lytton's *Life of Lord Palmerston.*

read through the accumulated correspondence of his rival, finding amongst the despatches many which seemed to derive from Whig diplomats who believed that the Tory victory was to be of long duration, and who trimmed their sails accordingly.

Moreover, as it turned out, Villiers found he was able to work very well with the Duke. There was a certain similarity in their attack upon the Spanish question. They were linked by a kindred sense of justice, common sense, and a knowledge of the country with which they were dealing. When Palmerston returned to office the British Minister at Madrid wrote rather ruefully, "The Duke is a great loss to Spain," and he found himself regretting, in the face of Palmerston's dilatory methods, the soldierly punctiliousness of the ducal replies to his despatches.

§ 7

Meanwhile the war gathered in intensity, and the terrible Zumalacarregui emerged, on the Carlist side, as a master of guerilla warfare. Bitterness and hatred increased, and the commanders of both armies began to indulge in reprisals of the most savage and revolting nature. In the theatre of operations Mina hanged every person found out of doors after nightfall. Zumalacarregui responded by shooting his prisoners. Valdez, who was sent to Navarre in the spring of 1835 to support Mina, was no better, and the honour of Spanish arms became stained by military crimes that would have disgraced the most degraded sections of a civil population.

It was impossible for the Allies to stand by and witness such conduct without a protest, and Villiers and the Duke, in April, 1835, devised the plan of sending a Commission from England to the Carlist headquarters which should have the double object of dispelling any hopes the Carlists might entertain that a change of Government in England had altered the views of Great Britain towards the conflict in Spain, and of drawing up some kind of convention which should bind the commanders of both sides to the common decencies of warfare. Lord Eliot and Colonel Wylde formed the Commission that the Duke sent out, and after much negotiation they obtained the signatures of Zumalacarregui and Valdez to the latter convention, while, at the same time, submitting a very plain statement that the Carlist cause could look for no assistance from England. The reaction of Madrid to the military convention was a curious one. The *madrilenos* resented it bitterly as placing the two armies on a level, whereas Don Carlos' troops were considered as rebels and traitors by the Queen's forces.

When Martinez de la Rosa rose to explain in the Cortes, he was met by a storm of criticism, and a vote for his impeachment was carried. As he left the building his carriage was surrounded by a howling mob, and only by a miracle did he reach his house in safety. Long into the night an angry crowd howled imprecations beneath his windows. " One wonders whether this people is worth saving!" sighs Villiers in despair.

The war had now reached a deadlock, and it became clear that the time had come for Great Britain and France to redeem their pledges as signatories to the Quadruple Alliance by rendering armed assistance to the Queen's cause, and at this juncture Martinez de la Rosa invited both Governments to do so. France flatly refused, and the Spanish Minister turned to England. The short-lived Tory Government had succumbed, and Palmerston was back at the Foreign Office. He was in an awkward position with regard to his Spanish policy. It was one thing to create, by the stroke of a pen, an abstract union of Powers to fulfil a certain purpose in Europe. But quite another to persuade English constituencies to pledge money and men to fight for a cause that they were perfectly incapable of understanding. Meanwhile he was bombarded by George Villiers with pleas for active intervention. In despatch after despatch the British Minister in Madrid argued the moral and political necessity of standing to our pledges, suggesting that the smallest British unit, ably equipped and commanded, would be sufficient to put shape into the muddle and confusion and bring the war to a successful conclusion. Palmerston temporised. In May, Villiers received a despatch in which he was instructed to inform Martinez that he must not look for foreign intervention *until all the resources of the Spanish Government had been brought into action*.

Villiers was in a state of towering indignation at this prevarication on the part of his Government. Palmerston wrote that he was well aware of the situation in Spain and the probable consequences of the decision he had come to. Granville wrote from Paris in the same vein:

"I can only say that if they are so they have carefully concealed their knowledge," writes Villiers bitterly to his brother Charles. "The only despatch I have received from Palmerston, and the several which de Broglie has written to Reyneval display an equal misapprehension of Spain, as she is, as she might be, or as she will be. I have seen no reasons given but inconvenience, or 'inexpediency under existing circumstances,' (that enormous political loophole), or any departure from the '*politique meticuleuse*,' which desires the end, but shrinks from the means. It may be inconvenient to grant Spain the assistance she demands, but then why make the Treaty, or enter into engagements if we are not prepared to accept the consequences?"

7

As for our telling Spain that she could expect no assistance from England till she had put into action all her existing resources, that, he considered, was a *mauvaise plaisanterie* of the first order. Had they any conception at home of the state of the country that they could have the want of imagination to say such a thing? " I confess," he concludes snappishly, " that the triumph we have given to the Holy Allies goes to my heart, or rather to my foot, for I have a sharp attack of gout."

He had good reason to deplore the effect that this betrayal would have on Spanish affairs. In fact, it created a political crisis. In June, 1835, the Spanish Government, disappointed in its hopes of Allied support, distraught by internal dissensions and incapable of controlling the mounting tide of crime and unrest in the country, tottered and fell. Martinez de la Rosa resigned, and his place was taken by Torreno, an aristocrat, a moderate liberal, believing in constitutional government, but retaining the strong prepossession of an aristocrat in favour of his own class and its privileges. He represented the liberal party of gentlemen in Spain as against the newer and more advanced liberals—or " progressionists "—who were headed by lawyers, doctors and soldiers risen from the middle classes. Torreno was strongly pro-French, having passed several years in Paris, where he had become intimate with the governing classes and all men and women of note in the political and social world. He was a man of great ability, both as states-man and as a debater; bold, not over-scrupulous, gallant, as fond of pleasure as of business, and accustomed to take the lead in both. " Two clever men," says Bulwer, in his *Life of Lord Palmerston*, " when brought together in public affairs, either like one another very much or not at all; M. de Torreno and Mr. George Villiers liked one another not at all. In the land of the serenade and the guitar," he adds mysteriously, " it is always pretended that love and politics go hand in hand, and the old question ' Qui est-elle?' was raised on this occasion."

Bulwer, who was a contemporary of George's, a diplomat and a politician, should certainly have known the gossip of the day. It is significant that Villiers is reticent on the subject of Torreno. Of all the other Spanish Ministers—Martinez, Isturitz, Mendizabal, Calatrava—he gives amusing, often brilliant, thumb-nail sketches in the course of his private correspondence home. But of Torreno never a word—save of the most formal character.

It may be that the two had sat together in the Paris salon of Mme. de Montijo three years before. If so, " the bone of con-tention " was still absent from Spain, and only returned to Madrid just before George left. But perhaps there was a lady nearer at hand; for the British Minister, despite an impeccable discretion, was by no means an anchorite, and had not been two years in

Spain without noting that Spanish women had beautiful feet and
walked with dignity and grace, "not a pit-a-pat and in a hurry
as the French women do." However this may have been, the
personal relations between Villiers and Torreno were cold and
restrained; and this was all the more unfortunate since they did
not see eye to eye with regard to policy. Villiers believed that the
future in Spain belonged to the progressive liberals: that power
would ultimately fall into their hands: that the one chance of
success that the Queen's cause had was to champion the advanced
party and to rely upon their support. Torreno, as a *moderado*,
feared the new liberalism, and, though a constitutionalist, frowned
upon the extension of democratic powers to local and municipal
bodies. Behind him was a large body of moderate, even reactionary, opinion, not wholly sound for the Queen's cause.
However, he was not strong enough to stem the tide of popular
feeling. The country was now in a state of seething unrest. In
Madrid the nightly robberies and assassinations increased—the
Jacobins were making trouble everywhere. In August a *junta*
was declared in the capital, and Torreno proclaimed a state of
siege. He himself retired to San Idelfonso, where the Court was,
and left the police to cope with the situation. The revolution, if
revolution it can be named, petered out, it is true; but a month
later every great town in Spain had its own *junta*, which addressed
its demands direct to the Queen. The authority of the Cortes had
vanished, and feeling ran so high that Torreno, incapable of controlling the situation, threw up his hands and resigned.

It was at this juncture that the Queen-Regent sent for the
British Minister and quite frankly asked him what she should do.
Distracted by factions, with the whole country in a state bordering
upon revolution, she turned to the one man in Spain whom she
thought would give her unbiassed advice.

That Villiers took upon himself the task of advising her may
seem on the face of it preposterous. But the wheel of events was
beginning to place these two in a curious psychological relation
to each other. More and more, as time went on, Maria-Christina
was to realise that the British Minister had no personal axe to
grind: that he was sincere in his enthusiasm for her own and her
daughter's cause: that his judgment of people and situations was
unbiassed, and that he was that very rare thing in politics—
rarest of all in Spanish politics—an honest man. And as the
political situation darkened, and the difficulty of her position
became more acute, she turned more and more to the British
Minister as the one person in Spain who could view a situation
with level eyes, and tell her what to do. Thus it came about
that by the end of his time in Spain, George Villiers occupied a
position which, if not unprecedented, is rare in the case of a

Minister accredited to a foreign court. His influence made and
unmade cabinets, appointed and dismissed military commanders,
created or shattered reputations. He advised what should be
done, and what should not be done, and in nine cases out of ten
his advice was taken. And it never occurred to him that his
position was a singular one. Nor was he, in any way, flattered
or exalted by it. He simply used his influence with the Queen
and her ministers to effect what he thought ought to be done in
the muddle and confusion of affairs. He was fully alive to the
advantage he had in being outside the complex of personal
intrigue that distorted every question as it presented itself, and
he eagerly responded to that kind of appeal to the judgment of
the "outsider," which people involved in affairs are sometimes
prone to make, and he was quick to turn such confidences to the
account of the legitimate cause.

On this occasion when she asked for his advice he had no doubt
in his mind as to what he should tell her to do. The only strong
man of the moment on the Queen's side was the Minister of
Finance, Mendizabal, a Jew. He was immensely popular, having
captured the imagination of the people by his wealth, his gifts,
his picturesque personality. He had character and determination; and whatever he might or might not prove to be in the
future, he was the only choice for the present. He was a member
of Torreno's Government; but Torreno had never liked him, for
there were rumours that he had been a revolutionary in his youth,
and anyhow he was known to hold advanced liberal views.
These, however, had not been much in evidence during his short
term of office in the Torreno Cabinet, as he had been almost
wholly occupied in the administrative task of saving the shattered finances of Spain.

Villiers knew that in giving the Queen this advice, he would
be accused of partisanship. For Mendizabal, in the first place,
was a Whig: he was also pro-English, having resided in England
and imbibed English traditions and sympathies; and he advocated
exactly that policy of concession to democratic forms of government against which Louis Philippe was secretly contending in
France. Indeed, Villiers was soon to realise that with Mendizabal's
appointment, the attitude of France towards the affairs of the
Peninsula was to undergo a change. A certain hostility to the
existing régime became apparent almost at once, and—more
significant—the frontier restrictions which prevented supplies
from France reaching the Carlist armies were quickly withdrawn,
with the result that by the end of 1835, long trains of munitions,
clothing and foodstuffs were streaming over the border and finding their way unmolested to the Carlist Headquarters. Both
Mendizabal and Villiers were alarmed at this manifestation, and

Villiers had grounds for suspecting that it was but a prelude to
an even more complete change of policy on the part of France,
and that Louis Philippe and his ministers were preparing to make
a treaty with Don Carlos himself. This change of front certainly
did not originate in Spain, where the French Ambassador, a wise
and slightly cynical old gentleman, was Villiers' very good friend
and ally. It originated in Paris and in London: in Paris where
the French foreign office were beginning to hold the view that
Spain was now plunged in irremediable anarchy and that the
policy of the Queen's Government was only making confusion
worse confounded: in London, indirectly, through old Talleyrand, who in the last years of his term as French Ambassador
there had failed to read the signs of the times: failed to understand such men as Palmerston, John Russell and Grey, and had
intimated to his royal master on his return to France (August,
1834) that England was rapidly declining in power, and would
soon be of little account in the politics of Europe. Heartened by
these doctrines, the French Government felt free to judge the
Spanish situation on its own merits. And what they now felt
was necessary for Spain—not only in her own interests, but in
theirs also—was some kind of "absolutism," as we should say
to-day, "dictatorship" to put shape into the chaos existing
there. And this, they felt, would hardly come from the Queen's
cause, which was supported by the advanced liberal sections of
the community, bolstered up by England and "international-
ised" by the Quadruple Alliance, concerning which they took a
very cynical view. Added to which the situation in Spain was
now dominated by Mendizabal, who was known to be Villiers'
choice, and would play into English hands. All these considerations together caused France, at this juncture, to veer round in
sympathy towards the Carlist side; and although, officially she
still gave lip-service to the Quadruple Alliance, a marked hostility towards Allied counsels in Spain was beginning to be
observed.

Both Villiers and Mendizabal became alarmed at these signs
and signals of French defection, and the tension between the two
countries over Spanish affairs was hardly relieved when it became
known in Paris that Villiers had drawn up a secret commercial
treaty with Mendizabal whereby in compensation for the loan of
a large capital sum on the part of Great Britain, Spain should
give preferential treatment to certain British raw materials entering the country. Villiers sketched such a treaty and sent it to
London as a suggestion, but was rebuked for his pains and curtly
informed "that His Majesty's Government did not consider that
it would be consistent with the spirit of the Quadruple Alliance,
for two out of the four nations to make separately and without

previous communication with others, an engagement . . ."
Although the greatest secrecy had been observed over the whole
affair only three people in Spain knew of the proposed treaty,
Villiers, Mendizabal and the Queen-Regent.   The French got
wind of it somehow, probably in London, and it was all over
Paris in twenty-four hours.   Louis Philippe and his Ministers
were furious, even though the treaty was never ratified, and
thereafter Villiers became both feared and hated in French official
circles.   It was lucky that a real friendship existed between him
and Reyneval, the French Ambassador in Madrid, and that
Reyneval was both experienced and cynical, and able to keep his
head, and perhaps Villiers' too, in the face of strained and trying
relations between the two countries.

If France was behaving in a most peculiar manner with regard
to the Quadruple Alliance, it cannot be said that England was
standing very firmly to her pledges.   However, although Palmerston, taken unawares by Spain's sudden request for "effective
aid" the year before (which in this case meant nothing less than
armed intervention), had had, in veiled language to refuse,
simply because in plain words there *was* no "armed intervention" to give, still his conscience had been by no means easy on
the matter ever since.   Nor, indeed, had he been inactive with
regard to it.   Far from it.   Spurred by the shame of having had
to refuse what he had quite obviously promised, he had out of
his own brain invented and brought into being an English volunteer unit, raised to fight for the Queen's cause; and there began
now to appear in the camps of Spain companies of perhaps one
of the strangest forces that has ever taken the field of battle.
Palmerston had been in a great fix.   Apart from the fact that
it would, he knew, be well-nigh impossible to involve the Whig
Government in a War for the Spanish succession, he knew that
France would never stand aside and see a British Expeditionary
Force operating in the Peninsula without joining in.   Above all
things, he did not wish to see a French Army in Spain.   The
problem was to discover a means whereby England—and France,
too—could give armed assistance to the Spanish forces, without
appearing to do so politically, and without officially involving
either country in a war against Don Carlos.   The forces in question, too, had to be such as not to be recognised by their respective Governments.   They must, so to speak, hang in the air; sub-
sist by themselves, and be unattached, save by the most incon-
spicuous threads, to any official source whatsoever.   Only under
such conditions as these could either country bear to see the
other operating in a military capacity in the Peninsula.   It was a
nice question, and the Foreign Secretary brooded over it for
some months.   But in the end light came to him.   He was visited

by what he considered a brilliant idea; and so marvellous a solution did he think it that he would brook no criticism or listen to any advice. He pushed the scheme through by Order in Council, sweeping all objections aside. The idea was this: the force that should fight for the Spanish succession should be a Volunteer Force, a "Foreign Legion," so to speak, enlisted in England for service in Spain. Propaganda for the young Queen's cause should be put on foot at once, and men of all classes should be invited to enlist for a period of two years. Gentlemen from the regular service could be seconded from their regiments to officer these irregulars while the expense of their sustenance and equipment would, of course, devolve upon the Spanish Government. For were they not risking honour and life itself in the cause of Spain? by a happy provision of Lord Sidmouth, it was enacted that such a force could not be trained in England. And this was most convenient as, on enlistment, its members would have to be drafted straight out to Spain to undergo their discipline there, under the benevolent eye of the Spanish Government. It was almost too good to be true, as this idea of a "Spanish Legion" seemed to fulfil all the necessary conditions of the kind of force required without costing the country a penny.

Villiers, from the start, was urgent in his opposition to the scheme. Had the force been equipped and trained in England, and furnished from there with stores and supplies for a regular campaign, it would have been another matter. But to throw a large unit of untrained, unequipped men upon a bankrupt nation, and expect a Spanish Quartermaster-General to furnish their only means of subsistence, was, he very well knew, heading for disaster. The old Duke also knew it. Villiers and he were the only two Englishmen at this juncture who had a real grasp of the state of affairs in Spain—Villiers from being on the spot, and the Duke from knowing his Spain too well to be deceived. They both protested, but in vain.

The history of this unhappy force would make a book in itself. As was to be expected, the exhausted state of the Spanish Treasury, and the dilatory methods of the Spanish Commissariat produced moments when the troops were forced to sell their accoutrements or starve. Although Villiers was ceaseless in his appeals to the Spanish authorities to fulfil their duties, he could not alter the Spanish character. Spain was Spain; delays were endless and corruption insatiable. Then, of the 9,600 men (under de Lacy Evans' command) over 2,000 never took the field, being unfit for military service at all. The rest, when at last they were launched as a fighting unit, did splendidly on several occasions, at times being a very marked factor in the military situation. But the term of enlistment was of two years' duration only, and just at the moment when their continued presence in Spain, might have made a difference, they were weakly disbanded, and sent home to England, "where they arrived," according to the Annual Register of 1937, "in the most miserable condition that can be conceived."

The whole scheme was a failure—one of those half-measures that, in the end, serve no purpose at all—as Villiers knew from the first it would be. And though he worked himself to the bone on behalf of the British troops, he was unfeignedly thankful to see the last of them.

§ 8

By the beginning of 1836, George Villiers was well into his third year as British Minister in Spain; and though he was always planning to come home on leave, the possibility of doing so for one reason or another seemed always to be disappearing into the future. Yet he was fascinated by his job and content to remain at his post:

"I have often asked myself, without getting a satisfactory answer, why I like being here separated from everything which my disposition, as well as habits, had rendered necessary to the enjoyment of life. I live in the midst of vice and intrigue; I have not, during two years, met with an honest man. There is no learning, no instruction, no taste, no conversation, and no objects, except to ascertain what party, be it of Princes or Ministers, is likely to prevail, for the purpose of being found on that side in good time. Still, it makes no difference to the satisfaction I feel in being here, or my unwillingness to accept any other diplomatic post so long as I could retain this . . . I feel so entirely embarked in the cause, the question, the country."

The truth was, George Villiers had now attained a position of considerable importance in the politics and social life of Madrid. His patent honesty, and his rather touchy sense of honour were disarming in a land where everything that was said had a double meaning, and honour meant little save in its respect to women. Gradually they thawed towards the enthusiastic young Englishman whose word—was it possible?—was as good as his bond. He entertained well, and on a princely scale; and in addition to the large official dinner-parties and receptions, which it is the function of a Minister in a foreign capital to give, at stated intervals, he had, early on in his career in Madrid, instituted a series of weekly *soirées* for men on Saturday evenings, "which," as he said, "served as a kind of club where men of different political opinions, who could never have met elsewhere, were thrown together. The house of a Foreign Minister," he adds, "should

be a mutual ground, where men of every shade of opinion may
congregate without compromise—that bug-bear of the Spaniard.''
These *soirées* had taken on, and the British Minister was wont to
receive nearly two hundred men of a Saturday evening. And
not only did these meetings serve the purpose for which they were
intended, but they also enabled Villiers to watch at close quarters
a number of men whom normally he would have had difficulty
in meeting, or at any rate in seeing together, and to circulate
easily and detachedly among politicians and men of affairs of
every sort and description. By this means he got to know everybody and everybody got to know him. He became a power, an
influence in the land. Some account of his direct intervention in
politics has been given. But his reputation, as a sort of dictator,
went far beyond that. At times it was most delicate and inconvenient. ''I cannot rid people,'' he writes at about this time,
''of the unshakable opinion that they have here, that I am all-
powerful, and can order and govern as I please. I therefore get
a levée of people every day upon their own business, who are full
of notions, passing strange, of what I can do. I will give you an
example of some cases occurring this week: Master Miraflores, a
rotund ball of conceit, came to state that the only salvation for
the country lay in my assisting him to form a Ministry. The
Neapolitan *chargé d'affaires* came to show me an insolent note
he had received from Mendizabal, and to request that I should
get it taken back again, and, at the same time, to speak about
the Court going into mourning for the Queen of Naples, which
he had some reason to think was not intended.

''Dal Borgo—who would be charged with Danish affairs if
Denmark *had* any business with this country—walked in upon
me, at the request of several of his neighbours, to represent the
scandalous state of the police, and to state that it was impossible
to stir after dark for fear of being assassinated, and would I get
it remedied. (I have done this, for it was quite true.) Then a
well-dressed, good-looking woman came in her carriage, but
would not give her name, and asked me for a blank passport for
an officer, whom she gave me to understand was her *cher ami*, and
who had killed a man in a duel and wanted to get out of the
country. Next came a gentleman, with whom I had not the
smallest acquaintance, to ask me to get him the Grand Cross of
the Order of Isabella la Catholica! Finally, came also Mendizabal
with a message from the Queen-Regent for—what do you think?
—to beg I would send away her brother, the Prince of Naples,
and Miss Penelope Smith (whom he had just married). I begged
to know how I could possibly do this. He said he did not know,
but that the Queen had no doubt I could contrive it!''

So the British Minister ''se faisait valoir'' at the Court of

Madrid, as befitted the representative of the most powerful of nations. From the first he had done things well. His cook was excellent, his domestic staff impeccable, and he was meticulous as to detail. Knowing, for instance, that the *kind* of horses he wanted for his carriage were difficult to procure in Spain, he arranged with "Poodle" Byng to send him out from England four matched bays from a particular stud. There was a good deal of correspondence about these favoured animals, and Emily Eden writes: "I fully expect that *the* decisive cavalry charge to decide the Spanish succession will be made by Don Carlos' troops, mounted on the horses the Poodle has sent you by the wrong road."

In Spain he contracted the habit of smoking, and years afterwards officials of the British Foreign Office were surprised to see the Secretary of State settling down to a night's work with a pile of red boxes on one side and a pile of cigarettes on the other. Moreover, this trick of turning night into day was probably begun in Spain. Madrid was too perfervid by day—at least in summer when the heat was terrific—to allow much time to be spent closeted in an Embassy study writing despatches. So it was mostly Villiers' habit to begin work in the evening, after dinner, and to labour on far into the night, rising late and dawdling the morning away in compensation. Such a course cannot have been very propitious to his constitution, but on the whole his health, but for one serious illness, was good during his time in Spain, and the heats kept his old enemy the gout at bay.

But to return to affairs. Mendizabal had disappointed his supporters. Looked on by all as the one man who could salvage the sunken finances of Spain, he had failed to fill the bill. You cannot make money without money, and there was nothing of any account left in the Spanish Treasury with which to bargain. A strong opposition began to form against him in the Cortes, headed by Isturitz, Anguella and Gallieno. "That bubble Mendizabal is about to burst," wrote Villiers rather snappishly in April, and in May his prophecy was realised. The Government fell, and a new Government was formed under Isturitz, leader of the popular party, of whose leadership he had been ousted by Mendizabal himself.

Meanwhile "the cannibal war" showed no signs of abatement. Indeed, the hatred and intensity redoubled itself on both sides, and the Eliot Convention was proving hopeless to stem the tide of outrage and violence that both sides complacently indulged in. In January, 1836, the Carlists, besieged in Barcelona, threw their prisoners from the walls and shot them as they fell. In March, Mina, who had had trouble with Cabrera, a Carlist

PLATE 3.—LORD CLARENDON
From a contemporary print.

chieftain on the borders of Catalonia, captured his mother and shot her. Cabrera retaliated by shooting the wives of some thirty royalist officers who happened to fall into his hands.

§ 9

The summer of 1836 was disturbed by a dangerous mutiny of the Queen's troops—almost a revolution—at La Granja. Maria-Christina herself became a hostage in the hands of the unruly soldiery, as in fact did the whole of the Court and most of the *corps diplomatique*, Villiers among them, who were spending the summer in the capacious palace and grounds of San Idelfonso, a few leagues from Madrid. It was a delicate situation, and had not the Queen and those about her behaved with commendable restraint and *sang-froid* the affair might have had the most disastrous results. As it was, the *émeute* was made to appear nothing more than a military demonstration; and with nice handling—and for once the Queen's Ministers kept their heads—it died down as rapidly as it had arisen, and though it shook the country momentarily it bore no evil effects to the Queen's cause. The origin of the revolt was probably financial. The Spanish Treasury was exhausted; the Queen's troops had not been paid for several months; and it was very much in keeping with the general slackness of the Spanish administration that the two regiments who were on duty as bodyguard to the Queen at San Idelfonso at this time should have been among the most flagrantly ill-treated in this respect. Grumbling and disaffected, any spark was sufficient to set them off. The spark in this case was Garcia, a big bullying sergeant with a taste for subversive politics. He preached the usual democratic gospel of government by parliament, instead of by Order in Council, and a return to the Constitution of 1812. "La Constituzion," cried the troops, many of them believing it to be a new name for the Queen, to whom they were devoted. On a night in August they marched to the palace, shouting and singing, broke their way in, and reached the State Apartments. The Queen, unmoved, received a deputation from among their number. "Liberty in the name of the Troops," said Gomez, their leader, as he knelt and kissed the Queen's hand. "But do you know, my son, what Liberty is?" asked the Queen gravely. "It is the rule of law," she said, "and obedience to authority." Other deputations arrived and sought to enforce their terms upon the Queen. Papers and documents were flourished in her face, but she remained cool and collected. She would call the Cortes on her return to Madrid, but she would sign no documents now. Finally came Garcia himself, and insisted that she should at least sign a paper stating that she would promulgate the Constitution pending the calling of the Cortes. "Have you read the Constitution of 1812?" asked Izaga, a Court official, of a soldier standing by. He replied that he could neither read nor write, but that his father had told him that the Constitution was a good thing, and that salt and tobacco would be cheaper if it were brought into force. A strained situation was turned to laughter and much merriment ensued. The Court officials behaved throughout with exemplary tact, keeping the surface of affairs friendly and light in hand. But beneath their easy *badinage* they were distraught with anxiety. What were they but a posse of defenceless individuals, the Queen among them, in the hands of armed troops, who were not clear what they wanted themselves and whose actions were completely unpredictable?

Meanwhile Villiers, who had made several attempts during the night to reach the Queen but had found his way barred on each occasion, finally managed to arrive in the State Apartments. The deputations had withdrawn temporarily, but the Queen was still in the hands of the troops. Villiers congratulated her on the courage and *sang-froid* which she had displayed, and she showed him the paper that Garcia insisted upon her signing. He read it through gravely and in the end advised her to sign it. She was, as he delicately intimated, a prisoner for the moment; and if a deadlock ensued between the Court and the troops no one could predict the consequences. The situation was too dangerous, and she was, he pointed out, powerless to do anything but to comply with this paper of Garcia's, which appeared, as a matter of fact, to be the least common multiple of the soldiers' demands. The Queen, after some discussion, consented to sign it, and Villiers went off to contrive a means of getting in touch with the Government in Madrid and to inform Ministers of the situation at San Idelfonso. It was a difficult task to achieve, as all the routes were, naturally, barred. But George, by now, was well versed in the ways and means of Spain, and he managed it somehow. The emissary arrived safely and gave his report to the Council. Quesada, the Captain-General, urged that he should be sent immediately to La Granja with sufficient troops to settle the affair off hand; but Mendez Vigo, the Minister for War, thought it better to adopt more prudent methods, and himself set forth to the scene of action to see what he could do. It was six o'clock in the evening when he arrived, and he found the troops completely out of hand, drunk with wine, singing and shouting. He made himself amiable and distributed money. Garcia, hearing of this, peremptorily ordered him to leave. Mendez readily complied, suggesting that he should take the Queen with him in order that no time should be lost in summoning the Cortes and swearing to the Constitution. But the ruse was too simple, and the Queen was detained. The next day was spent in pour-parlers between Garcia, Mendez Vigo and the Queen, and in the end the latter put her signature to a series of Decrees (one of which entailed the dismissal of Quesada). Mendez Vigo and Garcia together took these to Madrid, leaving the Queen at La Granja in charge of the soldiery. Meanwhile the members of the *corps diplomatique* were as much prisoners as the Queen, and Villiers spent the day the Decrees were being drawn up at the bedside of his old friend Reyneval, who had been taken ill some days before the mutiny had broken out and whose illness now took an alarming turn.

Mendez Vigo and Garcia on their arrival in Madrid found the town in a ferment. Indeed, it appeared that had it not been for the extraordinary courage of Quesada there must have been bloodshed.

With two companions he had dispersed a mob of several thousand armed men who had assembled in the Puerto del Sol. On the arrival of Mendez Vigo he learnt of his dismissal and tried at once to leave the city in disguise. He was recognised and lynched by the mob under circumstances of revolting barbarity. In him Spain lost one of the bravest of her Generals and by no means the least intelligent of her leaders.

When the Decrees had been promulgated and the Cortes convened, the Queen was permitted to return to Madrid. She was accompanied by the British Ambassador, but the French Ambassador was no longer at her side. Reyneval had died at La Granja, to Villiers' great grief.

The imminent danger was over, the Constitution was proclaimed; Garcia disappeared into obscurity, but the whole country was momentarily in a state of ferment; no one's life was safe.

During the next few weeks Villiers had several eminent politicians concealed in his house, with the intention of saving them from the fury of the mob, who had already murdered the Captain-General Quesada under circumstances of such unspeakable brutality. The Ducque de Ahunada, an important member of the Council of Regency, was hidden for ten days at the Embassy, and the Ducque de Ribas spent a fortnight there in concealment. And of Isturitz George writes: "I managed to despatch him to Lisbon, having myself fetched him at night, and got him into the stables without a single servant knowing it, or even the courier knowing who he was until they were out of the town."

The late Prime Minister passed safely through the guards that were set for him at the gates, and finally arrived in Portugal, where he broadcast the fact that George had saved his life, though Villiers had made only one condition in attempting to save him, namely that of absolute secrecy.   No wonder the British Minister was popular in Madrid.   But his heart was heavy, for to his reiterated appeals for more active intervention, there was, as usual, no response from the Government at home, and he was forced to stand by and watch the disintegration of affairs under the pressure of adverse events.

"This country," he writes at about this time, "is now a perfect political hell, as I remember in May 1835 I took the liberty of informing Lord Palmerston it would be, if England and France, having undertaken the affairs of Spain, did not proceed in their task with a firm hand."

Much capital was made out of the happenings at La Granja, and George Villiers was not a little surprised when he was told that all Europe believed that he himself had organised the revolution of La Granja, and that he had even been seen handing out pieces of gold to the disaffected troops.   It was a most astonishing and baseless scandal, which took a long time to die down.

§ 10

We must now pass swiftly over the events of the next two years.   If we have lingered in detail over the first part of Villiers' time in Spain it was in order to describe the complicated and dramatic political situation in which he found himself in the midst of his arrival at Madrid, to indicate the various threads of European diplomacy that gathered round the situation, and to show the manner in which Villiers conducted the business of British foreign politics in regard to it all.   Enough has been said to show that he took an independent line from the first, often correcting the views of his chiefs in Westminster, and urging lines of policy which were his own, gained from a knowledge of conditions on the spot, and when the Whig Government fell the Tory Ministry which took its place confirmed him in his post at Madrid.

As to the Carlist wars which we have followed in some detail, Villiers was not to see the end of them although he witnessed their outbreak, and we have not the space to do anything more than take a general survey of the circumstances which brought them to a close.   By the time the last shot had been fired in that unhappy conflict, Villiers was back in England, married, and a Cabinet Minister.

But to return to 1836.   In the winter of that year the anxiety of the political situation eventually undermined his health, and Villiers suffered a severe attack of dysentery which nearly cost

him his life. When it was known that he was seriously ill, the
greatest solicitude was shown in Madrid. He found afterwards
that a daily bulletin, signed by his doctors, had been posted at
the Porter's Lodge, and that crowds had waited daily to hear how
he was—a fact that amused and touched him when he recovered.

By the new year he was convalescent, and good news speeded
his recovery. For Esparterro, the new commander of the Royalist
forces, relieved Bilbao and inflicted a severe defeat on the
Carlists. Nor was this only a matter for public rejoicing, for
Algy, the youngest of the Villiers brothers, then a Lieutenant in
the Navy on H.M.S. *Ringdove*, was amongst the British volunteers
who aided in the relief of the town; and when George got the news
of the success of the expedition and of his brother's safety, which
he did whilst sitting down to a dinner of sixteen at the Embassy,
he was so excited that he translated the despatches of Wylde and
Hay into Spanish for the benefit of his guests and reported himself as ready to stand on his head with jubilation! A week later
Maitland, who had commanded the naval expedition, came to
Madrid and was fêted by all and sundry. At a dinner given in
his honour by the Deputies, Villiers rose to answer the toast of the
British Minister and pronounced a long political discourse in
Spanish which created the greatest excitement, being printed later
as a broadsheet and sold in the streets by the blind beggars of
Madrid. "El Magnifico Discorso que pronuncia el Señor Em-
bassador di Inglaterra. . . ." As he had spoken in no measured
terms of Allied intervention, his speech was not popular among
the French colony, and it resulted in a conversation between
Villiers and the new French Ambassador, Maubourg, which,
however, was perfectly satisfactory, since the latter was an insig-
nificant little man whom George could manage. But he regretted
Reyneval. Of the Maubourg "interior" he writes:

"Madame de Maubourg is a poor little thing, simple and surprised, without an idea in the world, very much bored with
Madrid, but having quite forgotten Paris; knows nobody; sees
nobody, and cares for nothing. She seems to respect her husband
because she married him. He is a dull, formal man; and when
they are together, and he is tired of reading *Le Journal des
Debats*, and wishing perdition to the liberals and success to the
doctrinaires, and she is tired of her worsted work, I am sure that
they both look together into the fire for hours without saying a
word."

A revolution in Barcelona next obscured the general situation—
all the more so when it was known that the outbreak was not of
Carlist origin, but was frankly republican in nature. The Court
was alarmed, and the Queen, distraught with anxiety and shaken

by her recent experiences at La Granja, weakened, and began
playing with the idea of coming to an arrangement with Don
Carlos. Villiers received despatches from home warning him that
she was considering the possibility of marrying the infant Queen,
her daughter, to Don Carlos' son. The difficulty, it appeared,
was which of the two should be considered " reigning monarch,"
which merely " consort." Villiers, knowing the character of the
two principals in this piece of political bargaining, did not imagine
that anything very tangible would come of it. Besides, he believed
in Maria-Christina—believed in her courage and determination,
and had full confidence that she would never set her hand to any
agreement that did not recognise her daughter unequivocally as
rightful Queen of Spain.

Moreover, on June 17th, 1837, she swore to the Constitution in
Madrid amidst scenes of the wildest enthusiasm, and there was a
great rallying to her cause, at least in the capital and the regions
round it. This was accentuated a thousandfold when in September
Don Carlos, after a series of small victories qualified by mild
defeats, much to his own surprise, blundered up to Madrid itself
and encamped within sight of it. He believed that half Madrid
would rise in his support and that the other half, fearing an
alliance between himself and the Queen-Regent, would proclaim
a republic. In this scene of confusion he saw himself taking possession of the city, being proclaimed King, and behaving with
perfect courtesy to his sister-in-law, and, it might be, even offering
her daughter his son's hand in marriage. But he was much mistaken in his predictions. Whilst the Carlists prepared banners
and streamers and printed proclamations to be used on the day of
their triumphal entry, the good Madrilenos, outraged at the sight
of the rebels outside their gates, rushed to arms. Those who had
been most disaffected were the first to offer their services to the
Queen-Regent. Never had there been so much military enthusiasm. And Christina herself was in no small measure
responsible for the sudden outburst of loyalty. She spared herself
nothing, riding up and down the lines within sight of the enemy
and in real personal danger, chatting to the men and to the non-
commissioned officers. For all her failings, she had many virtues
—a certain large-hearted jollity and real humanity, a great deal
of spirit and a physical courage that was absolute.

Never had a better feeling existed between the Queen and her
subjects; both were enjoying the danger, and so was the British
Ambassador. He was delighted with the Queen-Regent's conduct
and open in his admiration. He knew very well that messengers
went by night between the Queen's palace and the Pretender's
camp, but he had no fear that Christina would let down her
partisans; he knew too well how responsive she was to popularity

and how natural it was to her to endeavour to live up to the hopes which she had raised.

The whole affair was slightly ludicrous. The invading army sat in their camp awaiting the day on which they would be called upon to enter Madrid, and this day never dawned. No hostilities took place. The more fashionable members of Spanish society ordered their carriages and drove between the lines to have a look at the rebels. Villiers went on one of these expeditions and was little impressed by the Carlist troops, whom he describes as having the appearance of groups of picturesque gypsies, suitable for a water-colour of Theresa's.

Eventually it was borne in upon Don Carlos that he had made an egregious miscalculation. He was not going to be welcomed in Madrid either by his own partisans or by the Queen-Regent. Since he had not sufficient troops to take the city, he wisely decided to retreat before worse befell him. So one morning the Madrilenos woke to find that their enemies had quietly retired under cover of night. This ignominious effort to penetrate the Royalist stronghold was not effected without much loss on the part of Don Carlos' discouraged troops, who were harassed by the Royalist generals as they endeavoured to regain their bases. The retreat from Madrid marked the end of the serious stage of the Carlist war. From now onwards fighting was largely restricted to the provinces of the Basques and the Navarrese; and soon afterwards the unfortunate Pretender completed his series of errors by marrying his sister-in-law, the odious Princess de Beira, who soon lost him his few supporters.

In October, 1837, Villiers received the G.C.B. in recognition of his good work in Spain. He felt now that the Queen-Regent was in a position of comparative security, and he longed for leave to return to England, at least for a short time; but whenever he proposed to apply for leave some urgent matter immediately cropped up. The negotiation of a loan, followed by a commercial treaty; the strange activities of Mr. George Borrow, who would insist upon disseminating the Bible throughout Spain, and of Mr. Graydon, who publicly announced that "the Catholic religion was not the religion of God," and that he had been sent out from England to convert the Spaniards to Protestantism—all these affairs kept Villiers at his post for some time after he felt justified in returning to England, at least for a while. But in the end relief came, and in the summer of 1838 he applied for leave and it was granted him.

He had spent five years in Spain. He had negotiated two treaties: he had seen the Carlist danger arise and fade: he had stood by the Queen under circumstances of extreme peril: he had influenced her from despotism towards liberalism: he had done much to make the promulgation of the Constitution palatable to her: he had maintained British prestige in a remarkable fashion, despite the vacillations of the gentlemen at Westminster. On the whole he was well satisfied with his achievement.

As he journeyed towards Paris he anticipated a return journey in the late autumn. He felt himself so closely identified with Spanish politics that he could not visualise a final severance from them. Fate decided otherwise: he did return, but only for a few months, and with his head full of other matters. But his time of Minister in Madrid had covered a definite epoch.

And by the middle of 1839 Maroto, the Carlist General, was in treaty with Esparterro. Don Carlos reviewed his troops a last time. The men clamoured for peace. He turned his back upon them in disgust. On August 29th the Treaty of Verage was signed, and on August 31st the two armies met face to face and, following the example of their generals, embraced and then dispersed. The Carlist war was over and, though Cabrera fought on till 1840, a partial peace descended upon Spain. But this was a year ahead of the time at which Sir George Villiers disembarked at Dover.

CHAPTER V

LEAVE, SUCCESSION AND MARRIAGE

§ I

WHEN Villiers had seen his family, both immediate and distant, had made himself familiar with the circumstances of his brothers and discussed all and sundry with his mother, he decided to pay a few visits—Cirencester Park, Longleat, Petworth opened hospitable doors, and finally he went to stay with the Verulams at Gorhambury, a family who have not yet been mentioned, but who from now onwards played an important part in the life of George Villiers.

Not very far from The Grove stood the ruins of a beautiful Elizabethan manor house, once the home of Francis Bacon, where he had entertained Queen Elizabeth. Bacon's heirs dying out in the male line, the property had passed to a lady who first sold it to Sir Harbottle Grimston and then consolidated the position by marrying him. And here the Grimstons had lived till the end of the eighteenth century, when the eldest son, having married a lady of ample fortune, was persuaded to abandon the old house and build a fine palladian mansion on a neighbouring eminence. The Grimstons were Tories and, as such, were no doubt not only neighbours but also friends of Villiers' uncle, "the old Earl."

In a period of Tory ascendancy the head of the family received a peerage and took the title of Verulam, thus recalling at once his descent from Bacon and the site of the Roman town of Verulanium, remains of which were discovered in the park at Gorhambury.

The first Earl was a man altogether delightful and wholly typical of the early nineteenth century. He was honest, affectionate and entirely persuaded that life was good and enjoyable, and that he in particular was blessed in his family and in his station. Whether arrayed in his white top-hat he went down to visit his boys at Harrow, or taught them to play cricket on the lawns of Gorhambury; whether he was driving up to London in the curricle; frequenting Tattersalls, or helping to bring in a friend from Boodles; whether he was conducting family prayers, or writing invitations to Lady Verulam's parties, he was always the same contented, high-spirited schoolboy.

He might be occupied in "influencing" the election at St.

Albans, and refusing to go to church that he might not succumb to the sin of despising his political antagonists, whom he must inevitably see there; he might be entertaining Royal- or Hero-dukes for the purpose of shooting his aristocratic pheasants, or he might whilst riding with the girls be diverted from his path by the tale of "invaders in the furze fields" who must be captured and brought to trial; he might even be presenting addresses to the Lords against further concessions to Catholics, yet in all the grave and trivial occupations his equanimity was untouched. Not a shadow of doubt or dismay was ever known to trouble his simple and comfortable outlook.

One did one's duty, one accepted what came to one, and Providence looked after one; and to those to whom Providence's dispensations seemed less marked, one was kind. There was much in this robust and innocent creed to rest and vitalise the harassed minds of a later generation. People liked staying with old Lord Verulam; they might laugh a little at the undisguised wonder and admiration with which their host treated his wife; they might pause in astonishment at his incredible endurance upon which a broken arm or leg made not the slightest impression, but all the same they felt the better for their visit.

The first time Villiers had gone there was now many years ago; he had been taken by Charles Greville. But often since then he had strapped his guns to the back of a curricle, and driven down in answer to a hospitable invitation. Now, on leave from Spain, he proposed himself for a week-end. The children had grown up since his last visit and much had happened. There were Grim, Bob, Ned and Edward; Kathy, Emily, Mary and Jane. Kathy, the eldest daughter, whom he remembered as a red-headed child, was now not only married, but widowed. Whilst he had been in Spain he had heard something of her misfortunes. There had been a question of her marrying Lord Monson—"the little Lord," as he was called—and rumour had it that only Lord Verulam's kind intervention had saved a dutiful Kathy from her mother's schemes. And then, very soon afterwards, she had married John Barham, a rising young politician. Jamaica nabob on one side, he was, through his mother, heir to the fabulous Lord Thanet of incalculable wealth. Emily Eden had mentioned the marriage to Villiers in her letters in a waspish sentence: "Kathy Grimston was married to-day. Her mother is delighted—and I am sure the poor girl will like the diamonds very well."

Residence in London had brought Kathy Barham into Theresa Lister's circle, and a real friendship had sprung up between the two, so that in later letters Kathy's vicissitudes had been commented on in a kinder vein. Alas! the diamonds and the prospects had proved very poor counterweights to immediate unhappiness

and continued disaster. In the space of two short years Kathy
had lost a child, had seen her father-in-law go mad and die and
her own husband follow the same path. In less than three years
she had returned to Gorhambury with nothing but the diamonds,
a litigious pack of brothers and sisters-in-law, and a trunk full of
affidavits to remind her of her unhappy marriage.

In all these circumstances she had kept her head and acted
wisely and with forbearance, and Theresa Lister, looking on, had
judged her character and sung her praises to George with meaning.
It must be a great risk marrying a young girl out of the school-
room who, once parted from home influence, might develop into
almost anything. But in marrying a young woman such as Kathy
Barham there would be no risk; she had been tried and had
proved herself already. So to Theresa and to Mrs. George
the idea of a marriage between George and Kathy became an
ambition. They knew well that no one would be better pleased
than Lady Verulam (whose dying words later gossip reported to
have been, " Four daughters, four countesses "), and they felt
that Lord Verulam too (who had suffered as deeply as he was
capable of pain in his daughter's misfortunes) would be thankful
to know her united to one who would prove so utterly different
from her first husband. All that was necessary was to place the
situation before the interested parties in the light in which it appeared to their relations. So perhaps, after all, Villiers' visit to
Gorhambury was not quite so simply spontaneous as it appeared.

That he enjoyed his visit we know. The home life in this very
united family reminded him of his own youth. And if Lady
Verulam, rather querulous, rather fond of those dangerous "little
drops " which relieved her gout, bore no resemblance to Mrs.
George, the rôles were simply reversed. And whilst Lady
Verulam stood in the place of the Governor, to be placated and
managed and wheedled, Lord Verulam was the robust director
and confidante that Mrs. George had been.

Kathy, Villiers liked from the first. She was so reasonable, so
uncomplaining, despite misfortunes which might well have proved
the source of bitterness or romanticism to a less true realist. She
was to her brothers and sisters what George had been to his
family, adviser and model. They were well fitted to understand
each other. For that matter he liked them all, the quiet and
reserved Grim, the rollicking Bob, Ned, and Emily (who was
inclined to weep), Mary, who was so good-looking, and little
Jane, who played the latest French tunes on the piano and
waltzed till her feet nearly dropped off. But they were children
to be humoured and played with; and so, in their different ways,
were Lord and Lady Verulam themselves. Only he and Kathy
could talk together of life, hard, unpleasant, but vital, as they

knew it to be. When the time came for leaving he felt that he had made a real contact, inaugurated a friendship which might well have further developments.

But he said nothing. It was so short a time since Barham had died, and his own prospects were so vague. Now he must go back to Spain for an indefinite period; and though his pay was sufficient his private means were slender. If he left that post he would be in no position to support a wife and perhaps a family. And then too he had no idea what Kathy really thought about him; in general women had been complaisant in regard to him, but it is improbable that he had ever asked any woman to marry him.

§ 2

He left his affairs in the hands of his mother and Theresa. He did not wish Kathy to forget him; he wanted himself recalled to her memory at frequent intervals; he wanted her own feelings for him gauged by a less interested party. He could not have left his case in better hands. From the moment of his departure Mrs. George began a voluminous and almost daily correspondence with Kathy.

The ostensible pretext was to keep Kathy informed of Villiers' progress through the dangerous tracts of the North of Spain, where bandits and Carlist forces provided a very real source of peril. A few days later another letter was necessitated by a most unfortunate lapse on the part of Mrs. George.

"I have just done a shocking thing, and I want you to make my peace with Lord Verulam. A large parcel of letters was brought to me just now, some being from Theresa and the others from George. I suppose I did not exactly know what I was about and I opened one from Lord Verulam to George without even looking at the direction. I very soon folded it up, and it will go with my letter to George to-morrow unread by me."

A week passed and again Kathy was informed of the traveller's welfare. And it seems that she must have responded kindly to previous communications, for this time Mrs. George adds the comment: "I *do* and *will* allow myself to believe that you take an interest in him who is dearer than life to me." No response was apparently forthcoming to this advance, but undeterred Mrs. Villiers wrote four days later, "My own dear George arrived safe in Madrid on the morning of the 15th, and I am too thankful for such an enormous blessing, and too happy and too good-humoured to be able to scold *anybody* to-day, or I should scold *you*, you naughty child, for not having written sooner.

To this letter Kathy made a suitable reply, and then retaliated by speaking a little of her own affairs, the complicated situation which had arisen in regard to the Barham relations, Lord Thanet and herself as sole administrators of the wills of her husband and father-in-law. Here was a perfect opening for Mrs. Villiers' shaft, and she did not let it slip. After expressing some concern she goes on to say: "I am very glad you have got Lord Brougham as an adviser, for he must be a host in that way. I never much admired his politics, on which ever side he happened to be, but I believe he is a very kind and certainly a very able friend, though to be sure Lord B. and Croker form rather an unnatural coalition. I quite long for you to have done with it all. You will be so much happier, and I do suggest, if you can wait for a fortnight for an answer, that you write to George for his advice in the matter. If you did but know how happy it would make him to be consulted by you on any matter, and how sure I am that no quantity of public business, however pressing, would prevent his giving your concerns his very best attention. Indeed, George don't care for Spain and the Spaniards as he did. He lives on the hopes of getting away next spring and snapping his fingers at them all."

With what feelings Villiers himself would have read this description of his sentiments may be questioned, but Kathy fell into the trap and Mrs. George's next epistle is characteristic: "My dearest Kathy,—Yours just received has given me more pleasure than anything else could have done at this moment, for I know you must give pleasure to my own dear George by writing to him, that reflects pleasure back upon me. I thank and bless you for it."

For a month the correspondence continued in this vein, and then at last Lady Katherine admitted the true state of her feelings with regard to Villiers. Mrs. Villiers was triumphant, and let fly a pæan of thankfulness. Now she felt that George's happiness was secure. There might be difficulties, there might be delays, but the final consummation was no longer in doubt.

§ 3

Actually fate intervened within ten days of Kathy's declaration. On Christmas Eve, 1838, Mrs. Villiers wrote:

"My own dearest Kathy,
    "You must hear from me first of the death of poor Lord Clarendon. He expired at Deal on Saturday. A most unsatisfactory letter from his brother-in-law, Lord Maryboro' is my only announcement. Under other circumstances I should hope for George's return, but I cannot *now*—nor can any of us, when we think of the dangers of the journey. . . ."

Mrs. George had never liked her brother-in-law, but she was generous and his death instantly wiped out all her resentment. Unfortunately this forgiveness did not prove lasting, when it became apparent that ''nothing belonging to the Grove, *but the deer*! is left to George. It all went unreservedly to John by the late Lord Clarendon's will, and therefore is now Lady Clarendon's unreservedly.''

It was little comfort that Parkinson, Lord Clarendon's lawyer, should repeat sententiously, ''Sir G. will have no difficulty with his Aunt, it will all be right.'' For it was quite evident that Lady Clarendon was in no state to make a will, and Lord Maryboro' ''coming up to town *sly* on Friday'' gave food for the gravest fears that Lady Clarendon's relations might be endeavouring to secure a reversionary interest for themselves. It was also very humiliating not to have been informed as to when the funeral was to take place. . . . ''Would you believe it at this present writing we have never heard one word of the funeral except Lady M. saying *the dear remains* were to move yesterday.''

A week later they were still in doubt, and Mrs. Villiers, writing her bi-weekly report to Kathy, concludes: ''I will write every day that I hear anything of George or of 'the dear remains.' (Very wrong! but why do they make one wicked when one wanted to be good?)''

After all this it was something to learn from Leman that at least the pictures, plate and books at the Grove were heirlooms, and that Edward's drawing of George dressed in buckskins, driving a herd of deer through a turnpike, and the rest of the family seated round a camp-fire eating venison, *was* an under-statement of their financial prospects.

Finally, on January 3rd, Mrs. George went to visit the widow. ''You will naturally be glad to hear that I saw my dear sister Clarendon yesterday, and that I found the *visage de circonstance* which *I* put on for the occasion *quite* unnecessary, for anything more *gaillarde* I never saw—looking infinitely better than when I saw her last at the Grove. She told me all about Ld. C's illness and death and look after death, with the most perfect composure, but had evidently had her lesson given her for she repeated every two or three minutes . . . 'and the eldest will be chief mourner.' She had no notion which was the eldest, confused Montagu and Edward, and in short it is quite clear that the Maryboro's have the whole game in their hands. But, dear Kathy, only imagine how dangerous it is to talk to her, for she not only misunderstands but will actually misrepresent all one says. She was talking of how much Lord C. had always suffered from nerves and really for something to say, I replied how odd it was that all Villiers had such sensitive nerves, that I thought *the*

PLATE 4.—" KATHY ": LADY CLARENDON

From an oil painting (probably by Richmond) in the possession of the present Earl of Clarendon.

old Lord Clarendon had been the least nervous of the family. She looked rather confused (as she generally does) and said, 'When will he come?'—I naturally rejoined, 'Who?' and, after trying to recollect in vain, she said, 'from abroad.' 'Do you mean George?' said I. 'Yes,' she answered. 'I thought you called him Lord Clarendon.' Imagine, if I fired up, and I really exclaimed almost involuntarily, 'Good God! Lady Clarendon, you cannot for a moment suppose I could have called him so?' To which she very coolly replied, 'Oh, I didn't know—you know you might.' So I said as loud as I could, 'I spoke of the old Lord C., who died fourteen years ago,' to which she only said, 'Oh.'

"Now, *je vous demande un peu*, if it is not pleasant to talk to her, and I feel convinced she will tell everybody that I did nothing but talk to her of George as Lord C. I am now going to assist at the furor of opening the will, and Charles and Edward go too. And I know I shall laugh from the very fear of doing so. . . . We have agreed that none of us will say one word. The funeral will be on Saturday and 'the eldest is to be chief mourner.'

"There is something in the way she had got it by heart, that is more exquisitely ludicrous than I can describe. . . .

"P.S. . . . We have seen, we have heard, and it's all worse than we expected—everything left to her—not a hint even—not a suggestion to her, so that we must sit down with the painful conviction that all Lord C. said was a downright, premeditated lie. Lord C. leaves everything he possessed in the world—real and personal—to Lady C. and her heirs for ever! There can be no secret in this; perhaps it may be so far prudent to say that as Lord C. had told us, *all* what he intended (leaving the reversion to George) we can only suppose he knew that his wife would dispose of it in that way, and of course we must none of us allow that she is non-compos."

Even in the midst of her anxiety and distress Mrs. George tried to find some light in which her brother-in-law's conduct might appear less heartless.

"Yet I cannot see a loophole for believing that Lord C. did otherwise than tell a most deliberate lie, and though it may be very foolish, it does pain me more than anything else. Somehow I feel ashamed of it. He was my husband's brother, my children's Uncle. I cannot bear it. After an intercourse of apparent friendship for above forty years this crisis is very grating to one's feelings. I never had a great deal of respect for him, and thought there was a good deal of humbug in him, and yet when he appeared very kind, as he did sometimes, I have often accused myself of being unjust to him."

§ 4

The complication of the situation made Villiers' return from Madrid extremely desirable, and it was not long before Mrs. George was interviewing Palmerston and Melbourne on his behalf. Meanwhile there descended on George in Madrid a frightening avalanche of letters, and the more he read the more anxious he became. He had an unpleasant feeling that his mother had been and was being most hideously indiscreet. It seemed evident to him that she was blazoning his uncle's bad behaviour all over London, and at the same time quite frankly linking Kathy's name with his own. He feared that the results might be disastrous to his prospects in both fields, and he began to desire an immediate return to the scene of action. In addition he felt that the period of his usefulness in Spain was over. No one who was known to be leaving in the course of a few months could exert the influence which had formerly been his. Also he was beginning to lose heart. Conditions seemed to have changed so little during all the years of his service in Madrid. The Spaniards seemed incapable of saving themselves, and no foreign power was willing to take up the difficult and disinterested task of setting their house in order.

So it happened that he wrote letters to Palmerston and Melbourne supporting his mother's entreaties that he might be relieved as soon as possible. But since it was evident that at the best he must spend another couple of months at his post, he decided to do the only thing which might help to unravel one part of the tangle. He wrote and proposed to Lady Katherine Barham, and he was accepted.

On January 24th, 1839, Mrs. George writes thankfully: "Well, my own dear child, so the main object of my life is settled! and being settled is half accomplished. Only half! and these 'four mortal months,' as G. calls them, must intervene. Still it's being settled is a very great comfort, and now you may say all you please to each other."

The marriage was to prove all that both principals and even Mrs. Villiers had hoped of it. It inaugurated a perfect and lasting companionship to which only death put a term. For various reasons both George and Kathy urged that the engagement should remain a secret for some months. But Lady Verulam having confided in 'her dear friend the Duchess of Gloucester,' the rumour was soon spread all over the town. It then became a necessity to make a public announcement, and within the month Mrs. George was peacocking about receiving the congratulations of all and sundry. It was, perhaps, one of the happiest moments of her life. The relations between her and her future

daughter-in-law were of the happiest, and she writes enthusiastically: "I would rather you left off thinking of me as Mrs.
Villiers. A foolish joke in the olden time gave me the name of
'Mrs. George'—not Mrs. George Villiers, but 'Mrs. George'
by itself, and it has been so resolutely persevered in by all my
belongings and intimates, with only the variations of 'Mother
George' or 'old Mother George' that it gives me a stranger-
like feeling to be called Mrs. Villiers."

All was satisfactory, and not least the kindness of those in
power who furthered George's return to England. After "eating
and drinking his way out of Spain" in a series of dinner parties,
he reached London in the late spring, and was married in the
summer.

Aunt Clarendon proved herself more amenable to the charms
of the young couple than had been anticipated, and all seemed
couleur de rose as they set off on their marriage tour across Europe.
Before their return a new source of congratulation had come to
them, for George was invited to join the Government in the
capacity of Lord Privy Seal. This meant residence in London,
and completed his satisfaction. The years of distant and often
obscure labour had borne abundant fruit.

CHAPTER VI

LORD PRIVY SEAL

§ 1

SO Clarendon visited the Queen at Windsor, kissed hands and was sworn of the Privy Council as Lord Privy Seal. As such he became immediately a member of Lord Melbourne's Cabinet. As, on a former occasion, he had been raised from a mere clerk in the Customs to the position of Minister Plenipotentiary, so now, with equal swiftness, he found himself transformed from the character of a diplomat to that of a full-blown Cabinet statesman. And he reached the higher ranks of each profession without having served an apprenticeship in either. The service of the public was a less highly technical affair in those days than it is in these, and the business of the State was entrusted to persons whose worth, sincerity and capacity were proven not by competitive examinations but by their established character and behaviour. But the work and the ambience were new to Clarendon; and the ways of it must have necessitated a certain amount of adjustment in his mind before he became comfortable in his new post.

And what did he find when he joined his colleagues at Westminster? He found a semicircle of men, all of them friends, most of them related, governing England from little chairs round a table in Downing Street. They lounged and swore and chaffed each other. They broke up and dined in each other's houses and sat talking over the port half the night. Sometimes they slept in Council. A common background to life, a common point of view with regard to essentials, combined with an hereditary sense of responsibility, made them perfectly safe with each other. They talked the same language and held the same standards; there were no minutes of any meeting that took place between them and hardly any procedure. The Cabinet was a circle of friends considering together what was best to do under the circumstances that arose. That the business they conducted was the governance of England never occurred to them as strange or awe-inspiring. They were not weighted down by pledges to the constituencies; none of them had to stop to consider what Manchester might say or Sheffield think, though the Reform Bill was six years old. England was still, mercifully, the sole object of politics; and they were the lords of England. They knew their

England; they represented England, peer and commoner alike, and they governed the realm with a high-handed surety of touch which has never been equalled since. It was the last spell of pure aristocratic government in England, and there is a sort of charm about it as of a summer that won't break but continues far into the autumn. But though the warmth of summer still lingered on, nothing could stop the passage of time, and autumn was already implicit though hardly felt. Change—far-reaching change in the very nature of things—was already in the air. The passing of the great Reform Bill was a revolution in political theory. But its implications and the manifold social changes which the introduction of machinery were slowly to bring about over the face of England were mercifully hid from the group of individuals who governed the land in 1839. England was still the England of the stage-coach. There were no telegraph posts and no metal roads. Property was sacrosanct, and the price of corn was economically the measure of things.

Since the conduct of affairs was determined by talk from within, and not by pressure from without, the personalities within the Cabinet group counted for much; counted, indeed, for almost everything. For it was the inspiration and vision of individuals that gave birth to legislation, and it was the collective responsibility of individuals that shaped that vision into measures practical enough to be laid before the House. Politics were personal; and round the table in Downing Street were exhibited most of the passions and humours that flesh is heir to.

§ 2

At the head of it lounged Lord Melbourne, and if there was one statesman more than another that perfectly represented the type that ruled England in that age it was William Lamb, Viscount Melbourne. Easy-going, indolent, full of wild oaths and always for the middle course, he held the balance between the hot-headed reformers and the die-hards of his party, and kept a moribund Cabinet together as much by humour and common sense as by any other quality. With hardly any Ministerial apprenticeship to politics, he had found himself, by circumstance, thrust into the leadership of a great party pledged to Reform; and though he was far too much of a realist in life to believe that legislation could make a new heaven and a new earth, he was also far too much of a realist not to understand that change had come, far too judicious not to try and guide it wisely. It was, indeed, part of the whole irony of his life that he was called upon to lead a party whose political beliefs had gone far beyond the point to which he could honestly follow them. Though a member of

Lord Grey's Government, he had very little to do with the Reform Bill—nothing, indeed, with the drafting of it. He had had the Home Office at the time and had been chiefly occupied in quelling the very serious rioting and incendiarism that had affected whole counties. And though, since times were what they were, he concurred with his party in demanding the "Bill, the whole Bill, and nothing but the Bill," he suffered from none of the delusions common to his party as to the huge benefits the Bill would confer on the electorate. Change he regarded as a necessary evil, and on more than one occasion, when measures involving change were suggested, an irritable exclamation had escaped him, "Why the devil can't you leave things as they are?" But, all the same, beneath the cynicism and apparent indifference that he brought to the handling of affairs, beneath the studied inconsequence of manner and the high aristocratical bearing, there lay a keen sense of the actual. No philosophic radicalism tinged *his* outlook on the real. He knew men and the ways of men; he knew what could be done and what could not be done; he knew when to be firm and when to give way. And he was fully aware of the usefulness of this knowledge to the head of a Government whose members seemed bent upon tampering with the Constitution. For the past three years a still more difficult and delicate task had been thrust upon him than even the leadership of the Whig party—that of guiding and directing the first rather uncertain steps of Victoria down the path of her constitutional duties. And, although in the qualities of tact and taste, of tenderness, and of almost paternal understanding that this had required and called forth from him, his whole nature had known a late, an abundant flowering, the strain and responsibility of his position about the throne had taxed his powers to the utmost, and he had visibly aged in the past twelve months. Moreover, his Government, he knew, was doomed. It should have ceased to exist—and he knew it—more than six months before, when beaten on a vote in the Commons. It was only because of the loyalty of himself and his colleagues which forbade them to desert the young Queen in the crisis over the Bedchamber affair that they found themselves in office now. Their usefulness, their security had gone. They ruled on sufferance. The smallest combination against them and they must inevitably fall. But since he was in office the business of the country must be carried on; and each Cabinet meeting saw his portly form, his smiling, good-humoured countenance, his spruce grey whiskers and untidy white neckcloth at the top of the table, and Ministers at least guessed from his cheery greetings to each that no crisis to their affairs had occurred.

§ 3

Most often on his right at these meetings, as befitted the incumbent of the Home Office and the leader of the House of Commons, sat, very bolt upright and alert, as the pictures show, a tiny little man, hardly more than five feet high when he stood, and whose feet when he sat hardly reached the level of the floor. Very neat and trim and buttoned into a tight frock-coat, he gazed at his colleagues from candid innocent eyes, and his countenance exhibited at once the benevolence of an angel and the petulance of a child. No greater contrast could be conceived than that which at once separated and united Lord John Russell and Lord Melbourne. Melbourne regarded politics as a necessary responsibility incident to one's position in life. One was of the class that governed—well, one governed; one accepted one's duties and responsibilities. But it was often an infernal bore. But with Lord John politics were a passion. He had come early to them, entering the House when he was hardly of age, and gaining Cabinet rank almost as soon as his party came into power. Melbourne, on the contrary, had come late to them. He was fifty-two before he had a seat in the Cabinet, and though he had sat in the House of Commons for some years before that he had made no mark whatever there, and his friends had even suspected that his political career was going to be a failure. It was the sly evolution of circumstance that sent him to Ireland as Chief Secretary, that later installed him, much to his own surprise, at the Home Office, and, finally, upon the retirement of Lord Grey, forced the premiership upon him. In all this he was a passive agent, being totally devoid of personal ambition. Very different in this respect was John Russell. He conceived himself to have a mission: to be the harbinger of a new age of free institutions and reformed societies. To him the Whig doctrines had abstract and universal implications; and Reform was not merely the renovation of what was ageing or obsolete, but the bringing to birth of something new and enlightened in the hearts and minds of men. For this he was profoundly ambitious, with an ambition that was both dangerous to himself and to his colleagues, as subsequent events were to prove. His history in the present parliament is too well known to need recapitulation here. Unlike Lord Melbourne, he had been the prime mover in the agitation for Reform, and the Bill itself had been largely of his own drafting.

One of the finest leaders the House of Commons has ever had, he was a brilliant orator and a skilful debater. But his personal qualities made him a difficult colleague. Sensitive, proud, conscience-ridden; cold in temperament and manner often to the point of rudeness; uncertain in his loyalties, still more so in his behaviour; he was, however, redeemed by disarming qualities of frankness, a peculiar quaint charm all his own, and a naïveté which was almost childlike and certainly lovable. For gratuitous, and even monstrous, as his political conduct appeared on many occasions to his colleagues, they never quite lost their affection for him. And to the end they respected his singleness of purpose. Such was Lord John Russell, with whom Clarendon was destined to be closely associated for many years to come.

§ 4

Of a very different calibre was Lord Palmerston, Minister of Foreign Affairs. Gay, debonair, self-assured, the enormous optimism of this remarkable person overflowed in manner, in gesture, in attire. The expansive smile, the cheery wave of the hand, "the high metallic laugh," were not more expressive of Lord Palmerston than the huge white hat, the check trousers, the green gloves. He was all of a piece; and if the daring eccentricities of his policy found an echo in those of his dress, an irresistible, freakish charm set all to rights, and made Lord Palmerston one of the most forceful and fascinating of men. As he sat by the fire at Cabinet meetings, or leant across the table with finger raised to emphasise a point, the invincible self-possession, the sheer bluff force of the man would amaze his colleagues and carry all before it. To him politics—which meant at this period Foreign Politics—were a game; but a game that he played for the most part single-handed, his opponents being the Courts and crowned heads of Europe. With indomitable courage and a paramount sense of the dignity and weight of England, he warned Emperors of their misdemeanours and dictated policy to Kings. And quite often he omitted to tell his colleagues, till afterwards, the line he happened to be pursuing, so that they were suddenly faced with ugly upheavals and angry foreign despatches, the cause of which were unknown to them. But Lord Palmerston knew, and explained. And if his explanation proved to them all too clearly that, sitting alone among his red boxes in Whitehall, he had been adopting a line of conduct with regard to Russia, or France, or Spain at once preposterous and totally divergent from that which would have been advised in Cabinet, his courage and adroitness always managed to get them out of the scrape. And it was usually found that somehow the prestige of England had not suffered. Indeed—how was it?— it had generally increased. There was, indeed, something invincibly right about Lord Palmerston. And something, moreover, irresistibly dear to the English heart: so dear, indeed, that when he was seventy years of age he had so come to represent the English point of view, had triumphed so completely over his opponents and had yet remained so indomitably himself, unreformed and unrepentant, that the people of England made him Prime Minister, from which time onward, for nearly ten years, he ruled the country with an undivided sway, and no cabal or combination of political groups could break his ascendancy. When he died something died with him, never again to be recaptured in politics—a personal way of doing things, a sporting, gambling sense that suited the English well. After him came Gladstone and competitive examinations. And with them bureaucracy began. Off-hand, independent and shrewd, with generous sympathies and impulses, Lord Palmerston was endowed with superb common sense, a fighting spirit, and a distrust of foreigners. And what more do the English require of their statesmen?

Now it is in his relationship with these two men—Lord John Russell and Lord Palmerston—that the chief interest of Clarendon's future was to lie. The threads of his destiny were inseparably linked up with theirs. Both were to become Prime Minister, and Clarendon was to serve with each in various capacities in the years to come. To Palmerston he owed his first real chance in life, for it was Palmerston who picked him out of the obscurity of the Customs and Excise and sent him as Minister to Madrid. This Clarendon never forgot; and often as he had, at times, to disagree with Palmerston in matters of policy and method, his gratitude for this first opportunity offered him in life never permitted him radically to oppose him or to regard him in any other light but that of a close personal friend to whom he owed the utmost loyalty and affection. Nor was it difficult to love "Pam," for his optimistic nature and breezy manner were tonics in themselves and brought into the dusty council chambers a breath of fresh air, at once natural and stimulating. Moreover, in politics he was easy to deal with in this sense, that once he had made up his mind on any given subject nothing under heaven could shake his opinion, so that, although you might disagree with him, you at least knew where you were and what to expect. In this he differed profoundly from Lord John Russell, whose subtleties of mind and prickings of conscience were always causing him to change his mind at the most inconvenient moments. To him, as leader of the party now and for many years to come, Clarendon also owed the highest allegiance and loyalty, and these he gave unstintedly. But any dealings, personal or political, with John Russell were fraught with difficulty and danger, to say the least, and there were times when Clarendon was so enraged at his conduct that he could scarcely bring himself to speak to him. But in the end Russell

9

always managed to get himself reinstated in his colleagues' affections by means of a kind of unconscious innocence that there was
about him which purified his purposes whatever he did and made
his colleagues regard him in the light of some bright spirit from
another sphere who was imperfectly acquainted with the standards
of this, and who, for that reason, must be cajoled and helped back
into the normal paths of life. A quaint whimsical charm pervaded
his personality, and he had an undeniable touch of genius. In
spite of his manner, he inspired affection, and to the end, and in
spite of many differences, Clarendon remained on close personal
terms with him.

Now the destiny of these three forms the chief interest in the
years to come. Russell, subtle, uncertain, weak, but in spite of
this a leader with magnificent flashes of vision. Palmerston, downright, obstinate, opinionated and strong. Clarendon the mediator,
the perfect solvent, whose genius it was to serve rather than to
lead. Cabinet history for the next thirty years was intimately
affected by the interplay of these three personalities.

Other faces would come crowding in upon Clarendon's mind in
after-years as he called up the memory of this first Cabinet he
served in—Lord Holland, one of the most delightful and urbane
of colleagues, who combined a wide outlook on men and affairs
with a lifelong devotion to orthodox Whig principles; Lord
Lansdowne, who was to become the doyen of the party, and who
could always manage John Russell when he was in a difficult
mood; Macaulay, statesman, orator, historian, whose presence
was an ornament to any society; and many others too.

So Clarendon joined the Olympians and sat in conclave over
the affairs of men.

§ 5

When George returned from the Continent, all England was
sentimentalising over the royal romance, and the praises of Albert
were on everyone's lips. He had come, the tall, stiff, formal
German boy, hardly more than twenty, very reserved and shy
and conscious of his mission; and to him, dressed up in his
fanciful Coburg uniform, with his soulful eyes and barber's-block
whiskers, Victoria had succumbed with a surrender that was final
and absolute. And with that surrender the eighteenth century in
England utterly expired.

Clarendon missed the Privy Council meeting of November 23rd
(1839), at which the Queen formally announced her intention of
marrying Prince Albert of Saxe-Coburg and Gotha. But the first
Cabinets he attended were much occupied in discussing the for-
malities of the royal engagement, a point of law arising as to
whether or not the Prince was competent to make a marriage

treaty. Stockmar was very active these days, flooding the Cabinet with memoranda on all subjects relating to the marriage. Sometimes there were appendices (from other sources) to his memoranda to exemplify his points, and these, as often as not, were in German, and what was worse in German script. On more than one occasion we are presented with the spectacle of the members of Lord Melbourne's Cabinet staring helplessly at pages of angular calligraphy, totally unable to make out a word of their meaning. Here, however, the newcomer was of assistance, for Clarendon knew German well. On such occasions he would take the papers and, quickly reading them to himself, would expound their purport to astonished Ministers.*

The Government, when Clarendon joined it, were having a rough time in both Houses over the Nationalisation Bill, which they had just brought in in connection with the royal marriage. So long as Albert remained a German Prince the question of his precedence was reasonably clear. But if you divested him of his own nationality and turned him into an Englishman, then, as the Queen's husband, it was obvious that he must become the first gentleman of the land and take precedence of everyone—even members of the Royal Family. It was most unfortunate, but this was the clear implication of the Act as it stood, and needless to say the Tory Opposition were making great capital out of it. The Duke of Wellington, in opposition, was particularly strong on the subject, and the Government were perplexed and uncertain what to do. Clarendon offered to beard the old lion in his den, to see what conciliation could effect. The interview, though cordial, proved fruitless. Wellington was adamant. The Prince should take precedence of the Royal Family only over his dead body, and he would oppose that part of the Nationalisation Bill with all the means in his power. He said he had had to do with many sovereigns in his time, and had always found them reasonable in the last resort. Clarendon asked him whether he had ever had to do with a young Queen in love, which drew a smiling negative from the old warrior. In the end the Government had to drop the precedence clause out of the Nationalisation Bill altogether, after which the Tories were pacified and opposition died down.

So the winter and spring passed with solemn dinners at Buckingham Palace, at which Clarendon took the Queen in (" I did not know before that Lord Privy Seal ranked so high," wrote an awestruck Kathy), and frequent Cabinets, and little parties at the Grove, where Greville, Tom Moore, Macaulay, Lord John Russell and others sipped their port and discussed affairs. Victoria and Albert, happily married at last, retired to Windsor, and Ministers, with the immense business of the marriage over, could afford to

* Duke of Argyll.

relax. There was a Cabinet dinner about this time at the Palmerstons' to discuss among other things the territorial limits of
Canada and the vagaries of the Scottish kirk. But these grave
questions failed to capture the attention of tired Ministers, and one
by one they fell asleep, Lord Palmerston "meditatively," Lord
Lansdowne "gracefully," Macaulay "severely."

CHAPTER VII

THE EASTERN QUESTION

§ 1

THE Cabinet's well-earned slumbers were not suffered to last long. A cloud hung over the Near East, a cloud that thickened obstinately and ominously, and the thunder that eventually broke from it aroused Ministers to a startled realisation that, among other things, they were upon the brink of war with France.

It arose, this trouble, as most troubles in the Near East did in those days, from the invincible incapacity of Turkey to manage her own affairs. Over a considerable period of time she had allowed an Albanian adventurer, Mehemet Ali, slowly to accrue power to himself until the servant had become a menace to the master. It would be too long to recount the successive stages by which this enterprising warrior had made himself practically master of the Near East. Suffice it to say that by 1840 he held Egypt and Syria and was becoming a threat to the independent future of the Ottoman Empire. The Powers, though appealed to by the Porte at various times over the previous five years, had been preoccupied over their own affairs, and had let the matter be—all, that is, except Russia, who had come to the rescue of the Porte on terms very favourable to herself—terms embodied in the Treaty of Unkiar Skelessi, which, besides giving her an almost military ascendancy over other parts of the Ottoman Empire, virtually turned the Black Sea, as someone said, into a Russian lake. Palmerston, who had been Foreign Secretary at the time, was furious at the treaty, but powerless to prevent it. But now, when a fresh irruption of the subdued but unconquered Mehemet Ali forced Russia again to come to the assistance of Turkey, he was determined that she should not come alone. Abandoning the traditional Whig policy, which was apt to regard the Ottoman Empire as a moribund anachronism, he boldly determined that Great Britain should side with Russia in maintaining its integrity. Before the Cabinet were fully aware of what was really happening he had ordered Admiral Stopford to proceed with a flotilla to Alexandria and was consulting with Russia and Austria as to what steps should be taken next.

Now the danger in this situation lay in the fact that the sympathies and interests of France were all the other way. In the course of the past few years, by a series of amicable agreements with Mehemet Ali, France had been quietly and unobtrusively penetrating Egypt commercially to a very profitable extent. By this new and sudden awakening of the Powers to matters in the East she now saw the possibility of all her new-won gains going by the board, and, what was worse, the probability that the goose that laid the golden eggs would be stripped of its power to lay. So when Palmerston, *pro forma*, asked France if she would co-operate in the expedition to Alexandria, she demurred, and Palmerston, angry but not surprised, went ahead without her, nego-tiating with Russia and Austria the steps now to be taken. It was finally decided that Russia should move a fleet into the Dardanelles and an army to the Asiatic shores of the Bosphorus to protect Constantinople, while a joint British, Turkish and Austrian fleet was sent to blockade the ports of Syria. This was the situation at the beginning of 1840.

§ 2

By what hidden art Lord Palmerston was able to make tre-mendous undertakings appear as if they were mere matters of form, and gain the assent of his colleagues to measures of which he knew perfectly well they highly disapproved if they really understood their import, is a secret that we shall never know. That he did it again and again is a matter of history. It was only afterwards, when events began to move rapidly, that astonished Ministers found themselves deeply pledged to lines of conduct to which they never could remember giving their assent. It was so in this case. British warships were blockading the ports of Syria before Lord Melbourne's Government became fully aware that it was supporting Russia and Turkey against the interests of France. Lord Clarendon and Lord Holland were the first to awake from the spell that Lord Palmerston had put upon them, and when Clarendon turned his eyes towards the East and beheld what was going on there he became exceedingly alarmed. To him, as to most of the other members of the Whig Cabinet at that time, amity with France was a keystone of British policy. The Ottoman Empire was a cumbrous and ill-defined association of semi-barbaric states which was often enough changing its exact limita-tions. Moreover, it constituted an admirable cloak for Russia's stealthy advances in the Near East. Was Palmerston going to play into Russia's hands and embroil Great Britain with France for the sake of preserving that which, by its nature, was an anomaly and a danger to the society of European nations? He wrote a lengthy memorandum on the subject and circulated it amongst his colleagues, and Palmerston must have smiled at the ardour with which the views expressed in it clashed with his own. Meanwhile the tide of opinion was mounting against us in France, where the fiery Thiers was Prime Minister, and in England the colleagues stirred uneasily in their chairs. It was not till the end of May that the real trouble in the Cabinet began. But about that time Palmerston became aware that not only Clarendon, but five other members of the Ministry, disapproved of his Eastern policy—Lansdowne, Holland, Macaulay, Hobhouse and Labouchère. At a Cabinet meeting on May 23rd, Palmerston angrily addressed his colleagues and threatened to resign. Melbourne sat impassive at the head of the table, and it was left for Clarendon as the member of the Government who was known to be most opposed to Palmerston's policy to take the lead. He defended his position ably and pointed out that his disapproval had been openly avowed. If, he said, it reached a point which made it impossible for him to assent to Lord Palmerston's conduct of affairs, he would know what to do. Palmerston angrily resigned, and Clarendon also, and there was much heat, whereat Melbourne, who suddenly saw his Cabinet falling to pieces under his very eyes, bestirred himself. "We must have no resignations," he said firmly. "We cannot stand them, and what's more the country cannot stand them." Somehow he pacified the two angry Ministers, and persuaded both of them temporarily at least to withdraw their resignations. But thereafter matters went from bad to worse. By what one can only term a sleight of hand, Palmerston on July 8th persuaded his colleagues—all, that is, except Clarendon and Holland, who protested strongly—to sanction an ultimatum to be sent to Mehemet Ali, drafted by the four Powers, Great Britain, Russia, Prussia and Austria, with the notable exclusion of France. Palmerston justified this signal omission by pointing out that since months of negotiation had failed to make any headway against France's invincible prejudice in favour of Mehemet, it would have served no useful purpose to invite her to join in the ultimatum at this juncture. It was certainly plausible, but hideously dangerous under the circumstances, and Lord Holland and Lord Clarendon saw through the ruse. An angry altercation ensued, and both these Ministers refused to be associated with the ultimatum as it stood. Under ordinary circumstances they would have resigned. But so determined was Melbourne to keep the Government together till Victoria was more certain of her position that he positively forbade them to resign, and a rather unusual course was resorted to—that of presenting the Queen with two reports on the situation, a majority and a minority report. The latter was signed by Lords Clarendon and Holland alone. Once again the Foreign Secretary had thrown a wonder-working spell over the minds of his colleagues.

Now when it was known in France that the Powers had concerted a plan with regard to the Levant in direct opposition to
her known views on the subject, public opinion knew no bounds.
Thiers was in power at the time, and he immediately and osten-
tatiously set on foot the warlike conditioning of both the services.
The situation looked grim. And it hardly looked better, when
news was received that Mehemet Ali had rejected the terms of the
ultimatum. Orders were given, and the Allied fleets proceeded
at once to the blockade of the Syrian ports.

Palmerston was in great spirits. He was not in the least
frightened of France, being more than ever convinced that whatever precautions the French Cabinet might make, Louis Philippe
in the last resort would never endanger his new dynasty by a war
with England. So sure was he of this, that he even went so far
as to press arrogantly in Paris for an explanation of the preparations going on in France. Clarendon was appalled when he
heard of this, and appealed to Melbourne to have the despatch
to Lord Granville postponed for Cabinet consideration. But he
was too late: the despatch had already gone. A gloomy and
apprehensive Cabinet met at Melbourne's house on August 9th
to consider what steps to take in the event of France declaring
war. The Duke was consulted as to a Mediterranean expeditionary force, and preparations of all kinds were put on foot.

Now Lord John Russell had hitherto warmly supported Palmerston in his vigorous Eastern policy. But he came away from
the Cabinet of August 9th with certain doubts in his mind—
doubts as to the justice of the course the Government was pursuing with regard to France. At the beginning of September he
was at Minto, and there it was that his conscience began to trouble
him. When it became too uncomfortable he went up to London
to talk to Melbourne. Him he found in the greatest state of
anxiety declaring that he "could neither eat, nor drink, nor
sleep, so great was his disturbance." Next Lord John proceeded
to Windsor. From there he wrote to Melbourne urging that conciliatory overtures should be made to France. He also enclosed a
Memorandum on the Eastern situation and intimated that if the
Cabinet could not agree with it he would be compelled to resign.
Melbourne did nothing as was his wont in moments of difficulty.
Lord John, stung by hearing nothing from the Prime Minister on
so important a subject, wrote another letter asking Melbourne to
prepare the Queen for his resignation. But in the interim they
had changed places—Lord John was in London, and Melbourne had taken his place at Windsor. And what Melbourne
found at Windsor made him apprehensive on another score.
"For God's sake," he scrawled to Russell on September 26th,
"don't bring on a crisis: the Queen could really not go through

that now, and it might make her seriously ill if she were to be kept in a state of agitation and excitement."

What could Lord John do? A Cabinet was called for October 1st, and a good many ministers doubted whether the Government would survive it. However, Palmerston proved more conciliatory than usual, and agreed that certain overtures should be made to France on condition that Baron von Brunnow should obtain permission from St. Petersburg to co-operate with Great Britain in making them. A non-committal, but pacific despatch was also sent to Lord Ponsonby at Constantinople, and with this the meeting broke up. Ministers breathed again. Although the situation in the Cabinet was, to say the least, un-comfortable, no open rupture had as yet taken place between those who approved and those who disapproved of Palmerston's policy. But though within the Cabinet tempers were calm, and ministers who highly resented each other's conduct of affairs smiled blandly at each other, outside they expressed themselves with no uncertain voice. London was full of talk. The Palmer-stons were furious with Lord John, and went about saying that it was a pity that the policy of England should be disturbed because the two greatest fools outside the Cabinet had influence over the weakest man in it—the fools being Lord Spencer and the Duke of Bedford, and the weak man, Russell. They were also highly incensed with Clarendon for taking the line he did, and, although the latter all through this time was scrupulous in his attendance at Lady Palmerston's parties, and profuse and sincere in pro-testations of personal friendship for them both, nothing would make them believe that he was not plotting to overthrow his old chief and step into his shoes at the Foreign Office. And Lady Palmerston even went so far as to warn the ubiquitous Charles Greville that a sweet simple soul such as his own was incapable of realising the " depth of cunning of his friend George Villiers."

§ 3

But now it was that the results of Palmerston's strong line with France were beginning to take effect. Palmerston had judged right. Louis Philippe was not prepared to endanger his dynasty by a war with England. There never had been, in his opinion, the slightest danger of it. As long as Great Britain was firm in the pursuance of her policy, France in the last resort would truckle under. And in vindication of this view, Palmerston was able to produce at the Cabinet on October 10th a note from Thiers strangely pacific in tone, couched in quite a new language and positively decorated with olive. There is no doubt that it had great effect on the Cabinet, for whatever Ministers might now feel

as to Palmerston's conduct of affairs, they could not blind themselves to the fact that it was succeeding. In view of France's
new attitude, there really was no Cabinet crisis at all. Even
Lord John was completely disarmed for the moment, at any rate.
Ministers came away from the meeting almost in a dream to find
themselves still acting together as a Government. Palmerston
was now completely master of the situation.

"There is something grand," writes Kathy in her journal, "in
the very way he braves everything in spite of all opposition from
his colleagues—in spite of the Queen's fears—in spite of events at
home and abroad—he goes steadily on, undertaking the awful
responsibility which must fall on him from the course he pursues,
with a courage and calmness which would be admirable indeed,
if," she adds characteristically, "they did not proceed from a
crotchet."

The game is to the strong, and circumstances now began to
play shamelessly into Palmerston's hands. To begin with, every
mail brought fresh tidings of Allied successes along the coast of
Syria. Beyrout, Sidon, Saida—all fell before the victorious
Allied Squadron commanded by Lord Charles Napier. And on
November 3rd, Acre itself—considered the stronghold of the Near
East—was battered to a heap of ruins. Then Ibrahim, Mehemet
Ali's son, was routed from his new-won territory in Syria, and
Napier proceeded to Alexandria to demand from Mehemet the
restitution of the Turkish Fleet. News of these stirring events
was reaching the Cabinet all through the autumn and early winter.
It was also reaching the French Cabinet, where indeed it pre-
cipitated a crisis. Thiers was permitted to resign, and though
the speech that he made to the Chamber on retiring left no doubt
in anybody's mind as to what he thought of the July Convention
and the part England had played in it, it was equally clear that
Louis Philippe was parting with him for the very reason that he
held those views. His place was taken by the pacific and Anglo-
phil Guizot, who was withdrawn for the purpose from the Court
of St. James's, and Bourquenez was sent to London with instructions to pursue the path of peace. The King could hardly make
his intentions clearer. By the end of November the danger of
war with France was practically at an end, and, as usual,
Palmerston had imposed his will in Foreign Affairs over friends
and enemies alike, and been completely justified by events.
Although Lord John punctuated the late autumn by alternately
sending in and withdrawing his resignation, everyone knew that
the crisis was really over. As for Palmerston, he could handle
Russell at this juncture. In a series of letters he patiently removed one after another of the latter's objections. And at length

even Lord John, and even Clarendon, according to Greville, were converted. The letter in which Palmerston wound up the correspondence with Russell was a masterpiece:

> "CARLTON TERRACE,
> "*December 4th.*

"MY DEAR JOHN RUSSELL,

"It is quite true that our policy in the Levant has been more rapidly successful than the most sanguine of us could have ventured to hope; and I think you must feel gratified that it was your support of the Treaty of July which chiefly induced the Cabinet to support it. . . .

> "Yours sincerely,
> "PALMERSTON."

Was this irony, or supreme good taste? At any rate, a Christmas party at Broadlands completely healed the breach between these two, and all danger of a Government crisis was averted. But the part Clarendon played still rankled in Palmerston's mind, and was to for some time to come.

"I called on Palmerston," wrote Lord Broughton in his journal, "and congratulated him. He was in high spirits, but complained of the treatment he had received, particularly from Clarendon." Indeed, the distrust which the Palmerstons conceived for George at this time was to have important results on his career. The manner in which he finally routed it is an interesting episode in the history of his life. But it belongs to a later chapter.

The settlement of the Eastern crisis came in July, 1841, when a second *Treaty of London* was concluded between England, Russia, Austria, Prussia, and, be it observed, France. By its terms Syria and Arabia were restored to the Port: Mehemet was confined in the hereditary Pashalic of Egypt under the suzerainty of the Sultan: and the Powers agreed that the Dardanelles and the Bosphorus should be closed to all foreign ships of war so long as the Turkish Empire was at peace. In the words of Sir J. A. Marriot:

"The Treaties of London must be regarded as a conspicuous personal triumph for Palmerston. The Treaty of Unkiar Sjelessi was torn up; Turkey was rescued from the hostility of Mehemet Ali, and from the friendship of Russia; France was compelled to acquiescence, and the will of Great Britain was imposed upon Europe."*

* *England After Waterloo.*

CHAPTER VIII

FREE TRADE OR PROTECTION?

§ 1

DURING most of this time the Clarendons were busy decorating and moving into No. 1, Grosvenor Crescent, a house they had taken on a term of years, and which, as it proved, was to be their London home till Clarendon died in 1870. Here the pleasant pictures which George had acquired in Spain were hung, together with other relics of the Spanish years. Some pieces of furniture were brought from the Grove, others from Kent House, and a few were bought, to embellish this background against which so many of the famous political figures of the nineteenth century were to pass. John Russell—Macaulay—Palmerston—Granville—Gladstone—all were to know its hospital portals; and if it stands aside, its discreet frontage looking at, but set a little back, from the larger robuster porticoes of Belgrave Square, surely in this it was strangely symbolic of its owner. All was ready by the autumn of 1840, and here in September, while Cabinets raged over the Eastern question, Kathy Clarendon gave birth to her first-born, a girl. Three weeks later the child was duly christened Constance amidst much family rejoicing.*

All was now harmony among the colleagues. The Christmas spirit prevailed, and it seemed as if Lord Melbourne's Government were more firmly established than ever.

But a change in the weather of politics suddenly brought the vexed question of Free Trade to hang like an angry cloud in the otherwise bright firmament. That it was destined to destroy the last semblance of Whig Unity, to lead to the downfall of the Government and to split the Tory Party from end to end, was hardly suspected when Francis Baring raised the question from the Treasury. For it arose, as such questions usually do, from the efforts of a harassed Chancellor of the Exchequer to understand just why the revenue of the country refused to balance its expenditure. On this occasion, Mr. Baring among his friends at the Treasury, found himself faced with the prospect of introducing a Budget which showed a deficit of two millions and a

---

* Lady Constance Villiers, married in 1864 to the Hon. Frederick Stanley, who succeeded as 16th Earl of Derby. She died in 1922.

half—a large sum for those days. It was no surprise to him as he was perfectly well aware of the state of the country's finances. The Chancellor of the Exchequer, if anyone, should know the bareness of the land, and the trade returns and estimates that flowed in upon Mr. Baring from every side only confirmed his already fully formed impression that trade was stagnant, agriculture depressed and markets declining.

It was very odd; ten years of enlightened Whig rule seemed to have done nothing to disburden the country of its financial difficulties. The same problems, in slightly varying forms, raised their heads year after year, in a greater or less degree, were got over somehow, or happily shelved, but never solved. That they were acute enough this time for very serious reflection, was proved by the enormous figure of the deficit. There must, thought Mr. Baring, be something radically wrong.

The question, as he conceived it, therefore, was not only how to make good the deficit, but also how to ensure the future against the legacy of the past; how to liberate trade from the encumbrances with which it seemed burdened. There was the export question. Well, British manufacture was second to none: the mineral wealth of the country was enormous. Given good markets abroad—and this was a separate question—the export trade could look after itself. But there was also the import question, and that raised a great many problems. Mr. Baring determined to investigate the Excise system, and called for a list of Customs. He found upon that list no less than twelve hundred separate duties, "all placed upon it not for the purposes of Revenue but for purposes of Protection. It was true that he himself had worked through the Customs tariff; had, even the year before, considerably raised the duties it contained, in the pious hope that trade would expand and revenue increase. But the Budget of 1840 had proved no more successful than previous Budgets had been. Perhaps the whole system was wrong. Desperate cases need desperate remedies: and although he was very well aware that the Excise system had come to be regarded as a sacrosanct article of economic faith, Mr. Baring, sitting among his papers in the Treasury, began to analyse the theory of Protection with a logic born of despair. Who, in the last resort, he wondered, was protected, from what? There was a shortage of wheat in England, and yet there were large duties upon corn coming in from abroad. It is a fact of nature that the English climate is not such as will permit the sugar cane to flourish in this country. Yet Mr. Baring, looking at his Excise list, perceived that the duty upon sugar imported to Great Britain was exceptionally high. Might not the disease in the fiscal system, thought Mr. Baring, originate just here, in the Excise limb of the body economic, and the injudicious imposition of Customs upon the staple articles of food and use?

The idea, of course, was not a new one—at least, in respect of the abolition of the duties on corn. Charles Villiers had been ploughing a lonely furrow in this respect since 1834. Annually, and with commendable patience, he brought forward in the House of Commons a motion for the abolition of the Corn Laws, and up to 1839, at least, he had never received the support of more than ninety-five votes. The whole theory of abolition was sus-pect. It was a Radical cry, not worthy of the consideration of serious politicians. In 1839, however, the Corn Law League had made great strides towards the conversion of public opinion, and that year Charles Villiers was able to move a Committee of the whole House on the Corn Law of 1828. The vote in favour of abolition was larger than the year before by nearly a hundred, and a more respectable element of the House followed Charles Villiers into the lobby. They included Palmerston, Howick, Morpeth, Spring-Rice, Labouchère, and, be it observed, Mr. Baring himself. The debate had been lively; and to show the extent of feeling the question raised, it may be noted that while speaking upon the subject, Lord Melbourne "declared before God that he considered leaving the whole agricultural interest without protection the wildest and maddest scheme that had ever entered into the imagination of man."

§ 2

The question, therefore, had been sufficiently before the public for it to be no shock of surprise to Ministers, when, in a series of Cabinets in February and March, 1841, Mr. Baring introduced Budget proposals embodying reductions in the scale of duties upon goods coming into this country of so drastic a nature as to constitute a direct attack on the tariff system itself.

The colleagues reacted variously to the proposals. Rather un-expectedly Baring found a staunch supporter in Lord John Russell, whose restless mind had lately been probing into the question of food prices, and who had become as convinced as Baring himself upon the enormity of the high taxes on corn. With characteristic ardour he pressed his point in the Cabinet, and finally, for the old system, a moderate fixed duty of eight shillings a quarter was decided on.

It was a "revolutionary Budget," embodying a change of spirit from that of Protection to that of Free Trade; and the change was by no means popular among the rank and file of the party. The discussions in Cabinet were lively. They were also interminable and extremely intricate. So intricate, indeed, that the Prime Minister lost the thread of them; and at the last Cabinet before the Chancellor was to lay his proposals before the House, Lord Melbourne called his colleagues back as they were leaving the room and said: "By-the-bye, there is one thing we haven't agreed upon, which is, what we are to say. Is it to make our corn dearer or cheaper or to make the price steady? I don't care which; but we had better all be in the same story."

Clarendon had voted for the change. He had become a convinced Free Trader, though in many respects he would not go as far as his brother Charles. The theory of the "intaxability" of corn he thought ridiculous, and there was much in the theory and practice of the League of which he highly disapproved. But he thought the introduction of a modified form of Free Trade an indispensable necessity under the circumstances, and he sided with the majority in the Cabinet with a clear conscience.

The debates in the House, in which Baring supported by Lord John Russell introduced the reconstruction of the duties on timber and sugar, raged for eight consecutive nights. The House was not deceived. This was the thin end of the wedge. The reduction of duties was only a prelude to the complete acceptance by Lord Melbourne's Government of the principle of Free Trade in its entirety. Protection was still the centre plank of the Tory platform, and Sir Robert Peel summoned all his forces to defeat the Government. The issue was obscured by every legitimate means. It was, for instance, a great moment for the Tories when it was discovered that the reduction of the duties on sugar admitted a slave-grown product practically tax-free into the country. It was useless, in answer to this, for Lord John to depict in moving terms the conditions of simple peasants in the North of England who were substituting spirituous liquors for the tea and coffee that they loved simply because the sugar required to sweeten these beverages was too dear for them to buy. Why fix only on sugar? he asked. Was it not well known that slave-grown coffee was being shipped from Brazil to the Cape and re-shipped from the Cape to England for the sake of obtaining its admission under the preferential terms extended to the Colonies? Was philanthropy, he oratorically demanded, going to salve its conscience by dropping a lump of free-grown sugar into a cup of slave-grown coffee?

But it was of no use. The slavery question had roused the susceptibilities of every free-born Englishman, and the Whig party itself was in an uproar. The Tory ranks thickened grimly, and it became obvious that the Government couldn't possibly survive. The debate still raged on, but between the spasms of it, harassed Ministers had to decide the best course to take. Palmerston urged Melbourne to demand a dissolution. Clarendon was

for the alternative course of resigning.   Melbourne hesitated.
The racket about his ears was so great that at first he was for
resigning altogether.   But later he was converted by Palmerston,
and nothing Clarendon could say was able to shake him.   On
June 4th—the very day on which Lord John had announced his
intention of introducing the discussion on the Corn Laws—the
Government was defeated upon a motion of Sir Robert Peel's:
the necessary business was wound up and Parliament dissolved.

<h2 style="text-align:center">§ 3</h2>

So the Government that had ruled England for twelve eventful
years—the Government that had passed the great Reform Bill—
foundered at last.   There was no doubt in anybody's mind as
to the result of the elections.   Even Ministers, even Lord John,
knew very well that the end had come.   The party itself was
split on the corn question, on the sugar duties, on almost every
point of current policy.   Ministers had no following even in their
own ranks.   It was indeed time for someone with a united following to take over the governance of England.   A reformed electorate showed its sense of all this; for although a certain ardent
section of the Whigs went to the country with the battle-cry of
cheaper bread and cheaper sugar on their lips, the hard-headed
Yorkshire constituencies were not deceived and declared unanimously for the Tories.   Nor were the Whigs any more successful
in the South.   By the middle of July the issue was unequivocable,
and when the last returns came in August the state of the parties
showed a Tory majority of ninety-one.

There was a last Council, at Claremont, that autumn—a
melancholy affair—at which the out-going Ministers surrendered
their seals of office into the Queen's hands, and the members of
the Household their wands and other insignia.   Clarendon
attended with other members of the late Government; but Melbourne tactfully absented himself.   It was, for obvious reasons,
a great strain on the composure of the Queen, this saying good-
bye to the first friends and councillors of her reign.   Mr. Greville,
who, as Clerk of the Council, had charge of the ceremony, noted
that she behaved with great dignity, and that her self-control
never wavered for an instant.   "Though no courtier," he concludes, "I did feel a strong mixture of pity and admiration at
such a display of firmness."

Indeed, the blow had come at last, and Fate had removed her
beloved "Lord M" from about her person—for ever and a day,
as it proved—but she did not know this.   Nor did she know how
soon in the press of events and the development of her own character the vision of him would fade, fade right away into the past,

till she could write, as she did some six years later, with perfect equanimity to King Leopold: "You will grieve to hear that our good, dear old friend Melbourne is dying. . . . One cannot forget how good and kind and amiable he was, and it brings back so many recollections to my mind, though, God knows! I never wish that time back again."

So Clarendon, with the rest, was out of office, and had time to relax, to look around him; time to give to Kathy and the children (another daughter had been born to them in the interim*); time to write long gossiping letters to Emily Eden, still in India with her brother, but so soon coming home; to Lady Granville in Paris, giving her all the home news; time to give to the redecoration of the Grove; to the hanging of the Spanish pictures, "that looked so well in their new gilt frames," at Grosvenor Crescent; time, even, to have one's portrait painted by Grant and to watch the multiple spectacle of London life in the forties unroll itself across the stage of fashion. It was pleasant, too, to stroll down to the House of Lords and to sit, a detached onlooker, while the new Government took its first tottering steps in the path of office. So the year went out with pleasant little parties at the Grove, a little politics, a little talk, and much domesticity. The Clarendons were at Gorhambury for the New Year, and on the last day of the old, Clarendon writes to Lady Granville:

"I am living in the provinces, surrounded by Tories, who look upon us as the blackest of sheep, and I have consequently not an idea or a scrap of intelligence worth communicating, but I cannot let the year quite pass away without the good old custom of wishing you a happy new one. . . . Among the Tories there seems as much confidence in their tenure of office as if they had signed a twenty-one years' lease with the country. Among the Whigs, there is a kind of apathetic acquiescence in this, which looks as if all energy and intention were extinct, always except Palm, whose wishes, as usual, are fathers to his thoughts, and he accordingly believes that he shall rout the Tories foot and horse, and be re-established at the F.O. before six months are over. . . . Altogether we cut a sorry figure just now; but we are at our worst, and the Tories are at their best, and the fortune of war may bring us nearer to equality."

* Lady Alice Villiers, married Lord Skelmersdale in 1860, who was created Earl of Lathom in 1880. She died in 1897.

CHAPTER IX

THE CORN LAWS

§ I

LIFE in opposition is indeed pleasant and the Parliamentary spectacle by no means unamusing, especially when the responsibility of speaking for the party rests upon someone else's shoulders, and Clarendon was assiduous in his attendance at the House of Lords during the next two sessions. Never having served an apprenticeship in the Lower House, he was new to Parliament and diffident of his oratorical powers. With the exception, therefore, of one or two utterances on the corn question, he contented himself by being a silent spectator of events and by trying to learn all he could of the manner and methods of Parliament. When party issues were at stake there was always Lord Spencer to take the lead. Of the Clarendons' private life during these years we get occasional glimpses from letters, from Lady Clarendon's diary, and from Mrs. George's indefatigable pen.

During the parliamentary session they were mostly in London, where they were still busy putting the last touches to No. 1, Grosvenor Crescent; but being more fortunate than some in having their country seat so close to the capital, they frequently absented themselves for a few days, carrying friends and relations with them. And at the Grove, in these years, they must have created a very delightful atmosphere, for even Charles Greville's worldly pen grows quite lyrical on the subject:

". . . It is always refreshing," he writes, "in the midst of the cold hearts and indifferent tempers one sees in the world to behold such a spectacle of intimate union and warm affection as the Grove presents. A mother (Mrs. George) with a tribe of sons and daughters, and their respective husbands and wives, all knit together in the closest union and community of affections, feelings and interests—all, too, very intelligent people, lively, cheerful and striving to contribute to each other's social enjoyment as well as to their material interests. I have always thought Clarendon, the least selfish, most generous, and amiable man with whom I am acquainted."*

So the family had come into port at last. Mrs. George's efforts had been justified; and as she sat in the drawing-room at the

* Greville *Journals*.

Grove, surrounded by her children and grandchildren, she must have spared a thought or two to those other days, the days of struggle and uncertainty, of unremitting effort to keep up appearances on an insufficiency of means; days when she did not know where Theresa's new frock was to come from or the price of the braid on Algy's naval uniform. And perhaps she wished her crotchety old "Governor" back to see.

During 1842, and part of 1843, Clarendon carried out extensive alterations at the Grove. It is unlikely that Earl Thomas had done anything in the way of redecoration there for years before he died; and Uncle John had never had any money to spare for such things during his tenancy. So that the old house must have remained in very much the state that their father, the first earl, had left it. Since his succession, Clarendon had had little time to give to his private affairs. Once out of office, however, he was eager to carry out the plans for the Grove that he and Kathy had concerted together when first they went down there after their marriage; and the house was in the builders' and decorators' hands for nearly eighteen months.

They made excursions to watch progress during this time, and Kathy conscientiously records each one in her diary:

"Grove: George and I, Mrs. G., and Theresa and Villiers Lister* went there in Theresa's carriage with three relays of our horses, and returned the same afternoon, Friday, 30th June, 1843. We found things had not got on much since George was there last, but we spent a very pleasant day. We lunched at Fields'. The expedition did both Mrs. George and me much good."

While these alterations were going on at the big house, the Grove Mill, the little dower house in the park, where George had spent so many happy days as a boy, became the parking place of a second generation of Villiers children; and on one expedition to see them Kathy and Mrs. George narrowly escaped extinction, which Kathy makes the theme for moral reflection quite in the manner of the day:

"*Grove Mill House:* Mrs. George and I drove there and back again to London on Thursday the 8th to fetch Constance and Alice whom we had left there for a few days. I selected frames to be sent up for gilding, and we drove about. We had a most merciful and providential escape, an oak tree being blown down only a few yards from us, across the path we had just passed. We had been talking about the dispensations of Providence and of how useless it was to speculate upon future events in the world, and certainly it was clearly brought home to us by this event how

* Theresa's son.

entirely we were under the guidance and protection of a higher power, and how little we can settle for ourselves what is to be our fate the next hour or the next minute.''

Still another girl was born to the Clarendons during these years —Emily Theresa, born October 9th, 1843.* The parents were duly proud of their offspring, and Kathy relates in her diary the smallest happenings in the world of her progeny: ''Constance's birthday of three years old, kept by drinking tea in the garden at Kent House 2nd September '43. *So* excited with her presents.'' A note is added to this: ''Constance took her first walk to the toy-shop with George and me, 20th September, 1843.''

But life was social too. The Clarendons entertained a good deal at Grosvenor Crescent, and a short account of each party they gave or to which they were invited is duly recorded in the journal:

''*Dinner* at home consisting of Lord and Lady Clanricarde, Lord and Lady Seaford, Mr. and Mrs. Stanley, Lord Auckland and Miss Fanny Eden (his sister), Lord Minto and Mr. Macaulay. It was exceedingly agreeable, people in great force, especially Lady Clanricarde and Macaulay, the latter, after dinner particularly, was full of anecdote and fun.''

''*Russell.* Dinner at the John Russells' to celebrate the christening of their boy. I went there alone, George's influenza being too bad for him to go. Met there the Duke of Sussex, the Duchess of Inverness, the Duke and Duchess of Bedford, Lord Lansdowne, Lord Auckland and the Misses Eden, Lord Tavistock, Mr. Macdonald, Mr. Labouchère, Lord Minto, Harriet Lister, Lord William Russell, Lord John Russell, and,'' she adds characteristically, ''a seventeenth person (I believe) whom I forget. The Duke of Sussex made a good little speech after dinner in proposing the health of the child, Lord John made a short and good answer.''

''*Queen:* We dined with her Thursday, 16th March 1843, she was particularly gracious to George and me, and also so was Prince Albert. George talked and laughed with both to the surprise of the company, we thought. We met there Lord and Lady Wharncliffe——''

Then follows the inevitable catalogue of guests.

Nor were the arts neglected, for upon a certain spring afternoon of 1843, we are told, Lady Clarendon, Lady Morley and Theresa went a round of artists' studios, being much edified and delighted by what they were shown, especially at Landseer's, '' where we saw some very beautiful things, amongst others a domestic scene of Prince Albert just come in from shooting, the game scattered

* Lady Emily Villiers, married Hon. Odo Russell, 1868, who was raised to the peerage as Lord Ampthill in 1881. She died in 1927.

about the room for the Princess Royal to play with, who has got a kingfisher in her hand; a great many dogs in the room, and the Queen just coming in dressed for dinner to tell the Prince he will be too late." A remarkable composition!

So the Clarendons took their part in the social life of the forties, the broad, comfortable, easeful life of ninety years ago. But whilst they were enjoying the amenities in common with their generation, their private life was not exempt from misfortune. In June, 1842, Thomas Lister, Theresa's husband, died. He had been an ailing, delicate man for some time past, and the end was not wholly unexpected. But though Theresa had been happy with Lister, though community of interests and a certain similarity of temperament had made a lasting bond between them, her deepest feelings had remained untouched. Theresa was one of those people who can only give once, and though she mourned her husband sincerely, it was as the loss of a dear friend and not as a lover that she grieved for him. She was left with three children, Thomas Villiers-Lister, Maria Theresa and Alice Beatrice. But nearer to the heart of the family was the loss of poor Algy, Clarendon's youngest brother, who died July, 1843. Alarming reports had been received as to the state of his health, and in May it was decided to move him from Taunton, where he was in hospital, to Kent House. Fergusson, the much-trusted family doctor, saw him the evening he arrived, and pronounced him to be suffering from a rapid consumption. A consultation only confirmed Fergusson's opinion, and very little hope of his recovery was held out. Kathy writes: " As this is not a journal of private events, I will not attempt to describe the misery of the whole family about him." A temporary rally deceived them all into the belief that he might permanently recover, but the inevitable relapse ensued; he fell into a decline and died at Kent House on July 13th, 1843. And as if this was not enough, it was discovered that Edward, who had gone down to Taunton to fetch Algy up to London in May (and in so doing had contracted a severe chill), was also now affected with the same trouble. At first it was made light of; but Sir James Clerk, who visited him as a friend at Tunbridge, whither he and Elizabeth, his wife, had gone for his health, brought back the gloomiest account of him to Clarendon, who hurried down to see him. August brought no improvement, and early in September it was thought best that he should avoid the damps of an English winter, and Elizabeth determined to take him to Nice.

But Edward was a sick man, a very sick man, and not all the devoted care of his wife, nor the consultations of doctors, nor the gentle winter of the Riviera could arrest the ravages of the disease upon that delicate, nervous frame. He got steadily worse and died on October 30th. So passed that difficult and equivocal spirit from the earthly scene.

"He was a man little known of the world in general," writes Charles Greville, "shy, reserved to strangers, cold and rather austere in his manners. . . . He was not fitted to bustle into public notice, and such ambition as he had was not of the noisy, ostentatious kind. But no man was more beloved by his family and friends, and none could be more agreeable in any society when he was completely at ease . . . . The world, at large, will never know what virtues and talents have been prematurely snatched away from it, for those only who have seen Edward Villiers in the unrestraint and unreserve of domestic familiarity, can appreciate the charm of his disposition, and the vigour of his understanding."

So wrote Greville, who knew him well. In the last years of his life Edward had found solace for his difficult temperament in a marriage that was as perfect a union as such things can well be. Perhaps old Earl Thomas Clarendon's prediction was right, that only two people in the world ever really got to the bottom of Edward's nature—himself and Elizabeth Liddell.* "No one will love you better," he wrote, "till Mrs. Edward mixes love of a higher order in your cup. . . ." Edward left four children—a son, Edward Ernest; twin daughters, the late Dowager Lady Lytton and the late Dowager Lady Locke; and a third daughter, Maria Theresa, who married Colonel Earle, of the Rifle Brigade, and is the author of several books of family reminiscence.

Theresa Lister remarried in 1844, and the Clarendons received this piece of news at Wiesbaden, where they had repaired to take the waters. It astonished and delighted them, and in part compensated for the gloom of the past year. George Cornwall Lewis and Theresa had been friends for some time past, but few had attached any deeper meaning to their friendship. "I had seen them so often together that I had got quite accustomed to it," exclaimed Kathy. Not so Charles Villiers, who had perceived that something was in the wind, and had spoken both to Elizabeth and Theresa about it. George Lewis's father, Sir Thomas Franklin Lewis, Bart, M.P., is described by Torrens as "a careful and accomplished man, but formal, verbose and dull," and certainly there is a kind of aridness in George Lewis's written word that gives rise to the suspicion that the son was not in every respect unlike the father. His well-known remark that "life would be quite pleasant but for its amusements" gives an indication of his general outlook. His reticence was proverbial and frequently aggravating. Once whilst he and Theresa were staying

* Hon. Elizabeth Liddell, daughter of the First Baron Ravensworth.

at the Grove he was summoned to Windsor for the night. On his return he made no mention of any untoward incident, so that the party were surprised to see in the papers that the Round Tower had been ravaged by fire during the night that he had spent there. To Theresa's reproach, "Why, George, you never told us there had been a fire at Windsor," he replied simply, "Well, you never asked me." He was destined, however, to have a distinguished career, for his passionless and exact mind made him an admirable Chancellor of the Exchequer; and he was in and out of Whig Cabinets from shortly after his marriage to Theresa till his death in 1863. There was something in the detachment of his mind that was akin to Clarendon's, and these two were destined to become the closest of associates, both political and personal. He succeeded to the baronetcy on his father's death in 1855, as also to the family seat, Harpton Court, Radnorshire. He was kind, just and considerate, and made Theresa an admirable husband. They were married late in October, 1844. Shortly after the event Emily Eden writes to Clarendon:

"And so you came back to a wedding! You must have been pleased, as I know how much you have always liked Mr. Lewis, and Theresa seemed so thoroughly and *freshly* happy. Just tell me how the wedding went off—whether anybody cried, and how much you fraternised with old T. L. Between ourselves, I don't like his having the run of the Grove. Don't be hasty in swearing eternal friendship to him. It will be much more flattering if we let him into *our set* on further acquaintance."

§ 2

Meanwhile, politically, the years of which we have been speaking were not uneventful. In 1841, when the Whig Government were beaten at the polls, all eyes turned to Sir Robert Peel. Was he the man of Destiny? What would he do with his access to power; and what would he make of the Conservative party, which had practically been reborn under his influence? "You are a very clever man," thought Charles Greville to himself during a conversation he had with Sir Robert at about this time. He adds in the high-flown language of the day: "He may become as great a Minister as abilities can make any man, but," he adds, "to achieve real greatness, elevation of mind must be intermingled with intellectual capacity, and this I doubt his having."

Certainly Peel's administration laboured under no disadvantage at the outset. A large and unassailable majority in both Houses gave the Prime Minister a free hand for the legislation he wished to introduce; and if some of it had a familiar ring and to some wit suggested the criticism that the Prime Minister "had caught the Whigs bathing, and walked away with their clothes," still his measures "were framed with a breadth and propounded with a skill which no preceding financier, since the death of Mr. Pitt, had displayed."* He devised a new sliding scale of duties for corn; he imposed an income-tax, and with its aid he terminated the deficit which he had inherited from his predecessors; and, concurrently, he revised the whole Customs tariff.

There was no concerted opposition to these measures on the part of the Whigs. The condition of the Whig party was forlorn; it was spoken of as a corpse; it was treated as a phantom. Melbourne was gone into oblivion; Lord John was anathema to a large section of the party; Palmerston had a certain personal following, but any meeting of the party, as such, would only have disclosed and emphasised the differences and divisions of its members; and Lord John, as leader of the party, had to content himself with the private counsel of his immediate supporters—his brother, the Duke of Bedford, Lord Lansdowne, Lord Clarendon and others.

Meanwhile Peel's administration gathered strength. Like a great bird, this greatest of all Conservative leaders shook out his wings and soared to an altitude above party, an altitude wide and unrestricted, in which his legislative vision could have full play. In the session of '43, '44 and '45, overcoming all opposition, including the increasing dissatisfaction of his own party, he pushed forward a series of measures, great not only in themselves, but in the principles they introduced, and for which they formed precedents. In a series of Budgets during these years he did more to free trade from the shackles that encumbered it than any measure which had been proposed for a hundred years. He determined the position of the Bank of England, examined the credit of Great Britain and sanctioned the issue of paper money. He instituted the Metropolitan Constabulary as we know it now. He proposed and carried three great Irish measures. He raised the status of the Roman Catholic clergy, and increased the endowment to Maynooth. He promoted the higher education of the Irish people by establishing colleges—Queen's colleges, they were to be called—in three important Irish towns. He gave security to the Irish tenant by affording him compensation for unexhausted improvement in accordance with a Commission he had himself appointed. Nor was he afraid to tackle Irish disloyalty with spirit and determination. The Government was determined to repress with a strong hand all agitation for the repeal of the Union. A new Arms Act for Ireland was carried in 1843, in the teeth of opposition; and the prohibition of the Clonbarf meeting, with the

* *Life of Lord John Russell*, Spencer Walpole.

arrest and conviction of O'Connell, showed all sides plainly
enough the system on which the Government were determined to
act in the case of subversive propaganda. Such controversial
legislation and such determined policy were hardly likely to pass
unchallenged. For two years Peel dominated the political scene
to the exclusion of all else. The Tories sat open-mouthed in awed
admiration while their chief expounded his great measures in
speeches of unexampled eloquence. The Whigs were completely
converted. "Thank God Peel is Minister," cried one of the most
ardent of them at the Travellers' one night. "There is no doubt,"
reflects Greville, "that Peel *is* now a very great man." But it
was not long before Sir Robert's large and comprehensive policy
began to shock the extreme section of his own party. The die-
hards were beginning to complain that the Minister that had been
placed in power to further the cause of Protection was beginning
to coquet with Free Trade. The disintegration of the party that
three years later was to wreck the Government began visibly to
manifest itself in the session of 1843; and with the signs of weakness in the Government ranks the Whig Opposition took heart and
made itself felt. A Factory Act having to do with the education
of factory children, proposed by Sir James Graham as Home
Secretary in 1843, was vigorously assailed by Lord John Russell,
who came forward with the skilful proposition that the Church
was the pivot of the whole scheme. He then posed as the
champion of religious liberty, and introduced such controversial
matter into the debate that Graham had first to modify and then
to drop the Bill altogether. Nor did the Irish Arms Bill escape
unscathed. Lord John made a spirited attack on some of its
clauses and mutilated it considerably in committee. Parliament
was prorogued that year on August 24th. It had been a lively
session. "Peel is tired and dispirited," wrote Charles Greville.
"He ought to be blistered and turned out to grass for a year."*
But in the spring following the Prime Minister returned to the
breach and, with unabated vigour, introduced the series of commercial measures which culminated in the Bank of England Act.
But the tide of his followers was turning against him, and more
and more he had to rely on the support of the Opposition to pass
the more liberal and large-minded of his measures. A curious
situation. In the Maynooth Bill of 1845 he failed to command a
majority of his supporters. The third reading of the Bill was
carried by a majority consisting of 148 Tories and 169 Liberals
against a minority of 149 Tories and 35 Liberals. Disraeli led the
young Conservatives against their party chief, and the Bill was
only saved from disaster by the brilliant advocacy of Russell.
The party was beginning to split.

* Greville *Journals.*

Corn was the burning question of the times. The session of
1845 was marked by the increasing dissatisfaction of the Tories
with their party leader's views on the subject. There was no
doubt about it. Peel was steeped in heresy. Every measure he
proposed, every statement that he made, had so unmistakable a
Liberal ring to it that bull-dog Tory squires turned with rapture
to the invectives of the young Jew, Disraeli, as solace to their
outraged feelings. The path of the Prime Minister was not made
smooth for him that summer. The corn question hung like a
thunder-cloud over the land, and every other question that arose
took on that pale unnatural aspect that objects wear when a
storm is imminent. And in November the lightning flashed and
the floodgates were unloosed.

The corn harvest had been a bad one that year in England and
Ireland. This, in itself, would not have caused a crisis. There
had been many bad harvests, and the evil effects of them had
somehow always been circumvented. But this year the failure
of the cereals coincided with the complete failure of the potato
crop in both countries. The two together constituted a very
grave situation indeed, especially in Ireland. Peel and the
Government found themselves staring in horror at the gaunt
spectre of famine. The repeal of the Corn Law ceased at once
to be a matter of political opinion. It became an administrative
necessity. Something had to be done, and to be done quickly.
Food had to be rushed into the country. Every possible facility
had to be given to the machinery of importation. Peel summoned
a Cabinet, and fearlessly placed the issue before his assembled
Ministers. "Shall we maintain unaltered, shall we suspend, the
operation of the Corn Law?" If the choice was searching for
the Tories, it was no less so for the Whigs, and all eyes turned
to Lord John for a lead. Nor were they left long in doubt as to
their leader's opinion. On November 22nd he wrote a letter to
his constituents from Edinburgh, in which he announced his
complete conversion to the principle of Free Trade.

In Peel's mind there was no doubt as to the imperative need
of the hour. "The one remedy," he wrote to Goulburn (Chancellor of the Exchequer) on October 18th, "will be the removal
of impediments to the free import of those articles of which human
food consists." Nor did he labour under any delusion as to the
extent of the change. "The temporary remission of all duties
on corn is," he says, "in the present state of public feeling
tantamount to the permanent and total remission of those duties.
Once remitted, they will never be re-established."

So that it was with his eyes open to the full implication of what
he was doing that he met his Cabinet on October 31st and proposed to Ministers the immediate necessity of suspending the

operation of the Corn Law, and of summoning Parliament to review the whole question of agricultural protection. Ten out of his fourteen Tory colleagues looked at the Prime Minister, as he made his pronouncement, with expressions of horror and dismay. Lord Stanley and the Duke of Buccleuch resigned. The rest were silent. Only Wellington, Aberdeen, Sir James Graham and Sidney Herbert so far rose above party prejudice as to support him. With two pillars of the party gone and all but four of the remaining Ministers definitely hostile to his projects, Peel could no longer carry on. On December 6th he went to Osborne and placed his resignation in the hands of the Queen. Victoria was all in a flutter at the thought that her Whigs would be about her again. But much water had passed under the bridge in four years, and it was not for her beloved "Lord M." that she sent, but for John Russell.

§ 3

Now Russell was always optimistic in moments of party crisis, and after his visit to the Queen he sent delightedly for the leaders of the Whig party. The library in Chesham Place now became the theatre of politics; and there it was that the colleagues became gradually aware that, despite the very dubious unity of the Whig Party on the key question of the hour, John Russell was determined to make the attempt to form a Whig Government. Clarendon, who, of course, was present at these meetings, was doubtful of his chances of success, and urged the necessity of getting definite information as to the amount of support which Peel would and could give him. Russell agreed to the latter advice. Cottenham was against the undertaking altogether, and so was Macaulay. Palmerston listened but said little one way or the other. Peel at first declined to communicate his intentions to Russell. Sir James Graham's letter intimating this was read aloud at a second meeting of the Whig chiefs in Chesham Place, and it created a bad impression. However, nothing daunted, Russell was determined to persevere. It was finally decided that Lord Lansdowne and Lord John should go together to Windsor to tell the Queen what they proposed. This was that Peel should again be invited to state frankly what sort of measure he contemplated and would be prepared to support; and if he refused to do this, Lord John was to commit to paper a project, which was to be sent to Peel, desiring at the same time that he would say whether he would support it, and what amount of support he calculated he would be able to bring with him.

At Windsor their reception was cordial, but strange and wonderful in their eyes. It was now over four years since Whig Ministers had done political business with their Sovereign, and

during that time a change had been taking place, the extent of
which they were not aware, so that at the interview their bewildered vision lit upon two Sovereigns, and not one Sovereign,
and their slightly outraged ears detected the unmistakable "We"
—not the "we" of royalty, but the unequivocal pronoun plural
of two people speaking as one—as Victoria and Albert faced them
across the carpet. "The Prince has become so identified with
the Queen," snorts Greville, "that they are one person, and as
he likes business, it is obvious that while she has the title, he is
really discharging the functions of the Sovereign."*

Recovering somewhat from their shock, the two Whig leaders
stated their mission, and added that it was essential for them to
have some assurance that the dissentient section of the Cabinet
would in no case endeavour to form a Ministry.

Prince Albert undertook to write at once to Peel on this matter,
and with this they departed. In the course of the next day Peel's
answer was received, which was that the Protectionist section of
the Cabinet could not and would not attempt to form a Government. Upon this, and upon Peel's assurance that he would support any reasonable measure brought forward by the Whigs to
meet the existing situation, Lord John called another meeting at
Chesham Place with the intention of intimating to his friends that
the way was now clear for him to form a Government.

But now quite suddenly all his high hopes were flouted by a
circumstance of a personal rather than a political nature. It was
one of those unforeseen obstacles which Cabinets are apt to encounter. Lord Grey flatly refused to be a member of the Government if Palmerston was to have the Foreign Office. And Palmerston refused to join the Cabinet in any capacity save that of
Foreign Minister. The deadlock was complete, and no persuasive
and pacifying deputation of sweetly reasonable colleagues could
budge either gentleman from the position he had adopted. Russell
sat wringing his hands in Chesham Place. It was impossible to
go on with the business of forming a Government if Grey would
not serve in it. With Spencer gone (he had died that summer)
and Grey not one of them, their weakness in the Lords would be
deplorable, while any Whig Government without Palmerston
would be unthinkable. On December 18th he put pen to paper,
and wrote to Palmerston informing him that "one of his
colleagues objected to his taking the Foreign Office." Palmerston
answered with spirit "that this was additional reason for his
accepting no other."

By the evening of the same day it became known that Russell's
attempt to form a Government had failed. On December 21st
he went down to Windsor and resigned the attempt.

* Greville *Journals*.

The Queen accepted his resignation, and sent immediately for the late Prime Minister.

So did Lord John, in Disraeli's trenchant phrase, "hand back with courtesy the poisoned chalice to Sir Robert." And it must be owned that Sir Robert drank it down with a very good grace. "I will be your Minister, happen what may," he wrote to Her Majesty. "I will do without a colleague rather than leave you in this extremity." "Our worthy Peel," writes Victoria to Uncle Leopold, ". . . his conduct towards me has been chivalrous almost, I might say." Peel, however, had not to do without Ministers, for they all returned to his side at this crisis, all, that is, except Stanley. His place at the Colonial Office was filled by Mr. Gladstone.

§ 4

And now it was the turn of the great Conservative leader to pass, with the help of the Whigs, a measure dealing with repeal. The Queen opened Parliament in person on January 22nd, 1846. After moving and seconding the Address, Peel rose, and in a speech of commanding eloquence, fearlessly admitted his conversion to the principle of Free Trade. "Whether holding a private station or a public one," he declared, "I will assert the privilege of yielding to the force of argument and conviction, and acting upon the results of enlarged experience. It may be supposed there is something humiliating in making such admissions. Sir, I feel no such humiliation. I should feel humiliation if, having modified or changed my opinions, I declined to acknowledge that change for fear of incurring the imputation of inconsistency. The question is whether the facts are sufficient to account for the change. . . ."

When he sat down the applause was almost universal, though there were wry faces on the Conservative benches. One voice alone was raised in protest. For an hour, Disraeli denounced his own party leader with the barbed shafts of his invective, referring to Sir Robert's speech as "a glorious example of egotistical rhetoric," and his conversion to Free Trade as a betrayal of the party which had put him in power. Notwithstanding, the address was carried.

It was just about this time, when political tension was at its highest, that a longed-for event took place in the Clarendon household—Kathy gave birth to a son and heir, Edward Hyde, born February 26th, 1846.*

With the introduction and passing of the "Great Measure of

* Edward Hyde Villiers, Fifth Earl of Clarendon, P.C., G.C.B., G.C.V.O. He was sometime M.P. for Brecon, Lord Chamberlain of the Household and Lord Lieutenant of Co. Hertford. He died in 1914.

Free Trade which some men still regard as the chief glory and others as the chief reproach of his career," Peel reached the summit of his power. The descent was swift and precipitate. But he was prepared for that. He was asking the Conservative party to turn a *volte face*, to forsake their dearest principle. He knew what the end must be. The first critical reading of the Corn Bill was passed by a majority of 337, of which only 112 were Conservatives. On May 15th Peel carried the third reading in the Commons by a majority of 98. The Government, however, was balanced on a hair's breadth. With so deep a cleft in its ranks, it could only carry its measures by the co-operation and support of its political adversaries. The moment it brought forward a measure distasteful to the Whigs, Ministers knew very well that the dissentient members of their own party would join forces with the Opposition to defeat them. Such a measure, indeed, was the Irish Coercion Act of 1846, introduced by the Government to repress the savage outbreak of crime produced by the famine and distress in Ireland. A dispute over one of its clauses —here was the opportunity. Disraeli himself, in his *Life of Lord George Bentinck* gives us a picture of this division. Peel sat grim on the Treasury Bench "as the Protectionists passed in defile before the Minister to the hostile lobby. It was impossible that he could have marked them without emotion: the flower of that great party, which had been so proud to follow one who had been so proud to lead them. . . . They had extended to him an unlimited confidence, and an admiration without stint. . . . They had not only been his followers, but his friends. . . . They trooped on; all the men of mettle, and large-acred squires. . . . Sir Robert looked very grave. . . . He began to comprehend his position and that the Emperor was without an army." So Peel had his Waterloo. On the very night that the third reading of the Corn Bill passed the Lords without a division, June 25th, 1846, the Government was defeated on the Irish Coercion Bill in the Commons by a majority of 73. Peel resigned at once; but his Corn Bill had become law.

CHAPTER X

RETURN OF THE WHIGS

§ 1

THERE was now no question as to whether the Whigs should or should not take the Government. Peel had crashed, bringing down with him the whole Conservative party, which was split from end to end on the subject of Free Trade. For anybody on that side of politics to form a Government at this juncture would have been a sheer impossibility. The task of doing so now fell by necessity upon John Russell, and he set about the business of Cabinet making. It might be supposed that he would be faced with the same difficulty as had confronted him six months before with regard to Grey and Palmerston. But Grey, it was ascertained, was in a chastened mood and rather ashamed of the part he had played in the crisis of the previous December. Indeed, he was all tears and smiles and ready to serve with anybody in any capacity. As for Palmerston, who by now must have known who it was who refused to serve with him as Foreign Secretary, the intelligence left him completely unmoved, and he was as genial to Grey as if no incident had occurred. The only bitterness that remained was in the mind of John Russell, who was still furious with Grey's behaviour to him six months before and vowed he would never serve with him again. However, as expediency governs the game, Russell swallowed his pride and offered him the Colonies. "Lord Grey has thought better of it," scrawls Kathy in her diary, "and although Pam took the Foreign Office, Grey accepted the Colonial Office, which Clarendon was to have had if Grey remained obdurate." Clarendon, as before, was offered and accepted the Presidency of the Board of Trade.

Several Peelites, who had stood by Sir Robert in his late Free Trade venture, were invited to be members of the new Government, as it was thought desirable to strengthen the Free Trade element on the Treasury Bench. But these gentlemen politely declined, and Lord John was faced with the, to him, dubious advisability of inviting Richard Cobden to take office. The latter represented widespread interests, and had, of course, been the moving spirit in the agitation for repeal. He was an obvious choice; but at the same time he was, politically, a new and rather alarming portent, and it is not unamusing to note with what feelings of suspicion and distaste the aristocratical chiefs of the Whig Party regarded this first "man of the people" thrown up into politics by trade and a revised electorate. Lord Lansdowne thought that "the risk of inviting him would be greater than the gain," while Lord Beauvale, in whom John Russell seems to have confided at this time, used all his arts to dissuade him from making the offer. The rest felt uncomfortable, but hostile. Only Clarendon was whole-heartedly for Cobden's inclusion in the Government. "For years past," he writes of the Whig party, "its vitality and vigour have been failing . . . it no longer derives strength from public sympathy. It is considered to be aristocratical in its opinions, exclusive in its personnel, and guided by past historical reminiscences rather than by present public opinion. . . . Its reconstruction, on a far broader basis is now indispensable." These reflections he cast in the form of a memorandum and circulated among his colleagues. In the end the vexed question was settled by Cobden himself, who, when the offer was made to him, put Ministers out of their difficulty by declining on the grounds of health.

On Monday, July 6th, the new Ministers kissed hands at Osborne, and the same week they took up their labours in Parliament. The session was far advanced, but one or two matters had to be disposed of before the House rose. One was the question of the Sugar Duties. Now that the whole country had gone Free Trade, the huge preferential tariff against the slave-grown commodity had obviously to be lowered if not suppressed. Lord John decided to drop the tariff to equalisation with that imposed on the Colonial product. The Bill passed through the Commons with no difficulty. Clarendon offered to introduce it, and to look after its progress through the House of Lords. The summer was far advanced, and many peers had given up politics and retired to the country. But the personnel of the Upper House is a much more equivocal element than that of the Lower, and it happened that that uncertain wizard Brougham had come up from Cumberland especially to force a division on this issue. Now Brougham was a friend of Clarendon's, and was in the habit of writing him long political letters at this period. But he did not spare his language on this occasion. Added to which Wilberforce and Stanley were both in the House that night and the Government in a minority, so the situation looked gloomy enough. However, the Whips were sent out to search the highways and by-ways for party reinforcements, and in the end the Government carried the Division with a fair majority.

Parliament was prorogued by the Queen in person on August 28th, and tired politicians fled into the country. It had been a memorable session: the great Free Trade measure passed; Peel overthrown; the Tory party split for ever into two opposing camps; the Whigs united by the turn of events; and Russell in favour again. There was enough food for reflection in all this to carry members over till the autumn. The Clarendons retired to the Grove, where we get a glimpse of them in September from Greville's descriptive pen. "I came here (the Grove) on Friday," he says. "Half the Cabinet here, John Russell, the Woods, the Greys, Macaulay, very agreeable: capital table, Macaulay in great force. If it were possible to recollect all the stories, anecdotes, jests and scraps of poetry and prose he has given us, it would be well worth while writing down." A week later, he writes from Woburn: "Lord John went away the day I came. He is in high spirits, on good terms with the Queen, and well satisfied with the political aspect of his affairs."* All, indeed, seemed well for the moment.

In mid-September, however, an incident occurred over a Foreign Office despatch to Spain which indicated that Palmerston was at his old tricks again, and that the Queen was not as pliable as she used to be. It was over this affair that there began that tussle between Palmerston and the Court as to who should have the last say in matters relating to Foreign Affairs—a tussle in which John Russell was made to act, in his own words, as "umpire between Windsor and Broadlands," while the Cabinet played a kind of Greek Chorus to the historic contest. Times had changed since Lord Melbourne sat at the head of the Cabinet table, gazing into space and playing with his fob; since a young Queen at Windsor came in from the garden ready to be instructed in the gentle art of foreign diplomacy by wise and experienced councillors, who knew so much better than she how to frame a memorandum, how to draft a despatch. All this was over. In Melbourne's chair sat Russell, conscientious, alert and prim. And at Windsor a girl had become a woman and the woman was rapidly transforming herself into a ruler, with views of her own, obstinate, shrewd and clear. Despatches were returned with marginal corrections in the royal hand, and wide-eyed Ministers had to admit on occasions that the corrections were justified. The golden age of individualism in foreign politics seemed at an end, and a bureaucracy seemed about to control the State Department. So thought Clarendon, who told Greville that Palmerston's independent action at the Foreign Office had received a complete and final check. And Greville believed him. How wrong they were, subsequent events were to prove. However, the Court and the Cabinet seemed to have won the first round.

In this instance, Palmerston sent Lord John the despatch he

* Greville *Journals*.

was proposing to send to Spain. The latter, having read it, was alarmed at its contents, and intimated to Palmerston that it could not go to Madrid without the Queen's first seeing it. It was accordingly sent to Her Majesty, who kept it for two days and then returned it with her own comments and objections. Her letter was ably written, and her general survey of the situation exhibited a remarkably accurate knowledge of the state of the parties in Spain. As a consequence, John Russell called a Conference at his house consisting of himself and the Lords Lansdowne, Clarendon and Palmerston; and these four discussed the matter for over two hours. They finally agreed upon the drafting of a letter to be written in place of Palmerston's despatch. The letter was a lengthy affair, and although Ministers did not part till two o'clock in the morning, Palmerston wrote out the whole of it before he went to bed. It was sent down to the Queen the following morning, who returned it with her approval the same day.

The affair was comparatively unimportant, and it certainly passed off satisfactorily in every way. Palmerston had been in a pliable mood, and there had been no heat in the Queen's objections. But he was nettled by the incident, and it gave him food for thought. If such a pother was made when he sent his despatches to the proper sources for inspection, how much better it would be to send them off without having shown them to anybody at all. It was a dangerous thought, and the conduct derived from it was to lead him into a number of serious scrapes, from all but one of which, be it said, he extricated himself with colours flying. But in the end it proved his downfall.

The autumn and early winter were spent by Ministers in bandying papers and documents relative to the Spanish marriages, and the Cracow affair—both of them too slight to be touched on here—and in preparing for the coming session: but all interest in these subsided, as a new and more intimate cause of apprehension filled men's minds, and all eyes turned towards Ireland.

§ 2

The famine which had caused the change of policy at Westminster was gripping that unhappy country with an iron hand. The potato-crop had failed for the third year running. This year the cereals had failed also. It is almost impossible for us, in these days, to realise the appalling situation that such circumstances could create. There simply was not anything to eat, and the poor died in their hundreds. The distress knew no mitigation, and day by day the accounts that came into the towns from the outlying districts were of the most terrible nature. Within one week there had been ninety-five deaths from starvation in the

Lurgan Union Workhouse. In Sligo, so rapid had become the mortality that Coroners were totally unable to perform their duties. In many districts deaths were so numerous that coffin-burial became impossible and the corpses were rolled into pits outside the villages. Bands of starving peasants roamed the land in search of food, and a correspondent from Drogheda wrote that wretched women and children were to be seen on the decks of steamers trying to appease their hunger with the turnips half-eaten by the cattle on board. Needless to say, the famine and distress were all laid at the door of the English Government; and at an inquest held upon a starved girl in the Galway Workhouse, a verdict of "Wilful Murder" was brought in against Lord John Russell.

It is hardly surprising to learn that these conditions were accompanied by savage outbursts of crime all over the land. Nor will it astonish any who have the slightest acquaintance with Ireland and the Irish to hear that with the money they got from relief funds rushed over from England, the peasants, in many cases, bought arms instead of food, and then shot the officers who were sent over to regulate the distribution of relief. Menaced by a recurrence of famine the following year, they refused to cultivate the ground, and while they crowded to relief-bureaux with demands for employment, the landowners could not procure hands to till the unsown fields. From all points of view the situation was appalling. "We are all here of opinion," writes Greville, "that some tremendous catastrophe is inevitable. The evil is not in course of diminution, and what will happen and when it will happen, God only knows; but there must and will be some tremendous convulsion, and that before very long."*

Parliament met on January 19th, 1847, and on the 21st Lord John rushed legislation through both Houses, suspending the Corn and Navigation laws, while on the 25th he introduced a Government scheme for dealing with the general situation. The people were immediately to be taken off the roads and other works which had been instituted by the Government and enabled to work on their own holdings by being supplied with food by local relief committees. It was suggested that the funds for this purpose should be raised by a Government grant. It was the first of those palliative measures by which England poured money into Ireland in these years with a view to relieving distress. It was well-intentioned and sincere, but it was hardly constructive, and nothing in the clauses of the Bill suggested that a real legislative attempt was being made to put Ireland permanently on her feet. More practical perhaps, even in the existing crisis, would have been the Bill introduced by Lord George Bentinck, which

* Greville *Journals.*

provided that a large loan should be granted to Irish Railway Companies to develop a railway system throughout the island. It would have given immediate employment to multitudes of men, and focused them at points where food could be readily supplied. It would also have been the beginning of a system which would link up outlying districts with urban centres and make such a crisis as was then raging in Ireland impossible in the future. The proposal to read the Bill a second time was, however, vetoed by a majority of 214.

§ 3

As if the situation were not complicated enough for the Government, news now came that Lord Bessborough, the Viceroy, had fallen ill, and it was not long before it became apparent that he was going to die. But a respite in the course of his disorder gave John Russell time to reflect upon his successor, and when Lord Bessborough died in May, his plans were made. He had consulted Lord Lansdowne and the Duke of Bedford, and they were in agreement with his decision. He sent for Clarendon and offered him the post. The offer was made in Russell's most cold, short, abrupt, indifferent manner, "much as if he were disposing of a tide-waiter's plea to an applicant," to use Clarendon's own words in describing the scene. In after years Clarendon would have known that a certain inward diffidence often produced this outward effect in Russell. The more he asked people to do for him, the more off-hand his manner was apt to become.

And certainly it was a big sacrifice that he was asking Clarendon to make at this moment. The latter had been Minister now in two Cabinets and was just beginning to feel his feet in Parliament. He had a Department of State for the first time entrusted to him, and he was busy and interested in his work at the Board of Trade. He enjoyed the confidence and friendship of John Russell. He was on intimate terms with the rest of the Cabinet. Everything pointed to his remaining where he was, at the very centre of things, and developing the brilliant career that it seemed impossible should not open out before him if he remained in London. He knew that if he accepted the governance of Ireland at this moment his ideas as "man-on-the-spot" would inevitably clash with all sides, with all interests, with the Cabinet not least of all. He was under no illusions as to the task before him. "A man must indeed be sanguine who thought that the best-devised measures for Ireland were likely to work well," he writes to his brother-in-law in June. "I shall, however, hope to do whatever zeal, perseverance and honesty of purpose can effect." If he now accepted what John Russell referred to as the "odious and difficult task of the Lieutenancy,'' it was, we believe, for three reasons. First, because he knew that Russell wanted him to take it; and Russell was his party chief, for whom he felt great loyalty and affection. Secondly, because he had not forgotten his early interest in Irish affairs, when he had been a mere Commissioner of Customs in Dublin with no political power. And thirdly (a personal reason, but we think it weighed in the scale), his acceptance of the Viceroyalty at this moment would effectually allay Palmerston's suspicions that he had designs on the Foreign Office for himself. Ever since the Mehemet Ali affair the Palmerstons had been apt to regard him as a dangerous rival, an ambitious schemer, plotting to step into Palmerston's shoes. People already spoke of him for the Foreign Office. And although Clarendon had been scrupulously careful to avoid all possible occasion for strengthening this false belief, circumstances had had an unfortunate way at times of seeming to corroborate it. He was much consulted on foreign affairs. Russell confided in him. It was he he sent for, together with Lord Lansdowne, to confer upon the Queen's alteration of Palmerston's despatch. He was deferred to on the subject of the Spanish Marriages, owing to his knowledge of Spanish affairs. If Palmerston went from the Foreign Office, it was obvious who would be offered the post in his place, and it was difficult for some people to believe that he was not already scheming to get it. There was no open breach, of course, and the Clarendons were invited to the parties at Carlton Gardens. But they detected a coldness in Lady Palmerston's manner to them, and a forced geniality in Palmerston's greeting, and this distressed George greatly. Much as he had at times to disagree with Palmerston officially, he was personally attached to him, and he felt he owed him much. In becoming completely excluded from foreign affairs by a voluntary self-banishment to Dublin, might he not go some way towards clearing up this distressing and ridiculous misunderstanding?

All these reasons, we think, carried weight in his decision to accept the post.

For a month he remained in London winding up his affairs at the Board of Trade, and in the first fortnight of July, 1847, he sailed for Ireland.

CHAPTER XI
VICEROY OF IRELAND

§ 1

THE five years which Clarendon spent in Ireland, though an exile from politics at home, were by no means unfruitful from the point of view of his career. He lived through critical times; he handled difficult and dangerous situations with firmness and tact; he initiated legislation which, if it did not solve the Irish problem once and for all, at least did much to alleviate it temporarily; he took a strong line with the Government at home, and on several occasions forced its hand. He found Ireland in the grip of an appalling famine, with the whole machinery of the law broken down, crime rampant and revolution impending. He left it with law and order restored, trade reviving and the peaceable decencies of life so far reinstated that it was deemed safe for the Queen and the Prince Consort to pay a visit of state to Dublin while Clarendon was there, a course which would have been manifestly impossible even so much as to contemplate in the condition in which he found Ireland when he arrived there in 1847. During his Viceroyalty he was offered (and he accepted) the Garter, and when he left Ireland for good in 1852 there is no doubt that he was considered eligible for even the highest post in the Government.

The appointment in 1847 was a popular one. *The Times* reminded its readers of the good work that George Villiers had done in Spain; drew a parallel between the two countries, concluding, rather gloomily, by saying that the anarchy of Spain at its worst, even when darkened by the intrigues of Louis Philippe and Maria-Christina, were as nothing compared to the actual condition of Ireland at that moment.

The famine was at its height when Clarendon arrived in Dublin to take up his post. Conditions were appalling. Whole counties were on the move, men and women miserably patrolling the roads in search of food and work. Eyewitnesses of that time speak of long processions of starving individuals trailing over the countryside towards the nearest local workhouse. Some sank by the road and died where they were, while others passed by unheeding in their misery and want. In the Kenmare district the roads were congested for miles with men and women flocking into Killarney for relief. The temper of the people was sullen and savage.

Under the circumstances it could hardly be expected to be anything else. But it was dangerous and unfortunate that their reaction to the vast calamity that had befallen them should have
taken one shape, and one shape only, that of armed resistance to
the forces of law and order. By every means in their power they
contrived, they stole, they constructed arms for themselves; and
with these, in their misery, they shot all who were placed in
authority over them—even those who were trying to help them in
their need. The record of Clare, Limerick and Tipperary for 1847
is hardly credible. Assassination of landlords took place in broad
daylight before many witnesses; theft was universal, and convictions were impossible to obtain from juries who openly sided with
the miscreants. In a word, the administration of justice had
completely broken down.

Such a state of affairs, as might be expected, was eagerly seized
upon by the group of Irish politicals whose avowed aim, now that
O'Connell was dead, was to rid Ireland, by force, of the British
rule. Gavan Duffy, Mitchel, McGee, Smith O'Brien, Fintan
Lalor—these were the men who now swayed Irish politics, a
doctrinaire group who worked the clubs, set up a press and poured
out a never-ending stream of propaganda inciting to revolt. The
famine and the distress, the failure of the crops, the very murders
of rent-collectors—everything was laid at the door of the English
Administration, and their compatriots were invited to arise in their
might and drive the foul contamination of England once and for
all from their midst. These sincere and convinced men conceived
the masses to be in a highly inflammable state, awaiting but the
spark, which they could supply, to burst into the flame of open
political rebellion. How wrong they were, how little, being Irish,
they understood the psychology of their own countrymen will
come to light in due course.

Clarendon was nearer the mark when he realised, as he did at
once, that the crimes that were being perpetrated throughout
Ireland were not political in origin, but due solely to the prevalent
distress—a mere savage reaction to calamity. His eyes took in
the little group of political men in Dublin and elsewhere, and his
intelligence registered the effect they were having on the public.
He would deal with them later. His glance went beyond them
and out into the provinces, into the lonely countryside, where the
murder of landlords and resident magistrates, of rent-collectors
and rate-collectors, of farmholders and smallholders were of daily
occurrence. These, he saw, were sporadic and unorganised and
had nothing to do with politics. The law, as such, had broken
down, and men in their misery were taking advantage of the fact.
Very well, the law must be set up again, and he must be given
extraordinary powers (to be used at his own discretion) to see

that it was so set up throughout the length and breadth of the land. That was the first thing to do.

§ 2

He settled down that autumn to a correspondence, both personal and official, with John Russell, the object of which was to persuade the Government to strengthen his hands. He sketched an Arms Act and a Constabulary Act, which he sent to London for consideration. At the same time he applied for wider personal powers. Taking the bull by the horns, he boldly sued for a suspension of the Habeas Corpus—such suspension to be used, of course, at his own discretion, and only where he thought fit and proper. He knew he would not obtain this from Russell. But he suspected that the moment would come when it would have to be granted him, and it was just as well, he thought, to prepare the mind of the Government for such an eventuality. His predictions were right. John Russell blinked suspiciously at his demands. Surely Clarendon was being rather alarmist. Surely affairs in Ireland had not yet arrived at the point where a suspension of the Habeas Corpus could be envisaged. He wrote to Clarendon, arguing every point. He read Clarendon's letters to the Cabinet, and the colleagues debated the issues interminably. In the end the Constabulary Bill was accepted in principle, the Arms Act rejected and the suspension of Habeas Corpus shelved. Clarendon was furious. " I can hold out no hope of tranquillity being restored if some further power to protect life and property is not given to the Executive Government in Ireland," he wrote, and he continued to bombard Russell with appeals for further powers. Parliament was on the eve of assembling, and Clarendon began to hint that his continued presence in Ireland would have to depend on part, at any rate, of his representations being attended to. His retirement at this juncture would have been very awkward for the Government, and a paragraph was rushed into the Queen's speech asking for the " assistance of Parliament in taking further precautions against the perpetration of crime in certain countries and districts of Ireland." This assistance took the shape of a Bill introduced early in the session by Sir George Grey; and when Clarendon was sent the draft of it he was relieved (and amused) to see that it contained most of the clauses of his own Disarmament and Constabulary Bills. No mention was made of the Habeas Corpus. But that, he opined, would have to come later. The Bill met with a favourable reception in Parliament. Peel rallied his men to its support. Charles Greville, who met him in the park the morning after the first reading, remarked upon his support of the Government, to which Sir Robert replied:

"Yes, and I mean to support them; but they have made a great mistake, and missed a great opportunity. Parliament and the Country would have confided to the Lord Lieutenant any powers the Government chose to ask for; they have totally misunderstood the state of Ireland, and the feeling and opinions of this Country."*

The Bill passed through both Houses without misadventure, and Clarendon found his hands substantially strengthened. He now set about the task of restoring order with a will. At the same time he turned his eyes towards that group of politicians and journalists who were trying to transform the distress and degradation of their countrymen into open rebellion against the Crown.

The year 1848 dawned red with revolution. Revolution in France, revolution in Würtemberg; rumours, even, of a Chartist rising in England. The accounts of the February disturbances in Paris, in which Louis Philippe lost his throne and had to fly for asylum to England under the homely guise of Mr. Smith, sounded to the ears of *The Nation* as "a message from Heaven." To Mitchel of the *United Irishman* it sounded as a challenge to arms. He openly defied the Government and announced his intention of taking the field, while Smith O'Brien, the turbulent Irish member, made his last speech in the House of Commons, and left for Ireland with the purpose of founding a republic there on the French model. Clarendon, intent upon larger aspects of the Irish problem, was forced to turn a watchful eye upon this little group of confederates. Their first act was to send a congratulatory message to the new Government in France with a plea for help in their own cause. The result of this was rather depressing, for Lamartine replied that the French could not interfere in the internal affairs of the British Empire. Clarendon received the text of his reply and had copies posted on the walls of every police station in Ireland. He also concentrated a force of 12,000 troops in the Dublin area. Next the Confederates issued an attractive form of enlistment in a "National Guard," and spoke of the formation of a "Council of Three Hundred." The Government proscribed them both. But the clubs were organising and going forward with the collection of arms. On Duffy's showing, Dublin City and County had thirty clubs, Cork had eleven, Tipperary ten, County Wexford four, Ennis one. But there were no supplies and, above all, there was no money. Nothing daunted by these deficiencies, the *United Irishman* redoubled the ferocity of its articles.

Freedom of speech is desirable within limits, but when the limits are surpassed to the extent that Mitchel surpassed them in February, 1848, it becomes a nuisance; something must be done.

* Greville *Journals*.

Clarendon was determined to get Mitchel in the end. If he had not yet the machinery with which to arrest him, he would create it; he would force the Government to give it to him. Meanwhile the articles in the Press continued: "Let the man amongst you who has no gun sell his garment to buy one. Every street is an excellent shooting gallery for disciplined troops, but it is a better defile in which to take them. In the vocabulary of drilling is no such phrase as 'Infantry, prepare for window pots, brick-bats, logs of wood, chimney-pieces, heavy furniture, light pokers, etc., and these thrown vertically on the heads of a column below from the elevation of a parapet or top storey are irresistible." Such missiles as "broken glass for maiming the horses' feet" were freely advocated, and to these methods, the article continues, "revolutionary citizens add always boiling water, or grease, or, better, cold vitriol, if available. Molten lead is good, but too valuable; it should always be cast into bullets."

Waxing bolder, Mitchel addresses the Lord Lieutenant in an "open letter." "As for me, my lord, your lordship's humble correspondent, you have been told that I am mad—a dangerous lunatic, labouring under *cacoethes scribendi*. Do not believe it. I am merely possessed with a rebellious spirit; and think I have a mission to bear a hand in the final destruction of the bloody old British Empire, the greedy carnivorous old monster that has lain so long like a load upon the heart and limbs of England, and drunk the blood and sucked the marrow from the bones of Ireland. Against that Empire of hell, a thousand ghosts of my slaughtered countrymen shriek nightly for vengeance; their blood cries continually from the ground Vengeance! Vengeance! and Heaven has heard it. . . . Thank God, they are arming. Young men everywhere in Ireland begin to love the clear glancing of the steel, and to cherish their dainty rifles as the very apple of their eyes. They walk more proudly; they feel themselves more and more of men. Like the Prussian students (when the work had to be done for Prussia) they take the bright weapons to their hearts, and clasp their virgin swords, like virgin brides."

In case there should be any misunderstanding as to the scope and extent of these effusions, Mitchel writes:

"As for the warlike and treasonable articles in this newspaper, they will be steadily continued and improved upon, week after week, until they have produced their effect—the effect not of a street riot to break up a peaceable meeting, but of a deliberate and universal armament to sweep this island clear of British butchers, and plant the green flag on Dublin Castle."

This paper was published in Dublin itself, and placed weekly in the hands of thousands of discontented and disaffected persons all over the country. . . . There is no doubt at this time the life of the supreme symbol of British rule in Ireland was not very safe. "No Tipperary landlord," writes the Lord Lieutenant to Russell in March of this year, "ever received more threatening notices than I do, or more warnings as to *when* or *how* I am to be assassinated. I can't say that these disturb me at all; but as Dublin is full of the greatest ruffians on earth, I am obliged to observe a certain amount of precaution, and I only go out in the carriage for a short walk in the park, which makes me nearly a State prisoner."

There is no doubt that by March, Clarendon had "got across" to Lord John the danger of the situation, for we find the latter contemplating the suspension of the Habeas Corpus without a tremor. Lord Jocelyn was put up to try out the temper of the House on Ireland. In his speech he drew attention "to the language of certain mischievous and traitorous men, and went on to give an account of the subversive propaganda which was being disseminated broadcast in Ireland at the moment. Lord John replied amplifying Jocelyn's statement, and suggesting that a measure should be introduced to put a stop to such propaganda. The House was sympathetic, and the Government proceeded with a Bill known to history as The Crown and Government Security Act. The Bill did not involve the suspension of the Habeas Corpus; but it did give Clarendon the machinery with which to deal with Mitchel and the *United Irishman*. He struck at once. The premises of the revolutionary newspaper were raided, the presses and type confiscated, and Mitchel was arrested and charged under the provisions of the Act. The trial came on May 24th, and lasted two days. Clarendon was anxious for the result. The walls of Dublin were placarded with posters vowing vengeance on the jurors if they dared to convict. Every conceivable means of intimidation were applied, and the outcome looked uncertain. However, the jury, greatly daring, brought in a verdict of "guilty." The next day Mitchel was sentenced to fourteen years' transportation. Clarendon was taking no risks. It is probable that Mitchel's policy for the past six months had been dictated by the belief that if he were arrested the populace would rise to defend and rescue him, that Ireland would then be entered upon a path of revolution, the course of which it would be for fate to decide. Fully aware of this belief, Clarendon had taken ample precautions. And before the populace had had time to make up its mind as to a course of action, the prisoner was "hurried under an escort of cavalry through the streets of Dublin, put on board a waiting ship of war, and in a few hours was on his way to Bermuda."

The *United Irishman* was succeeded by the *Irish Felon* under the editorship of John Martin, and *The Nation* redoubled the fury of its language. Encouraged by the success of his action against Mitchel, Clarendon struck at the editors of these papers also, · and Gavan Duffy, Meagher and others were arrested. Whereupon Smith O'Brien and the leaders of the "young Ireland" party shook the dust of Dublin from their feet, and settled themselves in the country, where they gathered about them the nucleus of a revolutionary army, collected arms, and began to drill in earnest. Their proceedings were a direct declaration that they meant to resort to force. And now, indeed, it looked as if the long-expected revolution was about to take place, as if all the talk and blather of the past few years were going to be put to the test of action. Would all Ireland rise to the challenge of its leaders? Would the peasants of Connemara join forces with the down-trodden serfs at Waterford to sweep all Ireland free from the hated English rule, and plant the green flag of St. Patrick on Dublin Castle Tower? On the face of it, it seemed improbable. But still, one had to take precautions. Clarendon concentrated troops and constabulary at nodal points; and he sent his children home to England, and he and the faithful Kathy, almost prisoners now, sat and awaited events in Dublin.

The summer wore on, and as reports came in of the activities of the rebel army, the Lord Lieutenant passed them on with an ironical smile uncensored to the Cabinet. The tide of rumour mounted. England became at first alarmed, finally panic-stricken. Clarendon smiled, but offered no opinion. Let the full wave of panic fall upon the Cabinet: perhaps then they would give him the powers he needed. On July 20th the news was so grave that Lord John postponed his son's christening, which had been fixed for that day, and hurried up to London from Pembroke Lodge. On the following day the Cabinet at last and unanimously decided upon the suspension of the Habeas Corpus Act; and on the 22nd, Lord John introduced a measure for this purpose in the House of Commons. Contrary to all expectation, he rushed it through in a day. A guest who dined that night at Richmond with Lord John says: "The House of Commons was wonderful. . . . Nobody had the least idea of it, not the Cabinet. It was an inspiration of John Russell's; he began by making an excellent speech, an hour and a half. When they divided he made a speech in the lobby, begged the people not to go away, and said he meant to propose to go on with the Bill. To his own amazement, as much as to anybody's, he found no opposition, and carried the Bill through at a sitting. It was a great event for which the Lord Lieutenant nor anybody in Ireland will have been the least prepared."*

* Spencer Walpole, *Life of Lord John Russell.*

The fact was that Lord John had become thoroughly alarmed at the aspect of things in Ireland. Moreover, he managed most successfully to communicate his alarm to the House of Commons, and through the House of Commons to the country at large. All eyes turned towards Ireland. In London the anxiety was intense, the clubs buzzed with rumours. Everybody was in a state of the gravest apprehension. When would the blow fall? Was England prepared? Would the troops over there be loyal? In the middle of it all, a few days after the passage of the Bill, Lady Grey arrived at Pembroke Lodge, distraught, and without her husband, clamouring to see Lord John. All Southern Ireland had risen, she declared, and the troops had refused to act against the insurgents. The London evening papers corroborated her wild words: "Dublin. Wednesday. The whole of the South of Ireland is in rebellion. A special engine has just arrived in Dublin from four miles this side of Thurles. The station at Thurles is on fire. The rail for several miles torn up, and as the engines arrive, the mob intend detaining them. At Clonmel the fighting is dreadful; the people arrived in masses, the Dublin Club leaders are there; the troops were speedily overpowered. The military at Carrick have been driven back, and their quarters fired. At Kilkenny the contest is proceeding, and there the mob are also said to be successful. The Queen's messenger is just started with despatches for London."

Appalled, Lord John hurried up to London. Stopping at Apsley House on his way to Downing Street, he collected the Duke of Wellington, whom he found highly sceptical, especially of that part of the rumour which touched upon the disloyalty of the troops. Slightly comforted, the Prime Minister proceeded to Downing Street, from which he issued notes calling a Cabinet Council for that same evening. "John Russell," says one of his colleagues at that meeting, "tried to look firm, but was evidently much appalled, and we were all in dismay. The Duke of Wellington was sent for, and orders were issued for pouring reinforcements of infantry, cavalry, artillery and ships of war, into Ireland from all quarters." It was, indeed, something of an anti-climax to find next day that the whole story was a vicious lie fabricated in Liverpool; that no disturbances had taken place at all, and that the forces of the Crown were in complete command of the situation. The excitement in Ireland, however, was intense. The revolutionary Press, rising like a Phœnix from the ashes of its late persecution, surpassed itself. "Strike," screamed *The Nation*. "Rise, Men of Ireland, since Providence so wills it. Rise in your cities and in your fields, on your hills, in your valleys, by your dark mountain-passes, by your rivers and lakes, and ocean-washed shores. Rise, as a nation!" "In the case of

Ireland now," explains the *Irish Felon*, "there is but one fact to deal with, and one question to be considered. The fact is this: that there are at present in occupation of our country some 40,000 men in the livery and service of England; and the question is how best and soonest to kill and capture these 40,000 men." All was ready; and Clarendon sat waiting, waiting, waiting for the inevitable revolution. And then, on July 29th it came.

CHAPTER XII

THE REBELLION

I N all the history of the lost causes of the world, there is no
story more melancholy, more pathetic, and, at the same time,
more tragically ridiculous than the story of how in July, 1848,
Smith O'Brien and the Irish Confederates set out to sweep Ireland
free of the British occupation. They had no arms. They had no
supplies. They had no money, and what "army" they had was
perpetually melting away. They had, in fact, no resources whatsoever. And yet these convinced and earnest men, O'Brien,
Dillon, McGee and others, set out, like children playing at
soldiers, to conquer Ireland for the Irish, and to sweep the hated
foreigner for ever from the soil. The plan of campaign was
Dillon's—to seize Kilkenny, call the people to arms, and from
that ancient seat of Government proclaim the independence of
Ireland. This had a grand ring to it, and the rebel generals
adopted it unanimously. They proceeded, rather tamely, by the
Wexford coach to Loughlinstown, Co. Carlow. There they
joined up with O'Brien himself, and they all went on to Enniscorthy. Here they held a public meeting, and O'Brien proclaimed his intentions. "The People," says Gavan Duffy, in
Four Years of Irish History, "were greatly moved." And when
the four patriot generals left for Kilkenny "A large procession
on foot, and on horseback accompanied them, and left them with
passionate prayers for their success." It will be observed that
the procession returned to Enniscorthy, and that the rebel generals
went on their way alone. At Greiganmanagh another procession,
this time of "stout boatmen," was formed to escort O'Brien into
Kilkenny. At this junction someone warned them that Kilkenny
was strongly garrisoned, and that to attack it in their present circumstances would be to invite disaster. Whereupon the project
of entering Kilkenny in triumph, surrounded by "stout boatmen," was given up. The "stout boatmen," presumably, returned to their boats, and the General Staff, still in search of an
army, continued on its way alone.

It was now decided to veer towards County Tipperary, where,
if anywhere, they imagined their cause would find an immediate
response. On their way they passed by Callan, where their
coming was anticipated, "and that dull town, which never before
had such a lark, turned out to meet them. Bands, bonfires, green

boughs, all the evidences of popular favour awaited them." They held a hasty meeting and warned the people to be ready for a speedy summons to fight for Ireland. "Many of the Royal Irish Hussars," says Gavan Duffy, "attended the meeting, and it was noted they were amongst the most delighted of the audience."* No doubt they were. They had probably never heard such a joke before. At Carrick, where they next proceeded, we are told, "a memorable scene awaited them." A Council of War was held, and, although here there really seemed to be a nucleus of the male population ready and eager to fight, the vicinity of Pilltown, where 1,200 British troops were stationed, was thought to be an inauspicious neighbourhood in which to begin operations so the patriot generals trailed miserably on towards Cashel of the Kings. And here a great disappointment awaited them.

"Instead of sentinels and watchfires, columns of sturdy peasants, carts laden with provisions, flaming smithies where strong men were hammering iron and steel into serviceable weapons, and all the picturesque incidents of peasant war which their eager fancy had painted, Cashel was like the City of the Dead." So eschewing the towns where it appeared men had no heart in them, they turned with renewed hope to the rustics of the countryside. At Killenaule, a couple of hundred peasants showed great willingness to fight, but somehow melted into thin air when told to hold themselves in readiness. At Mullinahone the local smith said he was "killed" trying to hammer out pikeheads enough for the hands that itched to use them. At Kickham, it really looked as if an army was forthcoming, for as many as 6,000 men assembled armed with fowling pieces, impromptu pikes and pitchforks. Drill was necessary for such an irregular force, and drilled they were all through the night. In the morning they went off to breakfast and never appeared again. At last, in the neighbourhood of Killenaule, the rebel chieftains mustered a force of about a hundred and fifty, and with this "army" they proceeded to Ballingary. And at Ballingary, as it proved, they met their Waterloo; for here it was that on July 29th they finally clashed with the forces of the Crown in the shape of the Royal Irish Constabulary. A few shots were fired; the rebels ran away; and the great Irish Rebellion expired miserably in a back garden, with the Widow Cormack crying vengeance on both sides for the ruin of her cabbages.

The affray, indeed, has a touch of the divine absurdity of a Synge play. It is difficult really to discover what happened, but from the conflicting accounts of the incident a certain picture presents itself to the mind. And the central figure in this picture is the Widow Cormack herself. Towards the Widow Cormack

* O'Connor's *History of Ireland.*

peaceably at work upon her cabbage patch there advanced in all its panoply, and headed by Smith O'Brien in person, the rebel army. This was all very right and proper, and after giving it a tasteful glance she went on with her work in the garden. The times were disturbed, and it wasn't herself was going to be killed with seeing a few boys about with pikes in their hands. It wasn't till glancing by chance over her other shoulder that she caught sight of a body of policemen stealthily approaching from the far side. Then, in a horrified flash, she realised that a battle was impending, and that she and her cabbages were likely to be the scene of it. She threw down her tools, and, with shrill cries to her five youngest, who were scattered about the place, she scuttled like a frightened hen back into the house. Hardly had she reached sanctuary with her excited brood than there was a cheer from without, and she found the house suddenly full of the Irish Constabulary, who brushed past her unceremoniously, and began barricading the windows of her cabin on the garden side. Alarmed, she looked out for a moment at the late scene of her peaceful labours. At sight of her face at the window the rebels shook their pikes, for they thought she had betrayed them. This alarmed her still more, and, hardly knowing what she did, she rushed out of the house and accosted Smith O'Brien himself, whom she found sitting in the cabbages to avoid a cross fire from the house. The widow besought O'Brien to come and speak to the police. But that optimist told her to go back to them and explain that it was only their arms that he wanted. Only let the police give up their arms—that was all—and they would be allowed to depart in peace. The police greeted this proposal with shouts of laughter, and the infuriated widow returned again to the rebel leader, seized him boldly by the collar and began dragging him into the presence of Sub-Inspector Trant.

After that nobody knows quite what happened. The fire from the house suddenly increased. Bullets pinged and whistled through the garden. All was noise and confusion. There was a moment when Smith O'Brien was observed crawling on all fours from the scene of action. There was another moment when Mrs. Cormack found herself rushing for the village priest. And then, quite suddenly, it was all over. The firing stopped; all was quiet; and the police emerged, smiling, from the house of the widow. Nothing was to be seen of the rebels save the grim memento—seven dead—that they left on the field. How far they ran it has never been ascertained, but one thing was certain, and that is that they never came together as a body again. The last scene of all in this historic affray is the spectacle of the Widow Cormack lamenting over her ruinated cabbage patch and vowing vengeance on both sides for the damage created.

12

As for O'Brien, he wandered miserably about for a few days, and on the evening of August 5th he was found and arrested at Thurles Railway Station when on the point of leaving for Limerick. He made no resistance; and it was remarked that he carried no arms beyond a small fancy pistol in his waistcoat pocket. The law made great show of dealing with a dangerous traitor. At first he was condemned to be hanged, drawn and quartered. This sentence was immediately commuted to exportation to Van Diemen's Land. And the banishment was remitted altogether in 1856. Four other insurgent leaders—Meagher, McManus, Martin and O'Doherty—were tried at the same time as O'Brien, and all received the same fate at the hands of the Government. Gavan Duffy was tried four times, the jury disagreeing each time. Finally the case was abandoned. The fate of the others is interesting. O'Gorman escaped to America and became judge of the Superior Court of New York. Meagher also went to America and fought for the North in the War of Secession. He became acting Governor of Montana. McGee went to Canada, where he made a distinguished position for himself; Mitchel to America, where he continued his journalistic career. So the nest of disaffection and disturbance was cleaned out and its occupants dispersed over the earth.

Clarendon smiled. The end was certainly an anticlimax to all the talk and excitement in Ireland, to all the rumours and apprehension in England. But the consummation was all that could be wished. He had rid Ireland for a generation of the germ of revolution, and he had, safe in his pocket, what he had wanted so long, and what the Government had been so loath to concede into his hands, namely, the suspension, at his own will and when he thought fit, of the Habeas Corpus Act.

CHAPTER XIII

THE ROYAL VISIT

§ 1

IN October, John Russell came over to Ireland in person to stay with the Clarendons at Vice-Regal Lodge. He was accompanied by his wife, so that while the visit was of a social and private nature, which precluded the necessity of giving vast official receptions for the Prime Minister as such, the two statesmen could yet seize the opportunity of having long discussions on the subject of Ireland in the undisturbed privacy of a country house.

Clarendon was delighted. It was everything to have Russell here under his own roof, even for a few days. So much could, he thought, be explained and talked over by the two of them together that could hardly be expressed by writing. Personal contact meant so much in these situations, and it was personal contact with his colleagues that had been denied Clarendon for so long. So he made the most of the Prime Minister's stay. Long into the night they talked, according to a vigilant Kathy, Clarendon walking up and down smoking innumerable cigarettes, John Russell hunched in a chair, his feet hardly touching the ground, sometimes springing up to point an admonitory finger at the tall figure of his host. It was first and foremost of the land that they talked. And always they came back to that unalterable syllogism which governed then, and no doubt governs still, the intricacies of the Irish land problem. Tenants could not pay rents because the land produced so little; the land produced so little because landlords could afford to put nothing back into it; landlords could afford to put nothing back into it because they could not collect the rents. It is a known fact that thousands of acres of Irish soil were at this juncture in the hands of landowners who were scarcely in possession of the barest necessities of life. It was to mitigate this evil that Clarendon the year before had sketched out the Encumbered Estates Act, a scheme whereby impoverished landowners could be relieved of the burden of their estates by a fair sale to the Government. The Bill had passed in the session of '48, and already an extensive transference of lands was taking place all over Ireland. Clarendon and Russell discussed the workings of this, and Clarendon further developed to his guest

179

the outlines of an Emigration Bill that he had much at heart at this time. Russell was sympathetic to the idea, suggested modifications, and, on his side, proposed to Clarendon a scheme for giving financial aid to the Roman Catholic clergy, whose sufferings in the late famine had been as terrible as any. Owing, however, to their peculiar position, no form of Government relief or of organised private charity had ever seemed to reach them. Russell left Ireland well pleased, with his head full of schemes for the future.

§ 2

Meanwhile the session opened propitiously with a compliment for Clarendon in the speech from the throne:

"Organised Confederacies," read Victoria, "took advantage of the existing pressure to excite my suffering subjects to Rebellion. Hopes of Plunder and Confiscation were held out to tempt the distressed, while the most visionary Prospects were exhibited to the ambitious. In this conjuncture I applied to your loyalty and Wisdom for increased Powers, and, strengthened by your prompt concurrence, my Government was enabled to defeat in a few days Machinations, which had been prepared for many months. The energy and Decision shewn by the Lord Lieutenant of Ireland in this emergency deserve my warmest approbation."

But when Lord John circularised the Cabinet in favour of his own Roman Catholic Relief Bill and Clarendon's proposed Emigration Act, he received an unexpected shock. He became aware within the ranks of his colleagues of a compact little family group consisting of Lord Grey, his brother-in-law Sir Charles Wood, his cousin Sir George Grey, and his cousin by marriage Sir Francis Baring. These gentlemen were bent upon curbing the enormous expenditure of the Crown in Ireland at this juncture. As the schemes which Clarendon and Russell had at heart would have cost money, the family party closed its ranks and rigidly opposed them. Clarendon came over from Ireland to explain his Emigration Act in person to the Cabinet. But though there was much discussion of it, and though Lord Grey, seeing the possibility of doing some good to Canada, tried to hitch the scheme on to the desire of Canada to build a railway from Halifax to Quebec, it was in the end abandoned.

Lord John was furious. He had the mortification of realising that in the Cabinet, as it then stood, he was powerless to carry either of the schemes that he and Clarendon had intended for Ireland. Clarendon had gone back to Dublin by the time— early in January, 1849—that the breakdown of their hopes in regard to the emigration scheme became final. Lord John wrote a despairing letter to him, informing him of what was taking

place in the Cabinet and telling him of his fixed determination to
resign if he could not have his way.

The little man was in a dangerous mood, and ready, as alas!
he always was ready, to "upset the coach" if his schemes were
opposed.   Clarendon wrote from Ireland, pouring oil upon
troubled waters and preaching moderation.   Let Lord John
consider the other side of the picture—what had been already
done in Ireland.   The re-establishment of law and order was
going on apace: the Encumbered Estates Act was beginning to
work.   Would Lord John jeopardise this by resigning now, and
handing over the reins of government to new people, whose views
were known to be out of harmony with their own, and who, in
order to make an effect, might apply dangerous expedients to the
already dangerous situation?   His safe counsels prevailed in the
end.   Lord John was pacified, his exasperation subsided, and
Clarendon remained at his post in Dublin, where he felt he could
still effect much.

While he was over in England that autumn explaining his
emigration scheme to the Cabinet two things happened to him
which considerably enlightened him as to the position he was
beginning to hold in public affairs.

First, he was offered the Garter.   This in itself was no more
than a very high mark of personal esteem coming from the
Queen herself, and endorsed, of course, by her Ministers.   He
was, indeed, touched and delighted at the high honour bestowed
upon him and, urged by Russell, he accepted it.

More significant, however, was the intimation delicately conveyed to him through Wylde, the Prince Consort's secretary,
that in the most unlikely event of Lord John's health forcing him
to resign the post of Prime Minister the Queen had decided to send
for him, Clarendon.

Clarendon was genuinely alarmed at this piece of information,
and lost no time in letting it be known in high quarters that under
no consideration whatsoever would he accept the responsibility
of the premiership.   He knew very well the limit of his own
powers, and though he candidly admitted to himself the extent
of his own usefulness in certain spheres of government, he was
fully aware of his own limitations in respect of the highest political
office of all.   The place of Prime Minister was not for him, and
never would be.   He knew that, and he meant to hold to it; and
he was determined that the Queen should never make that particular overture towards him and give him the odium of having
to refuse it.   He confided his intentions to Greville.

"I told him," says Greville, "they would not accept his
excuses, because since his Irish Administration, he had acquired

a reputation which rendered him in the eyes of the world, fit for any post. He said he could not speak, and had not had parliamentary experience enough, having come too late into the House of Lords, and never having been in the House of Commons. Finally, he begged me to tell anybody who suggested such a possible contingency that no power on earth would ever induce him to take it. But," adds Greville cynically, "I don't think he was displeased when I told him I should certainly not say that . . . . The truth is, he is sincere in his disclaimer, but with an *arrière pensée* of ambition, which not unnaturally smiles on the idea of such prodigious elevation."*

By the end of January, 1849, the term allotted by Parliament to the suspension of the Habeas Corpus Act in Ireland was drawing to its close, and we find Clarendon pleading with the Cabinet for a further extension of it. As he wrote to the Home Secretary, such powers were necessary in order " to secure for Ireland that continued repose which is so vitally essential to her prosperity, to protect the country from the renewal of an agitation for objects that cannot be attained and which for many years has disturbed its tranquillity, scaring away capital, destroying confidence and rendering impossible the steady application of industry." When questioned by Russell, who thought rather optimistically that Ireland was entering upon a period of tranquillity, Clarendon replied that, if so, it was " a tranquillity of disaffection subdued by fear."

After this it is a little surprising to hear Clarendon suggesting a royal visit to Dublin. But it came to him as an idea out of heaven. Nothing, he conceived, would do more for the *morale* of the Irish people at this juncture than to present them with their Sovereign, a woman, young and charming, and surrounded, as she would be in the circumstances, by all the power and panoply of state. The Cabinet threw up their hands in horror at such a project. The responsibility would be overwhelming. No one would have a moment's peace until the royal party got safely back. How could Clarendon, who had just been granted a further suspension of the Habeas Corpus, in order the more quickly to deal with the disaffection which he pictured as still rampant, bring himself to suggest such a course?

Clarendon, however, gently persisted. Had not Lord Bessborough, shortly before he died, advocated a royal visit? Was the Government aware that no British Sovereign had set foot in Ireland for twenty-eight years? It was all very well to inculcate loyalty to the Crown, but how could unsophisticated peasants be expected to be loyal to what, after all, could only be to them the vaguest of ideas. Let the Sovereign appear in person; it would

* Greville *Journals.*

create an impression upon them such as nothing else in the world could. As for the responsibility, he could assure them that with the police and the troops at his disposal, and careful detective work prior to the Queen's arrival, there would be no danger.

With Clarendon's assurances the idea began to change its aspect a little. It would certainly be a great feather in the Government cap if, after all the public apprehension with regard to Ireland, they could bring off a successful royal visit. It was certainly a bold coup. The Cabinet consulted again upon the matter. Finally, they gave it their consent; the Queen was approached and the visit was fixed for a date in August.

The Times gives a good picture of the Lord Lieutenant's life at this period.

" To a man of Lord Clarendon's genial temperament it must be a disagreeable task to be compelled at every turn to curb the impetuosity of the warm-hearted people among whom his lot is cast, and to teach them how prosaic an affair is everyday life, but without it nothing can be done. Conceive what the situation of that man must be, who is daily called upon to discuss the merits of every panacea in turn with its enthusiastic inventor. Not a day passes but he must discard a sovereign remedy, and yet send the projector away contented from his presence.

"Repeal, tenant-right, colonisation, confiscation of Church property, destruction of entails, loans to landlords, Government reclamation of waste-lands and bogs, repudiation of debts, railroads, fisheries, all the *farrago* that the fruitful imagination of Ireland can devise must every day be bolted in his mill, and rejected as unfit for human use. The Poor Law, says one; No Poor Law, roars the other.

" In the midst of all this confusion, Lord Clarendon endeavours —as best he may—to suggest rather than command, to procure rather than to enforce obedience."

It is no wonder that the Lord Lieutenant was sometimes in a brown study when he took his walks abroad. There is a family story of him at this period which presents him in an amusingly absent-minded mood. A second boy had been born to the Clarendons in 1847, shortly after their arrival in Ireland, George Patrick Hyde, the author's father*; and some two months after the event Clarendon, it seems, was taking a short stroll in Phœnix Park when his meditations were broken into by the gentle approach of a pram. It was a very nice pram, he noted. Mechanically he stopped to inspect it. The nurse also stopped, and the Lord Lieutenant gazed absently down upon the sturdy

* Colonel the Hon. George Villiers, C.B., C.M.G., Colonel, Grenadier Guards. Sometime Military Attaché, St. Petersburg, Berlin and Paris. Military Secretary to the Governor-General in India. Died 1891.

infant inside it. " 'M," he said, " you've got a fine boy there. Whose is it?" " Yours, m'lord," came the reply.

Everything was ready for the royal visit when an incident occurred which darkened the skies and placed Clarendon in an awkward and painful situation. The action he took in regard to it made him the centre of a bitter controversy on both sides of the St. George's Channel, and finally compelled him to justify his conduct from his place in the House of Lords. Much political capital was made out of the Dolly's Brae affair, and the issues involved were obscured by every available means; but to anyone looking at the incident from the perspective of ninety years afterwards, and with the political animosities of the time removed, the principle involved seems simple enough, and Clarendon's action the only possible course under the circumstances. Briefly, what happened was this:

The Orangemen of County Down decided to form a procession and to pay a visit to their Grand Master, Lord Roden, at his country place, Tollymore Park, close to Castlewellan. The procession was fixed appropriately for July 12th, 1849, that date being the anniversary of the Battle of the Boyne. Lord Roden was Lord Lieutenant of the county and a justice of the peace. He was an honourable, an amiable, but a very stupid man. He received the deputation at Tollymore Park, offered them stimulating refreshments and permitted them to give a display of military manœuvres in the grounds; and then, instead of advising them to disperse and go away peaceably each man to his own home, he connived at their going back in procession by the way they came when it was known that a party of Ribbonmen were waiting to attack them. One of the stipendiary magistrates, a Mr. Fitzmaurice, who was present at Tollymore Park, begged Lord Roden to disadvise this course. But Lord Roden refused to interfere, and the inevitable occurred. A shot was fired, and in a minute the confusion became general. Four men were killed and thirty or forty wounded in the affray that ensued.

Clarendon was furious. He had known about the procession and had discouraged the idea. But since Lord Roden was a responsible person and Lord Lieutenant of the county, he had trusted to him to see that the demonstration, if it took place at all, was a peaceable one. Not that he himself had not taken ample precautions, sending both troops and police to act under the stipendiary magistrates of the district.

But between the incident itself and all that resulted from it there took place the State visit of the Queen to Ireland. And this, certainly, was the brightest event of 1849. It was a tremendous feather in Clarendon's cap that, given the state of the country when he arrived, he should so have restored the reign of law that the visit was possible at all. A great many people in both countries condemned the project as a premature and hazardous experiment, declaring that Clarendon alone would be responsible if anything untoward should happen.

The Cabinet were harassed and anxious. But Clarendon never doubted the reception that the Queen would have. And Clarendon was right. Nothing could have been more entirely successful than the week the Queen spent in Ireland. And nothing at that time could have done more to capture the straying affections of the Irish people and turn them and their thoughts towards loyalty than the sudden appearance in their midst of the young Queen herself, trustful and confiding, going about amongst them, busying herself with their affairs.

§ 3

The royal party arrived on August 6th and made a state entry into Dublin that day. The procession took an hour and a half to reach Viceregal Lodge, and the whole route was thronged with shouting multitudes. Clarendon was anxious, but not a single untoward incident occurred. In fact, the reception could not have been better. Never did a city pour out its inhabitants in vaster masses or enjoy a more triumphant holiday. The decoration of the streets was all that could be desired. "Invention," we are told by a journalist of the time, "had exhausted itself in diversifying the language of greeting and the symbols of welcome. The chariot of the gratified sovereign," continues the same chronicler, in the inimitable language of the time, "pursued its way among gay streamers, waving banners, festal garlands and under gigantic arches which seemed constructed of solid flowers, as if the hand of summer herself had raised them."

At Canal Bridge the Lord Mayor presented the Queen with keys of the city, and, in answering his address of welcome, Victoria happily referred to Dublin as the "Second City of my Empire." At long last they arrived at Viceregal Lodge, and Clarendon must have heaved a sigh of relief as they passed in under his roof from the shouting streets. A huge party they were, "requiring," as Kathy explicitly states, "seventeen *lits-de-maître*, and bringing with them nineteen servants." There was a vast official dinner that night. Next morning the Queen visited the National Schools, Trinity College and the Bank; and it was noted that whereas the day before she had entered Dublin surrounded by troops, on this occasion she was in an open carriage, preceded by a single outrider. And Clarendon did not omit to canvas the fact that it was by her express wish that she did so.

The next morning there was a review in Phœnix Park, and Albert flashed about in a Hussar uniform and was greatly admired.

In the afternoon the Queen held a Drawing-Room at the Castle.
There was another review, two more dinner-parties, more sight-
seeing, and then the party proceeded to Carton to visit the Duke
of Leinster. And at Carton, amongst other people of note, Mrs.
George was presented to the Queen—Mrs. George, well over
seventy now, but still pursuing the delights of earth with
unexampled fervour. There had been no room for her at Viceregal Lodge on the occasion of the Queen's visit. But she was not
going to miss seeing her own son, her beloved George, in the full
plumage of his exalted position, personally conducting the
Sovereign round the land that he ruled in her name. And at a
hint from Clarendon the Duke of Leinster included her in his party
at Carton; and there we have a glimpse of her from a letter of
Clarendon's. "A marvellous old lady," he says, "and so everybody thinks her. The Queen was very civil to her at Carton, and
I never saw anything better than her manner—so very *grande
dame* and *distinguée*—and she looked so well, and was so well
got up."

From Carton the royal party proceeded to Belfast, where there
were more addresses, another dinner-party, more sightseeing, and
the day after that the Royal Squadron stood out for the Firth of
Clyde. There was a frantic leave-taking, when Victoria stood
upon the paddle-box and ordered the Royal Standard to be
lowered thrice, an act which was considered on all sides to be the
limit of graciousness. And then the shouting and the waving died
away, the clouds of glory faded into the uninspired light of everyday, and suddenly the visit was over.

The Cabinet was pleased. It had been a great success. "A
thousand thanks for all the *gentil* things you say of us," Clarendon
writes to Sir George Grey. "We have certainly come out of the
mess with flying colours, and when one thinks of the many things
that might have gone wrong in bringing the Sovereign and this
strange people into communication for the first time, it is marvellous that during eight days not a single event occurred differently from what I wished. . . . My position of host, subject,
and Viceroy was rather anomalous, but the Queen bore it well in
mind, and she helped me in my rôle, and so far from impairing,
she rather added to the prestige of my office." The conduct of the
royal pair, he said, was the *beau idéal* of what was right under
the circumstances, and "their tact and kindness to us can never
be forgotten."

Greville writes:

"I saw Lord Lansdowne last night, just returned from Ireland.
He said nothing could have surpassed the Queen's visit in every
respect; every circumstance favourable, no drawbacks or mistakes, all persons and parties pleased, much owing to the tact of

Lord Clarendon, and the care he had bestowed on all arrangements and details which made it all go off so admirably. The Queen herself was delighted, and appears to have played the part remarkably well. Clarendon, of course, is overjoyed at the complete success of what was his own plan, and satisfied with the graciousness and attention of the Court to him. In the beginning, and while the details were in preparation, he was considerably disgusted at the petty difficulties that were made, but he is satisfied now.

Lord Lansdowne said that the departure was quite affecting; and he could not see it without being moved, and he thinks beyond doubt, that the visit will produce permanent good effects in Ireland."*

So everyone was pleased. The spectacular success of the visit, coming as it did after a period of great public anxiety over Irish affairs, seemed to prove that the Viceroy was a wizard who could work miracles. He was now looked upon, in Greville's own words, "as fit to fill any post."

* Greville *Journals*.

CHAPTER XIV

THE GOVERNMENT IN DIFFICULTIES

§ 1

THE Dolly's Brae incident had, perforce, to engage Clarendon's attention for most of that autumn and winter. For, by a sudden turn of events, what was in reality no more than a "regrettable incident" was turned into a burning political issue, which caused not only Clarendon, but the Government behind him, considerable pain and anxiety. The development of the situation was in this wise. Clarendon had very properly employed a competent Q.C. to investigate the circumstances that led to the affray on July 29th and to discover what, in reality, actually happened. This gentleman's report was completed in October; and, since the report made no doubt that the Orange party were the prime offenders in the matter, Clarendon instituted proceedings against certain of the Orangemen involved in the affair. If Lord Roden's action on July 29th were erratic and irresponsible, the course he now adopted seems to have been dictated by dementia. The evidence for the prosecution was submitted, as is usual, to the magistrates of the district where the delinquency occurred, which was, in this case, the bench of which Lord Roden was chairman. The magistrates, on this occasion, flatly refused to take the evidence submitted to them, and Lord Roden sanctioned their behaviour by his presence on the Bench at the time.

Clarendon was amazed, for Roden was a genial, kindly man to whom he owed much. But his stupid, ill-considered action on this occasion had created a very serious situation, for it involved the breach of a principle which could not be allowed to pass. However little Lord Roden may have meant it to appear as such, there was no getting away from the fact that his action constituted a direct challenge by a subordinate of the Viceregal authority in Ireland, in that, for party motives, he had sanctioned the refusal to take evidence in proceedings instituted by the Crown. Clarendon took what he conceived to be the only course open to him. He dismissed Lord Roden from the Commission of the Peace. He wrote to him in a perfectly friendly manner, explaining why he had to adopt this course, and hoping that his action would in no way influence the course of their personal relations.

The fat was in the fire. By his action Clarendon had incensed the whole of the powerful Orange organisation all over Ireland, and its Press set up a howl of remonstrance. Clarendon was reviled from one end of the country to the other. Wherever an Orange club or an Orange paper existed his name was execrated and his action condemned. That he should have had the injustice to strike against the very elements in Ireland that stood for law and order, for the maintenance of the Union and for loyalty to the Crown, whose help he had invoked in the late scare of revolution, whose support could have been called upon in any emergency— this could never be forgotten or forgiven.

There were monster meetings; there were manifestos; there were threatening articles in the Press. Nor were Lord Roden's friends behindhand in taking up the cause. Lord Downshire held a meeting of magistrates at Castlewellan, and suggested that all the magistrates of County Down should resign from the Commission of the Peace as a protest to the Viceroy's action.

Lord Roden himself sulked at Tollymore Park. He was hurt, aggrieved, and felt that he had been badly treated. The English Press, catching fire from across the Channel, took up the controversy with heat, and the Opposition papers made capital against the Government out of it. *The Times* stoutly upheld the Viceroy's action in a series of stern and slightly provocative articles.

These were answered with heat on both sides of the water, and the whole story was gone over again and again. Finally, the Opposition decided to make the incident the occasion of a parliamentary attack, and Stanley told Clanricarde that, though privately he did not think there was much of a case, he intended " to give the Government a gallop over it."

This information was more serious, and Russell intimated to Clarendon that he would have to come over to London to defend his action if the Opposition really meant to bring on a debate.

The controversy blazed through November and December, but it was not until after the Christmas recess that the Opposition took parliamentary action. Stanley's motion demanding papers on Ireland was timed for February 18th, 1850. On that night Clarendon was in his place in the House of Lords. It was a peculiarly odious ordeal. For not only had Clarendon, himself an indifferent speaker, to encounter Stanley, whose brilliant oratorical powers had earned for him the nickname of the " Rupert of Debate," but he had also to defend his action in front of the very man to whom his conduct was said to have been unjust; for Lord Roden had decided to be in the House that night.

Before Stanley opened his case he and Clarendon rushed to each other and shook hands very cordially, like a couple of boxers setting to. And then it began.

Stanley spoke for nearly three hours, and no metaphor, illustration or quotation from the Classics, or other oratorical trick, was spared or forgotten that could in any way help to bolster up the case against the Viceroy. A large portion of the harangue was devoted to an attempt to prove the legality of the proceedings on July 12th, 1848. A still larger part was devoted to an attack upon Berwick's report (upon which the proceedings were taken), which, it was attempted to prove, was a prejudicial and trumped-up affair, conducted in the interests of the Lord Lieutenant, who was determined upon a conviction against the Orange leaders. Finally, and with every art that oratory could devise, Lord Roden's presence upon the Bench when magistrates refused to take evidence, though stigmatised as possibly indiscreet, was vindicated in law and defended in fact. It was a brilliant discourse, delivered in Stanley's best style, and what it lacked in conviction it made up for in persuasive artifice, of which Stanley himself was a master.

In comparison with this finished work of art Clarendon's reply was a somewhat tame affair. But the facts were on his side, and his ungarnished statement of the course of events which led him to dismiss Lord Roden from the Commission of the Peace favourably impressed a House most of whose members were already convinced of the justice of his cause. Even Stanley knew that there was no case against the Government, and his attack was only in the nature of a demonstration. Clarendon, of course, had prepared his case with the aid of the highest legal experts in Ireland. When he sat down it was felt that he had completely vindicated his action and come honourably through a trying ordeal. Had he been a more practised debater he might have made more of the occasion. He might have pursued his adversaries and heaped ridicule and ignominy on their heads, for his case was watertight, and, moreover, it involved principles which might have been made to soar into heaven, to the burning shame of all who dared to attack them. In Stanley's hands the materials he had would have been crushing. "They would have been very powerful," sighs Greville, "if Lord Lansdowne had had them; but as it was," he concludes, "it was very well."*

All Clarendon's friends were pleased, and he had a very good Press next day. As for himself, he was satisfied at the result of his speech and immensely relieved that the whole affair was over. "Clarendon called on me yesterday," says Greville, "very happy at his success of the night before. There is a pretty general opinion that he made out a very good case and that Stanley's was a failure. The latter made one or two great mistakes, and was detected in one very discreditable attempt. He quoted from an

* Greville *Journals*.

My Lord Stanley

LORD CLARENDON SHAKING ALL THE BRAN OUT OF
THE DOLLY BRAE AFFAIR.

PLATE 5

Punch, March 2, 1850. *Reproduced by kind permission of the Editor.*

Act of Parliament, reading an extract from it, but stopping short at that part of the clause that would have upset his own argument."

This piece of chicanery was capped by Lord Roden, who read out to their lordships part of a letter written by himself to Clarendon, offering to resign from the magistracy, but stopped short of the second half of the letter, in which he said he hoped Clarendon would not accept his resignation because it would be such a triumph for the Catholics if he did, which would be a pity, because, as he said, "we had now got them down, and would be able to keep them down." Clarendon told Greville that he had been sorely tempted to quote the latter half of the letter, since Lord Roden himself had quoted the former, and that it was with great difficulty that he had refrained.

So the controversy which had blazed for six months died down, and Clarendon felt he had rid himself of an incubus by his speech in the House of Lords on February 18th.

§ 2

It was good to be in England again, and he stayed over for some days after the event. He found all London talking of foreign affairs, and it was gradually borne in upon him that Lord Palmerston had been behaving in a very peculiar manner. In fact, "Pam" was at his tricks again. Wherever he dined he heard talk of the monstrous action of the Foreign Minister in defending the cause of the dreadful Don Pacifico and the amiable, if slightly mad, Mr. Finlay, who was writing a history of Greece. What was it all about? Gradually he pieced the story together. Mr. Finlay, it appeared, owned a field in Athens, for which, as it transpired afterwards, he had paid the not extravagant sum of ten pounds. In the reorganisation of the Palace Gardens the Greek authorities had taken over Mr. Finlay's field without a by-your-leave or for-your-leave, and postponed the question of compensation indefinitely. But Mr. Finlay was very attached to his field, and with the months that elapsed between the time that the Athenians took it away from him and the always vanishing-into-the-future moment at which they promised compensation Mr. Finlay had ample time to assess it at its true value to himself.

He finally assessed this at £1,500. So much for Mr. Finlay.

Don Pacifico, on the other hand, was a rich Levantine Jew with a house in Athens. Technically he was a British subject, being a "scorpion," or native of Gibraltar.

In disturbances at Athens, not unconnected with religion, the house of the rich Levantine Jew was burnt. And though the house itself was valuable, it was as nothing, so the Jew alleged, to the value of its contents, which, he said, his conscience could not allow him to assess at a lower figure than £30,000. Both being British subjects, they turned to the British Government for help. Palmerston was sceptical of the extent of the claims, but he was determined that redress of some kind should be forthcoming.

After interminable negotiations in Athens and London had borne no fruit, Palmerston took action, and in January, 1850, Admiral Parker was instructed to call in at the Piræus with several ships of the line and to take his orders from the British Ambassador. Palmerston informed the British Ambassador that he should let the authorities know that the claims must be settled in forty-eight hours, or the fleet would take action. When the threat proved unavailing, Greek merchantmen lying in and around the Piræus were seized to the extent of the British claims. All Europe was startled at this provocative, high-handed action, and the Russian Ambassador asked angrily for explanations.

It was at this moment that the French Ambassador in London, Drouhyn de Lhuys, intervened and offered to mediate between the Greek and the British Governments. Matters had got to about this point when Clarendon was in London. Everyone was incensed at this diplomatic crisis which had appeared from nowhere.

At the outset Lord John had stigmatised the whole affair "as unworthy the interference of the British Lion," and had probably dismissed it temporarily from his mind. And then in the mass of official papers with which Cabinet statesmen are daily inundated much of the correspondence relating to it must have passed unnoticed. Palmerston had a conjuror's way of slipping material unassumingly through the hands of his colleagues without their being able to see it. Nor was he above altering a despatch unequivocally, when the red box returned to him, even when it returned to him from Windsor or Buckingham Palace. But if harassed Ministers in the thick of affairs were apt, at times, to miss the implication of a despatch, two pairs of ever-vigilant eyes in the calm palace atmosphere made up for their deficiencies, and their owners pounced like hawks upon the unwary phrase or hasty communication, and sent it back to its perpetrator bleeding and mutilated with corrections.

This was peculiarly galling to Palmerston. He could, with luck, slip past his colleagues. But the Court was different. The royal pair actually read his despatches; they really cared. It was very provoking. He took to not sending quite all his despatches to Victoria; to overlooking, most unfortunately and quite inadvertently, a correction of the Queen's (it shouldn't happen again); to misinterpreting a memorandum of the Consort's (how could he forgive himself?); and to other subterfuges. But Victoria was not deceived, nor was Albert duped. They had taken the measure of

the hated " Pilgerstein," and now they proceeded to call his bluff.
They stormed and raged. They complained bitterly to Lord John;
they wrote sharp reprimanding letters to Palmerston himself. But
to no avail. Lord John, they cried together, was completely
under the thumb of the wretched Palmerston; and Palmerston
himself, though proffering abject humility, went on just as
before.

Over the preliminaries of the Greek affair Palmerston, as usual,
disregarded an alteration made by the Queen in one of his despatches. She received a copy of the despatch itself, without her
correction, two days after it had been sent. Victoria was furious.
"This must not happen again," she wrote. "Lord Palmerston
has a perfect right to state to the Queen the reasons for his disagreeing with her views, but she cannot allow a servant of the
Crown, and *her* Minister, to act contrary to *her* orders, and this
without her knowledge."

Strong words. But what would he care? thought Victoria. He
was unfeeling, incorrigible. Could no one stiffen the good Russell
to make a stand against his intolerable behaviour?

Clarendon was surprised at the situation, the more so since he
thought that Palmerston had mended his ways since the affair
of the Spanish marriages, during which, as it will be remembered, a despatch of Palmerston's, which had passed the Cabinet,
had had, at the Queen's instigation, to be completely recast.
Surely he had learned wisdom from this incident? But here they
all were in London saying that he was behaving worse than ever;
that the Queen was nearly out of her mind with humiliation; that
Albert was beside himself with rage. And certainly, whoever was
to blame, there was a considerable stir in Europe over this Greek
affair.

It was, therefore, not without the gravest apprehension that
Clarendon received a summons to dine *en petite comité* with the
royal pair. As it happened, his worst fears were more than fulfilled. All went well at the dinner-table, where Clarendon strained
his powers to the utmost to keep the conversation from dangerous
topics. But he was their defenceless prey, and after dinner in the
drawing-room they fell upon him mercilessly.

"The Queen exploded," says Greville, who had the scene
direct from Clarendon himself, "and went with the utmost vehe-
mence and bitterness into the whole of Palmerston's conduct, the
effects produced by it all over the world and her own feelings and
sentiments about it. He (Clarendon) could only listen and profess
his almost entire ignorance of the details. After she had done,
Prince Albert began, but, not finding time and opportunity for all
he wished to say, he asked him to call on him next day."*

* Greville *Journals*.

13

This was hard; but there was nothing for it, and Clarendon duly presented himself at Albert's lodgings. That interview lasted two and a half hours; and in the course of it the Prince went into every detail and poured forth without stint or reserve all the pent-up indignation, resentment and bitterness with which the Queen and himself had been boiling for a long time since. The situation, he said, jeopardised the position of the Crown. The remonstrances and complaints, the sentiments and resentments of other sovereigns —of the King of Naples, the Emperor of Russia, for instance— directly affected the Queen's dignity as the sovereign and representative of the nation; and the consciousness that these sovereigns and all the world knew that she utterly disapproved of all that was done in her name, but that she was powerless to prevent it, was inconceivably mortifying and degrading.

In a pause in the harangue, Clarendon respectfully enquired whether the Queen or the Prince had remonstrated with the peccant Minister on those matters which so justly excited their strong feelings. Upon which Albert dilated upon the duplicity of the man; for, as he said, he was charming and reasonable to talk to—and, of course, they had talked to him on these matters, often, often—but although he promised everything at the time, he went on again just as before, and for a year now the Queen and he had never made mention of the matter to him, for they found it to be of no use.

Clarendon, through all this, was at pains to discover what was expected of him, and just why they had lit upon him as recipient of their confidences. The night before he had been unable to discover, but from something the Prince said in his interview with him the following day, it was borne in upon him that he was expected to go off and stiffen Russell against Palmerston's enormities, and to convey to the Prime Minister the full extent of royal feelings on the present conduct of foreign affairs.

This was both awkward and distasteful to Clarendon. It was one thing to disapprove of Palmerston's behaviour; it was quite another thing to have it attacked from outside and to be the recipient of confidences directly derogatory to a colleague. What made it all the more difficult was that Clarendon thoroughly sympathised with the Royals, and deprecated Palmerston's behaviour even as strongly as they did. And there was also his own peculiar position in regard to Palmerston to consider. That old distrust that the Palmerstons had conceived of him many years ago was by no means allayed yet, and if Pam got to hear that this interview which Clarendon had had with the Queen and the Prince Consort had exclusively concerned himself, his suspicions would be enhanced a hundredfold.

However, it was a royal command that he should go to the

Prime Minister with this tale of woe, and there was nothing for it but to obey.

Russell, whom he found in a conciliatory mood, blinked up at him sympathetically. "Oh, so you've had that, too," he said with a sigh. Clarendon impressed upon him the urgency of placing some sort of restraint upon Palmerston, since the Court were so enraged that, given some further provocation, the royal pair might take it into their heads to do something really rash. Russell promised to do what he could, and Clarendon left him, feeling that there his own responsibility in the matter ended.

But he was disquieted in mind. Nothing, he felt, could prevent a storm; and he only prayed that Russell, never a very tactful person, would have the sense to handle both Victoria and Palmerston with sufficient diplomacy to prevent disaster. He expected that Russell would try to induce Palmerston to accept the Colonies or some other post, where his interests and those of the Court would not be so likely to clash. But he knew Palmerston too well to imagine for a moment that he would accept it. The trouble was that the Court and Palmerston both suffered under the delusion that the conduct of foreign affairs was their own *exclusive* province, and both sides resented any interference from whatever quarter it came. It was a ticklish situation, for Clarendon was perfectly well aware that Russell's Government could not exist without Palmerston's presence in it. He wondered whether Russell was equally aware of this fact. He suspected not.

The storm, he thought, would break over the Greek affair, and, back in Ireland again, Clarendon awaited developments in that quarter with feelings of faint misgiving. And he had not long to wait.

Palmerston's overbearing treatment of Drouhyn de Lhuys in France's attempt to mediate between the Greek and British Governments caused that gentleman finally to lose his temper. He sued to his Government for leave to be withdrawn, and departed in a ruffle of fury on May 15th.

Simultaneously arrived a despatch from St. Petersburg angrily demanding whether England "intended to disengage herself from every obligation, as well as from all community of action, and to authorise all the Great Powers on every fitting opportunity to recognise towards the weak, no other rule but their own will, no other right but their own physical strength."

At this John Russell of a sudden came to life. And he was very, very angry. Hitherto, he had judged Palmerston's conduct more or less in a detached manner, and had concentrated his energies on keeping the peace between the Court and the Foreign Office. No particular incident had occurred up to now to bring home to him the possible dangers of Palmerston's behaviour. But now quite suddenly he found the Government of which he was the head involved in a first-class European row, with diplomats departing and monarchs raining despatches upon his defenceless head.

Charles Greville, nosing round for gossip in this truly exciting situation, found Russell very set and determined. Palmerston had overshot the limit, this time, he said. His action, of course, would have to be defended, since the responsibility for it fell upon the Cabinet as a whole. But after the Session, Palmerston must go from the Foreign Office. It was intolerable that the British Government should find itself perpetually at loggerheads with the whole civilised world through the independent action of one of its members.

§ 3

Such was John Russell's mood on the eve of Stanley's motion of no-confidence in the Government, which was arranged for June 17th. This time the facts were (or appeared to be) on Stanley's side, and he made a crushing attack on the Government. The House divided, and the Government was beaten by 37 votes. Now this, which was under the circumstances fairly inevitable, produced a curious reaction in Russell. And for this reason. It happened that that arch-intriguer, Dorothea de Lieven, was in England, and that she had been largely instrumental in rallying her Tory friends to the attack. Russell was furious with Palmerston; but he was not going to allow Russian backstair influence to change the course of English politics, and he hinted as much wherever he went.

All now depended on the House of Commons vote. That provocative gentleman, Mr. Roebuck, placed a motion defending the Government on the order paper for June 20th. The debate upon it began two nights later. Upon this debate depended the fate of the Ministry. It was a case of justification. Could the Government get away with it? Could Palmerston persuade the House, his fellow-countrymen, and the world at large that he was justified in the course he had taken? As a matter of fact he could, and, moreover, he did. But very few at the opening of that fateful debate imagined that the Government would be in at the end of it—still less that Palmerston would be more firmly established than ever at the Foreign Office. But so it proved.

On the first night, and while the attack upon him was developing and the despatches were being produced, Palmerston said nothing. Then, on the second night, he rose shortly before 10 o'clock. He spoke without a single note or memorandum for nearly five hours, from the dusk of a summer evening to the dawn of the next day. It was a remarkable feat of mental and physical endurance, since it must be remembered that he was then in his sixty-sixth year. He entered into the minutest analysis of his conduct of the Greek affair, taking always his stand upon the thesis that the life and property of British subjects abroad must be protected by the Home Government. He then went over a wider field, reviewing and vindicating the policy he had pursued in relation to Belgium, Holland, Spain, France, Switzerland and Italy. He concluded by challenging the verdict of the House whether the principles that had guided the foreign policy of the Government had been proper and fitting. Surely, as a subject of ancient Rome could hold himself free from indignity by saying "Civis Romanus sum," so also a British subject in a foreign land should be able with equal assurance to turn to his Government at home, certain he, too, of protection against injustice and wrong.

It was a brilliant and completely convincing piece of oratory. His stout defence of British interests: his "Civis Romanus sum": his masterly exposition of the Whig foreign policy—all carried the House with him. It was useless for Gladstone to leap to his feet and ask the House "what *was* a Roman citizen?" and to paint such a person as a member of a privileged caste holding all nations bound down by subjection and fear. The feeling in the House was better expressed by Sir Robert Peel—himself the leader of Opposition—who said that the "speech made them all proud of the man who delivered it."

It was nearly a quarter to three when Lord Palmerston sat down, and, as Kathy wrote in her journal two days afterwards, "at that moment he had triumphed over a great mass of educated opinion, over that mighty potentate, *The Times*, over two branches of the legislature, over the Queen and the Prince, and most of the Cabinet he sits in, besides all foreign nations."

It was true. From that moment Lord Palmerston became the most popular statesman in England, and he never lost his popularity. It was now more than ever impossible to dislodge him from the Foreign Office, and Russell was pledged to sink or swim with him in that capacity. As for the Court, they were routed foot and horse.

Clarendon, in spite of his disapproval, was genuinely delighted at the success of his old chief:

"I never read a speech," he writes to his brother-in-law, Cornewall Lewis, "with greater satisfaction . . . his perfect mastery of the subject—the order and lucid arrangement of his details—the well-sustained interest—the varied style of his oratory—the good temper and good taste with which he handled such a legion of bitter assailants—can never have been surpassed anywhere, notwithstanding the harassing ordeal he has gone through and the load of ordinary business pressing upon him.   To speak for five hours without turning a hair, or moistening his lips, or losing his voice, or missing any point that was useful, exhibits really an amount of physical and mental power almost incredible in a man of his age.   It places him on a pinnacle of popularity at home, whatever it may do abroad, and completely settles the question about which I never had a doubt, that no change in the Foreign Office is possible, and that Lord John must either go *on* with him, or go *out* with him."

CHAPTER XV

END OF THE VICEROYALTY

§ 1

BUT, eighteen months later, Nemesis overtook the resourceful Viscount; and this time his misdemeanour was not even made a question of argument, still less of parliamentary debate. He received his *démission* at the hands of Russell himself. The Prime Minister's patience was exhausted, and his temper was up. Not that he had any rancour against Palmerston personally. It was just that he found him impossible to work with as a Cabinet Minister, and he thought he had better go. What he did not realise was just how powerful Palmerston would be as a free lance. He thought he could carry on the Government without him. In an ideal society this might have been possible. Had the Foreign Secretary received his dismissal with a bow and a smile and a wave of the hand, all might have been well. What Russell did not allow for was an offended Palmerston, a bitterly hurt and infuriated Palmerston, a Palmerston who was not thinking in terms of pure politics at all, but in terms of brute personalities. Just how dangerous such an entity could be Russell was to find to his cost. It was, indeed, a most human situation, and, as it happened, Clarendon himself was involved.

As "men and not measures" was the crux of the affair, everything that resulted from it somehow took on a personal aspect. Public life, for a time, became split up into the human elements that composed it, and we find everybody connected with the incident—Clarendon not excepted—acting from deeply personal motives.

Clarendon's part in the affair, thrust upon him as it was, worked out well for him, better perhaps than he could have foreseen. But his behaviour (which in terms of politics was the refusal of the Foreign Office at this juncture) was very difficult to explain to a world that was not permitted behind the scenes; and the misunderstanding of his motives produced great bitterness in him, and enhanced a hundredfold his already growing distaste for public life.

We left him watching the development of the Don Pacifico affair from his desk in Dublin. Not much of interest happened

in Ireland in the months that followed. Clarendon's work there
was really finished. The famine was over, the seeds of revolution stamped out, law and order restored. Large tracts of land
were changing hands through the operation of the Encumbered
Estates Act, and in these favourable conditions trade was beginning to revive. Some excitement was caused over John Russell's
"No popery" cry in England, which had, as might be expected,
unfortunate repercussions in Ireland. Something of a stir was
also caused by the temporary eclipse of the Government over a
motion of Locke King's which took place in February, '51. A
Cabinet crisis ensued in which Stanley and Lord John fluttered
round Victoria, the Peelites sat in conclave, and Brougham wrote
post haste to Clarendon to say that he (Clarendon) was their only
hope and urging him to make the attempt to form a Government
if he were sent for. Every post brought contradictory accounts
of what was happening, and Clarendon was highly alarmed. He
was genuinely relieved when news came that the Queen had sent
for Lord John again and that the Cabinet had consented to
resume. All was quiet again in high places when in the early
days of December came the startling account of Louis Napoleon's
coup d'état.

Clarendon was interested. On the whole he approved. He
welcomed the change that threw one man's will across the inefficiency and intrigue of French affairs.

"Louis Napoleon seems likely to stand his ground," he writes
to Cornewall Lewis, "and it is impossible not to wish it: however
much we may dislike what he has done; for if he had failed, the
Socialist horrors that have taken place in some departments would
have been perpetrated all over France."

The British Government was cautious. Lord John watched
the trend of events with a puckered brow. He had no wish to
commit himself to the new régime in France till he had some kind
of assurance that it was likely to survive—for a time at any rate.
Revolutions in France were apt to repeat themselves, and it was
early days to pronounce with certainty upon the success of this
one. Lord Normanby was British Ambassador in Paris, and on
December 6th the Cabinet sent him instructions that he was to
refrain from any interference in the internal affairs of France, to
observe a perfect neutrality between conflicting parties, and not
to express himself in any way as to the Prince President's action.

Now Palmerston, as might be expected, highly approved of
the *coup d'état*, and thought it the best possible thing that could
have happened to France. Unfortunately he said as much, in
an expansive manner, to Walewski, the French Ambassador, who
had an interview with him during these days. In view of the
strict neutrality which the British Government were trying to

preserve his action was certainly indiscreet. But more indiscreet still was Walewski's reaction to it; for, whether innocently or not, he took Palmerston's personal view to be a pronouncement of Government policy, and he wrote immediately to the Quai d'Orsay intimating that the Prince President had nothing to fear from England in the existing crisis. That he should have done so was either very innocent or very malevolent, and in either case it was very unfortunate, for as Palmerston said later in his own defence, if every word a Secretary of State may let fall in friendly conversation with a foreign Ambassador is to be taken as a solemn pronouncement of policy, then the whole Foreign Office system is at fault and the relations between the Foreign Secretary and the Heads of Missions become a farce.

Perhaps, if matters had gone no further, Palmerston's mistake could have been covered up. But further the relentless Viscount insisted on pushing them. Truth to tell, he was thoroughly enlivened and excited over the French situation, and impartiality was never his strong suit. Lord Normanby in Paris was now surprised to receive a despatch, undoubtedly signed by his chief, expressing the highest approval of the Prince President's action and positively chiding the British Ambassador for his lukewarmness on the subject. This was very odd, thought Lord Normanby; and he referred back to a despatch that he had received no more than a week before, enjoining him to preserve the strictest neutrality and not to hint by so much as the lift of an eyebrow that the British Government favoured one side more than the other. His perplexities were hardly lightened when he met Turgot, who thanked him in the name of France for the loyal support of his Government. Lord Normanby was now seriously alarmed, and began to think that either he himself or the Government in Whitehall had been visited with madness. And he wrote post-haste to London to know what it all meant and what he was expected to say. And then it came out—the indiscreet conversation with Walewski, the despatch to Normanby, Turgot's misunderstanding—and Palmerston stood convicted without a word to say for himself, like a schoolboy caught robbing an orchard.

§ 2

Clarendon was watching events from Dublin, little dreaming that they would in any way affect himself, when on a certain night just before Christmas—it was December 21st—the bag arrived from London, and in it, among other things, was a sealed letter to himself in Lord John's handwriting. Opening it he read, and re-read, its contents with consternation and surprise. This is what he saw:

December 20th, 1851.

" Dear Clarendon,

" A serious difference has arisen between Palmerston and me. He had some conversation with Walewski about the President's *coup d'état*, which he (Palmerston) said he approved. A despatch was afterwards written by Palmerston, by the Queen's desire, prescribing strict abstinence from interference in the national affairs of France.

" Normanby reported that Turgot told him that Walewski had reported to his Government the approbation of the President's act by Palmerston, and that two of his colleagues had mentioned it as the approbation of the British Government. I asked for an explanation. No reply. The Queen asked for an explanation through me. Next came a second despatch to Normanby declaring his (Palmerston's) own opinion in favour of the President, sent off to Paris without my knowledge. After this an explanation to the Queen, consisting of a defence of the act of Louis Napoleon. I told him that was not the question—the question was whether, without concert, he should have expressed any opinion. I said that these violations of prudence and decorum had become so frequent that I thought he could not, with any advantage to the country, hold any longer the seals of Office. He declares himself ready to give them up. I have laid the correspondence before the Queen. Supposing the Cabinet to be of opinion that we can go on, the question of his successor arises. I am inclined to Granville, knowing your disinclination to succeed Palmerston, but everyone will look to you as the person most capable of holding the office. It is very possible that the Cabinet may say that no one but you is fit to succeed, and the country may echo that opinion. I wish you therefore to be prepared for what may happen. Any further lights on this subject I shall be glad to receive, as I am much in need of them."

So it had come at last—the blow that Clarendon had been dreading. It was exactly the concurrence of events which he most hoped would *not* happen. And it had happened. Everyone would now look to him to fill the vacant Foreign Office. Russell as much as said so in his letter. It was assumed on all sides that he would take it. He had been talked of for the Foreign Office for the past five years. It was known that his talents lay all in that direction and that he himself would care for the post. And he was going to refuse it—for two reasons, neither of which would sound satisfactory to his friends or to the public. The first was that he was determined not to accept the Foreign Office—never to accept the Foreign Office—save with the complete approbation of Palmerston. This, he knew, both *was* and would appear to be a confession of weakness. A man who believed in himself and his own powers, an ambitious man, would have seized the opportunity thus offered him, would have pushed through to success, whatever might be against him and whoever might be sore at his advancement. But Clarendon was not an ambitious man, nor was he a violent man; and he knew perfectly well that he could only be successful at the Foreign Office with Palmerston's whole-hearted approval. It would hardly be pleasant to have to admit as much. But, after all, the situation was none of his own choosing; it had been thrust upon him. He reacted to it in the only way he felt to be possible under the circumstances. His second reason for refusing also related to Palmerston. Clarendon was a politician, but he was also a human being; and the old distrust that the Palmerstons felt for him, dating back now for almost ten years, genuinely grieved him, was something he wished removed from his life on purely personal grounds. Life was not all politics nor all just a matter of "getting on." If he refused the Foreign Office at a moment when everybody expected him to take it, his action would at least have the effect of laying that inconvenient ghost for ever.

"I am exceedingly obliged to you," he wrote the following morning to Russell, "for having thought of my objections to occupy Palmerston's place, which are as strong as ever. For some utterly unfounded reason (as Heaven knows, I never coveted any office, much less his) Palmerston has always been suspicious of me, and if I become Foreign Secretary, nothing would ever persuade him or his numerous friends, in and out of Parliament, that I had not had some hand in his disgrace, and that they must avenge it, by thwarting me in every way that his vast knowledge and ingenuity can devise. This would be a great disadvantage, and my objection rests, therefore, quite as much on public as private grounds.

"I think Granville would do the business very well under your guidance. . . . Your expectation that the Cabinet and the Public might demand my services, is, of course, very gratifying to me; but you know how I estimate my own abilities, and I fear those who think better of them than I do, will be disappointed. I feel too, that an absence of four and a half years from the Cabinet, and from England, during which time I have only studied Foreign Affairs in the newspapers almost in itself disqualifies me for the Foreign Office at this critical moment.

"His dictis, I now leave my fate in your hands. If I can be spared from a task to which I don't feel equal, I shall be very happy. But if it be otherwise ordained, then I must rely upon your friendship clearly to explain to the Cabinet, and if possible, to Palmerston, that you are aware of my long-standing objections to the Foreign Office, that I accept it with reluctance, and that, until last night, I was totally unaware of any disagreement between yourself and Palmerston. You have my hearty prayers that whatever you resolve may be for the good of the country and your own honour and satisfaction."

Not a very pretty letter to feel obliged to write. But he wrote it; and, moreover, he wrote another in the same sense to the Duke of Bedford. For some reason this letter arrived first; and the greater part of the following from Lord John is based upon it:

"December 23rd. I will give you as fair an account as I can of what has passed since I wrote.

"The Cabinet in the first place approved of my conduct, and consented to go on as a Government. In the second place they gave me their opinion that although Granville was very fit for the Foreign Office, your appointment would give greater confidence and satisfaction to the public. I carried this opinion to the Queen, and told her, at the same time, of your letter to my brother. She expressed great esteem for you, and great admiration of your very handsome conduct. The result, however, was that it was plain to me that the anxieties consequent upon Palmerston's conduct had greatly preyed upon her peace of mind. There was an evident dread of intrigues so clearly pointed out by you as likely to be set on foot by the friends and admirers of Palmerston. Seeing this disposition and how much it was shared by the Prince, I proposed not to fill up the Office until I heard from you in reply to what I should write today.

"Seeing all the difficulties and grateful to you for the manner in which you have behaved to me, I tell you fairly that what would give me most ease would be that you should waive the Office for yourself and acquiesce in the appointment of Lord Granville. From what you wrote to the Duke, I conclude this course would be agreeable to you.

"I have had for five years a most harassing warfare, not in the Cabinet, but as Umpire between Windsor and Broadlands.

"I have just received your letter. It is as handsome as possible, and relieves me from all difficulty.

"2 p.m. I have seen Granville, and offered him the Office which he accepts."

But Clarendon was bitter—bitter at having to show himself up in a none too becoming light, bitter because the reasons he gave for declining the offer were accepted without demur. It is one thing to refuse a proffered crown, but quite another to have the thing snatched from one's gracefully declining hand with such evident alacrity and relief.

Against Russell he had no feeling. Russell had been placed in a very awkward position, and Clarendon had got him out of it. He felt quite magnanimous towards Russell. But that the Queen should have clutched so readily at what he knew must have seemed to her a very poor excuse filled him with surprise and resentment. He supposed he must have offended in some way, and he searched his memory for the cause. He mused aloud on the subject, rather viciously, to Cornewall Lewis.

"Once when I was in the Cabinet," he writes, "I told them *the truth* about their wish to send troops to defend the imbecile Queen of Portugal in her despotism; and, on other occasions, when I was not in the Cabinet, I gave them to understand that I was an unfit recipient of their grievances against Palmerston and Lord John. . . . Of course, this was all done most respectfully, and with ordinary men and women it would not have engendered distrust; but to Kings and Queens it probably appeared mutinous."

"The Queen and Prince," he continues, "are wrong in wishing that Courtiers rather than Ministers should conduct the affairs of the Country. . . . They labour under the curious mistake that the Foreign Office is their peculiar department, and that they have a right to control, if not to direct, the Foreign Policy of England."

There is no doubt that he was suffering a keen revulsion to public life at about this time. His family tried to spur him on to higher flights, but he would have none of their counsel.

"You and George Lewis," he writes to his sister, "are disposed to be complimentary to me, and to think I am ambitious, self-confident, full of zeal for public service, and capable of great and successful efforts; whereas the fact is that whatever may formerly have existed of these qualities, no longer does so; indeed, they have been smothered in this country where a residence of five years, nearly, has produced a contempt for human nature in general, and political life in particular that I cannot get over. You can have no idea what my depression of spirits and disgust of public life amount to."

And in answer to a letter of Cornewall Lewis to him he writes:

". . . I agree with your view of public life, but it leads me to a different conclusion to yours. It attracts you. It repels me. You would be satisfied with the ultimate appreciation of your conduct. I feel that having endured every kind of obloquy and moral torture, it is small satisfaction to be informed that you are not the scoundrel you are represented to be."

But to return to the crisis in London. There was a small core in the Whig party who, like the Court, feared and hated Palmerston for his dangerous and independent conduct of foreign affairs. It was with feelings of unmixed relief that this group heard of the tyrant's downfall.

"Palmerston is out!" shouted young Granville as he burst into Greville's room at five o'clock on December 22nd. "Palmerston is actually, really, irretrievably out!" and Greville nearly fell off his chair with excitement. It was just after the Cabinet had broken up. Granville had been asked not to attend, and told that he would be informed the reasons why afterwards. "It is none of the things we talked over," he cried excitedly. "Pam is out; the offer of the Foreign Office goes to Clarendon to-night, and if he refuses, which, of course, he will not, it is to be offered to me."

Two days later Greville writes in his journal:

"To my unspeakable astonishment Granville informed me yesterday that Clarendon had refused the Foreign Office, and that he had accepted it. . . . I have not yet heard from Clarendon and am curious to know his motives for refusing an appointment which I should have thought would be not only peculiarly agreeable to him, but which would have enabled him to quit Ireland in so honourable a manner."

If Clarendon was sore at the lack of enthusiasm shown for his services, Palmerston was far more so at the treatment which had been meted out to him. Indeed, he was deeply mortified and hurt. He argued that the grounds for his dismissal were totally insufficient, alleging, with some truth, that his conversation with Walewski had been a purely personal affair. When he went on to say that his letter to Normanby was also of a private nature, those who had seen a copy of it lifted their eyebrows, for, as a matter of fact, the letter was couched in the strongest possible terms, and anybody might have been excused for considering it as a definite injunction.

When the Cabinet met on December 22nd the Palmerstons believed that the colleagues would rally to Palmerston's defence and refuse to sanction his dismissal. That they did not do so was a further mortification; and their wrath fell all the more heavily upon Lord John and the Court.

". . . John has behaved like a little blackguard," writes Emily to her brother Frederick Lamb, "giving in to their (the Court's) plans, and trying to put it upon a private opinion expressed to Walewski (which bound the Government to no course, and left it quite unshackled).

"I think the House of Commons will be very angry at this Granville appointment—a young lordling who has done nothing but dance attendance on Albert, and patch up differences among the Palace Commissioners, who has whispered a speech or two about the Board of Trade and the one at Paris, in which he put forward his having passed his holidays in his Father's home at Paris, and having married a French woman. . . . It is so lucky," she adds, throwing grammar to the winds, "for an effervescing woman to have such a calm and placid husband which no events can irritate or make him lose his temper."*

* Quoted from Guedalla's *Palmerston*.

So Granville went to the Foreign Office, and Clarendon remained on at his post in Dublin.

But now there was a visible term to his labours in Ireland. Lord John, sincerely grateful to him for his behaviour to himself, was willing to offer him anything—the Embassy at Paris, for instance. "This George declines," writes Kathy in her journal, "but begs on the score of the expense and annoyance of the Dublin season and the ill-health that it entails upon him, that the offer to the Duke of Newcastle should be made immediately. This," she adds ominously, "Lord John ought to do. And I mean to insist on it." The entry was made on Christmas Eve, 1851. And on Christmas Day, Charles Greville was writing in his diary:

"I received a letter from Clarendon yesterday afternoon with his reasons for declining [the Foreign Office]. They are very poor ones, and amount to little more than his being afraid of Palmerston, first of his (Palmerston's) suspecting it was an intrigue to get rid of him, and, secondly, of the difficulties Palmerston would throw in his way at the Foreign Office. He had advised Lord John to take Granville, but he said if it was absolutely necessary, he would accept. I can't help thinking he will be mortified at his advice being so immediately taken. His conduct has been, to my mind, very pusillanimous and unworthy of him."*

Yes, they would all be saying that of him. But it couldn't be helped. . . .

§ 3

Meanwhile Palmerston, though outwardly his bland, unruffled self, was by no means calm and placid within. In fact he was in a blind rage with John Russell. He considered that that little man had stabbed him in the back, but he was very far from crumpling up, like Cæsar, with a mere "*Et tu, Brute.*" The noble Viscount was all for stabbing back—hard. And, indeed, when they saw him take his place in the House of Commons—not as usual on the Treasury Bench but as a mere rank-and-filer of the party—the Whigs, or some of them, were filled with feelings of apprehension and alarm. The same smiling countenance, the same foppish exterior, the dyed whiskers, the tightly fitting frock-coat, the extravagant waistcoat—what machinations might not be going on beneath this smooth and polished façade? True, he came badly out of the debate upon his dismissal, but John Russell, so to speak, hid behind the Crown, and Palmerston could only rebut his accusations by raising a constitutional point on just how far the Crown has a right to interfere in the matter

* Greville *Journals.*

of despatches and letters of instruction, and he was not prepared to do this for many reasons. He contented himself by defending his action on more general grounds, but the House was not convinced.

He had burked the question, and everybody, including himself, was aware of it. The general belief was that he was done for politically, and Disraeli at an evening party was even heard to remark that "there once *was* a Palmerston." But it was all very well to dismiss him with a shrug of the shoulders and a wave of the glove. There he was, bland and smiling, a little ominous in his new seat in the House, himself and yet not himself. The Tories took heart, and looked him up and down with new eyes. He would be a great acquisition to the party; so forcible, a little independent-minded, perhaps, but what vigour. . . . The Peelites, too, regarded him a little wistfully. After all, he *was* sound on Free Trade, but, then, perhaps a little too uncertain and not quite orthodox, if you came to think of it, on any article of party creed, and, of course, anathema to the Court. But still, the House of Commons was full of regretful sighs and questioning looks. But Palmerston sat in his seat unmoved. He was a Whig, and he meant to remain a Whig. The party might think they were done with him. That was curious, because he was by no means done with the party.

The Session opened briskly, and Russell explained a new franchise scheme. All seemed well, and he followed it up with a Militia Bill. In the debate upon this Palmerston innocently proposed an amendment. It was no direct opposition to the Bill, but merely the suggested alteration of one word, the word "regular" for the word "local," with its implication that men raised and serving in one part of the country could, at need, be drilled and made to serve in another.

It was a mild enough proposition, and so far from combating the principle of the Bill, it seemed in reality to extend it. But there was the glint of steel in the Viscount's little amendment. And in the lobbies it flashed out and was thrust right home. The amendment was carried against the Government by a majority of thirteen, and Russell, taking it as a vote of no confidence, resigned at once. Of course, it was most unfortunate, and Emily wrote round to say that her husband "did not intend to put out the Government." And Palmerston hardly supposed that the Government chose the Militia Bill "as a Parachute to avoid a ruder descent." But not so in private.

In private he wrote like a naughty schoolboy to his brother:

"I have had my tit-for-tat with John Russell," he said, "and I turned him out on Friday last."

There was, for Clarendon at least, a sequel to this exhibition of ill-feeling and all that it had given rise to. And this sequel was altogether for the good. The Government was turned out in February. In March the Clarendons were home again for good. One of the first engagements that Clarendon fulfilled in London on his return was to call at Carlton Gardens in answer to an invitation from Palmerston himself. He found the late Foreign Secretary alone, and for two hours he discussed with Clarendon all that had happened in the past two months. He produced the letters and papers, going into everything in the greatest detail. They talked as friends together; and from the complete frankness of Palmerston's manner towards him, Clarendon realised that that old cloud of distrust which had laid so heavily across their relationship for the past ten years had been lifted once and for all.

CHAPTER XVI
SECRETARY OF STATE

§ 1

SO the Clarendons were back in England after their five years' exile in Ireland. The farewells were said; the testimonials and addresses received and answered; the valedictory speeches delivered and replied to. It had been quite an arduous task, this doffing of the intricate harness of State, and it had taken the best part of two months to accomplish. But now that it was all over and they were home again, they could assess what in Ireland it had been impossible to assess—the extent to which the Irish Lieutenancy had increased Clarendon's reputation as a personage of weight in public affairs. Wherever they went they were looked upon with new eyes; and there is no doubt that Clarendon was now considered as one of the leaders of the Whig party. This, as may be imagined, was very gratifying; and it was all the more apparent since the accommodating part that Clarendon had played in the late Government crisis had set him right with all sides. The Queen and the Prince Consort received him with open arms, feeling, as they did, that he had saved them from Palmerston's vengeance. Lord John became quite human when he saw him, conscious that Clarendon had got him out of a grave difficulty; while Palmerston, as we have already described, finally forgot the old distrust he had of him and greeted him as a friend and equal.

Now an ambitious politician could have made much capital out of this favourable situation. Indeed, had he been one of the strong, un-silent men of that age, Clarendon might—he almost certainly would—have become leader of the Whig party in the political orientations that followed the fall of the Government. For the rift between Russell and Palmerston seemed absolute at the moment; Lord Lansdowne's age and health hardly permitted him to assume such a post; and Gladstone's hour had not yet struck. There were not a few among the Whig party who looked with a new interest at Clarendon as he went about London picking up the old threads of his life again after his five years' exile.

But the Court knew his wishes on the subject of ever becoming Prime Minister, and so, for that matter, did John Russell, while Palmerston, who did not, expressed himself perfectly ready to serve under him. But Clarendon was not going to put his head into that noose. He was, he knew, efficient and useful. He was a good friend to the great ones of the earth. He could work with them, advise them, and propitiate them. But he was not one of themselves; and it irked him when people thought that he was. He had no political initiative—he made no claim to it—and no individual political vision such as drives men on to seize the reins of power in order to put their vision to the test. So, after basking pleasantly in the warmth of approbation with which he found himself temporarily surrounded in London and making it clear to all and sundry that, whatever happened, it would not be he that would be coming forward to lead the Whigs, he retired with much relief to the Grove, which needed his attention after five years' absence.

And at the Grove, too, Clarendon settled down to enjoy the family life of which he had been deprived for so long. There were great tribal reunions in Hertfordshire that summer; and the Grove became the dumping-ground for innumerable children of Villiers origin. Theresa came with her three Lister children—Villiers, Thérèse and Alice. Then there was Edward's widow, Elizabeth —vivacious and lisping as ever—with *her* brood, the boy Ernest and the girls Maria-Theresa, Edith and Elizabeth (twins these last); not to speak of a surge of progeny from brother Montague's vicarage (not yet exchanged for the Bishop's Palace at Durham).

As hosts to this large and motley flock, of all sizes and ages, were Clarendon's own children—Constance, Alice, Emily, and the two boys Hyde and George. Of these, Constance was the eldest, a girl of almost twelve now, and Alice was scarcely a year younger. Then came the eldest son, Lord Hyde, a boy of seven, then Emily, then George, who was only five at the time of which we are speaking. True to mid-Victorian traditions of motherhood, Kathy, though she had been married for nearly thirteen years, was still producing. Indeed, an " interesting event " was expected that summer. (It occurred on August 13th, when a third boy, Francis,* was born to the Clarendons.)

So the Grove came alive again, and the grazing deer raised surprised and angry heads as their peace was broken into by the shrill, unpleasant cries of children. In the frightful ginghams and pork-pie hats of the period the girls bowled their hoops and plagued their governesses, while the boys, proud of the strange old muzzle-loading weapons looted from the gun-room, went ferreting under the vigilant eye of a wildly bearded keeper, or set up cricket-stumps and bowled to each other in the park.

* Rt. Hon. Sir Francis Hyde Villiers, P.C., G.C.M.G., G.C.V.O., C.B. Sometime Assistant Under-Secretary for Foreign Affairs. Ambassador, Brussels. Died 1925.

And over this wide cousinship of leggy girls and large-limbed Villiers-looking boys, Clarendon presided in a genial and generous fashion. There are very few alive to-day who can remember the "Uncle Clarendon" of that period; but those who do, recall a tall, spare figure, slightly stooping at the shoulders, a face, chiselled and sensitive, with greying Regency whiskers, and fine-spun, thinning hair. They remember how he used to romp with them and play with them; and, above all, they recollect his laugh —infectious and delightful—that started as a slow gurgle and spread into a long, unrestrained ripple of amusement.

So the children played that summer, and Kathy lay out on the lawns expecting her child, with Mrs. George in attendance, very old now but still passionately interested in anything that concerned the family in any way. And sometimes through the hot afternoon would come the crunch of wheels on gravel, and a brake would arrive from Gorhambury full of Kathy's sisters and their progeny—Jane Caledon, fresh from Ireland, Emily Craven and Mary Folkestone. A second generation of Grimstons would descend and shout for their Villiers cousins while their mammas trooped decorously on to the lawn, wrapped in voluminous shawls, to enquire how "their Angel" was standing the heat.

The elections wore on, and it became obvious that the Whigs would be out. But—Whigs or Tories—did it seem to matter very much? The heavy, placid rule of Victoria absorbed them both and continued in undisturbed enchantment across the realm.

§ 2

Then, just to remind people, steeped as they were in the enormous security of a workable system, that after all even the socially august—even the great Victorians—were heirs to mortality at large, came the terrible, the shocking news from Walmer. The Duke was dead. It was impossible: it was incredible: but it was true. He died at twenty-five minutes past three on the afternoon of September 14th, sitting bolt upright in his chair at the castle. He was eighty-three, and deplorably deaf, but otherwise his faculties had remained unimpaired. And somehow people had come to look upon him as eternal, as if England without the Duke of Wellington was an idea impossible to conceive. Although he had been regular in his attendance in the House of Lords, he had spoken little and had not taken much active part in politics for the last three years before his death. But he had been there in the midst of things, an honoured and venerable figure, seeming, with his dignity and weight and the achievements imperishably associated with his name, to shed lustre on the present by recalling the glory of the past, England's prowess in the field, her prescience and her power. The whole nation mourned. Victoria rushed to her tablets.

"England's, or rather Britain's pride, her glory, her hero, the greatest man she ever produced, is no more," she wrote from Balmoral. . . . "One cannot think of this country without the Duke—an immortal hero! In him," she continues rapturously, "centred almost every honour a subject could possess. His position was the highest a subject ever had; above party, looked up to by all, revered by the whole nation, the friend of the Sovereign; and how simply he carried these honours! Not an eye," she concluded, knowing her England, "will be dry in the whole country."*

The new Parliament opened on November 11th, and on the 18th the State funeral took place. From Whitehall, up Constitution Hill and along Piccadilly, St. James' Street, Pall Mall, Charing Cross, the Strand, Fleet Street, Ludgate Hill to St. Paul's went the funeral car through streets lined with sorrowing spectators. On the steps of St. Paul's it was met by Prince Albert and the great officers of State. Following the choristers along the nave came the foreign marshals carrying the Duke's colours, and Prince Albert with the Sword of State before him. The coffin was conveyed upon a wheeled bier, the pall being flung back and the white feathers of the Duke's hat waving in the wind which swept up the nave. Dr. Milman, we are told, read the service in a clear and sonorous voice. At its conclusion, Garter-King-at-Arms stepped forward and proclaimed the style and titles of the Duke. A wand was broken and thrown down on the coffin, and the ceremony closed with the benediction pronounced by the Bishop of London. General officers were seen with tears openly coursing down their cheeks as they looked for the last time upon all that was mortal of their hero. "Honour to the people who so well knew how to reverence the illustrious dead!" exclaimed the new Prime Minister, Lord Derby, in the House of Lords, pronouncing his set funeral oration, while Disraeli signalised his first leadership of the Commons by a similar effusion in the Lower House. Similar? No, hardly. The stilted language, the mechanical periods, the hackneyed Classical allusion—what was all this from Disraeli, who knew so well how to move the House when he chose? The whole speech—how was it?—had a foreign, almost a Latin ring to it. Members were bored, disappointed and a little puzzled. Next day enlightenment came. It was discovered that he had lifted the whole speech, word for word, from Thiers' eulogy of a second-rate French marshal, Gouvion St. Cyr; and the *Daily News* published it side by side

* Queen Victoria's Diary.

with its French original, neatly prefixing it by a passage from his own father's works on literary plagiarism! And the world hardly knew whether to be more amused or outraged by this cynical imposture.

§ 3

Politically, two facts had become obvious from the moment John Russell resigned in February. One was that the Whigs, momentarily eclipsed and all at sixes and sevens over the rift between their party leaders, would be beaten at the elections. And the second was that given the state of the Tory Party, no team that Derby could get together would last for more than a few months. The Whigs might be disunited amongst themselves, but they could at least be trusted to vote in the same lobby in opposition to any controversial legislation that the Tories might bring in. It was correctly surmised that Derby would not command a settled majority in either House.

That being the case, it was necessary for Whig statesmen to look ahead and plan for that return to power which everyone felt could not be delayed for long.

The autumn was full of *pour-parlers* and suggestions for "shadow-Cabinets," and the exchange of views between the Duke of Bedford, Clarendon, Russell and Sir James Graham.

It was just at this moment that had Clarendon felt it in him to lead the Whig party he might have come forward and been first choice for the post of future Whig Prime Minister. Under his propitiatory sway, it is possible that Russell and Palmerston would have consented to serve together, forgetting the hateful past. As this was out of the question, and as no other purely Whig leader seemed forthcoming, a Coalition Government seemed indicated, and much correspondence passed between statesmen on this fruitful subject.

The difficulty was to make John Russell understand that he could not be at the head of a Coalition Government: that with the rift between himself and Palmerston still unbridged he could not, even in a Coalition Government, command a sufficient following in his own party to make his position as head of a combined Government at all feasible. Sir James Graham, with whom Russell was on very cordial terms at this time, undertook the task of gently intimating this to him. Russell replied without anger but with great firmness that he had long made up his mind that he would belong to no Government unless he could be its head. To accept any other post, he averred, would be "a degradation." Graham combated this idea, and dangled the memory of Fox in 1806 before his eyes.

Russell looked at the picture with the grave, uncertain eyes of a child, but found it unconvincing. The Duke of Bedford also reasoned with his brother, but received an angry letter for his pains.

Abandoning this line for the moment, they approached him delicately on the vexed question of Parliamentary Reform. Here he could not command a unanimity even in his own party. Palmerston and Lansdowne were vehemently against any further tampering with the franchise—at least for the present—and it was thought that the latter would refuse to join a Government if it were pledged to anything like the extent of reform which Russell had supposedly in mind. But here they found the little man unexpectedly amenable. Clarendon received a letter from him in which he said that he was not disposed to insist on the franchise question, and certainly should not propose it against the opinions and wishes of his many friends. This was much. And Clarendon took the letter hot-foot to the Duke of Bedford, who was greatly surprised at his brother's sudden yielding on this point. Emboldened by this news, the Duke invited Russell to meet Lord Aberdeen and Lord Lansdowne at Woburn, where, in the quiet atmosphere of a country house, they might have an opportunity of compounding their difficulties. By what arts of flattery, cajolery and temptation the two older statesmen charmed the reluctant Russell from his perch is not known. But when at the end of their conversations the Duke, who had not been present at them, asked his brother what course he thought the Queen ought to take in the event of a Ministerial crisis, he replied that, in his opinion, she ought to send first for Lord Lansdowne and then for Lord Aberdeen, and the intimation was that he would be willing to serve under either.

All seemed now ready for the future. And, as it proved, the future came upon them with a rush. The conversations at Woburn took place at the beginning of December. Three days later the Tory Government fell, and the Queen, as designed, immediately sent for Lord Lansdowne. But he excused himself from undertaking the task of forming a Government on the score of his age and ill-health. He was seventy-two and crippled with gout. The Queen, accordingly, sent for Lord Aberdeen. A day later she wrote to Russell in the following terms:

" Osborne,
" *December 19th, 1852.*

" The Queen has to-day charged Lord Aberdeen with the duty of forming an Administration, which he has accepted. The Queen thinks the moment to have arrived when a popular, efficient and durable Government could be formed by the sincere and united

efforts of all parties professing Conservative and Liberal opinions.
The Queen knowing this can only be effected by the patriotic
sacrifice of personal interests and feelings to the public, trusts
that Lord John Russell will, as far as he is able, give his valuable
and powerful assistance to the realisation of this object.''

So the gentle Aberdeen—loyal, conscientious, tolerant and just
—became head of the fateful Administration associated with his
name, and the struggle for places began.

It was an ironical Fate which at this moment called to the head
of affairs a man whose qualities and aspirations were set at naught
by the implacable march of events. For, loving peace, he was
dragged inevitably into war: and loving harmony, he was forced
to preside over a Cabinet the members of which were highly
individual and, in notable cases, mistrustful, jealous and scheming.
A true and loyal friend, his Administration was to fall from a
blow delivered from within, and by a colleague from whom he
had every reason to expect the highest consideration. That his
gentleness and high sense of behaviour never deserted him even
in this extremity is a tribute to the innate quality of the man; and
though his Government goes down to history as weak, unwieldy,
and almost criminally inefficient, nothing that can be said of it
seems in the least applicable to himself. He stands, unscathed,
a statesman of rare gifts, a gentleman of high honour and distinction. Fate, and his colleagues, were too much for him: that
was all.

From the outset his path was hardly a smooth one. ''I have
never passed a week so unpleasantly,'' writes Sir James Graham.
''It was a battle for places in hostile camps, and the Whigs disregarded fitness for the Public Service altogether. They fought
for their men as partisans, and all other considerations as well as
consequences were disregarded.'' That the Whigs said the same
of the Peelites cannot be denied; and it is difficult to discover
which side scrambled most for the plums of office. The disruption of the Whig party and the bitterness of the place-hunting
are amusingly reflected in a letter to Clarendon from Emily Eden
at about this time.

''Yesterday,'' she writes, ''Lady Mary Wood'' [Lord Grey's
daughter-in-law] ''called, in the last stages of Grey 'pee-aw-
ishness''—a rigid, despairing peevishness, which, in many people
would imply confirmed bad health with loss of friends and fortune, but with her meant that all the Greys had not got places.
Sir Charles Wood thought she had much better hold her tongue,
and indeed said so several times; and when she said if Lord John
went on in that way, he would lose all his followers, I said that
then I thought he might have a chance! . . .

''But then she went back to . . . the Militia Bill, and things

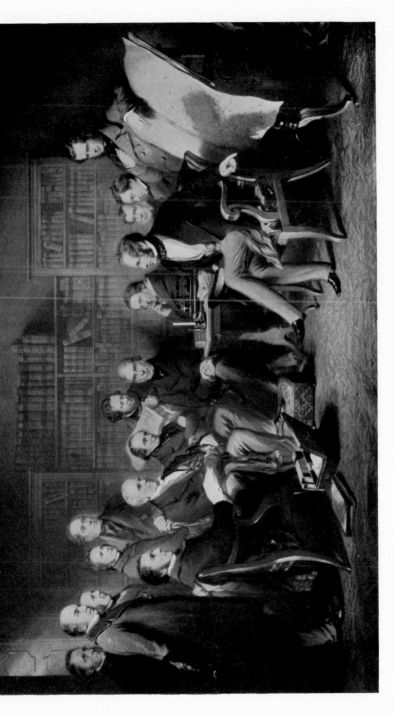

PLATE 6.—LORD ABERDEEN'S GOVERNMENT

From a print in the Author's possession.

Standing (left to right) : Sir Charles Wood, Sir C. Molesworth, Sir James Grahame, The Duke of Argyll, Lord Clarendon, Lord Granville, The Duke of Newcastle *(on the extreme right).*

Seated (left to right) : W. E. Gladstone, Lord Lansdowne, Lord John Russell, Lord Aberdeen, Lord Cranworth, Lord Palmerston *(with hand pointing to the map),* Sir George Grey, Sidney Herbert.

that are, or ought to be, in the first volume of Hume's History, and then came down to Lord Carlisle, and some Scotch appointment.

" 'You can't think what an effect it had on Lord Rutherford,' she said (which is quite true, as I never knew and doubt whether I shall ever think of what affects Lord Rutherford!) and then the dreadful climax of the paragraph in the Globe newspaper which somehow prevented her and Charles from walking home from Church on Sunday. It stopped them at every corner, and I do not know how they ever got home. She began so often, 'But what I blame Lord John for is,' that when she said that they had taken a house close by him, I think she blamed him for being in Chesham Place. I wish these wives of political men would hold their tongues or elope."

The battle for places raged for ten days, and arrangements might have broken down altogether but for Lord Aberdeen, who exhibited an extremity of tact at a moment when his patience was stretched to the limit. But at last it was all settled and appointments allotted and the list of places announced. Palmerston was offered, and accepted without demur, the Home Office; the Duke of Newcastle, a Peelite, took over the Colonies; Sidney Herbert, also a Peelite, Secretary-at-War; Sir James Graham was First Lord of the Admiralty, and Lord Granville was President of the Council. Sir Charles Wood, late of the Exchequer, became President of the Board of Control, and Sir William Molesworth was Commissioner of Works.

And Russell? Russell wavered as to what he should have. First he claimed the Foreign Office and the leadership of the House of Commons. Then he began to wonder whether his health would stand the strain of conducting the affairs of the House, and at the same time of undertaking the added labour of a great Department of State. On December 20th, he betook himself to Berkeley Square to ask Lord Lansdowne's advice on the matter, and there we are presented with a very characteristic little mid-Victorian scene.

As the two were talking in the library at Lansdowne House, Macaulay was announced and shown in. When he became acquainted with what the two statesmen were discussing, the great historian cleared his throat and turned to Russell.

"You said, Lord John," he declared (referring to the latter's eulogism in the House of Commons on the late Duke of Wellington): "You said, Lord John" (and one can almost see the right hand slip Napoleonically into the breast and the left go flourishing under the coat-tails), "You said that we could not all win Battles of Waterloo, but that we might all imitate the old man's patriotism and sense of duty, and indifference to selfish interest and vanities when the public welfare is concerned; and now is the time for you to make a sacrifice. Your past services and your name give us a right to expect it."

These were the kind of sentiments which mid-Victorian statesmen liked to declaim to each other. Anyhow, Lord John was deeply moved, and departed from the scene determined to take office. But the more he thought of his health the less possible did it seem for him to undertake the vast labours incurred by his position in the House of Commons, coupled with the work involved in being head of a great Department. He wrote to Aberdeen and said that he would accept office and undertake the leadership in the House of Commons, if he should be allowed to do so without portfolio.

A great deal of discussion took place on this score. But at last a compromise was found. And the compromise was Clarendon. It was decided that Lord John should adorn the Foreign Office until such time as Parliament met, and that he should then hand it over to Clarendon, who would be ready and willing to receive it. It appeared a reasonable arrangement, and Lord Aberdeen accepted it with a good grace. On December 23rd, Lady John Russell wrote in her diary: "Lords Aberdeen and Clarendon gave me their words of honour as gentlemen that, on the meeting of Parliament, John should leave the Foreign Office, and not be asked to take any other office." And now Clarendon found himself able to accept the post without a qualm. Palmerston was in such a position that he could neither be offered nor could accept the Foreign Office, and could therefore watch Clarendon take over his old post with perfect composure. Far from there being any objection in anyone's mind about his now taking it, Clarendon found himself, by the tide of events, manœuvred into the position of being actually able to save an awkward situation by accepting it, as he had saved an awkward situation before by refusing it. And everyone was pleased. Russell was pleased; Palmerston was pleased; and, now that Palmerston was out of harm's way and safely ensconced in the Home Office, the Court was pleased.

The old year went out, and on January 9th, 1853, Lord Aberdeen gave a Foreign Office dinner, which the heads of Foreign Missions attended. The Clarendons went; and Aberdeen, talking to Clarendon, waved an arm in the direction of the Foreign Ambassadors, and referred to them as "your future flock," and Kathy notes in her diary that the latter were particularly attentive to her as the wife of the future Foreign Secretary. Clarendon also spent a night at Windsor at this time, and the Queen informed him that she was aware of his "noble disinterestedness." So all seemed now for the best.

Parliament was to meet on February 10th, and Lord John informed Clarendon that he thought he should give up the seals of office about the 15th.

Now, although the arrangement about the Foreign Office was common knowledge in political circles, the fact that it had been planned beforehand was never meant to be made public. When the time came for handing over, it was assumed by all those in the know that Lord John would make some public statement about his health preventing him from continuing to discharge the arduous duties of the Foreign Department, and that with the approval of Lord Aberdeen the Queen had graciously commanded Lord Clarendon to undertake to fill the post.

The political world was, therefore, somewhat surprised one day in the middle of January to open their *Globe* newspaper and to read there a paragraph giving a full account of the arrangement. Now the *Globe* was "inspired" by Russell, so everybody knew the source from which it gathered this piece of information. It put everybody concerned in a most awkward and embarrassing situation. Russell, at times most formal and correct about affairs of this kind, was given also to sudden and appalling lapses. This was one of them. Victoria and Albert were furious and fell upon Clarendon, who was paying a second visit to Windsor at about this time. They were all graciousness again when they discovered that the paragraph was as much a surprise to himself as to them. He smoothed them down and promised to do what he could with Lord John. Meanwhile Aberdeen, sorely provoked at the incident, had put pen to paper in Lord John's direction. On his way back from Windsor to the Grove, Clarendon paused in London to go and see Russell.

He found Lord John having that very moment composed a letter to Aberdeen, in answer to the latter's recent one to himself. Being slightly nettled at the criticism of his conduct, Lord John's epistle was not the most tactful of documents. The letter was actually on the table ready to go off, and he read it to Clarendon. Clarendon thought it injudicious, and said so. At that moment the door opened, and in came Aberdeen himself. Whereupon, with a delicious naïveté, Russell, waving the very letter in his hand, turned to Aberdeen and explained that he had just written to him, but that Clarendon, to whom he had read the letter, thought it a bad one, so he had decided not to send it. Aberdeen burst out laughing, and said that it was a good thing to take counsel; perhaps his own letter had been a bad one, but then he had not taken counsel!

Thus, by a kind of divine frankness, Russell always managed to get himself out of trouble.

Parliament opened on February 10th. A week passed, and

Lord John made no sign of handing over. On the 15th, Clarendon mentioned to Russell that he was going down to the Grove that Saturday. The look on the little man's face at this information was comical to behold. "Saturday," he said. "But that is the day . . ." oblivious of the fact that he had omitted to tell Clarendon that a Council was being called that very Saturday to install him as head of the Foreign Department. However, Lord John was profuse in his apologies; and certainly Clarendon was amused rather than annoyed at his forgetfulness. All was therefore put right. A Council was held on February 19th, and at it, with the solemn ritual proper to such occasions, Russell relinquished, and Clarendon accepted, the seals of the Foreign Office, and on the 21st he accompanied Clarendon to Buckingham Palace, when he kissed hands on appointment.

And what did Palmerston think? He thought, apparently, that Clarendon should have been Prime Minister at this moment, and said as much to Lord Stanley of Alderney. Kathy, hearing of the conversation, begins an entry in her diary with:

"Wonders will never cease! When one remembers Lord Palmerston's apparent jealousy of George, and now hears this, added to Lord Palmerston's own admission to George that he had for years thought him the fittest man to be Prime Minister, it makes one marvel. . . ."

Perhaps it was less of a marvel to Clarendon himself. He had played his cards well in that quarter: he had been content to wait; and now his policy was bearing a rich harvest in the approval of the very man without whose support he knew that his labours in Whitehall would have been fruitless. All had turned out for the best, and he must have felt well content as he drove from Grosvenor Crescent to the Foreign Office that first morning as Secretary of State for Foreign Affairs.

The new session opened favourably enough. The curious assortment of Ministers shuffled down into their places. Cabinet meetings were frequent and amicable; all seemed for the best. The portent was Gladstone, unfolding his Budget schemes to wondering colleagues "in a conversational exposition which endured without a moment's interruption for more than three hours." The vast structure of finance that he built up, brick by brick, before their astonished gaze completely dumbfounded the Ministers. Argyle referred to it as "by far the most wonderful effort that I have ever heard from the lips of Man," and his colleagues agreed with him. They were, moreover, surprised beyond measure. They knew and respected Gladstone as a politician of weight. They recognised his abilities and admired his oratory. But they hardly realised till then how mighty a phœnix they were cherishing in their midst. And they were duly grateful. Aberdeen wrote post-haste to the Lieven:

"The Government is infinitely stronger than I ever expected to see it. The truth is Gladstone has raised himself to the highest pitch of financial reputation, and has given a strength and lustre to the Government which it could not have derived from anything else."*

It was true; for if the effect he had on Ministers in the privacy of the Cabinet was overwhelming, even more so was the effect he had upon the House when, a week after his private exposition to Ministers, he rose and unfolded his Budget scheme in the Commons, in a speech that lasted for nearly five hours. "It was," says one of his colleagues, writing many years after the event, "one of those rare occasions on which a really fine speech not only decides the fate of a Government, but enlightens the mind of a people, and determines for an indefinite time to come the course of national legislation."

And it is a tribute to the soundness of this—Gladstone's first and greatest Budget—that England came through the coming war financially unscathed. All seemed well. Only Clarendon, peering out over Europe across the barrier of his red boxes, perceived an angry, sullen cloud hanging obstinately over the Near East. Eventually—despite the frantic efforts of them all—it broke in thunder and lightning—over the distant Crimea.

* Life of George, Fourth Earl of Aberdeen, by Lady Frances Balfour.

CHAPTER XVII
CAUSES OF THE CRIMEAN WAR

§ 1

THE incident which disturbed the vast nexus of interests and counter-interests upon which Europe was poised in those days, and which finally tipped the nations over into that welter of bloodshed and suffering, of fortitude and heroism, which is known to history as the Crimean War, was a simple and innocent enough affair in itself. It seemed, indeed, to bear no relation whatsoever to the magnitude of the forces that it brought into play. But, simple as it was, it turned out to be no less than the lever which set in motion a huge and complicated piece of machinery that could only cease functioning when a number of intricate, correlated and, as it proved, disastrous movements had been completed. The lever, in this case, was a diplomatic tussle of the mildest order. It was a wrangle between the Greek and Latin Churches as to which of them should have the custodianship of some of the Holy Places in Palestine.

Now, human ingenuity was hardly so bankrupt that it could not solve such a problem. Indeed it could, and did, solve it. A perfectly fair and just compromise was come to in the matter of the Holy Places. But by the time it was reached the question had given rise to issues far beyond itself, and higher problems affecting the whole political situation in Europe were discovered to be involved.

The wrangle over the Holy Places was as between France, whose new ruler posed as the champion of Latin Christianity, on the one hand, and Russia, whose age-old protectorate of the Greek Orthodox Church was universally admitted, on the other. But the irony of the situation lay in the fact that Turkey had the casting vote in the matter; for the soil upon which the Holy Places stood was Turkish soil.

The question had arisen two years previously, and a faint reverberation of it had reached the ears of Palmerston, who was Foreign Secretary at that time. He dismissed it summarily as a wrangle " hardly suited to the times in which we live," and turned to other matters. For once he had been wrong. For once he failed to see the dangerous implications lying at the root of a European question. And now, in the spring of 1853, those sinister implications began to unfold. For, pressed hotly by French diplomacy in the matter of the Eastern claims, Turkey, with one rather fearful but also slightly defiant eye on Russia, conceded the custodianship of the Holy Places in question to France.

Russia, in the persons of the Emperor Nicholas and his advisers, was furious. But not, as it happened, so furious with France for gaining her point as with Turkey for conceding it. It was just at this moment that the question of the custodianship was lost sight of in higher political issues. For it was at this moment that Nicholas decided that Turkey—that hateful, heathen anomaly, the Sick Man of Europe, the huge, monstrous entity that sprawled across his southern frontiers, that persecuted the Christian minorities under his protection, that held together as an entity only with the goodwill of the Western Powers, the so-called Ottoman Empire, the perennial nuisance of Europe—should die.

There is no doubt that Russia, after Turkey's concession to France, was determined upon the complete destruction and distribution of the Ottoman inheritance. For some time past the Turkish administration had gone from bad to worse. The rule of the Sublime Porte was venal, corrupt, inefficient and weak. The Sultan, indolent and debauched, was powerless in the hands of a number of scheming viziers as bad as, or worse than, himself. Nicholas had been watching their proceedings with interest for nine years past. He considered the whole Turkish system was collapsing, and now in the spring of 1853 he judged the moment ripe for giving it just that extra push that would make its dissolution an immediate certainty. He was quite frank about it. "I tell you," he said to the British Ambassador in St. Petersburg, "that if your Government has been led to believe that Turkey retains any element of existence, your Government must have received incorrect information. I report to you that the Sick Man is dying, and we can never allow such an event to take us by surprise." With even more frankness he went on to discuss the heritage of the empire of which Great Britain and Russia, it appeared, were to be the residuary legatees.

Unfortunately, in proposing to put an end to Turkey, he was, consciously or unconsciously, proposing to put an end to the *status quo* in Europe. In proposing to destroy the Ottoman Empire he was proposing to do away with what was considered by all sound European statesmen to be the only counterweight to himself, to Russia, in the Europe of those days. Russia and Turkey, equal and opposite; they were the essential weights in the scale. The balance of power was said to depend upon them.

Turkey, therefore, must never be allowed to dissolve. Turkey in Europe, dominating the Near East, or at any rate cohering and subsisting as a corporate entity in the eastern waters of the Mediterranean—this was a cardinal maxim of Western European statesmanship, and strong men blenched at the thought of its extinction. If the Turkish Empire did not exist as a fact, it must at least continue to exist as a convention; and the moribund, decaying thing must be bolstered up and made to grimace, and dance, and show its teeth, even if in reality it was nothing more than a political ghost. Otherwise Russia would have it all her own way.

§ 2

Russia, the terrible, almost mythical autocratic state of the North—Russia with no counterweight in the South and East—unadulterated Russia—the contemplation of such a thing brought an icy chill to the spines of the Foreign Secretaries of the day. For consider its mere size on the map. Peering at the globe through their spectacles, the statesmen of the day were appalled—as anyone might be—at the enormous, preponderating space, the huge, amorphous area assumed by Russia as compared to any other country represented. The Austrian Empire, they noted, would fit into a corner of it; France might be duplicated in an endless series across its length and breadth; whilst all that is assumed under the term " the British Isles " might be made to recur across its colossal expanse with the monotonous insistence of the pattern on a wallpaper. That it was much less dangerous than it looked on the map; that its huge area was sparsely populated by an agricultural, not an industrial, people; that it had no railway system whatsoever and was perennially unprepared for war—these facts were hardly taken into account at all, and Russia remained a " name of fear " in all the Foreign Departments of Europe.

Moreover—and this circumstance made it all the more terrifying and difficult to deal with—the methods and practice of the Russian rule were completely at variance with the liberal trend of the Western democracies. By an ironical turn of fate Russia, in these days, is looked upon as a paradise for Communists. To our grandfathers she was looked upon as the perfect example of " the Fascist State." For consider: the policy internal and external of this vast empire was in the hands of one person, the Emperor himself, who acted (or did not act) on the advice of a camarilla of unelected aristocrats and men of affairs. There was no parliament, and—oh, shame! —there was nothing remotely resembling an elective principle. The power and the glory were all centred in one person, who assumed, in popular imagination, almost the stature of a god. A wide-flung, intricate espionage kept the system in being and swept into the terrible confines of Siberia all who dared oppose it in thought or deed.

Such was the political picture of Russia firmly rooted in the minds of mid-nineteenth-century statesmen.

The sinister power, they noted, already sprawled across the north and west of Europe. It was essential that its stealthy advance to the ports of the south and east should be circumvented at all costs. Russia must never reach Constantinople. She must never even be permitted to dominate the Black Sea. So thought France and Great Britain. So thought every country that was not bound or compromised or blackmailed into an opposite opinion by geographical propinquity or treaty obligation. With great force did England hold these views, for England had much at stake. Russia must never, we held, be allowed to penetrate Asia Minor and steal down through Persia to threaten our Indian interests.

Now, geographically, the one barrier against this feared southern encroachment of Russia was the unwieldy conglomeration of states and peoples roughly held together under the name of the Ottoman Empire. That its rulers were heathen and oriental by nature; that its Government was just as much—if not more—of an autocracy than that of Russia; that its rule was inefficient and given to the persecution of Christian minorities—these facts were conveniently forgotten in the contemplation of more material and profitable considerations. For Turkey in Europe possessed this sovereign virtue in the eyes of European statesmen of the day: its northern and western boundaries were spread out in a convenient curtain right across Russia's way to the Mediterranean, which was further stayed by the geographical position of three stretches of water—mercifully all in Turkish hands—the Bosphorus, the Sea of Marmora and the Dardanelles. Not until Russia so dominated Turkey as to be able to use these seas as if they were her own could she have free access to the Mediterranean. That day must never come.

Unfortunately the Turkish Empire, as a military and political unit, was always on the verge of crumbling to pieces. Twelve years previously, it will be remembered, it nearly fell to pieces under the hammer-blows of Mehemet Ali. It will also be remembered at what pains England had been then to preserve its integrity—even to the point of nearly going to war with France, who, for reasons of her own, was interested in the preservation of Mehemet Ali in the Pashalik of Egypt. Any threat of the demise of Turkey was a matter of the highest concern to the diplomats of the Western States; and, as for Great Britain, she had in the past been prepared to sacrifice a very great deal to preserve the Turkish Empire intact.

So when the Emperor Nicholas of Russia calmly assumed that Turkey was about to die, and rather hinted that he was preparing to hasten her end (and what did we mean to do about it?), Europe woke up to the fact that far more than the custodianship of the Holy Places was at stake: that, in fact, a very dangerous situation indeed had arisen in the Near East. Statesmen were appalled quite suddenly to find themselves looking down a long vista of difficulties at the end of which was war.

That Russia meant business this time was certain. Her diplomatic methods with the Sublime Porte in the spring of 1853 left no room for doubt. Nor did she conceive war as the only possible means of gaining her ends. Indeed, Nicholas thought that war would hardly be necessary. He thought that by forcing harsh terms upon Turkey—the kind of terms that Austria sought to impose upon Serbia in the summer of 1914—he would amply achieve his purpose. For he judged that Turkey, harassed by internal and external dissensions, would be too weak to resist them. He sought, therefore, to extort from Turkey an offensive and defensive alliance framed in such a way that it would virtually reduce her to a state of vassalage, rob her progressively of her power over her own subjects, and put an end for ever to her empery in the Near East. When this happy consummation had been reached he was quite prepared to discuss the Ottoman inheritance with the Western Powers—with Great Britain, for instance. But first Turkey must die.

When the terms of the alliance were examined and their implications realised, Europe understood that a convulsion was taking place the magnitude of which could hardly be estimated. Patiently, resolutely, honestly and, be it said, unintelligently, the diplomatists of Europe worked for peace. Month in, month out, for a year and more, with diminishing hope, but unrelenting energy, they toiled to prevent a conflict. Every conceivable demand, every possible ruse was tried in a vain attempt to save the situation—even, on one occasion, to issuing an identical despatch to Russia and Turkey in the childish hope that Russia would read it in one sense and Turkey in another. International machinery was set up in Vienna, and from Vienna rained an unremitting stream of notes, memoranda, despatches, suggestions and propaganda. But all to no avail. The situation moved slowly and ruthlessly on to its inevitable climax. The deeper Russia became involved in the net of diplomacy with which it was sought to restrain her, the angrier, the more resolute she became. And the more resolute and threatening she became the more fearfully Turkey turned to England and to France for protection against her wild behaviour. France and Great Britain were irretrievably pledged to Turkey—she was our ally, how could we desert her? In July, '53, the Russian troops crossed the Pruth, and hostilities between Russia and Turkey commenced.

But even then a last passionate attempt was made over a number of months to limit the conflict. It was not till January, '54, that the situation was considered without hope. In February the ultimatum of England and France was sent to St. Petersburg. In March we were at war.

And so it happened that the two great liberal Powers of the West went crusading, not in defence of the Holy Places, not in defence of Christianity and the rights of Christian worship, but in support of a dusky Moslem Power, whose presence in the comity of Christian nations was in itself an anomaly, whose rule was a rule of oppression, and whose methods were those of barbarism. To the many the truth was obscured and the issues falsified. "In a palace on the Bosphorus," says a modern historian, "sat the Sultan, a fleshy and irascible debauchee, usually intoxicated, and always lethargic, surrounded by a group of Mohammedan fanatics, of whose plots to supplant him he was dimly aware and whose ability to raise the fury of a priest-ridden mob kept him in abject terror and peevish submission. In England were public halls, crowded with respectable shop-keepers, evangelical maiden ladies and stolid artisans, enthusiastically proffering their lives and money in the service of this obese little tyrant in a fez, whose name they could not pronounce and whose habits of life were as unknown to them as those of a prehistoric monster."

§ 3

Clarendon received the seals of the Foreign Office on February 21st, 1853, and it did not take him a week to discover that he had put his foot into a hornet's nest. He discovered, for instance, that a large semi-military mission was descending out of Russia upon the Sublime Porte. The head of this mission was Prince Menchikoff, a soldier rather than a diplomat. The object of the mission was to "discuss," but of course in reality to *impose*, the terms of the alliance with which Russia was seeking to bind Turkey to her for ever. This mission was on its way to Constantinople at the moment that Clarendon took over at the Foreign Office. Hamilton Seymour was writing the gloomiest despatches from St. Petersburg, and the whole situation was as dark as it could be.

Not much had been done to alleviate it in the time that had elapsed between the Aberdeen Government's accession to power and the moment when Russell handed over his department to Clarendon. In the wrangle for places and the general disturbance created by a Coalition Government shuffling into office, the attention of Ministers had been focused more on the immediate domestic scene than upon the vagaries of the foreign situation. And Lord John, anxious alike over his health and his rather

peculiar position in the new Government, had done little more in
the matter than write an angry despatch to France pointing out
the extent to which she had disturbed the *status quo* in the East,
and asking her what she meant to do about it. One other step
he took, however, and it was an important one. He sent Lord
Stratford de Redcliffe, who was on leave in England at the time,
post haste back to Constantinople. Now Stratford de Redcliffe
had been for years in the Near East and probably knew more
about its problems than any other statesman or diplomat then
living. He was British Minister at Constantinople. To send him
back to his post at this moment of crisis for Turkey was the
obvious thing to do. But opinions are divided as to the ultimate
wisdom of the course. Stratford de Redcliffe was of a strong and
slightly over-bearing character, and one school of thought is inclined to believe that the Crimean War might never have taken
place but for the presence of this man at this juncture at Constantinople. Another believes that he was the only man in Europe
who could have saved Turkey from dismemberment by Russia,
and that, given Russia's attitude, no one could have prevented the
war. Be that as it may, the fact that he was actually on his way
back to Turkey was a great relief to Clarendon as he first looked
out at the situation in Europe from the standpoint of Minister of
Foreign Affairs. The only other ray of light in the gathering
gloom was the presence of Count Brunow in London. Brunow
had been many years Russia's Ambassador in England. He knew
and understood the English point of view, and was sympathetic
to all and sundry. Clarendon and he from the first worked un-
remittingly for peace.

It is impossible in a work of this kind to enter in detail into
the immense series of negotiations that now ensued. The web of
diplomacy thickened round an angry and determined Russia. We
get glimpses of her floundering this way and that in an attempt
to get free. We see Stratford de Redcliffe manœuvring Prince
Menchikoff into a position in which by rights he should not have
had the face to present the Russian terms to Turkey. And we
see him presenting them all the same. We see the massing of
Russian troops on the Danubian frontiers, and watch Sir James
Graham knocking up Clarendon in the middle of the night with
a despatch from Admiral Dundas intimating that Constantinople
itself was in danger, should he go with a squadron to Besika Bay
to protect it? And we picture Clarendon's grave face as he explained the situation, next morning, to a hastily gathered
quorum of Ministers at the Admiralty. We seem to hear him
pleading, as he did, for delay. The misunderstanding of a signal
—a hasty command—a random shot, he says, and a situation

would arise from which there would be no going back. We hear
Lord Aberdeen, in perfect accord with Clarendon, throwing his
whole weight into the scale for peace; the others uncertain, but
in the end convinced.

An immense amount of responsible work was now, necessarily,
thrown upon Clarendon, and he emerges as a strong and skilful
negotiator, even if, as was the case, the ultimate issue was beyond
his control. Moreover, he had a humour and lightness of touch—
saving graces in the interminable and intricate labours in which
he and his colleagues were now embarrassed. Cabinet meetings
on the Eastern question were frequent, and he had endlessly to
explain the situation and read the despatches he was sending to
the various countries involved. "There is in all such documents," writes the Duke of Argyll, "a great amount of repetition,
and the phrases of diplomacy are to a large extent so artificial and
conventional that the work did sometimes seem wearisome beyond
endurance. But we had two great alleviations. The first was
the constant recollection that apparently on the most trivial points
before us the issues of peace or a bloody war depended. The
second source of relief was the liveliness and humour which characterised the reading of our Foreign Secretary, Lord Clarendon.
His moving comments were inimitable. His readings of the character of each diplomatist were often as good as a play, and were
a real help in enabling us to judge how far we could trust each
separate element of the situation at the separate Courts."

And Palmerston was pleased with his pupil.

"I admired greatly your letter to Seymour," he writes to
Clarendon, after one such Cabinet meeting, "but I did not like to
say too much in its praise in the Cabinet for fear that by doing
so I should lead others to think it too strong. I can assure you
that it is a great comfort and satisfaction to me to know that the
conduct of our foreign relations is in such able hands as yours,
and your administration of your important department is attended
with this advantage to the country, that, from a variety of circumstances, you can say and do things which could not so easily
have been said or done by me."

Nor was Clarendon's ordeal of having to step into the position
of Foreign Secretary at such a grave moment unrecognised by
him:

"You have had the most difficult part assigned to you that
ever man had to play. You have been put into the position of a
general, who, having taken command of an army one day, should
be called upon to go into action the next, before he had made himself acquainted with the qualities, habits, dispositions of his
officers, and before he had time to sound the tactics of his
opponents; and who, moreover, should find himself fettered by a

council of war some of whose members," he adds, making a sly hit at Aberdeen, "were of the slow-march school."

All that spring of 1853 Clarendon tirelessly and impartially admonished both sides. ". . . Nor will you disguise from the Sultan and his Ministers that perseverance in his present course must end in alienating the sympathies of the British nation, and making it impossible to overlook the exigencies of Christendom, exposed to the consequences of their unwise policy and reckless administration." The despatches passed backwards and forwards. It was not until the end of May, when the full enormity of Russia's demands were made known, that Clarendon's attitude definitely stiffened and that he became convinced in his own mind that war was inevitable.

"It is indispensable," he writes on May 26th, "to take measures for the protection of the Sultan, and to aid His Highness in repelling any attack that might be made upon his territory. . . . No sovereign," he continues two days later, "having a proper regard for his own dignity and independence, could admit proposals which conferred upon another and more powerful sovereign, a right of protection over his own subjects. . . . Fourteen millions of Greeks would henceforth regard the Emperor as their sole protector, and their allegiance to the Sultan would be little more than nominal, while his own independence would dwindle to vassalage."

In July—after Turkey and Russia had broken off diplomatic relations—Clarendon, with the assent of the Cabinet, set up an international conference at Vienna in order that the two countries, even though they had ceased to be on speaking terms, could still communicate with each other through this impartial and helpful tribunal. And Vienna rained notes and despatches and protocols. But to no avail. Russia and Turkey were at daggers drawn, and in October the fighting began.

"The beastly Turks have actually declared war," writes Clarendon to Kathy, "so there's an end of the Olmütz arrangement out of which something might possibly have been made; but it's all over now."

Russia and Turkey were at war; but as yet Great Britain and France were not involved, and a last frantic effort was made to limit hostilities. The Aberdeen Government peered bodefully at the situation like a group of frightened hens. Lord Aberdeen, distracted at the prospect of war, spent hours of Clarendon's time, walking backwards and forwards across the carpet of the Foreign Secretary's room, racking his brains out loud in an endeavour to find a solution. Clarendon watched him from over the pile of red boxes on his table, and shrugged his shoulders. Everything was being done; everything had been done. Fate must decide. . . . The other colleagues circularised each other in ceaseless memoranda. "The present situation," began one of Lord John's innumerable minutes, "makes it necessary to look back, around us and forward. . . ."

§ 4

And then in the autumn, quite suddenly the public became alive to the situation in the East. Not that the man in the street understood much of what was going on there, nor could enter into the intricate causes of peace or war—but for some time past he had seen Turkey referred to in the papers as the "Sick Man of Europe," and by association the term had a kind of appealing ring to it. One is sorry for sick people. One enquires at their hospital, one takes them grapes. Turkey was the "Sick Man of Europe." Poor Turkey, one must see how his condition is today; and every morning as "paterfamilias" spread his *Times*, he began almost unconsciously to scan the columns for news of the patient. Moreover, in contrast to the "Sick Man" (still feverish apparently, but holding his own), there began to loom across the public mind another portent, another phenomenon, large, lowering and slightly sinister. This was the "Bear"—the "Russian Bear." The "Bear" was a bully and was harrying the poor "Sick Man" and trying to take his coat from him. It is impossible to imagine anything more unsporting, more contrary to the public-school spirit, more un-English than to take the coat from the back of a poor sick man. But this apparently was what the "Bear" was trying to do. He is represented, the "Bear," in the cartoons of the period, as a large black animal with a small head, standing upon his hind paws, the imperial crown of Russia perched provocatively between his alert little ears, his forearms curved in a peculiarly grasping and significant manner. Poor Turkey, poor "Sick Man of Europe," how will he stand up for his rights against so large and overbearing a monster? Manchester wondered darkly, London glowered. Meetings were held; halls were thronged; pamphlets were printed and disseminated. By the beginning of November the "Bear" was rapidly turning into the "Bug-Bear." Public opinion had indeed shifted from the summer, when, in a test debate on Eastern affairs in the House of Commons, Cobden, representing thousands of solid nonconformists, championed the cause of Russia and Christendom against the Moslem hordes of Turkey, and was cheered to the echo. Since then the question of injustice had crept in. And if there is one thing that rouses the apathetic heart of the English people more than another it is the spectacle of injustice, especially if injustice is accompanied by coercion, more especially if that coercion is from a stronger to a weaker nation. It now mattered little to the public that Russia in the present quarrel was suing for the rights of Christian subjects against the tyranny of Moslem overlords: that in the past there had been grave abuses, massacres even of Christians, and that Russia was determining that this should not happen again. All the public now saw was the huge figure of the "Bear" stripping the coat from the poor "Sick Man," preparatory to encircling him with those long curved forearms, and squeezing him gently but firmly to death. And no one was going to stand for that. However, the "patient" seemed to be doing well, and by the look of it was attacking vigorously along the whole Danubian front. "Well done, Turkey! Well done, the Sick Man of Europe!" Was the "Bear" going to be routed after all? And then at the beginning of December came a staggering piece of news. On November 30th, it appeared, the Russian Admiral Nachimoff basely attacked the Turkish fleet at anchor off Sinope and sunk it to a ship, killing some 4,000 Turkish seamen. Indignation in England knew no bounds. It was "a dastardly act," "a crime," "a massacre"; and the Government were loudly called upon to revenge this outrage.

It was, of course, not an "outrage," not a "massacre," but a perfectly legitimate act of war. But by this time public opinion was inflamed to such a degree that no act of Russia could be looked upon other than as the work of a cad and a bully. Why did we not at once go to war to avenge this wrong? The pacific Aberdeen became unpopular.

The whole Government was looked upon with suspicion. Some sinister cause must be at work which prevented Ministers from acting in the only British way possible after the "massacre" of Sinope. What could it be? It must be a foreign influence of some sort. Some high-placed foreigner moving darkly and secretly behind the scenes, some—— And then, with a sudden rush of horror, enlightenment came to the public mind. Albert. It was Albert, of course. Why hadn't they realised it before? Albert had access to the State papers of Victoria, Albert had a secret key to the red boxes that were placed on Victoria's table, and Albert was intriguing with Russia. Albert had won Victoria over to his Russian sympathies. The whole Court was pro-Russian. They were intriguing with the Coburg-Orleans clique, who were known to be the tools of Russia. The situation was really desperate. Could nothing be done about it? And while butcher boys went on their rounds singing:

> " Little Al, the royal pal,
> They say has turned a Russian,"

their elders and betters met darkly in newspaper offices and canvassed the chances of being able to bring about Albert's arrest for high treason! Rumour, on one occasion, had it that he actually *had* been so arrested; and a large crowd gathered on Tower Hill to watch him enter the Tower by "Traitor's Gate." The Queen was deeply hurt, and confided her sentiments to the sympathetic ear of Aberdeen. But Albert, with the dispassionate precision of a German scientist, drew up a list in writing of the causes for his unpopularity, and considered them one by one. All responsible people felt for the Queen and the Prince, and were deeply shocked at this exhibition of public hysteria. But there was nothing to be done about it. It just had to wear itself out, which it did in the early months of 1854.

The movements of the fleets had, all along, measured the successive stages in the failure of negotiations. At first they had been at Malta, threatening the Eastern waters of the Mediterranean. They had then moved up to Besika Bay, a small harbourage at the south-western entrance to the Dardanelles. As the situation darkened they received instructions to move up the Dardanelles into the Sea of Marmora, to Constantinople itself. As Russia's language became more insolent, they were moved into the Bosphorus. And now, as all hopes of peace seemed rapidly disappearing, they were instructed to push on into the Black Sea, and to "invite" all Russian ships to return to harbour. But though Clarendon was writing the despatch authorising this on November 30th, this "momentous" order to the Fleets was only executed on January 4th, 1854. Christmas fell on a darkening world, and January was spent in last efforts to maintain the equilibrium. Parliament opened on January 31st, and the Debate upon the Address was almost entirely devoted to the Eastern Question. All sides rallied to the Government. Lord John made a firm speech, and Disraeli protested loyally "that no future Wellesley on the banks of the Danube" would have to complain of the obstruction of Her Majesty's Opposition.

But the situation was puzzling enough. Every negotiation had apparently broken down, and the mine of possible negotiations seemed exhausted. The Allied fleet was in the Black Sea. Yet no shot had been fired and no ultimatum had been sent. Were we at war or were we not at war? An enterprising member of the Upper House actually asked this question of the Foreign Secretary on the evening of February 14th. It was an awkward question. It must be remembered that the Congress of Powers was still in session at Vienna. A last-moment compromise might be arrived at. As long as that body was actually operative anything might happen. Clarendon answered cautiously. "I consider," he said, "that we are in the intermediate state: that our desire for peace is just as sincere as ever; but then I must say that our hopes of maintaining it are gradually dwindling away, and that we are drifting towards war."

A week later Austria gave the *coup de grâce* to what Mr. Alfred Tennyson, lately called to the laureateship, called "the peace that I deemed no peace," by asking the Powers to demand from Russia the immediate evacuation of the Danubian Principalities. Russia refused this demand on March 19th. And on March 27th and 28th the Western Powers declared war.

CHAPTER XVIII

THE WAR

§ 1

THE real "Crimean" War began in September. Before that date operations had been confined to the Balkans, the troops from England having been landed in Gallipoli with the object of pushing into the interior, and of helping the Turks to repel the advance of the Russians on the Danube. But so successful had the Turks been in this campaign that in July the Russians began the evacuation of the Principalities. By the first week in August not a Russian was left west of the Pruth. The question now presented itself: Where should the blow against Russia be struck?

All eyes turned towards the Crimea, towards the great fortress of Sebastopol, the nerve-centre of Russia's power in and about the Black Sea. Here was a harbour fit for a fleet's anchorage; here was the base, full of stores and ammunition and guarded by fortresses, from which whoever held it could command without question the Black Sea trade. Tremendous preparations had been made at Sebastopol. It was here that Russia expected to be attacked, and it was here that it was essential to attack her. So urged Palmerston in and out of the Cabinet, and his colleagues were inclined to agree with him.

The march on Sebastopol began on September 19th. On the 20th the Allies crossed the Alma, and stormed the heights beyond it, in the face of a fierce resistance. This was the first considerable action of the war in which British and French troops took part, and the excitement over every detail concerning it was immense. It was not until the beginning of October that the full accounts of the action reached London, and then the battle in all its military details was fought and refought again in the clubs, at dinner-tables, in the letters and correspondence of the time. It was told and retold how our gallant men flung themselves into the waters of the Alma, which were literally churned into foam by the round-shot and canister of the opposing batteries; how Lord Raglan and his staff dashed over the bridge, wildly cheering on the advancing battalions, while the Duke of Cambridge brought his division into action with great ability, and had, for the first time, "an opportunity of showing the enemy his devotion to

Her Majesty.'' Great and memorable were the feats of arms on this historic occasion. Sir George Brown, conspicuous on a grey horse, rode in front of his light division, ''urging them with voice and gesture.'' A sudden shell burst, and he disappeared from view, only to reappear again, horseless but waving his sword, and crying, ''23rd, I am all right! But sure I'll remember this day!'' It was told and retold how the Guards passed up to the attack ''almost as if they were in Hyde Park'' (which is always said of the Guards), but how a tornado of ''round and grape'' thinned out their front ranks. It was told how Sir Colin Campbell, admonishing his men, said, ''Highlanders, I am going to ask a favour of you. I am going to ask you so to act this day, that I may be justified in asking the Queen for permission for you to wear a bonnet,'' and how fully they obeyed their Chieftain's wishes. It was told of the rivalry between the Guards and Highlanders and of how, when finally a detachment of the Guards reached the summit, Sir Colin Campbell, with his men close on his heels, was heard shouting, ''We'll have none but Highlanders here.'' It was told and retold how personal encounters, bayonet to bayonet, crowned the day; and how finally the enemy fled down the slopes to the south and east, leaving three generals, 700 prisoners and 4,000 killed on the field of battle.

It was war in the grand manner. It was glorious, it was epic; but it was also tragic. The Allied casualties were very heavy. ''I am not fit for anything,'' writes Emily Eden to Clarendon, ''but to sit and wait for the paper, and then to cry over it, as I did yesterday, partly from excitement, for it is a stirring thing to read of our men marching through that river, and up that hill as they did; and partly from thinking of all the miserable wives and mothers and sisters then reading that same paper, and the happiness of their whole lives slipping away from them. ''Une seule ligne pour l'annoncer—un instant pour le lire, et tout est fini pour elles, fini sans retour. I cannot recollect taking the war so to heart in young days—did you? To be sure, I was sixteen when it ended, and you were younger, and then it had gone on so long. . . .''

After the victory of the Alma, nothing stood between the Allies and their objective, Sebastopol. Exhausted though the troops were, Raglan was for pushing on and taking the fortress by a coup de main. It probably could have been done, and had it been done, the course of the Crimean War would have been very different from what it was. But the cautious St. Arnaud, already dying, would not hear of it, and Lord Raglan could not carry his point in the Allied Council of War. The troops marched soberly towards the great citadel, and the long investment began.

§ 2

And now began, too, that terrible Crimean winter, that epic of hardship and helpless endurance, in which the armies, inadequately equipped and inadequately supplied with medical stores and services of all kinds, lost more in the enforced inactivity of the trenches than if they had been engaged in a series of bloody encounters. It was some time, however, before the conditions obtaining at the front became known in England; and during the first weeks of October repeated rumours of the fall of Sebastopol circulated in London. The war was popular among all classes. The rights and wrongs of the case seemed to matter not at all; or rather they were obscured by other considerations. One voice alone—John Bright—spoke fearlessly above the tumult but was hardly heard in the hubbub of it all. In answer to an invitation to be present at a war-meeting in Manchester, he wrote:

"My doctrine would have been non-intervention in this case. The danger of the Russian power was a phantom; the necessity of permanently upholding the Mahometan rule in Europe is an absurdity. Our love of civilisation, when we subject the Greeks and Christians to the Turks, is a sham; and our sacrifices for freedom, when working out the behest of the Emperor of the French, and coaxing Austria to help us, are pitiful impostures. The evils of non-intervention were remote and vague, and could neither be weighed nor described in any accurate terms. . . . You must excuse me if I cannot go with you; I will have no part in this terrible crime. . . ."*

Such an opinion was rare, and the people who held it formed a negligible minority.

As for Greek Christianity, the average Englishman knew very little about that, and what he did know he did not like very much; and though eccentric Englishmen sometimes thought fit to give their lives for the cause of Greek freedom, the great majority of Englishmen openly preferred the Turk, whom they considered, and still persist in considering, "the only gentleman of the Levant." Moreover, by then, the anti-Russian feeling had grown to such proportions that, in taking up arms against Russia, the nation had the feeling that it was really taking up arms against the powers of darkness. And with this laudable but erroneous sentiment, it embarked upon a conflict that in the end cost nearly twenty-three thousand men and all of seventy-six million of money.

And now the old and cumbrous machinery of war, put into

* *Annual Register.*

action again after nearly forty years of peace, began to strain and creak with an ominous and unhopeful sound. For nearly the whole of that period the great Duke of Wellington had sat at the Horse Guards, and nobody had ever dared to question his absolute authority and wisdom on all that pertained to the Army. And as in 1830 he considered that the British Parliament was as perfect an organism as was possible, and any attempt to alter or extend the workings of it would undoubtedly lead to disaster, so during the whole of that period he must also have considered the Army administration as perfect as anything may be in a man-made world. For nothing, materially, had been changed since Waterloo; and when the Aberdeen Government took stock of the machinery at their disposal for the conduct and maintenance of an army in the field, they found a strange state of affairs. They found, for instance, that the nominal control of the Army was entrusted to the Secretary of State for the Colonies. The Ordnance was under a separate Administration Board; the Commissariat was directly under the Treasury; while the Militia was under the Home Office. There was no central control whatsoever, and departmental jealousy ran hot and strong. It was soon discovered that the multifarious demands of the army in the trenches were producing hopeless confusion among these scattered fragments of abrogated authority. The Duke of Newcastle, an honourable and worthy man, but possibly not among our most brilliant administrators, occupied at this time the unenviable position of Secretary of State for the Colonies. Hopelessly overworked, and handicapped by being in the House of Lords and not in the House of Commons, this conscientious nobleman did what he could to sort out the various tangled threads entrusted to his hands. Admittedly it was not much, for the existing machinery would not admit of much. But as the demands of the Army became more insistent it became apparent that the Duke's efforts to produce order among chaos were not proving sufficient. Something was wrong.

Lord John's restless eye was the first to detect an anomaly, and he spent the early part of the year 1854 bickering with Lord Aberdeen as to the necessity of separating the War Department from that of the Colonies. At first Lord Aberdeen did nothing. The arrangements for war were immemorial. They had been sanctioned by the Duke of Wellington; Waterloo had been fought and won under their ægis. They did, indeed, appear to be a little strange, a little awkward in their working. But it would be a rash Government which tried to change them in the midst of a war. So thought Aberdeen in May. But Lord John was not to be put off. He returned again and again to the attack, and by June he was daily threatening to resign if the two Departments were not separated. By this time, also, he had been successful in persuading some of his colleagues that all was not well, and a question in the House finally clinched the matter. Aberdeen gave way, and in June the change was effected. The Duke of Newcastle left the Colonies to found a new 'War Office,' and Sir George Grey took over the Colonial Office. But John Russell's inquisitive glance did not rest there. It followed the unfortunate Duke of New-castle into the very sanctum of his new Department; it watched with relentless attention his floundering efforts to create a new staff (the old war staff had, quaintly, been left behind to deal with colonial affairs); it noted with unpitying accuracy the general muddle, misunderstanding and overlapping of functions which the new Department exhibited, and Lord John's intelligence behind that candid, inquiring stare decided that Newcastle was inefficient and that Newcastle must go. Not only must he go, but he must be replaced by Palmerston. For, strangely enough, Palmerston had now become for John Russell the hero of the hour. Palmerston could do everything. He was the one strong, fearless man who was worthy of the war situation. He must be in charge of the new War Department, whose efficiency would be assured in his hands. From his seat in the House of Commons he could answer all questions relating to the conduct of the war. It was right and proper and convenient in every way. Newcastle must go, and Palmerston must have his place. How and when this grand reconciliation between the dove and the eagle took place it is difficult to discover. It is true Palmerston had lately made a speech described by Lady Palmerston as "so courteous and so kind to that wayward Johnny," and this may have had its effect. By the late autumn of 1854, this determination of Lord John's that Newcastle must go and that Palmerston must replace him was already pronounced in Cabinet affairs.

Now most of the colleagues felt that, though Newcastle might be somewhat slow, he was sound and thorough in his methods, and they had come to believe that the evils of the administrative side of the war lay not so much in the personality of the man in charge of the War Department as in the inherent weakness of the machinery at his command. They also felt a certain loyalty as colleagues to the man upon whose head fell so grave a responsibility. It was their responsibility as well, and, as Lord John's insinuations began to mark upon their intelligences, they insensibly drew closer to the man to whom in loyalty they felt bound. Thus the disintegration of the Aberdeen Cabinet began.

Meanwhile the army starved and wasted before Sebastopol. The list of casualties through sickness and disease increased by leaps and bounds; whole regiments were put out of action by the

losses incurred. The medical services were hopelessly ill-equipped
for the task set before them; and until Miss Nightingale and her
devoted women arrived on the scene the hospital base at Scutari
was a crying disgrace. The stagnation of the military situation
was as complete as was the ground itself, held in the iron frosts
of the winter that was now descending upon that unhappy region.
Alma, Inkermann, Balaclava, glorious feats of open warfare, were
things of the past. No news of battles reached England now;
only terrible tales of hardship and endurance, the sickening
wastage of disease. By the middle of November a gloom had
settled down upon the nation which news from the front did little
to dispel. In a series of fearless articles *The Times* correspondent
in the Crimea described to the nation the full horror of the conditions of the troops in the trenches, the inadequacy of their
equipment for a winter campaign, the absence of transport, the
shortage of food, the breakdown of the medical services. And he
laid the full responsibility for the general muddle and inefficiency
at the front solely upon the shoulders of the Government.

In reality, it was nobody's fault; it was everyone's fault. What
had happened, of course, was that during forty years of peace no
one had thought of looking at the war machine or of bringing it
up to date. Quite suddenly Great Britain found herself involved
in hostilities in a distant land, and the machinery at the disposal
of Ministers was hopelessly inadequate to the task imposed upon
it. No one realised this more fully than the Prime Minister and
the Duke of Newcastle. In his biography of the Prince Consort,
Martin speaks, with truth, of these Ministers, who " toiled night
and day, meeting to the utmost of their ability every want which
was brought to their notice from headquarters, and anticipating
others which the best practical advice within their reach at home
suggested as likely to arise. Knowing better than any other men
could know what the evils were that demanded the cure, their days
and nights were racked with anxiety from the consciousness that
any complete cure was beyond their reach." But the nation was
not in a mood to go into the rights and wrongs of the case. The
facts portrayed in *The Times* articles were corroborated by the
thousands of private letters which were reaching England from
the theatre of war at this time. Blame attached somewhere. The
nation became sullen and angry.

Meanwhile the colleagues themselves were at sixes and sevens.
In and out of season John Russell tried to force Aberdeen's hands
with regard to Newcastle, and Ministers, feeling that a loyal companion was being attacked, closed their ranks against Russell's
insinuations. At the beginning of the session, which opened on
December 12th, both Disraeli and Layard assailed the Government
fiercely on the conduct of the war. It was, everyone thought,

only a matter of time before a motion of no-confidence was brought in. And then the Government would fall.

And, try as they could, honestly and by every means in their power, the Government were powerless to control the appalling situation before Sebastopol. "The splendid army of 30,000 men which he had organised, and had sent with such brilliant success to the Crimea," writes the Duke of Argyll, who was President of the Council at the time, "was reported to us as dying by inches in the besieging lines. Yet we were kept in complete ignorance of the causes. . . . The silence of Lord Raglan was positively excruciating. Nothing came from him but the driest facts." Cabinet meetings were frequent, and Ministers laboured to find a solution to the wastage in the Crimea. At one of the meetings it was stated that the army, in casualties and disease, was losing an average of a regiment a week. Palmerston sprang to his feet. "But why should this be?" he cried. "This," says the Duke of Argyll in describing the scene, "was the question we were all asking, and were all equally defeated in getting any guidance in reply."

The course that John Russell now took has been variously criticised. By most of his contemporaries it was considered base in the highest degree; by his colleagues in the Cabinet it was considered an act of the grossest treachery. To his dying day Russell himself considered it, in his own words, "one of the wisest and most useful acts of my life"; and it is by no means certain that posterity is not with him. The Aberdeen Cabinet was an unwieldy affair; there were difficulties and jealousies which made it well-nigh impossible for Ministers to pull whole-heartedly together as a team. The country was involved in a distant war; the machinery for conducting it was obsolete, and the Aberdeen Government would not face up to the drastic reforms necessary to set it right. It was too grave a moment to allow personal loyalties to stand in the way of national necessity. Russell felt that the Aberdeen Government must go. And he took a step that he knew would expedite its going. He resigned. Moreover, he resigned on the eve of Roebuck's motion of inquiry into the causes of the condition of the army in the Crimea. By his resignation at that moment he clearly showed the Opposition, the nation, the whole world that the counsels of the Government were divided and that he himself, the leader of the House of Commons, had no more confidence in the Cabinet as it stood.

As so often happened in John Russell's career, he took a perfectly legitimate step, but at the wrong moment, and in the wrong manner. Had he resigned a month before, no one could have accused him of treachery. After all, no Minister is necessarily bound for ever to a Government in which he serves; and when he honestly feels he can no longer be party to proceedings with which

16

he disagrees, to resign becomes a conscientious necessity. But to wait, as Russell did, till the moment when the Government was about to be attacked from without, and then to resign, is to point your resignation with a barb that no conditions can warrant. And then the manner of his going was such as only John Russell could have devised. There had been Cabinet meetings on January 18th, 19th and 20th, in all of which Russell had taken an active part. He was introducing measures of his own on education, Church rates, etc., and he spoke upon these at these meetings, "thus giving us," says the Duke of Argyll, " every indication of his continuous membership and fellowship with us." On January 24th the Duke came early to the Cabinet room, but not so early as Palmerston, whom he found with an open letter in his hand. "Read that," he said in amazement, handing the letter to the Duke. It was a note from Lord John, telling Palmerston in three lines that he would hear a letter from himself read to the Cabinet by Lord Aberdeen that day, and that the letter was his own resignation. It was, he said, "a painful but necessary step." Not a word to Aberdeen, to any of them, before that moment; not a week to fill his place and reorganise their ranks before meeting Parliament and the debate on Roebuck's motion. It was hardly a resignation: it was a flight. And it is no wonder that the colleagues considered it an act of the basest treachery. But if Russell's action was treachery, not much can be said for the step that the Government took as a result of it. Pulverised by Lord John's resignation at such a moment and in such a manner, the colleagues, after a lengthy Cabinet meeting, could think of nothing better to do than to resign themselves in a body. Lord Aberdeen was charged with the duty of taking their resignations to Windsor that same afternoon.

Victoria was furious—furious with Lord John for once more "upsetting the coach," but even more furious with Aberdeen and his colleagues for weakly resigning as a result of it. In fact, she would not hear of the resignation of the Government. She told him frankly that such conduct was unjust towards herself, injurious to the character of Ministers and indefensible to the country at large. And she sent him back with instructions to tell the others so, and with definite injunctions to carry on until the Government was defeated in the House. "Ministers," says the Duke of Argyll, " differed in the wisdom of carrying on; none of them differed in recognising that the Queen had exercised her prerogative with wisdom and strength."

In the Cabinet meetings that followed it was unanimously decided to uphold Newcastle and to resist Roebuck's motion to the utmost. But Newcastle informed his colleagues that whatever might be the result of the debate he intended to resign after it.

The nation needed a scapegoat, and he was perfectly prepared to act as such. But first they must close their ranks and fight the motion as a united team. This was reasonable, and Ministers reluctantly—for they thought he had been very badly treated—accepted his decision.

The debate came on on January 29th, 1855, but the result was a foregone conclusion. Although Gladstone expended all the powers of his oratory in an attempt to prove that the enquiry was unprecedented, Disraeli for the Opposition made short work of his arguments and turned the debate into one of no confidence in the Government. "Sir," he said, "I have no confidence whatever in the existing Government. I told them a year ago . . . that as they had no confidence in each other a vote of want of confidence was superfluous. I ask the House of Commons to decide if twelve months have not proved that I was right in that assumption?" He continued: "The late President of the Council (Lord John), in scattering some compliments among the colleagues he was quitting, dilated upon the patience and ability with which the Secretary of State for Foreign Affairs had conducted the duties of his department. I am not here to question these valuable qualities or that patience, but I say that all the patience and all the ability with which the Earl of Clarendon may have wrought are completely lost by scenes like this; and when Ministers of this country have themselves revealed their weakness to foreign courts, all the ability and all the patience of that statesman cannot make up for the weakness which is known to prevail in the councils of England. . . ."* The debate extended over two nights, and in the division on the second night the motion was carried by 157, only 148 voting with Ministers, and the whole of the Opposition, including many Liberals, voting against them. On January 30th Lord Aberdeen placed his resignation and those of his colleagues once more in the hands of the Queen. This time she was bound to accept them.

§ 3

And now began an absurd comedy of musical chairs, in which the members of the defunct Ministry, aided at first by the Leader of the Opposition, danced and pranced round each other, sparring for the vacant seat at the top of the Treasury Bench until Fate, growing weary of the game, played the wildest prank of all and enthroned in it the most unlikely of all the players, much to his own and everybody else's surprise.

The Queen sent for Lord Derby, as leader of the numerically strongest party now that the coalition was out. But Derby had no luck. He went off to canvass Palmerston, for he well knew

* *Annual Register.*

that any War Cabinet without Palmerston would be unthinkable. But Palmerston made Clarendon's continued presence at the Foreign Office a condition of his own association with Derby's Government. And on approaching Clarendon, Derby met with a polite but categorical refusal. There were many things which Clarendon was prepared to do for the common good, but serve under Derby was not one of them. Baulked thus of the two essential planks upon which he might construct a Government, Derby retired from the game, and the Queen sent for Lord Lansdowne. But Lansdowne, emphasising his gout and his age, declined to make the attempt himself, but suggested that the Queen should send for Clarendon. But this did not smile upon Victoria. She well knew that Clarendon would not make the attempt to form a Government. Besides, he was very well where he was, at the Foreign Office. The irony of it was that John Russell was now the only person left she could send for. Victoria demurred. It seemed ridiculous to ask him—the author of all the trouble— to form a Government. Not one of his late colleagues, she guessed, would consent to serve with him. Finally, however, deciding that his eyes had better be opened, she sent for him and asked tentatively whether he was willing to try his hand. And Lord John, perfectly confident and misdoubting nothing, blandly replied that he was very well pleased to make the attempt, though he *did* add that without the Peelites it would be impossible, without Palmerston it would be inconceivable, and that he considered "the co-operation of Lord Clarendon indispensable." The Queen, greatly marvelling, promised to send for Clarendon, to sound his views, and Lord John tripped off gaily to charm the Peelites.

The conversation between Clarendon and the Queen was very frank. He told Her Majesty that the views of his colleagues towards Lord John were so obvious to everyone that it was inconceivable that he should be rash enough to try to form a Government at this moment. So inconceivable, indeed, that people were beginning to say that the only reason the Queen sent for Lord John at this moment was in order *not* to have to send for Lord Palmerston. Clarendon begged her that in the event of Lord John's not being able to form a Government—which, indeed, was a foregone conclusion—that she would not set her face against Palmerston in memory of the old days, but that she would bring herself to send for him, though Clarendon could not say whether he would or could form a Government.

The Queen said that this, indeed, was her intention. But she was much distracted by the political crisis. As Clarendon was leaving, she said rather pathetically to him: "Lord John Russell can resign, and Lord Aberdeen can resign. But I can't resign. I sometimes wish that I could."

The same afternoon Clarendon went off to Lord John's house in Chesham Place to inform him of his views. He had studiously avoided meeting Lord John since the latter's resignation and the fall of the Ministry. But as Russell was now endeavouring to form a Government of which he hoped Clarendon would form a part, the sooner "Johnnie" knew his views the better. Lord John he found closeted alone with Palmerston; and Clarendon told him to his face that he considered he was trifling with the gravest interests of the country in trying to form a Government that he knew could not possibly last. Had he no conception of the feelings of his colleagues, and the feeling of the country generally concerning his late conduct to the Aberdeen Government? Russell replied in the words we have quoted, that he still thought that to be "one of the wisest and most useful acts of his life." He then asked Clarendon blandly whether he might submit his name to the Queen as Secretary of State for Foreign Affairs. "Certainly not," came the instant reply. Palmerston, who had sat silent while this colloquy was taking place, screening his face from the fire with a newspaper, now—to use Clarendon's own phrase—"hummed and hawed" in his usual way, and said to Lord John, "I told you that you would meet with some trouble."

Russell took all that was said in good part, and when they separated, as he was going to the Queen and had his carriage waiting outside, he insisted upon dropping Clarendon at home. Clarendon, who privately wished to have a few words with Palmerston alone, demurred and said that it would take him out of his way. But Lord John insisted, and they drove the few hundred yards between Chesham Place and Grosvenor Crescent in the most amicable manner. But nothing would turn Clarendon from his decision, and that night he wrote to Russell, informing him that he found himself unable to join any Government that Russell might form at this moment. Palmerston the same evening wrote to the same effect. Nor was Lord John any more successful with any of the other colleagues. In forty-eight hours he experienced a heavier fall than the Prime Minister whom he had jockeyed out of office. Grudgingly he relinquished the impossible task. There was a short pause and then Clarendon received the following note from Palmerston:

> " PICCADILLY,
> " *February 4th*, 1855.

" My dear Clarendon,—I have just received an authority from the Queen to endeavour to form a Government, and I hasten to say that I must say to yourself that which I said to Derby and to John Russell—that I could not belong to any Government in the present state of affairs in which the conduct of our foreign relations was not placed in your hands. I hope and trust that you will enable me to go on by saying that you will do so too.

"Yours sincerely,
"PALMERSTON.

"I am going off to Lansdowne, and then to Aberdeen. I will take my chance of finding you at home during the evening."

At half-past eleven that night the indomitable Viscount walked in on George and Kathy as they were sitting in the drawing-room at Grosvenor Crescent. Hale and hearty and in very good humour, it seemed nothing to him that he was undertaking the post of Prime Minister at the age of seventy-two, at a time when Great Britain was engaged upon a perilous and distant war. Perfectly confident in his own capacity and his power of cajoling his colleagues, he was busy picking up the wreckage of the late Ministry and hammering it into a ship of state. He had a long interview with Clarendon, who was eager and willing to serve with his old chief; after which, though the hour was late, he went cheerfully off into the night to canvass some of the others. The next day was taken up with interviews and consultations of all kinds.

Towards evening on February 5th Palmerston had got his team together. Clarendon remained at the Foreign Office; Palmerston, Prime Minister; Gladstone, Chancellor of the Exchequer; Sidney Herbert, the Colonies (his former office of Secretary-at-War was abolished); Lord Panmure, the new "War Office." Russell flickered round the edge of office, but at first refused to take any post in the Government.

Armed with this list, Palmerston repaired to Buckingham Palace to inform the Queen of the successful issue out of their difficulties. And Victoria, who could not herself resign, had to accept the inevitable. It was unthinkable, it was inconceivable, but it was a fact. "Pilgerstein" was Prime Minister!

CHAPTER XIX

NAPOLEON CAUSES ANXIETY

§ I

"A MONTH ago," wrote Palmerston to his brother about this time, "if any man had asked me to say what was one of the most improbable events, I should have said my being Prime Minister. Aberdeen was there; Derby was head of one great party; John Russell of the other; and yet, in about ten days' time they all gave way like straws before the wind; and so here I am, writing to you from Downing Street as First Lord of the Treasury."* There is an impish glee, something of the triumphant and slightly unrepentant schoolboy in the tone of this letter, which carries the irresistible *panache* of the man down to us through eighty years of time, and explains more than printed documents can how he came to be where he was at this time. Palmerston, Prime Minister! To some it came as a shock of surprise. "An impostor," wrote Disraeli, "utterly exhausted, and at the best only ginger-beer, not champagne, and now an old painted pantaloon, very deaf, very blind, and with false teeth, which would fall out of his mouth while speaking if he did not hesitate and halt so in his talk—here is a man which the country resolves to associate with energy, wisdom and eloquence."† He was wrong. The "old painted pantaloon" took hold of the governance of England at a moment of great national danger; steered her through the last stages of the war with Russia; through the peace-making that followed that war; through the long-drawn anxiety of the Indian Mutiny; and with only one short intermission through the eight years of peace and prosperity that ensued. With Clarendon's help he lifted England high in the councils and Courts of Europe; and when he died his loss was felt almost as much on the Continent as it was in England itself. He was seventy when he became Prime Minister, and in his eighty-first year he died, and he died Prime Minister.

Meanwhile, with perfect self-confidence and a commanding optimism, the septuagenarian installed himself at Downing Street. Clarendon found him there pursing his lips over a letter from the Queen "which," he declared to Clarendon, "he found eminently

* Quoted from Guedalla's *Palmerston.*
† *Idem.*

characteristic of the writer, full of good sense and decision." This gave Clarendon to think. If this was the line he was going to take with the Court, Clarendon's own task would be lighter. This new mood of the Prime Minister caused Clarendon to nick-name him "the Babe of Grace."

And now there was the question of John Russell to consider.

It was unthinkable that John Russell, with his now vast par-liamentary experience and his staunch Whig principles, should rest idle when what was virtually a Whig Government was in power. Moreover, it would be highly inconvenient to have John Russell without Cabinet responsibility, a free-lance, enfilading the Government from any angle he chose. The "Babe of Grace" was as much perplexed as any of his colleagues. It was now that an idea occurred to Clarendon which was, after much cautious thought, acted upon; and if it led to further entangle-ments and bitterness all round it was hardly Clarendon's fault that it did so.

It must be remembered that during the whole of the past crisis Clarendon had been fishing in the troubled waters of the European Courts for a basis upon which peace negotiations could begin. The allies, by this time, were clear enough (or thought they were) upon the essential points of negotiation to meet the Russian dele-gates at a conference. The congress was about to meet again in Vienna, under the presidency of the aged Westmorland, for the purpose of examining a possible basis for peace.

Clarendon's suggestion was that Russell should attend the meet-ing in Vienna as British delegate.

With the approval of the Queen and of Palmerston, Clarendon approached Russell on the subject. Russell was flattered and inclined to accept. Yes, he thought he might go. Finally he said he would go. Then, when it was all settled, he wrote to Clarendon to say that he had caught cold going to Windsor and couldn't possibly start for some days, that no doubt Westmor-land could open the conference, and that anyhow it was all a "wild goose chase," the search for peace at this juncture. Clarendon was furious at this change of attitude. It appears that Lord Minto had been with John Russell, rather putting him off the conference. Whereupon Clarendon sought out Lord Minto and stormed at that astonished peer, with the good result that the latter hurried off to undo his evil work. It soon became known that Lord John was starting immediately.

But hardly had he got as far as Paris when a Government crisis at home gave Palmerston the opportunity of definitely offering him a post in the Cabinet.

Palmerston found himself forced by the pressure of public opinion into allowing a Commission to be appointed to enquire into the conduct of the war. On hearing this, the Peelite members of the Government resigned in a body. Such a crisis at such a moment would have been sufficient to upset most Governments and most Prime Ministers. But nothing daunted the septuagenarian at this time. Three gaps appeared in his ranks. He simply filled them up. He offered John Russell the Colonial Office with a suave forgetfulness of past bitterness, and Russell accepted with alacrity. Sir George Lewis, Clarendon's brother-in-law, succeeded Gladstone as Chancellor of the Exchequer, and Sir Charles Wood went to the Admiralty. It was arranged that Russell, in spite of becoming a member of the Government, should still proceed to the congress at Vienna. Cabinet rank, it was thought, would give an added weight to his position there. So with closed ranks and colours flying, Palmerston's administration proceeded on its way.

§ 2

The prospect was far from pleasing.

The war dragged hopelessly on. Sebastopol was becoming a sore in people's minds. It seemed impossible to take, and it seemed equally impossible to leave off trying to take it. The deadlock was complete. Raglan vouchsafed no military opinion whatsoever on the subject. When a battle took place he dutifully recorded it in an able and clear despatch. When no battle took place he sent home endless Q.M.G. returns, lists of promotions, and reports on boots. The Cabinet were distracted. No one seemed to know exactly what the situation was out there, since it was impossible to get anything out of Raglan. In the clean sweep that had hoisted Lord Panmure into the War Office, it was suggested that General Simpson should be despatched to Headquarters to confer with Raglan and to report to the War Office. Accordingly, this gentleman started for the front at about this time.

To add to the embarrassment of the military situation, disquieting rumours now came from France that the Emperor was shortly proposing to go to the Crimea himself, to take over the dual command and to put an end to the interminable siege by storming the citadel at the head of 62,000 reservists. This was a horrifying project, and Clarendon immediately wrote a lengthy despatch to Cowley for the edification of Drouhyn de Lhuys and others whom it might concern, giving a hundred tactful reasons why the Emperor of the French should remain in France at this juncture. He also conferred with Walewski, who was as concerned as the British Government could be at the project; but he added that from the information he had it seemed that the Emperor was set upon it, and that they would have to make the best of it. This was startling. But more was to come. On February 26th their worst fears were realised in the shape of a letter to Palmerston in the Imperial hand itself, making the proposal and asking for the concurrence and approval of the British Government.

The Queen was greatly agitated. Indeed, she was perfectly furious. The idea of this political adventurer, this usurper of thrones, this pinchbeck Emperor, commanding her troops—*her* troops in the field—filled her with a blind rage. She summoned Palmerston and told him that Clarendon must go over to France in person immediately, see the Emperor, and put an end once and for all to this preposterous idea. Lord Clarendon was so clever at smoothing over difficulties, at putting disagreeable things to people in a pleasant way. Did not Lord Palmerston think that it was a good idea that he should go over and see the Emperor at once? Palmerston, who had already secretly decided that Clarendon should go, was able to applaud the idea as emanating entirely from Her Majesty.

So Clarendon steeled himself for the unpleasant task. But just before he started rumours were afloat that Nicholas of Russia, who was known to be suffering from a sharp attack of influenza, was now in a critical condition; and on the afternoon before his departure Clarendon announced in the House of Lords that a telegraphic communication had just arrived with the intelligence that the Czar was dead. This was a staggering piece of news, and no one at first could measure its significance. But for the moment the live Emperor of the French gave more cause for alarm than the dead Emperor of all the Russias, and Clarendon proceeded to France.

Napoleon III he found in the full panoply of war at his camp at Boulogne: very astute, very determined and fully aware of the nature of Clarendon's mission. And the setting was all in the Emperor's favour. General officers clanked in and out of the large, cold, empty house in which the Emperor had installed himself; A.D.C.s ran hither and thither on important messages; maps were spread and councils held as if the theatre of operations were just over the hill behind the town. And into this highly charged war atmosphere came the pacific Clarendon with the delicate mission of persuading the second Napoleon that the mantle of the first had not descended upon him. A whispered word from Colonel Fleury, who was sent to meet him on the quay at Boulogne, confirmed Clarendon's secret belief that the army, at least, was not in favour of this Crimean venture on the part of the Emperor. Heirs to the finest technical military tradition in the world, they were in no mood to be commanded by someone outside that tradition who had never been through the intensive training that goes to the making of a French general. The Emperor as an ideal, as the head of the State, as France personified—yes, they would die for that. But the Emperor as a commander in the field —no, *soyons raisonable*. With this helpful intelligence in reserve Clarendon was ushered into the presence.

The Emperor greeted him with the utmost cordiality, and in the conversations that ensued the greatest friendliness was preserved on both sides. Clarendon was unexpectedly impressed. It was impossible to come in contact with this strange, exotic, forceful little man with his impenetrable gaze and his bemused, almost snake-like eyes without becoming aware of the strange atmosphere of destiny that hung about him like an aura, without succumbing a little, after a first repugnance, to the fascination of that complex, that extraordinary personality. And Clarendon was no exception to the rule. He admitted afterwards to being both impressed and charmed with him. It was not the first time he had met him. But it was the first time that he had met him and done business with him—alone. And now, after polite preliminaries, they came to the point. The damping of ardour is always a thankless task; and as Clarendon unpacked his *chiffres* with Spencer-Ponsonby at his elbow, he frankly hated his mission; but he had no doubt of the success of it. He was fully equal to it, and knew it. Delay was the first veil to throw across the hectic picture that the Emperor had made for himself, and, armed with indubitable facts and figures, Clarendon proceeded to show how impossible it would be for the British Government to transport even as much as ten thousand French reservists to the scene of action within, say, two months at least from the date of embarkation. And then as to the situation before Sebastopol: granted the men were landed, the material and supplies at hand, what with the nature of the ground and the strength of the fortresses against them, what with the necessary engineering preparations to be made and the plans to be constructed, did the Emperor not think, with his own military experience, that four months would be the shortest possible time in which such a campaign as he conceived could be successfully carried out? Could he spare all that time away from Paris? that was the point. There was the political situation to consider. He was head of the State as well as Commander-in-Chief of the Army. . . . Having sowed this uncomfortable seed in the mind of the Emperor, Clarendon wisely let it germinate while turning to other aspects of the case. In a subsequent conversation that day, which measured the increasing intimacy between the two men, Clarendon drove his former point home by asking the Emperor to consider his position in the event of the campaign not proving successful. And then Clarendon said no more. He knew perfectly well that his task was accomplished.

That night there was a dinner, and Clarendon sat by the

Emperor, surrounded by the military splendour of the Second Empire. The polite pretence of imminent departure was preserved, but Clarendon was not deceived. His last word to the Emperor the following morning was in the nature of a gift—the gift of a phrase, a convenient, an accommodating phrase. Clarendon said that he thought that the Emperor should not move till everything was ready. And then he should go and give ' le dernier coup de main.' "C'est le mot," cried the Emperor, catching at it delightedly, "le dernier coup de main." But Clarendon thought he knew, as he sailed back in the man-of-war which had been sent to fetch him, that the hand that delivered that last coup at Sebastopol would not be that of the Emperor.

Arrived in London, he hurried to Buckingham Palace, where the Queen was eagerly expecting him. And what had he said to the Emperor, and what had the Emperor said to him? Had Lord Clarendon made sufficiently clear to the Emperor the difficulty there would be in his taking over the command of her troops? He had. That was most satisfactory. And the Emperor quite understood, did he not, that it would strain the alliance considerably were the French to reap all the honours of victory, while the British troops, her troops, were to act merely as transport carriers to the Imperial armies? He did. That was good. And what else had the Emperor said? Victoria was beginning to be interested in this "sire, her good brother," across the Channel. Of course, when it was a question of his commanding her troops, he was an adventurer, an upstart, a usurper of thrones and worse besides, but when he was not actively misbehaving himself she was inclined to be interested in what she heard about his strange personality. She was much pleased with Clarendon's mission. And she wrote to thank him the same day. If the grammar is a little mixed, the sense is at least gratifying.

"She is anxious to express to Lord Clarendon how much gratified we have been by the manner in which Lord Clarendon put the state of affairs before the Emperor of the French, and we are certain that it will have been of immense use, in every way. The Queen is especially pleased at the frank and high tone which Lord Clarendon held in talking of this country and of her noble and much calumniated Army. We were also much gratified by all the Emperor said to him."

A fortnight elapsed, and the Imperial sword still lay in its scabbard. Then came the gratifying enquiry as to whether a visit of the Emperor and Empress to the Queen about the middle of April would be acceptable. Clarendon breathed again. He knew that his arguments had prevailed.

§ 3

And hardly a month later—on April 16th—the Imperial pair actually came on a state visit to Windsor.

The Queen was in a great flutter at the prospect of meeting this exotic new Sovereign and his beautiful wife, of whom she had heard so much. Great preparations were made at Windsor for their reception, and no expense was spared. The State apartments in which they were to be housed were completely redecorated, and Victoria and Albert spent many anxious hours supervising the work. The day arrived, a fine spring day, " lovely and so warm, but the sun shining and making everything look so pretty." They were six hours late, having encountered fog in the Channel and narrowly escaped running into the South Foreland. But at last they arrived.

Clarendon was with the Queen at Windsor, in full fig, to assist at their official reception, and Kathy saw them pass down Piccadilly from Lady Palmerston's balcony at Cambridge House. " The carriages were open so we had good looks at them—the Emperor and Empress side by side in the first carriage, with Prince Albert who sat with his back to the horses. As they passed Lady Palmerston's house, Prince Albert pointed *it* or *her* out to them, and they looked up and bowed—the Empress struck me as very pretty, with a quiet pale face."

At Windsor, Victoria was in an agony of expectation, all the more so for the long delay. " News arrived that the Emperor had reached London at ten minutes to five," she writes in her journal. " I hurried to be ready, and went over to the other side of the Castle, where we waited in one of the tapestry rooms near the guard-room. It seemed very long. At length, at a quarter to seven, we heard that the train had left Paddington. The expectation and agitation grew more intense. The evening was fine and bright. At length the crowd of anxious spectators lining the road seemed to move, then came a groom, then we heard a gun, and we moved towards the staircase. Another groom came. Then we saw the *avant-garde* of the escort; then the cheers of the crowd burst forth. The outriders appeared, the doors opened, I stepped out, the children and princes close behind me; the band struck up ' *Partant pour la Syrie*,' the trumpets sounded, and the open carriage, with the Emperor and Empress, Albert sitting opposite them, drove up, and they got out. I cannot say what indescribable emotions filled me, how much all seemed like a wonderful dream." And then with a superb touch she adds: " These great meetings of Sovereigns, surrounded by every exciting accompaniment, are always very agitating."

She stepped forward and embraced the Emperor on both cheeks, and also "the very gentle, graceful and evidently very nervous Empress." A solemn procession was formed, and they proceeded upstairs to the Throne Room, where the great officers of State, Clarendon amongst them, were assembled.

Next day Kathy and Lady Palmerston travelled to Windsor together, and there was a great dinner that night in St. George's Hall. The Queen presented Lady Clarendon to the Empress before dinner, and Clarendon presented her to the Emperor after dinner. The Empress, Kathy found "very gracious, very pleasing and very pretty: she evidently enjoys fun, and is now clearly comfortable and at her ease with the Queen. The enormous size of the petticoats of the Empress and her ladies," she adds, " is quite remarkable, a complete return to the old fashion of hoops." It will be remembered that the Empress, at the time, was expecting a child (the Prince Imperial, born in December of that year), and had invented the crinoline to draw a veil over her condition. Perhaps this was the first time that the crinoline had been seen in England. " The Emperor's countenance," continues Kathy, " is very curious, there is something melancholy about it. But it strikes me also," she adds darkly, with many underlinings, " that it might look very savage. There is a want of proportion about his figure which takes much off from grace, his head and shoulders have the appearance of belonging to a much taller man than he is—his legs are much too short—yet his manners are dignified from their composure, and he plays his part in the best taste, a very difficult part to play." After dinner that night there was a ball, which Kathy thought " rather solemn," " the pauses between the dances rather too long, and not enough girls invited." Next day the Emperor was invested a Knight of the Garter, and Clarendon, who attended the ceremony, told Kathy that Napoleon " did not quite kneel while the Queen ' fumbled ostensibly as she always does,' to show her unfamiliarity with the slightly indiscreet article of male attire."

After the ceremony the Emperor declared that he had taken an oath of fidelity to the Queen, and that his whole life would be a proof that he would faithfully adhere to it. Victoria was delighted. The more she saw of him, the more delighted she was with him. None of the sovereigns of Europe had ever treated her like this before, and she liked it.

Between festivities they had long perambulations on the terrace together, and the Emperor referred to Albert as " Le Prince, votre époux," and everything was very homely and gemütlich.

There was a reception at the Guildhall by the City of London, the Lord Mayor in full panoply having with him as guest the Préfet of the Seine and other high notables of the Paris Municipality. It was an impressive affair. The Emperor delivered an

admirable speech, in which, among other things, he made a graceful allusion to the days of his exile in England, and this was very
well received.   Clarendon, of, course, was on duty during the
whole of the visit, and wrote hourly notes to Kathy about it all.
" A very bad despatch from Vienna," he writes at the end of one
of them.   " The Russians decline, and I am horribly afraid that
J. R. is making a mess "—a premonition of the trouble that was
coming.

The festivities continued.   A gala performance at the opera; a
visit to the Crystal Palace; a reception to meet the *Corps Diplomatique* at the Walewskis'; a Council of War at Buckingham
Palace.   At last on Saturday, April 21st, it was all over, and the
Imperial pair departed in a cloud of glory, while " the common
light of day " descended with a rush once more upon London and
Windsor, and Victoria admitted to feeling very flat.   She had
fallen completely for the exotic little man who paid her compliments, who treated her at once with the exaggerated respect due
to the Queen of England, but knew so artfully how to mingle with
this the more subtle flavour of a hardly disguised liking and
admiration for her as a woman.   This she had not had from
anyone, not even from Albert.   It was a form of flattery which
she (unconsciously) found to be extremely congenial to her.
Years afterwards she was to have it again, from a very different
source—from Disraeli.   And she reacted then as she reacted now.
The response was identical and immediate.   She liked it, and she
liked the people who gave it her.   And she had no conception of
the reason why.

CHAPTER XX
THE RETURN VISIT

§ 1

AND now came murmurs of Johnny's doings in Vienna. For a month the high-minded, conscientious but impulsive Russell had sat at the Conference table surrounded by the subtlest diplomatists in Europe.

From the first it was apparent that Russia would not consent to the limitation of her naval forces in the Black Sea. This was unhopeful, as the point represented one of the four bases of peace which the Allies were determined to build on. The other three were as follows: (1) The Russian protectorate of the Principalities to be replaced by a "Collective Guarantee"; (2) the navigation of the mouths of the Danube to be free; (3) the renunciation by Russia of any political protectorate over the Sultan's subjects of whatever religion.

Russell himself thought the limitation of Russia's armaments in the Black Sea was not a vital point, and his view became known both in Vienna and at home. The Government were not pleased, and Palmerston wrote tetchily to Clarendon:

"What Cowley says of John Russell is true—he has never been accustomed to deal *personally* with artful negotiators, and he has an unlucky habit of suddenly giving way on matters in regard to which he had previously taken an irrevocable stand. Horace Walpole, I think, says of the Duke of Bedford of his day, that he was never immovable upon any opinion unless it was one which had been instilled into him by somebody else, in direct opposition to his own previous convictions."

Worse was to follow. When Count Buol, the Austrian Envoy, suggested a plan by which, instead of limiting the Russian forces in the Black Sea, Turkey, France and England were to increase theirs, Russell, instead of saying that for practical and economic reasons the scheme was a *mauvaise plaisanterie*, took it up with enthusiasm, and returned home to press it upon Palmerston and Clarendon, who were furious at this defection. Aware of their disapproval, Russell, as usual, offered his resignation.

This was extremely awkward. For the Government's sake, for the Emperor's sake, for Lord John's own sake, it must never be thought that the British Plenipotentiary had been a party to the *débâcle* at Vienna over this point. There must be no explanations.

Clarendon, who still held the threads of negotiations in his hands, was determined that the Government should show a united front to what had taken place at Vienna. Buol's scheme should be shown to have received no support from any source. It must be shown that, although Lord John as plenipotentiary at Vienna may have temporarily approved the scheme, on returning home and in consultation with his Government, he became quite convinced of its inadvisability, and was as sound as any other member of the Government in condemning it. Only so was there any prospect of reopening the *pour-parlers* on the subject of peace. Any weakening on the part of the Allies would immeasurably postpone the prospects of a settlement. For three days Palmerston and he worked upon Russell to prevent his resigning, and in the end they won. He gave in, pocketed his pride, and resumed. It cost him a great deal; and still more did it cost him to get up in his place in the House on May 24th, and answer a vote of censure introduced by Disraeli with special reference to the Vienna negotiations. He replied at length. It was a fine, fighting speech expressing the Government's resolute determination to carry on the war, and to curb the power of Russia. He went into no particulars with regard to the negotiations, and of course no reference whatever was made to Buol's scheme, which he himself had thought a fair basis upon which to negotiate. The speech was well received by the House, and the motion of censure was routed from the field. Unfortunately, Buol himself read the speech and was dumbfounded.

How could it possibly be that Lord John Russell, with whom he had parted on terms of perfect understanding with regard to the scheme for the third point, should have spoken thus in Parliament? How was it that the British plenipotentiary should hold one language in Vienna, and quite another in London? He could hardly believe his eyes as he looked at the text of the speech. When repeated perusals convinced him of the truth, he was at first shocked and surprised. Finally, he became very angry. It seemed to him as bad a piece of political treachery as he had ever met with in the course of a long and artful life. He determined that the British Government should not get away with it. With the utmost cynicism—for what good it could possibly do it is hard to conjecture—he proceeded to let the cat out of the bag. He accordingly issued a circular to the representatives of Austria at foreign Courts in which he stated his version of the story, disclosed for the first time the proposals he had made for the termination of the dispute over the Black Sea

17

point, and added wickedly, "The Ministers of France and England, in confidential interviews, showed themselves decidedly inclined to recommend the same to their Governments with all their influence."

This was appalling; and the effect throughout Europe was electric. In England all eyes turned upon Russell, who stood out upon a very white sheet.

There was a pause, and then the tempest broke. The Press fell upon Lord John with a fury that was both unprecedented and unashamed. And the attack of course, was not confined to the newspapers. Lord John was asked in the House whether Count Buol's statements were accurate, and he had to admit that they were so. The debate that ensued, though it afforded Lord John an opportunity for explanation, only increased his difficulties, and accentuated his embarrassment. For while, on the one hand, he could not avoid speaking, on the other he could not give the true reasons that influenced him. Thus his explanation fell flat and inadequate upon his audience. It looked as if nothing could save the Government if John Russell remained in it. Palmerston and Clarendon and such other members of the Cabinet as were in possession of the facts about Vienna (not all of them were) were ready to stand by Russell, and to face the motion in the House. But Russell did the only possible, the only generous thing under the circumstances. He resigned himself. And this time he went with the goodwill of all his colleagues, for in going he had undoubtedly saved the Government.

§ 2

In August took place the return visit of the English Royals to Paris; and as was fitting, Clarendon accompanied them as Minister-in-waiting. Napoleon was determined that his visit should clinch the impression he knew he had made upon Victoria at Windsor, and he spared no pains to make it a success. Moreover, it should be magnificent and the entertainment far more beautiful and impressive than that with which he and Eugénie had been regaled in England, magnificent though that had been. The Second Empire should coruscate and be made to display all the beauty of its manifold, changing colours before the astonished, unsophisticated gaze of England's royal Mistress. The Alliance at this juncture was important to him. Not only should Victoria be dazzled by the magnificence of her reception; she should also —he would see to it—be struck by the frankness and simplicity of his bearing towards her. Victoria should become his *friend*.

Surrounded by a brilliant staff he was there to meet her on the Quay at Boulogne. He rode by her carriage to the station, a gay and gallant cavalier. The reception in Paris was overwhelming, and, late though the hour was, they trotted the whole seven and a half miles to St. Cloud through roaring multitudes. Ninety thousand troops, including National Guards, lined the way: and that night Marshal Magnan told Clarendon that he had known Paris in all its phases for fifty years, but that he had never seen it like that—not even when Napoleon returned after Austerlitz. This was a good beginning. But it was nothing to what followed. A fête at Versailles, where the Grandes Eaux were made to play, followed by lunch at the Trianon, all done with *équipages* and a *train* that had not been seen since the days of Louis XIV. A gala performance at the Opera; a review; a State visit to the Exhibition; a visit to the Tuileries; three and a half hours' sight-seeing at the Louvre; and—perhaps the high-water mark in point of magnificence—a ball at the Hotel de Ville, of which Clarendon says: "Nothing in the Arabian Nights could equal the enchanted Palace of the Hotel de Ville. I never dreamt of anything so fairylike, but I will not attempt a description that our own correspondents will do, of course, far better than I."

Victoria went through it all in a dream. Before the visit, she had been slightly apprehensive, and rather fearful lest the programme should prove too much for her. She had made Clarendon write to Cowley and let it be intimated to the Emperor that she was easily tired. But *l'appétit vient en mangeant*. When presented for the first time in a European capital with foreign multitudes, all acclaiming *her*, all scrambling for a glimpse of *her*, all projecting large waves of goodwill and pleasure towards *her*, she came to life in an astonishing manner; she expanded like a flower; she responded eagerly, with dignity and grace. By the second day she was settling down quite frankly to enjoy herself. With the true German passion for sight-seeing she insisted upon being shown *everything*. As for it tiring her, she had quite forgotten all about that. "As for the Queen," writes Clarendon, "no Royal Person ever yet known or to be known in history comes up to her in *indefatigability*. Conceive her walking in the heat here for an hour in the morning, then going over the Tuileries, and then for three and a half hours perambulating the Louvre, knowing that she had the Ball at the Hotel de Louvre in prospect, the weather being the sort of sirocco we had at Nola di Gaeta—do you remember?"

At the Louvre, Victoria quite knocked everybody up, "the Emperor during the last league going in great distress," and some of the Courtiers showing visible signs of wear and tear. But Victoria, sublimely unconscious, marched ruthlessly on down gallery after gallery, looking, asking, and being informed. A very fat male member of the French entourage, tightly uniformed, and perspiring profusely, murmured in Clarendon's ear, "*Je donnerais tout—tout—la Venus de Milo y incluse—pour un verre de limonade.*" At the end of this expedition, when Clarendon expressed a hope that she was not more tired than she looked, Victoria replied sweetly that she was not in the least tired, but that perhaps her feet ached a little. And it was because she was so natural, because she was obviously enjoying herself among them, that all Paris went mad about her. Her graciousness, her dignity, her smile, all were eagerly canvassed and approved; some even going so far as to think her looks enchanting. "The unaccountable dignity with the short stature, and *bienveillance* of manner have walked into their hearts," wrote Clarendon to his wife, "I thought the Dames de la Halle would have kissed her this morning."

And Napoleon led her on from triumph to triumph. Perhaps the *comble* of the whole visit was the moment when, torch in hand, he conducted her through the shadowy outer spaces of the Invalides at dusk to the circular ramp that guards the sunken chapel where the first Napoleon lies in his great porphyry sarcophagus. Here in the presence of his nephew and of the great officers of state of both nations, Victoria of England gazed down upon the resting place of England's greatest enemy, while the organ, discreetly muffled, gave out the strains of "God Save the Queen." All were deeply moved and impressed at the scene. "What a page of history," wrote Clarendon.

During the whole visit, Clarendon's time, as may be imagined, was more than fully occupied. Not only was he Minister-in-waiting, and required to take part, fully uniformed, in every function and ceremony, but he was also Minister of Foreign Affairs, and the State visit to Paris by no means diminished his work in that capacity. By daily messenger, the red boxes streamed in as usual from the Foreign Office, and his powers of sheer endurance were taxed to the utmost. "We dine in full uniform at 6.15," he writes, "and then go to the Grand Opera, so that the scramble is greater and the time for doing anything less even than I thought, for the accumulation of undone business is quite frightful to look at and think of, and I have not been in bed above five hours any night yet, so you may suppose I am getting a little tired, but I am quite well, and the being so much in the air takes the place of sleep, I suppose."

But he managed to snatch moments for writing to Kathy. "There," he cries in the middle of one of them, "I had got so far when a horrified footman rushed into my room to say that the Queen was already gone and that the last carriage of the cortège was kept waiting for me."

No sooner had Clarendon started upon this State visit than an

invitation arrived for Kathy and the two elder girls to go over
to Paris and to take part in the festivities. The notice was so
short and the difficulties so great that Lady Clarendon decided
against it. It would have been a difficult situation for her to
have been placed in. She could not have taken her rightful
place with Clarendon in the various ceremonies and festivities,
and at moments it would have been very awkward for her. The
same contingency had arisen in the spring visit of the French
Royals to Windsor with regard to Lady Cowley and her daughters,
who were invited to England for the occasion. But Lord Cowley,
foreseeing the difficulties they would sometimes have been placed
in, had not allowed them to go. Clarendon warmly approved his
wife's decision. "The Empress," he writes, "asked directly
after you and seemed rather surprised that you were not at Paris,
and I could not help saying how much you would have liked it,
but on an occasion like the present it would have been disagreeable for you, '*de ne pas nous trouver ensemble.*' She looked a
leetle put out." In a later letter he refers to it again. "I could
never have borne that at the Theatres and Fêtes, etc., I should
have been going off in comfortable state in the next carriage to
the Emperor's, and that you should have been *à la bonne aven-
ture*, to be taken care of by *anybody*, for the Cowleys being in
the same boat as myself, could have done nothing for you. In
short," he adds, "we should both have *lost caste*, by *submitting*
to it."

The Empress herself took very little part in the visit. Her
condition made it impossible for her to assist at the long and
tiring festivities. Pale and nervous ("she can talk to the ladies
of nothing but her condition," wrote Clarendon), she floated
across the background, a kind, attentive hostess.

In the midst of all the shouting, Clarendon could not resist
snatching a moment to call upon his old friend Madame de
Montijo, and to congratulate her on the brilliant destiny of her
daughter, that daughter that he remembered so well in '31, a
fair-haired child, when he himself, a young and aspiring diplomat,
had come to spend long hours in her mother's apartment which
held so many associations for him. In different circumstances he
found her on this occasion, yet there was much that had not
altered. The Emperor had given her a charming house and here
he found her surrounded by the *bibelots* and pretty things that he
remembered so well. He had not seen her for years. She had aged
and grown stout, but otherwise the years had not changed her. She
was still invincibly the same, and her position as mother of the
Empress touched her not at all. She took no rank other than that
her birth allowed her, nor did she wish for any; and she remained,
just as he remembered her, astute, worldly, frank and completely

unprincipled. Clarendon she received with a mocking gaiety redolent of the past. She was delighted to see Milord, who had grown so great a personage in Europe these days. Everybody was talking about him and saying pretty things about him; and to think she had known him when he was plain George Villiers, hein? Well, well, the ways of Providence were strange indeed. To think of la petite Eugénie, now! Who would have thought it? Ah, but she was beautiful. Did he not think her beautiful, now? And she was going to have a child, this time for sure. That mishap of the year before; it was not natural, no; it had been brought on by those who did not wish her to have an heir. She knew what she knew. But this time, for sure; and pray God it might be a boy. The Emperor now, he quite doted on her. And did Milord know that when the marriage was already declared the Emperor came to her in great distress of mind with a letter in his hand from some busybody who stated, what do you think?—oh, no really, it was too good—it stated that Eugénie was *Milord's daughter*! "And what did you say to him?" asked Clarendon. The old Spanish woman looked at him with the utmost simplicity. "'Sire,' I said, 'les dates ne correspondent pas.'"

Clarendon told Kathy of this interview, and she dutifully records it in her journal with the icy comment: "Funny story to repeat to George himself. I did not know that she was aware of the report which has been so prevalent that the Empress was George's daughter, and as it is by no means a flattering report to her character, it seems queer that she should talk about it thus to him."

And so he left his old friend, glad to have touched again for a moment the hand that had been so kind to him in the past, and returned to his duties in the present, to find the Queen just returned from a fête, and *would* Lord Clarendon kindly make a *brouillon* for a letter of thanks to the Préfet. . . .

But at last it all came to an end, and Victoria departed with a flourish from St. Cloud in an open carriage drawn by eight horses with postilions. The night before the departure Clarendon came upon her in a pensive mood. "Isn't it odd, Lord Clarendon," she said, "the Emperor remembers every frock he has ever seen me in!"

CHAPTER XXI

THE END OF THE WAR

§ 1

ON Monday, September 18th (1855), the longed-for news arrived. Despatches were received in London with the intelligence that Sebastopol was a smoking ruin in the hands of the allies. The long agony was over. The impregnable place had fallen. It was as if a shadow had passed from the face of the sun. The relief was immense and the rejoicings universal.

Clarendon's despatch informing the Queen reached her after dinner at Balmoral, whereupon the entire party, headed by Albert and joined by gillies, keepers and half the village, proceeded up the cairn to light the bonfire that had long been prepared for this historic occasion. "Our children," wrote Kathy proudly in her journal, "received the news . . . with truly British cheers." For her, as for the nation at large, there was only one fly in the ointment, "the despatch received late last night," she says, "gave Mrs. G. and me pain and anxiety, for it announced that the French had taken the Malakoff, but that the British had failed to take the Redan, and one's British feelings are hurt by this apparent contrast." However, these sad reflections were soon effaced by the fact that "dear little Emily's birthday was kept to-day by a rural tea-drinking and cooking for themselves at the Temple of Pan . . . it was very pretty."

However disappointing it might be that the final and successful *coup de main* was delivered by the French, the great fact remained—the city was in the hands of the allies and the Russians were in full retreat. The right to impose what conditions we chose concerning the Black Sea had been justified by arms. So far, so good. But victory was not yet pushed home, and it all too soon became apparent that with the fall of Sebastopol the French were of opinion that "honour was satisfied," and the entire autumn and winter were occupied by the Cabinet, and Clarendon in particular, aided by the Court, in attempting to prevent the Emperor from being inveigled into a premature peace.

§ 2

France and England stood in quite different relations to the peace question. The French had gone into the war on a particular point—the guardianship of the Holy Places. A great many other questions had been involved as well, but fundamentally the issue was clear. And now that the Russian power had been smashed in the Near East and the glory of the French arms vindicated, it was difficult to see reason to continue a war which was daily becoming more unpopular.

England, on the other hand, desired no less than the complete future security of the Ottoman Empire. Her arms had not been graced with signal victory, and an incensed public demanded the prosecution of the war. When, as was the case, Austria and France began to negotiate separately with Russia, and only invited England's consent to terms which had already been formulated, Palmerston, voicing the feeling of the country, was ferocious. Clarendon restrained him in so far as to make him send back a *modification* of the terms suggested, and not a *refusal* of them. Not trusting his suave and conciliatory Foreign Secretary to put into words all that he felt upon the subject, Palmerston himself wrote an angry and offensive letter to Persigny, the French Ambassador in London, for transmission to Walewski, in which he asked whether the French Government was aware of the fact that England was a principal in this affair and not a mere political and diplomatic contingency. He also stated that rather than be dragged into an unsatisfactory peace, England would sustain the struggle with the aid of Turkey alone, and that he was at liberty to tell his Government as much. The copy of this letter—it had already been sent—fell out of a red-box one November morning on Clarendon's writing-table, and annoyed him very much. The trouble was done and remonstrance was useless, but it all could have been put so much less offensively. Was this Palmerston, Prime Minister? Was this the "Babe of Grace"? And of course it was left to the Secretary of State to smooth the troubled waters that would arise.

Persigny would demand explanations. Sure enough the next day Clarendon writes:

"I had not been here ten minutes this morning before the French Ambassador wished to see me, and I was surprised that he walked in with his usual *gaillard*, good-humoured look. He began, however, by saying, '*J'ai eu une lettre de Lord Palmerston qui m'a beaucoup emotionné tant par la substance que par la forme, qui est bien dure.*' He then pulled out the letter which, of course, I made as if I had not seen, and I managed partly by agreeing with what Palmerston said, and at the last paragraph by saying, 'Oh, that's a form of expression used by a man who feels strongly, and Palmerston *is* in a position that makes him feel strongly,' to calm the little man and make him perfectly reasonable."

Even so, Clarendon did not spare France over her attitude to the modifications, and he adds:

"I must own that I was in better humour with Palmerston's letter from having just read one from Cowley, giving an account of Walewski's insolence, and his surprise at our having ventured to suggest any modifications. I was boiling with rage and therefore defended Palmerston *con amore*, nor could I deny when Palmerston asked me this afternoon whether with reference to Cowley's letter, I now thought his too strong, I really could not say I did. We mean to adhere to our modifications, and I convinced Persigny that they were right."

But Clarendon was anxious.

"The French," he wrote, "have been screaming for peace so loudly that I expect Austria will be frightened at the hard terms she has imposed upon Russia, and may want to back out of them. In short, it is a very nervous moment."

But, in all this, the Emperor was by no means as identified with his Government as was thought over here. He was anxious for peace. He thought the time had come to make peace. But he was no more desirous than we were to make a peace which would not show unequivocally upon which side victory lay. And he was sound upon one point: he would not enter into a peace in which England would not concur.

But with Paris demanding that the war should end he had to play a difficult game. He himself thought the Austrian proposals sufficient. To these he intended to adhere, and his policy was to bring England to adhere to them as well. The feeling between the two countries was running somewhat high at the moment— at least, in Government circles. He now used his high prerogative to overreach it. He sat down and wrote a letter to the Queen herself, as one monarch to another. The letter is an interesting document. It is at once affectionate and frank; sincere and to the point. And quite short, a statement of difficulties between friends.

First, he emphasised the independence of both nations: "We are both of us free in our actions, we have the same interests, and we wish the same thing—an honourable peace." What alternatives lay before them? To *conquer* Russia was impossible; to blockade her useless; to try to coerce all nations to take part against her in a crusade to free Poland, Finland and Circassia would be dangerous. Was it not best, then, to secure Austrian co-operation in negotiating peace terms which France and Austria both considered reasonable, which Russia seemed prepared to accept, and which, moreover, differed so very little from those with which Lord Palmerston had been ready to concur? He remained, with further protestations of affection and goodwill, Her Majesty's devoted and true brother, Napoleon.

Victoria was pleased and touched at this letter, and also slightly agitated. It was an important letter and needed a clear and carefully worded reply. Albert made *brouillons* for two days and finally arrived at a version which they both thought adequate. But the Queen was loath to despatch so significant a document without the approval of her Ministers-in-Chief. It was a Sunday, and Clarendon was snatching a rare interval of rest at the Grove. But a royal messenger arrived across country from Windsor with an urgent request from the Queen that he would come to her at once on important business, and there was nothing for it but to obey. On arriving at Windsor he found Palmerston already ensconced, and the four of them—Victoria, Albert, Palmerston and himself—immediately proceeded to the business of drafting the letter. It was a very long letter that they finally agreed to. In the first place it pointed out, rather carefully, the differences between their relative positions as monarchs. Next Victoria was allowed to comment tartly on the want of courtesy involved in France's action of concerting a plan with Austria and of placing it as a *fait accompli* before England for acceptance or rejection. The letter then stressed three points: (1) That England, even if she agreed to the scheme, could not be bound to the letter of proposals which she had not discussed; (2) that Austria should be made to stand to her ultimatum, and to break off negotiations if it were not accepted; (3) that any arrangements concerning the neutralisation of the Black Sea should be such as England was known to consider satisfactory.

Victoria then warned the Emperor of the disadvantage to France if it were loudly proclaimed, as it was beginning to be, that France could not carry on the war any longer owing to financial difficulties. Finally, she assured him that she was convinced of the good that would come of these frank and direct communications between sovereigns, and she remained his very affectionate sister and friend, Victoria R.

This letter had its effect. The Emperor frankly admitted our right to take exception to the way the terms of the ultimatum had been settled without consultation with England. He went more closely himself into the question of "the modifications," which had been represented to him by his Government as mere "microscopical advantages," which we were trying to gain, and had to admit the justice of some of them. Above all, the hint in the Queen's letter that efforts everywhere were being made to have it supposed that France was willing to make peace on any terms annoyed him exceedingly. His attitude stiffened. He let it be known that whatever peace rumours might be circulated for the benefit of the Bourse, he would not be a party to a peace of which England disapproved. "Rest assured," he said to Lord Cowley, "whatever I think right I will do, and I shall not be afraid of making my conduct understood in France."

§ 3

December dawned wanly over a distracted Europe.

The diplomatic world flickered with uncertain fires. The weather was depressing: there were interminable fogs in London. However, a sparkle of amusement was afforded by the King of Sardinia's visit to England. A contingent of brave Sardinians were at the moment in the Crimea. So the King was, of course, "our gallant ally." He came, a huge figure of a man with fierce moustaches and rolling eyes, accompanied by a small, round, inquisitive-looking secretary and Minister-in-attendance, who blinked discreetly through his glasses, and to whom nobody at the time paid much attention. But his name happened to be Cavour, and Europe was to ring with it in a few years' time. The King was completely unsophisticated. He had no small talk whatsoever. The great ladies who were asked to meet him terrified him beyond measure. He whispered to Clarendon that the Queen "*lui avait joué un joli tour*" in having presented him to a circle of them and left him alone to deal with them. Clearing his throat portentously, he shouted at Lady Granville: "*Eh bien, madame, qu'avez vous fait de beau?*" And that lady, equal as she was to most situations, was so taken aback that she could only stammer weakly: "*Pas grand'chose, Sire!*" He told the Queen that he never lived in society and that he always dined alone, "*seul avec mes chagrins*," which touched her very much. He rolled his eyes meditatively upon the Princess Royal—but not for long. During the visit he had a talk with Clarendon, in which he asked whether Milord, in the general settlement that was so soon coming now, could not manage for him *une petite extension de territoire*, and took Clarendon's contemptuous shrug of the shoulders in quite good part. Albert showed him Woolwich Arsenal, and Victoria was up at five o'clock in the morning to see him off. He gained nothing by the visit and departed amid a little ripple of laughter. But a high destiny awaited him. His hour had not yet struck, that was all.

§ 4

Christmas came and went, and the bells rang in the New Year —1856. Europe still simmered angrily, and the despatches

flowed from the Foreign Office in a constant stream, where
Clarendon sat like a patient fisherman casting his line endlessly
backwards and forwards over the troubled waters. But in the
first fortnight of the year an event took place which shattered the
harmony of his personal life and was a great blow to the whole
Villiers family.

Mrs. George, now in her eightieth year, was suddenly taken ill.
She lingered for a few days in a twilight of consciousness, very
feeble, but not suffering, and died on George's birthday, January
12th. It was almost inconceivable to the Villiers as they gathered
at her bedside that the inveterate old woman, so part and parcel of
their lives, so gallant and undefeated, so kind and so gay, was
really going to leave them for good. What would life be without
that laugh, without that insatiable zest for news, for human gossip
of all kind that it was the joy of each member of the family to
play up to? What would life be without those long, detailed
letters that told them all so little that they did not know before,
but so much about the indomitable spirit that indited them. A
long life she had had, and in the main a happy one. She had had
struggles, but in the end all obstacles had given way before her
sheer zest for life. All her dearest wishes were at last accomplished. She had lived to see Theresa happily married and her
beloved George Secretary of State. So identified had she become
of late years with all that touched or concerned her children and
her grandchildren that it seemed almost a reversal of nature to
them that she should so suddenly be gone from them for ever.

It was at once a consolation and an anxiety to Clarendon that,
being in the midst of affairs important to the whole nation, it was
his bounden duty to wrench his mind from his own personal
sorrow to the business of State. On first hearing that Mrs. Villiers
was dying, the Queen hastened to write a line of sympathy, and
in the course of his reply Clarendon said: '' Your Majesty may
rest assured that no affliction of his own could make Lord
Clarendon unmindful of his duty to Your Majesty, and he trusts
that the public business will not suffer from the calamity that has
befallen him.'' The next day—his birthday—the end came. And
the Queen wrote from Windsor:

'' . . . It is with deep concern we learn that the last sad scene
is closed, and that Lord Clarendon has lost his beloved mother.
Such a loss is one that can never be repaired. It is one of the
links which is broken on earth; but at the same time, one which,
as it were, seems to connect us already with another and a better
world.

'' It must be a consolation in the midst of his grief for Lord
Clarendon to think that the last days—indeed, the Queen believes,
weeks—of his dear mother's life were spent in happiness under

his roof'' (she had been moved to Grosvenor Crescent), ''surrounded by his children, and cheered by the pride she must have felt in having a son who rendered such invaluable services to his country and his Sovereign.''

'' These were no mere words of courtesy,'' says Theodore Martin in his *Life of the Prince Consort*, from which the above is quoted: '' they were prompted by regard for the statesman to whose friendship and sagacity the Queen and Prince knew by experience they could appeal with confidence in all circumstances of nicety and difficulty, and whose ability in his conduct of Foreign Affairs, since they had been under his charge, had been of no small importance in consolidating the Alliance between France and Sardinia, and in bringing the great conflict in which we were engaged to the point at which Russia found it necessary to negotiate for peace.''

CHAPTER XXII
THE PEACE TREATY

§ 1

AND now hardly had Mrs. George been laid in her grave than a turn in the European situation called for Clarendon's whole attention. On January 15th Russia accepted the Austrian ultimatum and declared herself ready to come to the conference table. Two months had been spent by the British Government in pressing amendments to the Austrian proposals, and in the end the substance of our "modifications" were embodied in the ultimatum that Prince Esterhazy submitted to the Czar. Russia had made one last wriggle in the shape of a number of modifications, but when she found these were not countenanced she had given way.

Clarendon considered that we had gained the substance of that for which we went to war—namely, the salvation of the Ottoman Empire, the denial of Russia's right of suzerainty over the Christian subjects of the Sultan, the destruction of Russia's power in the Black Sea. He himself was ready for peace, but he had no doubt that the nation at large would not be satisfied with such a peace and would vent their hatred and contempt upon the negotiator of the treaty which should now be made.

Under the circumstances it required no little self-sacrifice to offer himself as the victim, and to suggest Paris, and not London, as the seat of the *pour-parlers*. But he knew, none better, that the Emperor was the lock to the door of peace, and that he, Clarendon, alone amongst the English statesmen possessed the key to its secret mechanism. The Queen appreciated his disinterested motive and was convinced by his argument, as indeed was Palmerston. So the matter was settled, and Clarendon undertook the thankless task of Chief British Plenipotentiary (with Lord Cowley as his second) simply because, having the whole threads in his hands, he knew himself to be the only man fitted to lead the deliberations and bring them to a sound conclusion in accordance with the minimum demands of Great Britain.

And now in the weeks that followed Clarendon reached, perhaps, the climax of his career. The part of plenipotentiary—of negotiator in matters of policy between the great European nations—was one peculiarly suited to his gifts and talents. At the conference table he was forceful, he was persuasive, he was firm. All the diffidence that he felt when faced with a debate in the House of Lords fell away from him. He could command a situation and drive his will across opposing wills. He had an instinctive sense for the European polity. Unlike John Russell, he was a realist in foreign affairs, and he knew every move of the game. Armed with a complete knowledge of all the negotiations which had led to the conference, he was, as he admitted to the Queen, the person best fitted to sit with Lord Cowley at the conference table on behalf of Great Britain. And the result justified this assumption. By persuasion, by firmness and insistence, and by sheer force of character it was he who dominated the situation in Paris and gained a peace which, if it did not completely overthrow Russia (which was what the warmongers in England still wished), yet embodied all we had a right to ask, conceded all that we had gone to war for and was a peace honourable to England, and very different, be it said, to that which the Emperor or Walewski would have concluded, had they been left to their own devices.

But in a Paris wearied of war, the dominance of Clarendon's personality in the council chamber, the unyielding nature of his insistence upon points that the Emperor and Walewski considered of secondary importance, his severity with the Russians and his influence over the Emperor were all looked upon with suspicion amounting to dislike. But much of it was laid at Palmerston's door. "I understand that I am not considered by nature a wild beast," he writes to the Prime Minister, "but that I am a slave of the English newspapers and the representative of your anti-Russian feelings; and that as peace would be fatal to your Government, I am here for the purpose of making it impossible."

From the outset his difficulties were enormous. To stiffen the Emperor and Walewski to accept nothing short of the full extent of the Austrian peace proposals, read, moreover, in the light of his own and the British Cabinet's interpretation of them, this was the nature of his task. The full measure of the Austrian proposals with certain material guarantees for their proper execution demanded by Great Britain would *just* be acceptable as peace terms. Anything short of this, any weakening as to the guarantees, any swerving from any of the points involved, would mean a peace that would fall short of the minimum that England felt justified in demanding. Unfortunately, there was considerable divergence of opinion between the French and English Governments upon the relative importance of certain of the pledges and guarantees. Worse still, the Emperor and Walewski did not see the English point of view in the matter, and Clarendon, knowing that peace had to be made, realised that he must use all his arts and devices to stage an act of wholesale bluff. Moreover, the Russians were

not unaware of this division of opinion, and their plenipotentiaries
would have constant access to the Emperor, whilst Walewski's
Russian sympathies were, of course, well known to them.
Napoleon's views were a mystery, but there was at least one
personal reason which made him desire peace. Eugénie was
about to have a child; and if this proved to be a boy, what more
fitting entrance into the world for the eaglet than the celebration
of a great European peace, concluded at Paris under his father's
ægis, with guns firing and the people cheering?

The opening of the conference was fixed for February 26th, but
Clarendon thought it advisable to be in Paris well before that date,
and he arrived there on February 16th. That night he dined with
the Emperor at the Tuileries, and afterwards, alone in the
Emperor's study, they talked of European affairs: of Sardinia and
the future of Italy—and here Clarendon put in a plea that the
Sardinian delegates might be treated at the conference on terms of
perfect equality with the great nations, and the Emperor agreed
that this should be so. They talked frankly of the Alliance, and
the Emperor said pretty things of the letter from Victoria of which
Clarendon had been the bearer. And then Clarendon unburdened
himself of his views with regard to the coming conference. He
said that peace—even such a peace as they had a right to expect—
would be certain to result if only Great Britain and France were
unyielding in their demands upon Russia to fulfil in spirit and in
letter the full terms of the Austrian proposals. He warned the
Emperor that every species of flattery and machination would be
employed—was already being employed in Paris—to gain concessions and to deflect the purpose of the Alliance, and he begged
the Emperor to be very careful in his language to the Russian
plenipotentiaries, Brunnow and Orloff, when he should see them.
He even went so far as to intimate that he knew that persons of
high standing who were for " peace at any price " had daily access
to the Emperor, and he ventured to hope that His Majesty was
lending a deaf ear to counsels that were not in perfect harmony
with the spirit of the Alliance. This touched the Emperor upon a
point of honour and roused him from his lethargy. He said that
if Russia refused to fulfil the conditions agreed to he would have
no more difficulty in continuing the war now than he had had two
years before in declaring it. The conversation was important, not
so much for what it actually effected as for the fact that at the
outset it established the tone of intimacy and frankness in which,
as it proved, all their subsequent conversations were to be held,
and which did so much to enable Clarendon to gain an influence
over the mind and heart of the Emperor. There is no doubt that
the Emperor liked Clarendon personally. And that was half the
battle.

On arriving in Paris the British Minister was not best pleased to hear from Walewski that Brunnow was already ensconced there. Part of his object in going to Paris so soon was to forestall the arrival of the Russians. However, Walewski informed him that Brunnow was anxious to meet him before the opening of the conference, and this at least seemed to show a conciliatory spirit. Accordingly he asked Brunnow to call upon him.

It was a curious meeting. They had known each other well in the past. And the last time they had met was at the British Foreign Office, when Brunnow, almost in tears, had come to demand his passports on the eve of war. Now he found him in a highly conciliatory mood, anxious to blame the policy of his late master and to assure Clarendon that the new Czar held very different views of Russia's Eastern policy. They discussed the origins of the war, and Brunnow laid the blame largely upon Menchikoff's high-handed, injudicious diplomacy—or lack of it— in Constantinople. But Clarendon came away from the conversation with the impression that there was going to be trouble over two points—the fortress of Kars and the Bessarabian frontier line.

§ 2

The conference opened formally on February 26th, when twelve statesmen met round a green baize table to try to unravel the complicated tangle into which the affairs of Europe had got themselves. Lord Clarendon and Lord Cowley represented Great Britain, Count Walewski and Baron de Bourquenay, France, Ali Pascha and Mehemet Djemal Bey, Turkey. Count Buol and Baron Hubner represented Austria, Count Cavour and the Marquis of Villamarina Sardinia; and Count Orloff and Baron de Brunnow were the Russian plenipotentiaries. Six countries were involved, and the niceties and distinctions of their separate interests in relation to the common object—peace—made, to say the least, an interesting psychological display. France played for safety. Peace must be concluded, and Walewski, the Emperor and Bourquenay were for ever trying to keep the balance between the stringent demands of Great Britain and the attempt of Russia to evade them.

Austria, the official mediator, whose part in the war had not been very creditable, was distrusted by all: by Russia because she thought that Austria was the tool of England and France in an attempt to humiliate her; by France because the Emperor and Walewski were veering away from her politically and turning their eyes towards Russia; by England because she suspected that Austria would in the last resort, and through fear, attempt to gain concessions for Russia at the conference table. Sardinia was

18

there to press the affairs of Italy against Austria, who herself had
strongly objected to Sardinia's being represented at the conference
at all. And Prussia, whose vaunted neutrality during the war
only admitted her to the conference after the disputes between the
belligerents had been settled, signalised her entry by attempting to
get the preamble to the treaty so worded as to make it appear that
she had been a party to the deliberations of the conference from
the first. It was a hotch-potch of opposing interests and conflicting wills.

As the long sessions succeeded each other the conference more
and more resolved itself into a battle between Clarendon and the
Russians, with Walewski, so to speak, keeping the ring. Time
and time again Clarendon, with the haughty assumption of the
spokesman of victorious peoples imposing their wills upon the
vanquished, rose to quash Orloff's objections, to point out that his
protests were out of order, that his suggested modifications were
inadmissible. Taking his stand rigorously on the letter of the
Austrian proposals, he exacted the fullest acceptance of them by
Russia, accompanied by the material pledges demanded by the
allies. He pushed Russia far. So far that on more than one
occasion it looked as if the negotiations must break down. The
Emperor and Walewski wavered, and it was nice handling for
Clarendon. Not only had he to impose his will upon the plenipotentiaries in open conference, but he had to go behind the scenes
as well. Again and again in the privacy of that little *cabinet-de-
travail*—that overheated little den where the master of France took
his ease—in an atmosphere of cigar smoke and after-dinner relaxa-
tion, it was Clarendon's task to bring the great Napoleon's nephew
to face up to the facts of Europe, to leave his dreams and his
schemes, to cease drifting, to take decisions. The Emperor
allowed the British statesman to be fearlessly frank with him.
Behind Clarendon was England and the stubborn little figure of
Victoria, with her statesmen, ruling the world—or seeming to.
And in the end England was always right. He must be careful.
But at times Clarendon would *dépasser la limite*. The Emperor
would flare up. "*Permettez-moi de vous dire, milord,*" he
snapped on one occasion, "*que je suis complètement d'un avis
contraire,*" and the tone in which this was said admitted of no
further discussion upon the point—for that evening. But such
outbreaks were rare. Clarendon found that, in the last resort, he
could nearly always stiffen the Emperor's attitude upon any point
that he himself considered really vital. But it was anxious work.

Bessarabia nearly broke the conference. The cession of that
strip of territory was considered vital by Clarendon and Palmerston. But of all the clauses of the Treaty it was the most distasteful to Russia. In Count Orloff she had a negotiator of no

mean powers. Versed in every trick of the game, he exerted his whole energy and all his arts to obtain the deletion of the hated clause—even to raising such geographical questions as to whether a certain chain of mountains purporting to form one of the new frontiers existed anywhere but on the map! Moreover, he said, it was useless for him to consult St. Petersburg. His Government, he said, were unyielding on the question. He and Count Brunnow argued interminably with Walewski in private, and sought repeated audiences of the Emperor. But Clarendon remained perfectly unmoved, even when the Emperor and Walewski seemed to waver. He was civil, courteous, but adamant. And in the end he triumphed.

At a session within the first fortnight of March, Orloff rose to say curtly that he had received instructions from St. Petersburg to accept the frontier line in Bessarabia as proposed by the allies. And the rustle of papers round the conference table which greeted this announcement was more eloquent than words to display the relief of tension felt.

The attempt to "immunise" Turkey from the stealthy aggression of Russia in the countries east of the Black Sea next held the attention of the conference. Circassia became a household word among the plenipotentiaries over several sessions, and long and tedious hours were spent in debating frontiers and discussing protectorates. The Black Sea clauses, contrary to expectation, went through pretty easily. They were the last obstacle to peace, and Russia accepted them. The game was up, and she threw in her hand.

With brighter prospects in the conference chamber and rumours of imminent peace, Paris became en fête. The streets were gay with foreign uniforms, and dazzling equipages swept by carrying important functionaries hither and thither on the business of state or pleasure. As peace was now certain and the tension relaxed, Kathy came out to Paris to be with Clarendon for the celebrations. A large and comfortable house had been placed at their disposal, and here, when peace became assured, they entertained officially and in the grand manner.

In the midst of all the festivities the long-expected event occurred. On March 16th Eugénie gave birth to a boy. The Emperor was beside himself with excitement and delight, and there were tears in his eyes when Clarendon called to offer the congratulations of the Queen on the event. The cup of fulfilment was now full for him. But he became more politically elusive than ever. New schemes, new ideas, new horizons were opening out before his eyes. The glamour of his position in Europe was beginning to take hold of his imagination. With the brilliant success of his arms in the Crimea, with the dynasty established and the succession secured, who could dictate to him, who would be so bold as to bind him against his will? Clarendon was not slow to detect the new orientations of his mind. He had occasion to seek an audience with him at about this time. The attention of the conference was now almost wholly devoted to the drafting of the Treaty, and Walewski was perpetually playing into the hands of the Russians by allowing the wording of it to read as if the pledges demanded by the allies were in reality voluntary concessions made by Russia of her own accord. It was to complain of this travesty of truth that Clarendon had sought an interview with the Emperor. He found him indifferent, wayward, his mind filled with new problems and new ideas. In his despatch to Palmerston that night Clarendon sounded a warning note:

". . . the impression left on my mind," he writes, "was not satisfactory. The Emperor wishes peace to be signed, and he has ceased to care much for the conditions upon which peace is to be made, and he does not care at all for the form in which those conditions are framed."

The Emperor no longer sought an Austrian Alliance, nor did he longer consider, Clarendon felt, his commitments clearly bound up with the Anglo-French Alliance. It was certainly a paradox, but it seemed none the less true that the war and the peace had turned the Court pro-Russian.

CHAPTER XXIII

THE REPERCUSSIONS OF PEACE

§ 1

ON Sunday, March 30th, 1856, peace was signed. "*Au Nom de Dieu, Tout-Puissant,*" to the booming of guns and the ringing of bells. All Paris was in the streets that night to view the illuminations. There was a great dinner at the Tuileries and the Emperor made a speech. It was a creditable and honourable peace, and Clarendon had had enormous difficulties in achieving it. He had done well and he knew it. From the first he had made the French feel that, though the English were ready to continue the war alone, they were yet not determined to break honest efforts for a reasonable settlement. And now such a settlement had been reached.

The stealthy aggression of Russia in the Levant was checked for a generation. Her whole Near Eastern policy was challenged and destroyed. The position of Turkey in Europe was vindicated and secured by material pledges and guarantees. Russian supremacy in the Black Sea was overthrown and its waters freed to the merchant shipping of the world, but permanently interdicted to the flag of war. Russia's claim to a protectorate over the Christian populations within the Ottoman Empire was categorically denied; and the Powers, including Russia, bound themselves not to interfere with the internal affairs of Turkey. The fortress of Kars, taken by the Russians in open warfare, was unconditionally surrendered to Turkey. Russia was to retire from the shores of the Danube by ceding a strip of Bessarabia to Moldavia, and both provinces were to be in future under the suzerainty of the Porte, the contracting Powers collectively guaranteeing their privileges. It seems difficult to conceive what else we could have demanded. Indeed, it was known that we could not have gained more, and those in the heart of affairs were surprised we had gained as much.

"The Queen thanks Lord Clarendon much for his two letters of Saturday and yesterday: and we congratulate him on the success of his efforts in obtaining the peace, for to him alone it is due, and also to him alone is due the dignified position the Queen's beloved country holds, thanks to a straightforward, steady and unselfish policy throughout. . . .

"The Queen finds Lord Palmerston very well pleased with the peace, though he struggled as long as he could for better conditions."

The next day she wrote to King Leopold.

"That so good a peace has been attained, and that this country stands in the high position she now does, by having made peace, and not yielding to unworthy and dishonourable terms, is all owing to Lord Clarendon, whose difficulties were immense, and who cannot be too highly praised."

The Emperor also was very pleased. There had been tricky moments, but Clarendon had been right when he had predicted that if France and England stood firm, Russia would give way. The Anglo-French Alliance had stood the test of a trying strain, and if, as Clarendon feared, it was a trifle stretched at the moment, he had, in reality, little doubt but that it would ease back into position when the tension was released. His work was over and, breathing a sigh of relief, he wrote a letter of congratulation to Queen Victoria.

The Emperor, too, wrote a letter to "Madam and very dear Sister," which proved what Clarendon had opined—namely, that whatever new orientations might attract him he was by no means finished with the old. And he was at pains to show the world that the Anglo-French Alliance was of paramount importance to him by publicly honouring Clarendon in every way. To tell the truth, he had been careful of the Alliance in his public behaviour all through the conference. However much he might wriggle in private, in public he was scrupulous to show how much store he set by the friendship of England. At official receptions, at parties, at the Tuilieries, it was Clarendon he singled out, it was Clarendon he called up to him to confer with in the eyes of the world, while the guests whispered and nodded. But in the end he went further. In the speech he made to the assembled delegates after the signing of the peace, he turned to Clarendon and Cowley and said that peace was due to the spirit of conciliation they had exhibited, and his words clearly gave the congress to understand that in the opinion of the Emperor the question of peace or war had rested with England all along. "The Emperor's remark," wrote Clarendon to the Queen, "has produced a great effect. It was uncalled for, but generous on the part of the Emperor, and Lord Clarendon trusts that it will be satisfactory to Your Majesty."

Napoleon was very anxious that Clarendon should receive the Grand Cross of the Legion of Honour, and was not best pleased when, according to the English custom existing then with regard to foreign orders, he was compelled to decline it. A few days later an enormous van arrived at the Clarendons' house in Paris containing a priceless piece of Gobelin tapestry and a magnificent set of books, *Iconographie Grecque et Romaine*, accompanied by a dedicatory letter in the Emperor's hand. The tapestry was so large that it could not be got into the house, no door being wide enough. "It seems it was exhibited in the Great French Exhibition," writes Lady Clarendon in her journal, "and was reckoned so fine that the Emperor would not allow it to be sold, though he had some great offer either from the British Museum or some other English institution. I believe he makes these presents of large pieces of Gobelin tapestry only to crowned heads or great potentates, so this is intended as a very special honour; but, alas! I fear it is a very inconvenient one, or may be so, if our dread is realised that we have no wall large enough to hang it on." (Her fears were groundless, for it hung for many years in the hall at the Grove.)

And now honours began to fall thick and fast. Walewski received the Gold Cross of the Legion and Bourquenay was made a Senator. The Queen bestowed the Garter upon Lord Palmerston and offered Clarendon and Cowley steps in the peerage. Both the latter declined: Clarendon on the score that he did not wish his sons to be "hampered" in earning their living by the burden of courtesy titles; and Cowley on the score of the inadequacy of his means to bear a higher position than that which he already bore. In declining the honour, Clarendon wrote: "The Queen's gracious intention is the best proof to Cowley and myself that we have had the good fortune to merit Her Majesty's approbation. . . . Lord Clarendon hopes it is not presumptuous in him to say that he would not exchange Your Majesty's letters of approval for any public mark of Your Majesty's favour."

Though the peace treaty was signed on March 30th, the Congress of Powers continued its labours well on into April, and the chestnuts were out in Hyde Park before Clarendon was back in London again. The peace was accompanied by a declaration abolishing privateering and establishing a new "maritime law of nations"; it established the position of neutral vessels carrying enemy goods and *vice versa* in a series of declarations which remained valid till the late war. So much sound sense and goodwill were displayed by the plenipotentiaries in conducting this part of the negotiations that the mind of Louis Napoleon became captivated by the idea that the congress should remain in session until all the anomalies in the map of Europe should be adjusted. Though Clarendon had to point out to him that this would mean the Rhine for France, to which Germany would never consent; an independent Poland, to which Russia would never agree; a liberated Italy, which could hardly come to pass without a war with Austria, the *ideés Napoléoniennes* took shape enough in the mind of Clarendon for the conference to end upon a " League of Nations " note, with himself making an impassioned appeal to the Powers to bring their disputes to the conference table before having recourse to arms.   And with this his labours in Paris came to an end.

When he rose a few days later in the House of Lords to lay the Treaty of Peace upon the table, he was cheered to the echo, and it was some time before he was allowed to speak. By this time rumours of the difficulties he had had to overcome in Paris had got abroad, and he was considered to have conducted the negotiations with brilliance and decision. His old political enemy, Derby, the " Rupert of Debate," it is true, attacked his proceedings with vigour in the true party spirit, calling the peace the " Clarendon Capitulations "; but he made no impression on his audience, and the result of a division showed a sweeping victory for the Government.

CHAPTER XXIV

MID-CENTURY

§ 1

SO the bands played and the troops came home, and Victoria pinned medals on the proud breasts of heroes who had fought at Balaclava, Alma, Inkerman—names that still ring in the mind and evoke visions of a tradition of arms, a method of warfare, a view of life that has utterly passed away. For although certain rubicund old gentlemen with snow-white hair into whose presence, in boyhood, one was gently pushed with the breathless whisper, "He lost his arm at the Redan," provide a link with that legendary past, the age, and all that it stood for and all that it was, has more completely faded into history, is more strange to us now in thought and spirit than almost any other age we can think of.

Post-Crimean England—the age of Trollope, of Surtees, of John Leech's sporting pictures, when humour and fashion were alike fantastic, yet life ambled pleasantly to the sound of horses' hoofs. A certain distinction, a certain individuality of manner and behaviour still clung, like a perfume, over the late fifties. Another decade, and a mechanical identity, begotten of the greed of gain out of mass-production, was to settle like a locust-cloud upon the tree of life and strip it bare. But in the fifties there was still choice, discrimination and style. Middle-aged men had passed their youth under the Regency; their fathers had been sheer eighteenth-century. And so in the mid-nineteenth there still lingered something of that old elegance of life, that raffishness, that freedom to be oneself that, for all its formalism, was the heart of the eighteenth century. Men's dress had not yet settled in to the deadly uniformity of our days. Attire was still open to the nuances of selection, and the trouser was no fixed thing. A hundred varieties existed, and were worn and indulged, from the extravagant baggy peg-top to the skin-tight riding hose. Collars, stocks, cravats—none of these were fixed commercial objects, but matters of consideration and high art. Prodigious and absurd as some of the costumes of that age appear to us now, they at least proclaimed what their wearers were *like*, and bring to the mind a generation of men to whom the "grand manner" still meant something.

And so the last great aristocratic scene passes before us in retrospect, a scene in which peers and their eldest sons still governed the land with the unquestioned assurance with which they conducted the business of their private estates; a scene of harvest and achievement, when a rich, established sense of things still prompted men to build for the future because there seemed so little reason to believe that the future would be any different from the past. Alas for their optimism! It was the "Twilight of the Gods," and the great luminaries of those days were all too soon to suffer an increasing and in the end a total and perpetual eclipse. New suns were to appear, had already appeared, in the firmament of things, and prodigies such as Gladstone and Disraeli, Cobden, Bright and Goschen—men of the rising middle classes—were now to electrify the heavens with new forces of attraction and repulsion, while the old stars shone fitfully for a generation, lapsed and then faded out at last into the outer night.

And Clarendon was very much of his age. He was as old as the century—fifty-six now, and full of honours. Tall, spare, a little bent, with thinning grey hair and whiskers, he could be seen any day strolling across the Horse Guards or getting into his brougham in Downing Street, an amused, quizzical expression on his face. He was the doyen of the Foreign Office, the specialist on Foreign Affairs. Nowadays, when you thought of our foreign relations, you no longer conjured up a terrifying spectacle of Lord Palmerston sitting like a fierce red spider in a web of machinations and war plots, nor even the less alarming if hardly less assuring one of Lord John's puzzled little countenance bending dubiously over a foreign despatch. No, you thought rather of Lord Clarendon, courteous and smiling, smoothing out difficulties and explaining everything to everybody, to everybody's complete satisfaction—Lord Clarendon, who could be as firm as he was suave in manner, and who had brought home from Paris a just and desirable peace and terminated, not without honour to England, the late disastrous war in the East.

That summer the University of Oxford marked its approval of the Secretary of State by conferring upon him an honorary D.C.L., and a nice irony compelled him to receive the degree from the hands of Derby himself. Kathy was rather apprehensive of his welcome by Tory undergraduates, but the result quite reassured her.

Later he was at Holyrood as Minister-in-Attendance, and moved with the Court from there to Balmoral, Balmoral rebuilt and refurnished after Albert's own designs—all pitch-pine and red tartans and Landseer pictures. The keen Scottish air undoubtedly did him good, but he felt permanently frozen.

Victoria was most attentive and insisted that the Minister-in-Waiting should himself join in the happy family life which she delighted to lead in the romantic paradise of pine and heather which constituted her Scottish home. Here, divesting herself of royalty—almost—she achieved the freedom of the common life of humanity—almost. Surrounded by dogs and trailing her shawls across the terrace, she would set up her easel just at the point where the garden gave on to the moor (so romantic).

' Didn't Lord Clarendon think that a sketch from just here would be delightful? If she could only catch the light on that group of trees properly! But oh, how difficult it was! Had Lord Clarendon ever tried to sketch? No? Lady Clarendon was *very* good at it, she had been told. Albert always said . . .'

Or there would be picnics in the hills in the high northern light, with ghillies, unpacking grouse and cold ham from huge baskets, while Victoria, blushing and laughing, would actually help to pass round the plates, while horrified ladies exclaimed, "Oh, ma'am," and the gentlemen—Clarendon amongst them—in impossible plaid capes, rushed gallantly to her assistance. And then there was the Highland Gathering, where one watched innumerable sets of reels, 'all danced so beautifully by the simple Highlanders from the country round about, and one tried to judge which sets were best. It was all very wonderful—and how dearest Albert entered into it all!'

§ 2

The international situation was far from reassuring. The execution of a highly complicated Treaty afforded innumerable opportunities for chicanery, and Russia was taking every opportunity to evade her obligations. There were interminable wrangles over the frontier questions, and nearly a breakdown over the town of Bolgrad. France was lukewarm in her support of our policy, and the Alliance was strained to the utmost. Meanwhile, King Bomba of Naples was giving trouble, and in the East a Persian situation was developing. Clarendon was at his wits' end to cope with it all.

By December the work at the Foreign Office had become appalling. Accelerated methods of communication, petty wars (in China and Persia), the perplexing difficulties arising out of the carrying out of the Treaty of Paris, brought a constant stream of despatches, telegrams, reports and the like from all quarters of the habitable globe.

Clarendon and some of his staff worked fourteen hours a day. He abjured society and was scarcely seen abroad at all that winter. In a letter to Normanby he states that the year previously 56,000 despatches had been received and sent, and that the number had undoubtedly increased for the current year.

Palmerston grew alarmed for Clarendon's health:

"Peel said that no man should give advice till he is called in," he wrote to him, "and you have not called me in, but I am called in by the interest we all take in your health. What, then, should be the objection to the following suggestion? You want more air and exercise; much you cannot have; a little you might, and every mickle makes a muckle—a little every day tells in the course of the year. Why should you not provide yourself with a steady hack with good action, who would give you no trouble when on him, and not prevent you thinking over the next draft you are going to write? Why should not the aforesaid quadruped be at your door every morning just as you finish your breakfast? And why should you not ride him to the end of Hyde Park and back again? It would only take you half-an-hour; but that half-hour, if daily taken, would have in some degree the effect of Balmoral air . . ."

History does not relate whether or not this advice was taken. Probably not, as Clarendon was, at no time of his life, very 'horse-minded.'

Christmas came, and he tore himself away from his desk to spend a few days only at the Grove. But the new year (1857) saw him hurrying back to deal with matters in China. An awkward situation had arisen there, and since the feeling evoked by it was, as it turned out, sufficient to cause the temporary eclipse of the Government, we must pause for a moment to consider it.

The incident is not without a recent parallel. A vessel, China built, China owned and manned by a crew partly British and partly Chinese, had acquired a technical right to fly the British flag. Unfortunately, the Chinese authorities refused to be impressed by this transfer. The ship was known to have been engaged in dubious operations off the coast for some time past, and when they saw their chance, the ship being in Canton harbour, the Chinese authorities took action. A boarding party tore down the British flag and carried off the crew, British and Chinese alike, loudly declaring that the ship was, in reality, Chinese. The British Ambassador protested and demanded an explanation. The Imperial Commissioner became truculent, whereupon the British fleet proceeded to exact satisfaction by destroying the river forts. The Chinese reply was to put a price of thirty dollars on the head of every Englishman, with the result that by Christmas war loomed imminent.

As we who live in the twentieth century have cause to know, this is the type of incident which must always create a sharp cleavage of views and give rise to strong emotions, since some will argue that the incident is trivial, others that the principles involved are fundamental.

Derby, in the Lords, deplored the punitive action taken by the British Admiral, since it involved the shedding of blood without a declaration of war. He failed to convince, and the Government came through with a majority of thirty-six. In the Commons, Cobden, censuring the reprisal and demanding an enquiry, described the Chinese as " an ingenious and civilised people who were learned when our Plantagenet kings could neither read nor write; who had logic before Aristotle, and morals before Socrates." Lord John, Disraeli and Gladstone supported him, and the Government found themselves in a minority of sixteen.

Palmerston thereon decided to go to the country. He knew that the temper of the House did not always represent the temper of the electorate. And he had a good cry—a variation of the " Civis Romanus Sum." The Chinese had violated the British flag; they had broken their treaties; they had offered a reward for the heads of British subjects. Was the country going to stand for that? And yet the leaders of the Opposition were ready to accept such humiliations, any humiliations, it appeared, rather than stand fast for the rights of British citizens all over the world. Against such a cry it was useless for Cobden to try to stir up the stolid artisans of the North to a sense of kinship with their learned " yellow brothers." Useless for Gladstone to embark on the first of those tremendous canvassing expeditions which Disraeli, later, was to dub " Pilgrimages of Passion." " What," asked Palmerston and his colleagues, " did the British public think of such folly, of such cowardice, of such duplicity?" What they thought was recorded in their vote, which gave a smashing victory to the Government. Cobden and Bright lost their seats, and Palmerston returned to Westminster stronger than ever before. Satisfaction was extorted from the authorities at Canton, and the Chinese incident blew over. Everyone was pleased. Even the Court was relieved that Palmerston was back.

"I sat next the Queen at dinner," writes Clarendon on May 29th, "and never saw her in better spirits, or more gracious. I had a long talk with her afterwards, too, and she made me tell her what I thought of Palmerston's health, about which she was evidently anxious; which is curious," he adds, "considering how particularly she would have liked him to die two or three years ago."

Palmerston himself told Ministers sententiously that " it is a great satisfaction and a great support to us all to have the Court so friendly." So the old breach was healed as much as temperament and divergence of view would permit.

§ 3

Into this peaceful scene, at the height of the season, and ironically enough at a moment when all England was celebrating the centenary of the Battle of Plassey, came the appalling news from India.

"Well do I remember," writes the Duke of Argyll, "that morning on which we read of this disastrous event. It was our custom at that time to breakfast at an open window, a little above the level of a very pretty parterred garden. It still comes back to me how sick we felt with anxiety, how alarming the prospect appeared, and how all our flowers had lost their glory."*

The news was already seven weeks old when it arrived, and Palmerston, who had as yet hardly taken in the gravity of the situation, informed the Queen that an extensive mutiny had broken out among her Indian troops, but that he had no fear of the results. But the terrifying news of the shooting of British officers and the massacre of British civilians evoked a storm of angry protest from the country. The demobilisation of home-coming reservists from the Crimea had been so complete that at the moment at which the news from India arrived we had only 8,000 troops available for active service abroad. Palmerston immediately despatched the greater part of these under Sir Colin Campbell to the scene of action, and Lord Elgin, whom Clarendon had sent out to China as plenipotentiary in the late dispute, acting brilliantly on his own initiative, intercepted substantial reinforcements as they were on their way to Canton and diverted them to Calcutta.

In answer to a question in the House, the President of the Board of Control said that 14,000 men would be in India by the middle of July.

Clarendon, save as Minister of the Crown, had no responsibility with regard to Indian affairs. From the first he took a very gloomy view of the situation.

"The enormous distances are our difficulty," he writes, "because before our troops can reach India and begin their march of a thousand miles, the Mutiny may spread beyond control. On the whole," he adds, "the conduct of Foreign Governments has been sympathising and friendly—just what ours would be to any of them under circumstances at all similar."

Palmerston was consistently optimistic and thought that in the end the overcoming of the Mutiny (of which he had no doubt) would enormously increase our reputation in the East and enable

* Diary of the Duke of Argyll.

us to pull the strings of administration tighter throughout the Indian continent.

By the middle of July it was known that Delhi was in the hands of the rebels, and Ministers began to shake their heads in earnest. But Palmerston was invincibly cheerful. "While you are shaving or taking a walk or a ride, turn over in your mind what will be the best thing to do as to the future government of India," he said offhandedly to Clarendon one day. Clarendon gasped. "He has a jolly way of looking at disasters," he wrote that night to Kathy.

But though the Mutiny was the chief topic at this season, there were not lacking other troubles, troubles which darkened the international horizon and gave Clarendon constant anxiety. Chief amongst these was the state of the Anglo-French Alliance, which was showing distinct signs of wear and tear.

However, the personal relations between Victoria and the Emperor were still intact, and it was thought advisable to profit by them and to have the French Royals over on a visit that summer. The idea of the visit was that it should be a purely private affair; that they should, as it were, call in as by chance at Osborne, where the Queen and Prince would be at that season; that there should be no official reception, and that the royal pair should not even go as far as London; that they should remain a few days quietly sharing in the life that Victoria and Albert normally led at Osborne; and that they should then depart as unobtrusively as they came. Of course, the Prime Minister and the Foreign Secretary would be asked to come down for the day from London some time during their stay, and if, as they strolled amicably about the grounds together, the gentlemen found it in them to open their minds to each other on various interesting points of international policy—well, it was thought nothing but good could come of that in so friendly and natural a setting.

They duly arrived on August 6th, sailing up the Solent in the *Reine Hortense*. The weather was fine for their visit, and the gardens at Osborne all that could be desired. There were picnics and expeditions, and even, one night, a ball. And, as was fitting, Palmerston and Clarendon went down from London to pay their respects. They found Napoleon in a good humour, and a great deal of business was transacted which never found its way on to paper. ". . . Good things were done, and bad ones averted at Osborne," writes Clarendon after the interview. "A very black cloud hung over the alliance when the Emperor came there; but all was sunshine before he departed." A question was asked in the House of Lords as to the result of the visit, and Clarendon was able to give a satisfactory account of it. He was, it is evident, much relieved in his own mind on the subject.

A fortnight later he was at Balmoral again, shaking his head over the Indian news and wondering that "Mars" (Lord Panmure), who was also in Scotland, could have the heart to go deer-stalking at such a time.

It was a gloomy winter with bad news coming from India by every mail, and, in the middle of November, one of the worst financial crises that the country had ever been through. One great house after another failed, and the funds fell alarmingly. There were emergency Cabinets, and on November 12th the Government decided to suspend temporarily the Bank Charter Act. This produced the effect of a "moratorium," and gave the banks a respite from the drain on their resources caused by public panic. Sir George Cornewall Lewis, Theresa's husband, was Chancellor of the Exchequer at the time, and behaved throughout with admirable firmness and judgment. Of him, the Duke of Argyll writes in his memoirs:

"His calm and judicial mind, and the utter absence in him of political passion of any kind, made him an invaluable counsellor. I have never seen in any man, except in Lord Aberdeen, a mind so singularly dispassionate, combined with such wide knowledge, and perfect integrity of character."

A ray of hope, however, permeated the general gloom when, just before Christmas, news reached England of the relief of Lucknow. Moreover, Delhi was ours again, and by the turn of the year even the most pessimistic were inclined to believe that we had the Mutiny well in hand.

A new year dawned, and by January 8th the Calcutta correspondents were writing:

"Our prospects brighten rapidly. In almost every part of the disturbed districts we have encountered the rebels and beaten them. In almost every part we have opened the roads, and communication with Delhi is now direct."

§ 4

The Indian Mutiny, to all intents and purposes, was over. There now only remained the rounding up and punishment of rebels and the general pacification of the affected districts. But for the Government there loomed, in regard to the situation, a vastly more important and difficult problem—the whole problem, indeed, of the future administration of India—that problem which "Pam" had so off-handedly asked Clarendon to solve while he was shaving or having his bath! It was an absurd anomaly that a vast continent numbering some three hundred millions of people of every race, caste, and creed, should be virtually under the sole administration of a private trading company. For some time past reasoning Englishmen had had an uneasy conscience with regard to this state of affairs. It was obvious that the ultimate authority in India should be vested in Crown and Parliament. Palmerston was determined upon it and was preparing a Bill on the subject. But the East India Company was immensely strong, had an almost glamorous prestige and a remarkable history. Moreover, the ramifications of its vested interests touched the pockets of countless Englishmen. When the Company became aware that their prerogative was about to be attacked, the Corporation prepared to do battle. It passed resolutions and got up a petition to Parliament. But Palmerston was bent upon his course, and all interest was centred upon the impending struggle, when a purely fortuitous incident changed the outlook, removed Palmerston temporarily from political supremacy and handed to his rival, Lord Derby, the honour of piloting an India Bill through Parliament.

The incident was the abortive attempt on the life of the Emperor Louis Napoleon by Orsini and other revolutionaries in the Rue Lepelletier. At first it was difficult to imagine that the incident, however regrettable, would cause any political reaction in England —least of all that it would have power to turn out the Government. But, unfortunately, it was discovered that Orsini had lately been in England; that the bombs thrown in the Rue Lepelletier were actually made in England and that, in effect, the whole plot had been hatched, in all its devilish details, by individuals basking in the benignant incuriosity of the English law. Feeling in France ran high. Paris was infuriated; and Walewski wrote an injudicious despatch to Persigny, in which he asked rhetorically whether the "right of asylum" should protect such a state of things, and whether "hospitality was due to assassins."

Clarendon poured oil upon the waters sufficient to calm the agitated spirit of Persigny, but the matter was one for the Home Office, and more especially for the Prime Minister. Palmerston asked Ministers tetchily why, if the French found it necessary to expel dangerous foreigners from their midst, they didn't send them to America instead of shipping them to England. However, something had to be done to salve French pride, and he thought out a Conspiracy to Murder Bill, the clauses of which were designed to remove conspiracy from the class of misdemeanours to that of felony, punishable with penal servitude and other rigours. This he introduced himself on February 9th. But between the date of the crime and the introduction of the Bill, feeling on both sides of the Channel had had time to mount. In an access of loyalty, the officers of the French Army memorialised their sovereign in addresses bristling with offensive allusions to England. Thus the 59th Regiment were "moved to demand an account from the land of impunity which contains the haunts of the monsters who are sheltered by its Laws. Give us the order, Sire," concluded the address, "and we will pursue them to their strongholds." Another memorial concluded with the words: "Let the infamous haunt in which machinations so infernal are planned be destroyed for ever." This was going a bit far, and the British public, which at first was as outraged by the news of the attempt on the Emperor's life as any good Frenchmen could desire, hotly resented these gibes and threats, and began to view the situation in a different light. So when Palmerston introduced the Conspiracy to Murder Bill, there were not lacking those in Parliament who regarded this piece of legislation as a truckling under to France, and Kinglake moved an amendment:

"That this House, while sympathising with the French nation in its indignant abhorrence of the late atrocious attempt against the life of the Emperor . . . deems it inexpedient to legislate in compliance with the demand made in Count Walewski's despatch of the 20th January, until further information is before it of the Communications between the two Governments subsequent to the date of that despatch."

It was a direct attempt to block legislation on the subject. But luckily, when put to the vote, the Government came through with flying colours. However, Milner-Gibson, in anticipation of the second reading, submitted as an amendment:

"That this House hears with much concern that it is alleged that the recent attempt on the life of the Emperor of the French has been devised in England, and expresses its detestation for such a wicked enterprise, and that, while the House is ready at all times to assist in remedying any defects in the Criminal Law, which after due investigation are proved to exist, it cannot but regret that Her Majesty's Government (previously to wanting the House to amend the laws relating to conspiracy at the present time) have not felt it to be their duty to reply to the despatch received from the French Government, dated Paris, January 20th."

Clarendon, indeed, had stayed his hand. To have replied in official language to Walewski's despatch would have been to court disaster. Feeling was far too high to have risked the further aggravation of it on both sides of the Channel, which a despatch, couched in strong enough terms to have rebutted Walewski's allegations, would have afforded. It would have been so easy to write, and have looked so well when placed upon the table of the House. It would have gained for its author immense prestige and a cheap popularity, born of the feeling of the times. A weaker man might have succumbed, a less wise one have blundered. But Clarendon refrained. What made him a great Foreign Secretary was just this innate sense of how to act and how *not* to act in moments of strain between two countries. Lord Cowley, Ambassador in Paris, had no doubts as to the wisdom of the course. Indignant at the behaviour of the House of Commons, he sent the following communication to Clarendon:

" Having learnt by telegraph that certain resolutions imputing blame to H.M. Government for not having made reply to Count Walewski's despatch to Count Persigny, dated January 20th, had been affirmed by a majority in the House of Commons, I think it a duty to your Lordship to place on record that, although I have not been charged to make any official communication to the French Government, in answer to that despatch, I have been enabled by your Lordship's private instructions to place before the French Government the views of H.M. Government far more fully, and, I cannot but believe, far more satisfactorily, than would have been the case had my language been clothed in more official garb. . . . I know not what may be the result of last night's vote, but at all events I lose no time in stating my conviction that to your Lordship's judicious and prudent conduct at a very critical moment it is owing that, without the shadow of the sacrifice of a single principle, our relations with this Government have not received a check which might have been fatal to the friendship which yet happily prevails between the two nations."

However, failure to answer Walewski's despatch was only the Opposition's excuse for attacking the whole theory of Palmerston's Bill, and the chief thesis of Milner-Gibson's amendment was soon lost sight of in a welter of protest against altering the law at all at the bidding of France. Hysteria prevailed, and French parallels to the present situation were even sought for in the allegation that the Great Napoleon had left considerable sums in his will to one Cantillon for having promised to try to murder the Duke of Wellington! The press joined the critics of the Government, and by February 17th the whole pack was in full cry. Radicals, Peelites, the scattered remnants of all parties joined in the chase, and as a result of a division on the 19th, Palmerston found he was out by sixteen votes. He immediately placed his resignation in the hands of the Queen, who at once sent for Lord Derby.

So ended Clarendon's first term of office as Secretary of State for Foreign Affairs. For five years he had held the delicate threads of our international relations in his anxious but competent hands. He had steered England, not without honour, through one grave crisis after another. Taking up the seals of office on the eve of a general European disturbance, and powerless as he was—as anybody would have been—to avert the disastrous war that followed, he picked his way delicately through the maze of continental intrigue and chicanery, and himself negotiated an honourable and lasting peace.   In the process of all this he became a statesman, not in the narrower fields of home politics, but in the wider one of European affairs, where his personality was felt, his power recognised, and his word respected.

But the strain of the last five years had had its effect on his health.   He had lost a certain resilience that he had had, and his enemy, the gout, was a more frequent visitor.   He was not old; but he had got to that point in life when people say of a man, "He is not so young as he was."   His mind and faculties were at their height.   The strain of using them to their utmost was beginning to tell on his frame, that was all.   He had been constantly in the public service since his youth.   Hard work, difficult, uphill, irritating work had been his portion for years now.

But he had been young once, and behaved as young men should.

" 'We have heard the chimes at midnight, Master Shallow,' " writes a reminiscent Emily Eden.   " I wonder whether you recollect a particular evening at Greenwich, when you and Francis Baring, and 'Pow' (C. E. Poulett, later Governor-General of Canada) and G. Tierney dined with us.   White-bait, of course, and after dinner, when the park was locked up, we let ourselves into it through the little garden gate, and had coffee.   G. Tierney tied a shawl over his head and gave us imitations of Mrs. Siddons."

Mrs. Siddons. . . . Regency days.   How distant they seemed now. . . .   Almacks—with Lady Jersey coruscating in her diamonds, and the Regent's pawky countenance nodding in the distance.   An evening at the Opera with Bob Grosvenor, and "Boy" Elliot, and Theresa, when Grisi sang, and the Ballet had been particularly fine: early days at Kent House, when he and Hyde were young men-about-town, and improved the shining hour in the London of the eighteen-twenties.   It all seemed another life, and himself another person.   It was pleasant to turn from these dream-like recollections to the firm realities of the present— to Kathy and the children, to the peace and recreation of the Grove after the last five strenuous years.

CHAPTER XXV

THE VISIT TO COMPIÈGNE

§ I

CLARENDON spent the early spring and summer mostly in Hertfordshire, basking in an unwonted leisure and the fact of having time to give to his household and his estates. It was pleasant to walk the fields with Hyde and George—such fine boys now, and so likeable. And how they were growing up. . . . He was to take Georgey in April to school for the first time —to Mr. Essex's at Malvern Wells (for there were preparatory schools nowadays); and Hyde was going to Harrow this term. It was pleasant to drive over with Kathy and Constance to Gorhambury, where "Grim"* and his beautiful wife now held sway; to picnic and romp with the younger children in the woods; to laugh and be at ease with one's own. And there was the library, and after the business of the day what more delightful (since politics, after all, was the one really enthralling occupation) to sit down and write on current events to Palmerston, to George Cornewall Lewis, to Delane of *The Times*?

The summer passed, and the tranquil autumn days were taking their uneventful course at the Grove, when, on October 21st, something of a bombshell arrived in the shape of an invitation to Clarendon (and a like sent simultaneously to Palmerston) to spend a week in November at Compiègne with the Emperor of the French. Nor did it appear that the visit was to be of a purely private character. The two ex-Cabinet Statesmen were not asked primarily as friends—though that, too—but as members of the late Government that had done so much to preserve and strengthen the Anglo-French Alliance. For the Court was to be there; and certain of the Ministers. There were to be entertainments, a shoot, a hunt, and other festivities.

It placed them in a highly delicate situation, and one for which, as far as they could see, there was no precedent. It was certain that if they went, the Emperor, on some occasion during their visit, would talk politics to each or to both of them. And then how could they answer? For they represented no Government at the moment, and what they might say could only be the expression

---

* Lord Grimston—always known as "Grim"—succeeded to the earldom on the death of his father, the first Earl of Verulam, in 1845.

of their own private opinion, whereas the Emperor would be sure to take it as the opinion of Great Britain at large. The Emperor seemed to overlook the Derby Government altogether, and to turn to Clarendon and Palmerston as the only people who counted in England—at least, in respect of foreign affairs. Why, in heaven's name, if he wanted to do honour to England, couldn't he have asked Derby and Malmesbury over? On the other hand, it was a gesture conceived in the friendliest spirit, and it was essential not to give the Emperor cause for believing that any unpleasant feeling remained as the result of the crisis in the spring.

"The more I think of the Compiègne invitation," writes Palmerston tetchily to Clarendon on November 2nd, "the more I wish to get off, if it could be managed without offence to the Emperor. It would be a considerable bore to go thither, and one cannot say how our going thither might, under certain circumstances, be taken by our Liberal friends, and the public at large. On the other hand, one would be very sorry to do anything on the subject which could be taken amiss by the Emperor. I shall be glad to receive your opinion on the matter."

Clarendon thought that there was no valid excuse for them not to go, and in the end they went on November 13th. As might have been expected, their conduct raised a storm of criticism—especially among their own party.

"Did anyone ever hear such folly as this visit of Palmerston and Clarendon to Compiègne?" wrote Delane to Bernal Osborne. ". . . I think you may safely recant your allegiance to both these luminaries. No star shines very bright above the horizon; but these two seem to have hopelessly set."

Articles appeared in the *Daily News* and *Saturday Review* soundly rating them for their indiscretion, and Lord John Russell was heard to remark that henceforward they must both be regarded "more as courtiers of the Tuileries than subjects of St. James's."

Theresa grew alarmed for her brother's reputation and deplored the Compiègne visit for the effect it might have against him politically. "I do regret that you went to Compiègne," she wrote to him when he had got back, "as it is of much more consequence to England that honest men should not be misinterpreted than that they should run the risk of slightly offending the Emperor, who would make war upon us to-morrow if it suited his purpose. Of course, as you went on public grounds, I only hope that you were right; but you can hardly expect those to whom you are a first-class object can like any step that attaches abuse to your name."

The visit itself proved a very brilliant affair.

"I think I left off writing to you when I was sent for to go a-gunning at Compiègne," wrote Clarendon to the Duchess of Manchester, "but the *chasse* was given up as it rained too hard, and the day was got through by such pastimes as *conversation spirituelle*, kept up by thirty people, football in the gallery, and quadrilles on horseback in the *manège*, the Emperor doing lance-exercises, and other equestrian feats, *à la Francone*, for the amusement of the Court. The next day was fine, and we had *chasse au tir*; each tireur had four guns provided for him with four loaders in cocked hats; the beaters were a squadron of lancers in boots and spurs, with a trumpeter who signified to them what they should do. It was a pretty, gay scene; but I believe that most of the creatures had been turned out the day before, or were let out of traps as the Emperor approached."

That night there was a great dinner with charades after, and Princess Mathilde was in high good humour, chaffing everybody, Lord Hertford in particular, "but she could make nothing of Palmerston, who sat next to her at dinner and was exclusively occupied with his comestibles." The next day it poured again, and what happened to the gentlemen is not recorded; but Kathy, who on this occasion accompanied her husband, notes in her diary that M. Jules Sansleau "told the Empress and Ladies a ghost story." There was an expedition to the ruins of Pierrepons; there was a play acted " by common soldiers," and another— strange contrast—acted by the comedians of the Théâtre Français. There were more dinners and more charades, and eventually the gay party broke up, the Clarendons arriving back in London at two o'clock on the morning of November 20th. The next day they went down to the Grove, and thither not many days later came Charles Greville, intent upon the inner history of the Compiègne visit. He was not disappointed:

"I went to the Grove on Wednesday last, and came back on Friday. There I had long talks with Clarendon for the first time for many a day, when he told me a great deal that was interesting, just as he used to do formerly, first about his visit to Compiègne, and his conversations with the Emperor. . . . They had a great deal of conversation about Italy and the anti-Austrian projects attributed to France, about which the Emperor's ideas were most strange and extravagant. He said that the two questions in which France had been interested were, one, the regeneration of Poland, and the other the regeneration of Italy; that in pursuit of the first, France became naturally the ally of Austria against Russia; that in pursuit of the other she became the ally of Russia and Sardinia against Austria; that since the peace with Russia had put an end to anything being done about the first, the second alone became possible. Claren-don then pointed out to him all the difficulties of involving him-self in such a contest as this scheme supposed, stating that Austria would sacrifice her last florin and her last man in defence of her Italian possessions; that to go to war with her would almost inevitably, sooner or later, plunge all Europe into war, and that the object to be gained by it would be wholly incommensurate with the cost and danger that would be incurred. The Emperor appeared to have no reply to make to Clarendon's remonstrances, nor did I gather that His Majesty had any *casus belli* against Austria, nor even any just cause to urge against her. . . .

"Another day the Emperor asked Clarendon to come to his room when he told him that he wanted his advice, that he was in a great dilemma and embarrassment in regard to his Roman occupation, and in a false position from which he did not know how to extricate himself. He was dying to recall the French troops, but did not know how to do it. He had always hoped to get the policy, laid down in the Ney letter, carried out, but as soon as the Pope and his ecclesiastical councillors returned to Rome, they refused to do anything, and whenever he held out any threats of withdrawing his troops, they always said he might do so whenever he liked, for they very well knew the reasons which prevented him doing it: the moment the French troops marched out, there would be an uprising in Rome and the Papal provinces. The religious party in France would deeply resent his exposing the Pope to any such danger, and as soon as the French army went away, the Austrians would march in, and be masters of the whole country. Clarendon acknowledged the gravity of the situation, and the difficulty, but could suggest no solution to it. They discussed the possibility of inducing the Pope to relinquish his temporal sovereignty, and to accept a great revenue instead, but neither of them thought this plan feasible."*

Was it love of double-dealing for its own sake, was it a desire to throw dust in the eyes of his distinguished guests, or what other motive prompted the strange and mercurial sovereign of France to hold such language with Whig statesmen at that par-ticular moment? For his plans regarding Italy were all laid. He had a treaty with Cavour, pledging France to armed intervention in Italy, in his pocket when he talked thus with Clarendon; and hardly a month was to pass before he was to pick a quarrel with Austria; and to follow this up (so as to make his intentions with regard to Italy perfectly clear) with the announcement that the Prince Napoleon was to marry the King of Sardinia's daughter. Afterwards, it was some satisfaction to Clarendon to think that he had not minced his words as to the plausibility of intervening in Italy.

* Greville *Journals.*

§ 2

The year 1859 opened menacingly at home and abroad—abroad with the Emperor Napoleon's extraordinary speech to the Corps Diplomatique on New Year's Day, in which he practically insulted the Austrian Ambassador to his face; at home with John Bright thundering doctrines of revolutionary franchise reform to sullen Northern audiences, who, it must be said, showed peculiarly little enthusiasm for his schemes.   His health had forbidden him to take any part in politics for the past year, and his sudden and violent re-incursion into the political arena was a shock to all parties, and caused Clarendon to quote Byron's dictum on his mother-in-law, changing only the personal pronoun, "he has been dangerously ill: he is now dangerously well again."

Clarendon met the eminent demagogue in the street about this time, and described wonderingly to Kathy "his insolent and swaggering way of saying that he and Lords like himself [Clarendon] had no idea of the extent of Reform which they would be obliged to swallow, and other radical speeches which Clarendon seems to have answered with contempt and spirit, and felt an almost unconquerable desire to give him a good thrashing, which he felt he *could* do, and would have liked intensely " (Lady Clarendon's journal).

However, Derby was conscientiously anxious to enlarge the basis of parliamentary election, if only to keep such a measure of reform out of the hands of John Bright and his colleagues, and the Derby-Disraeli Reform Bill was introduced on February 28th. This measure was Disraeli's own particular child, and he and Derby worked out its nature and extent with very little reference to their colleagues in the Cabinet.   When the clauses of it were known to the Cabinet at large, just prior to its introduction in the Commons, Spencer Walpole and Henley resigned at once. Nothing daunted, Derby and Disraeli went forward with the Bill. In spite of Disraeli's eloquent and lucid explanation of its clauses, it was received with a certain flatness by the House of Commons.   There were other matters to occupy the attention of members than that of the eternal reform question.   However, when implored by Disraeli to examine the Bill in detail, some thought it went too far in lowering the county franchise, while some complained that it did not also lower the borough franchise.   A desultory debate ensued, which was adjourned to the second reading, fixed for March 21st.

On that night John Russell moved a resolution cleverly worded so as to win the approval of both classes of objectors, and the result of a division a few evenings later showed a majority against the Government. This defeat was to be expected on so highly controversial a question as that of reform. The Derby Government existed only on sufferance. Any combination of the scattered Peelite, Whig and Radical elements which were disunited upon most subjects would certainly unseat the Government. It speaks volumes for the crafty words of John Russell's resolution that it got Palmerston and John Bright into the same lobby for very different reasons.

Disraeli was bitter to the core with Russell, and in summing up the situation after the Government defeat he made a brilliant attack upon him.

"There was one quality," he said, "which had rather marred than made his fortune—a sort of restlessness that will not brook that delay and that patience which are sometimes needed in our constitutional Government for the conduct of public affairs. The moment the noble lord is not in power, he appears to me to live in an atmosphere of coalitions, combinations, *coups d'états*, and cunning resolutions. An 'appropriation clause' may happen to everyone once in his life. But there is only one man living of whom it can be said that in 1835 he overthrew the Government of Sir Robert Peel upon an impracticable pretext; that in 1852 he overthrew the Government of Lord Derby with an objectless coalition; that in 1855 he overthrew the Government of Lord Aberdeen by a personal *coup d'état*; and that in 1857 he overthrew the Government of the member for Tiverton by a Parliamentary manœuvre. . . ."

Then, sounding a graver note, he referred once more to the measure of reform that had been before Parliament:

"There is the Conservative view of the question," he said, "and there is—not to use the epithet in the least degree offensively—the revolutionary view of the Question. That is to say there is that Conservative view, which, in any change that it recommends, would wish to preserve and maintain the present character of the House of Commons, which is a representation of the various interests and classes of the country. And there is the revolutionary view which would attempt to alter the character of the House of Commons, and make it a representation merely of the voice of a numerical majority."

The tone and accent of the great Jew as he spoke these words were sober and thoughtful, and he wagged a warning finger at the House of Commons. In eight years' time the same Jew was to pass the most revolutionary of all the Reform Bills of the nineteenth century, a measure that entrusted the electoral function to the countless unlettered masses—that swelled the register by over a million voters—the first of those measures that have ended by giving the supreme governance of England into the hands of that very "numerical majority" against which, on this occasion, he warned the House of Commons—a measure that even his party chief and staunch supporter termed "a leap in the dark."

CHAPTER XXVI

ITALIAN INTERLUDE

§ I

AFTER the defeat of the Government in March, Derby decided to go to the country, and April that year was noisy with elections. The result was a Conservative gain of thirty seats; but even this spectacular victory only brought up the strength of the party to within fifty of the total that might, on any occasion, vote against them in the House of Commons. There was a general feeling that the Government was doomed, and Whig statesmen that spring engaged in the enthralling occupation of Cabinet making "before the event."

One Sunday, Palmerston came round to Grosvenor Crescent and sounded Clarendon as to what he ought to do if the Queen sent for him and charged him to form a Government. The situation between himself and Lord John was, of course, the difficulty. Clarendon advised him to drive straight from the Palace to Lord John's house and appeal to him to help him. Clarendon smiled and asked him what he would do if the unexpected happened, and the rôles were reversed, the Queen sending for Lord John, and Lord John driving straight from the Palace to *his* (Palmerston's) door to ask for *his* help. Whereupon the old lion grunted and said that he had much enjoyed being out of office and having had time to look after his affairs and that he should remain as he was, he thought. The fact was that both he and Lord John had got to that point of eminence in the party wherein they were both, so to speak, co-equal and co-eternal, and it was difficult to know which had most claim to form a Government in the name of the Whigs; and though the personal breach between them was healed, they were both touchy concerning their precedence and authority.

The Queen was fully alive to the dilemma, and when the expected happened and the Government fell on June 10th she sent for neither. In her perplexity she summoned Lord Granville. Now Granville was some thirty years younger than Palmerston and not very much less younger than Lord John; Granville, "the polite," as he had been called eight years before, an able statesman, gracious and amenable to everybody, but hardly competent to weld the stubborn factors of the great Liberal party into a united whole at this juncture.

It now became Granville's unpleasant task to go the round of the statesmen who might have expected to be chosen before him, and, after announcing his elevation, enquire whether they would serve under him. Clarendon, unself-seeking as usual, consented; Palmerston expressed surprise, but also professed his readiness to serve, under certain conditions; Lord John, as usual, proved intractable, and insisted on retaining the leadership of the House. The moment he heard this, Palmerston began to make difficulties. Granville ran distractedly from Chesham Place to Cambridge House, till Clarendon urged him to give up the undertaking, and in the end he found himself obliged to do so.

The Queen had now positively to choose between Palmerston and Russell, and she chose Palmerston. The choice was in reality inevitable. Despite his high position in the party, Lord John's recent political history had not been such as to inspire the rank and file with confidence sufficient for them to give him the whole-hearted support necessary to form a Government. So Palmerston, in his turn, began the task of Cabinet making. Now the Queen desired to retain Clarendon at the Foreign Office. So did Palmerston. But Clarendon, guessing that his acceptance might exclude Lord John from the Government—who would never be content with anything less than the Premiership, the Leadership of the House of Commons, or the Foreign Office—urged that his own claim should be waived. "How few men are like Clarendon," writes an adoring but disappointed Kathy, "so unselfish, so unambitious."

George had judged Lord John rightly. On June 13th came a letter from Palmerston stating that Russell had claimed the Foreign Office as the price of his co-operation. At the same time the Prime Minister offered Clarendon a choice of several other posts in the Government, but he politely declined them. His dislike of office was genuine, and nothing but the belief that his knowledge of Foreign Affairs might be useful to the Government would tempt him to shoulder the burden. So a Government was built on Clarendon's self-suppression. One afternoon, a little later, Jord John, who had always the courage of self-justification, came to call on Clarendon to explain to him why he considered himself essential to the Foreign Office. Clarendon was slightly amused, slightly cynical. "Johnnie" had always such high motives for doing himself a good turn.

The leading posts in the new Ministry called for little comment —it was the old gang with certain adjustments. Palmerston and Russell were the leading lights. The Duke of Newcastle was Colonial Secretary, and Sir Charles Wood adorned the new post of Secretary of State for India. Sidney Herbert was Secretary-at-War, and Lord Granville President of the Council. There was

much feeling in the Villiers family over Gladstone's appointment
as Chancellor of the Exchequer. This had been promised to Sir
George Cornewall Lewis, since he had already proved himself
an able Chancellor in the late Whig Government. Theresa was
furious, and asked rhetorically whether it was necessary for the
"finances of the country to be set to music."

§ 2

Great events were happening in Europe that summer, where the
Emperor Napoleon and his armies coruscated bravely in the Italian
sunlight; and when the excitement attendant upon a change of
Government had subsided, all attention in England was directed to
the struggle that was taking place beyond the Alps. The Governments of Europe were aghast at this new manifestation of independence on the part of the Emperor, and some looked to England
for a lead. Palmerston, who was Austria's very good friend north
of the Alps, was her implacable enemy south of them. "The
Austrians have no business in Italy," he declared to Granville,
"and are a public nuisance there." From the first he supported
the cause of Italian independence. In this he was vehemently
supported by Russell, and it is questionable whether these two
statesmen ever worked in greater accord than they did during the
two years that followed. Fate had been kind to Clarendon in
excluding him from the Foreign Office at this moment, for he was
hopelessly out of sympathy with Palmerston's Italian policy.
He was too level-headed to be carried away by the romantic
exploits of Garibaldi, too much of a realist in foreign politics to
be moved, as Russell was certainly moved, by the spectacle of a
nation struggling for its national rights. He did not "see" Italy
as a single nation, but as a number of small states, racially and
linguistically connected, but having very distinct and in many
cases divergent customs and traditions. He saw Italy as Venice,
Piedmont, Tuscany; and he was highly sceptical of a unity which
obliterated the distinctions which such names inevitably recalled
to the mind.

Holding these views, so fundamentally at variance with those
of Palmerston and Russell, had Clarendon been at the Foreign
Office, his position would have been an extremely difficult one.
For both these elder statesmen had become passionate advocates
of a united Italy. As for Russell, during the year 1859, his
mind was almost wholly occupied with the Italian question.
"Italy has become Johnnie's latest fad," was the Cabinet phrase,
and Ministers grew weary of Cabinet meetings largely devoted to
the development of his ideas on the subject, all the more so since
the policy that he and Palmerston were pursuing embroiled the

Cabinet with the Court and was inexplicable to most of the other Governments of Europe.

We have no space to give a detailed survey of the origins of the Italian situation. Suffice it to remember that in the revolutionary year of 1848, when Germany, Bohemia, Hungary and Austria were in a ferment, Charles Albert, King of Sardinia, placed himself at the head of the national movement in Italy and achieved the independence of the northern states—Lombardy, Venice, Parma, Piacenza and Modena. This at the time had delighted Palmerston as much as it had distressed Queen Victoria. Yet in a year the situation was reversed. Austria managed to re-establish her rule, and Charles Albert's last army experienced defeat. For a decade it had seemed as though " united Italy " had been a mirage; but beneath the smooth surface of ordered rule four men had worked for the defeat of Austria: two men of action, Charles Albert and Giuseppe Garibaldi; a poet and theorist, Mazzini; a statesman, Cavour.

All four had kept their eyes upon two European figures—those of Palmerston and of Napoleon III. Both these were known to have strong Italian sympathies, and the Emperor was said to desire an arena in which to exhibit the valour of his Imperial troops.

Cavour, the statesman of this group of four, had the brilliant plan (and had carried it through) of sending a contingent of Sardinian troops to the Crimea to fight for the allies. By this means he had obtained a seat for himself, as representing Sardinia, at the Congress of Paris, and it was not chiefly of Crimean affairs that he had talked at that council table. Moreover, he had seen much of the Emperor privately—he had managed that—and he had left Paris with a secret pact in his wallet. Austria was to be driven from Italy when circumstances seemed propitious. In return France should acquire Savoy. In 1858 Cavour called upon Napoleon to redeem his pledges, and by New Year's Day, 1859, it became evident that France and Sardinia were seeking to provoke Austria to war. Suspecting a pact, but not officially apprised of its existence, England endeavoured to mediate, but without success. On April 23rd Austria sent an ultimatum to Sardinia demanding her disarmament. Cavour gleefully accepted the challenge, and the Austrian troops crossed the Ticino. Napoleon stood by his promise, and on May 13th, 1859, Charles Albert, now become "Victor Emmanuel," met at Genoa "the magnanimous ally who had come to liberate Italy from the Alps to the Adriatic." Behind "the magnanimous ally" were 100,000 men.

There followed a brief and brilliant campaign, whereby the whole of the north of Italy fell to the victorious arms of the allies. But just as their success was at its height, and after the great

Franco-Italian victory of Solferino, when everything seemed possible, Europe rubbed its eyes to discover that the two Emperors had met and were discussing peace terms at Villafranca.

"On Friday morning," writes Charles Greville in his journal on July 12th, "the world was electrified by reading in the *Times* that an armistice had been arranged between the belligerent Emperors in Italy, and the subsequent announcement that they were to have a personal meeting yesterday morning, and the armistice to last five weeks (till August 15th) led to a pretty general conclusion that peace would be the result."*

Not many weeks elapsed before these prognostications were proved correct. The war was over; peace was proclaimed. Italy was to be free, not to the Adriatic, but to the Mincio. Austria was to retain Venetia and the Quadrilateral. Leopold of Tuscany and Francis of Modena were to be restored to their ducal thrones. Piedmont was to annex Lombardy, and Central Italy was to be federated under the presidency of the Pope. This, as can be well imagined, was hardly the consummation that Victor Emmanuel, Cavour and the Italian liberals had looked for. It was bitterly resented by Sardinia; and Cavour resigned office, a disillusioned man. But Victor Emmanuel made a brave show of jubilation with his new subjects. The truth was that Napoleon soon found that he had not the means for subduing the great fortress of the Quadrilateral. This the young Emperor of Austria, Francis Joseph, very well knew. He realised that he had only to retreat into that mountainous region to bring the French to a standstill. Napoleon saw this, and saw also that if the war were prolonged the Germanic federation, with Prussia at its head, might very well take the field against France.

But though Victor Emmanuel had not gained everything, he had gained something. And he went slowly forward with the unification of Italy. During the year 1859, Tuscany, Parma, Modena and the northern half of the Papal Dominions declared by plebiscite for union with Sardinia. On April 2nd, 1860, a Parliament representing 11,000,000 Italian people assembled at Turin.

As a result of all this the affairs of Europe were in a deplorable state, and Napoleon now attempted to throw upon Great Britain the onus of disentangling the knotted threads by suggesting a conference at Paris. Lord Cowley was highly sceptical of the good that such a congress would do. But at first Palmerston and Russell were not too unfavourable to the idea. It is significant of the divergence of view that existed between Clarendon and his two Whig confrères at this moment that, although the Emperor had

* Greville *Journals.*

expressed to Persigny an ardent desire that Clarendon should be nominated as first British plenipotentiary upon this mission, and although Cowley himself wished it, although his name was suggested in the Cabinet by the Duke of Newcastle and warmly advocated by other members of the Government, both Palmerston and Russell showed by their silence that the suggestion was not agreeable to them.

"When hard pressed," writes Kathy, "they merely said that no one but a Cabinet Minister could be sent to be put over Lord Cowley, thus making it appear to be tenderness for Lord Cowley's feelings, whom they both dislike, that made them refrain from asking Clarendon to be plenipotentiary."

The reason for their reluctance was, of course, not far to seek. It was not likely that they would send a man to the conference table who did not share their views on the Italo-Austrian question.

But although at first the idea of a congress had seemed feasible, Palmerston soon came to the conclusion that, with Austria at the conference table, an attempt would be made to whittle away all the advantages that Italy had gained by arms and by her plebiscites that summer; and to this he would be no party. He stuck to his guns, "Italy for the Italians," and refused the presence of Great Britain at the congress. Other nations made other difficulties, and in the end the idea of the congress was abandoned.

The Court was profoundly shocked at the line the Government were taking in the Italian controversy. Albert and Victoria, though fully alive to the flagrant abuses of Austrian government in Italy, thought it monstrous that a people should throw off their rulers, and the Queen considered it outrageous that *her* Government, *her* Ministers should aid and abet them to do so. Clarendon, who stayed with her at Osborne in August of that year, found her beside herself with rage and mortification.

"The Queen thinks of nothing but Foreign Affairs," he writes to Cornewall Lewis, "and spoke to me with great bitterness about Palmerston and John Russell. She said she was unhappy, and in a state of constant nervousness from the fear that some trick would be played upon her, and that without her being able to prevent it, the country would be involved in a wrong policy. Lord John, she said, had not written one despatch which she did not wish he had *not* written; but she admitted that he had adopted all her numerous corrections with good humour, and that, as yet, his letters had not been as rude as formerly. I tried," he adds, "and not in vain, I hope, to moderate her views, and those of the Prince on the subject."

Writing on the same theme to Theresa Lewis:

"Her old feeling against Palmerston," he says, "is quite
returned, and she spoke with bitterness of him and of Lord John.
It is evident that these two men sit upon her mind like lead, and
give it a permanent indigestion. I saw Palmerston on Tuesday,
and put some water into his wine, for he was very unjust about
the Austrian tendencies of the Prince, who is as much alive to the
brutal stupidity and shortcomings of Austria as Pam himself; but
the latter dubs everyone Austrian and anti-English who won't go
all lengths with him in trusting France, and backing Sardinia."

The more passionately Italian in sympathy the policy of the
great Whig leaders grew, the more sensitive and impatient they
became to any breath of censure or interference; and although the
Queen admitted in August that Lord John's letters were not as
rude as they formerly were, by November she could hardly say as
much, for he went so far on one occasion as to write a letter to
her beginning, "Lord John Russell unfortunately does not par-
take of Your Majesty's opinion in regard to Italy," covertly in-
sinuating that the Queen "was no well-wisher of mankind, and
indifferent to his freedom and happiness." And turning to Palmerston with a mild reproach concerning the "annexation" of
the Duchies, she was cheerfully informed that "the people of the
Duchies have as good a right to change their rulers as the people
of England, France, Belgium and Sweden; and the annexation of
the Duchies would be an unmixed good for Italy, for France and
for Europe." Victoria was not used to this kind of language. To
Lord John she administered a sharp rebuke. She sent the peccant
letter to the Prime Minister with a sharply worded intimation that
"she must demand that respect which is due from a Minister to
his Sovereign." It was 1852 over again, but this time with
Russell added. And as for Palmerston—oh, what a falling off!
Clarendon's "Babe of Grace" had put on the "old man" again,
and it is to be feared that he had become "Pilgerstein" once
more in the private colloquies of Victoria and the Prince.

That autumn Garibaldi and Victor Emmanuel made themselves
masters of Italy from Sicily to Turin. The Papal States had been
entered, and the fortress succumbed. Only Venetia remained in
Austrian hands. To all intents and purposes the union of Italy
was a *fait accompli*. France and Russia marked their disapproval
by withdrawing their diplomatic representatives from Turin.
Great Britain showed her approval by Russell's glowing despatch
to Sir James Hudson.

Palmerston and Russell were jubilant. *The Times* hedged, dis-
approving of all that the "Sardinians" said, but approving all
that they did. But there were other sections of opinion:

"Are we to sanction and uphold an open violation of every
principle which has hitherto been deemed sacred," writes Charles

Greville, "and by the maintenance of which the moral elements of the world have been held together? Is our policy, too, so changed that we can regard with satisfaction and approbation a course of combat by which the very existence of Austria will be directly or indirectly threatened?"*

And though Clarendon, always a realist in foreign affairs, was hardly borne away by such exalted sentiments, he did think Italian unity the first step in the progressive dismemberment of the Austrian Empire. And with Austria enfeebled, what then? His eyes turned apprehensively northwards, towards Prussia.

* Greville *Journals*.

CHAPTER XXVII
DEATH OF THE PRINCE CONSORT

§ 1

DESPITE these hurricanes abroad, 1861 dawned quietly and sedately over the English world. The Conservative home policy of Palmerston reflected the mood of the country, and the parliamentary session hardly produced changes worth recording. Lord John, old now, and wearied of the rough-and-tumble of the Commons, retired to the less exacting atmosphere of the Upper House. But this event, so long expected, did not break in upon the discreet hush which enveloped the outward trend of events.

It was the dead-level of the mid-Victorian epoch, and everything seemed rooted in an unassailable security. The solemn procession of life went unalterably forward; everybody knew his exact position in the scheme of things, and change of any kind appeared an impossibility. The virginia-creeper crept imperceptibly up the hideous face of the houses; the croquet balls clicked on the lawns; in the sacred precincts of the Universities tremendous Dons expounded Plato to Prime-Ministers-to-be; while if any event called for national comment, there was Alfred Tennyson at hand to turn it into melodious English verse. All was for the best in the best of all possible worlds. Earth reflected the placid smile of heaven. Life was decent, quiet and ordered.

Clarendon, out of office, had no more arduous task than to go on a mission to Berlin to be present at the coronation of William I of Prussia and to invest him with the Garter in the name of the Queen. But tragedy lay in wait for the English world, and hardly had he arrived home from his mission than it fell like a thunderbolt on an unsuspecting people. England lost the one man who for years had consistently stood as buffer between unruly English-minded politicians and the world at large. And the Queen lost the whole mainstay and inspiration of her life.

Everybody knows the story. The Prince had been ill for some days—taken suddenly ill after a flying visit to the Prince of Wales at Cambridge. At first it was lightly thought of; a severe chill, with some fever. The Queen was not anxious. She had full confidence in Sir James Clark. He was there. He assured her that all was going well. She went about her ways as usual. But Palmerston, who was at Windsor early that week, thought other-

wise. So did the Prince himself, who had a presentiment that he
was going to die. But the Queen continued to read *Peveril of the
Peak* out loud to him, and to make plans for his convalescence.
Palmerston was anxious. As bad luck would have it, he was laid
low himself with an attack of gout the moment he got back to
Broadlands from Windsor. It is just possible that events might
have turned out differently had he been active and on the spot.
From the first he had very little confidence in Clark, and would
have insisted upon a second opinion earlier. As it was he wrote
to Windsor three times a day, and himself was so anxious, so
white and drawn at dinner one night, that Em grew frightened
for his health. It was not till after the Prince had been ill, and
quite ill, for some days that the public became aware that anything was seriously amiss. But the bulletin of December 11th
had an ominous ring. "His Royal Highness is suffering from
fever unattended by unfavourable symptoms, but likely, from
its symptoms, to continue for some time." An ill-worded,
equivocal statement that turned every eye upon Windsor. And
thereafter, and with appalling swiftness, the tragedy that none
had foreseen, that none had allowed for, came suddenly close.
The eleventh—the date of the issue of the bulletin—was a Wednesday. On Thursday the news was worse. And when, on Friday,
Clarendon, restless and ill at ease himself, went down to Windsor
to enquire, the entourage met him with white, hopeless faces. It
was a question of hours, they said, and everyone knew it, except
the Queen. Princess Alice was showing a fortitude beyond her
years. She had tried gently but firmly to warn her mother of
what was coming. But though by now Victoria realised that he
was very ill indeed, nothing would bring her to believe that she
might lose him. The thought simply refused to enter her head.
Clarendon was stunned by what he had heard at Windsor. Next
day he wrote to the Duchess of Manchester:

"When I was there yesterday the anxiety was extreme . . .
I can think of nothing else, and yet I can't bear to think of the
consequences that his death must entail. I am sure you will have
the same feeling, for you know, just as I do, what the real relations were between him and her, and how different they were
from those of any other man and wife; for no other woman has
the same responsibility or the same motive for being absolutely
guided by the superior mind of her husband. The habit or rather
necessity, together with her intense love for him, which has
increased rather than become weaker with years, has so engrafted
her on him that to lose him will be like parting with her heart
and soul."

The next day, Friday the 13th, while Londoners went un-
concerned, or nearly so, about their Christmas shopping, and the

shops themselves were gay with Christmas garlands, those who knew and loved Victoria were praying in their inmost hearts that the cloud might be lifted from Windsor. Saturday dawned, and the bulletin announced a slight improvement in the Prince's condition. All day London was distraught by contradictory rumours —he was better; the crisis in the disease had been reached; if he could be carried over the next few hours (and surely he would be) the worst would be over—and others which said that he was sinking fast; that he could not last out the day; that he was dying.

At half-past four that afternoon a bulletin was issued at Windsor which allowed of very little hope. ''His Royal Highness the Prince Consort is in a most critical state,'' it said, and faces in the London clubs grew grave. It was too appalling to contemplate. . . . The hours dragged on. And then about midnight people in bed, people at parties, people coming home and in the streets were startled by a strange, unwonted sound—the tolling of the great bell of St. Paul's. All rumours died down in the face of the sullen fact that that sound denoted. Next morning the Gazette announced the following:

'' WHITEHALL,
'' *December 15th.*

''On Saturday night, the 14th instant, at ten minutes before eleven o'clock, His Royal Highness the Prince Consort departed this life at Windsor Castle to the inexpressible grief of Her Majesty and of all the Royal family. The Queen, His Royal Highness the Prince of Wales, Their Royal Highnesses the Princess Alice and the Princess Helena, and their Serene Highnesses the Prince and Princess of Leiningen, were all present when His Royal Highness expired. The death of this illustrious Prince will be deeply mourned by all Her Majesty's faithful and attached subjects, as an irreparable loss to Her Majesty, the Royal family and the nation.''

Early on Sunday morning the telegraph spread the news far and wide across the land ''in time sufficient,'' says the official account, ''to permit references being made to the calamity in most of the churches throughout the Kingdom.'' And no one had any thought that day but for the Queen. The news produced a commotion of feelings, ''which,'' as the account aptly states, ''almost forbade the use of the ordinary language of respect and sorrow.'' All that day Windsor was shrouded in impenetrable silence. No intimate word reached the outside world—nothing, save the bare official statement issued at noon on Sunday that ''the Queen, although overwhelmed with grief, bears her bereavement with coolness, and has not suffered in health.''

The castle walls frowned bleakly down, and no one dared conjecture what was passing within.

Clarendon was shocked beyond measure. He threw up his
hands when he heard the news. ''A national calamity,'' he exclaimed, ''of far greater importance than the public dream of!''
Bit by bit the scattered facts of the last hours were pieced
together.

''On Friday,'' writes Lady Clarendon, ''the Prince of Wales
was sent for from Cambridge. He arrived in the middle of the
night. It seemed a little doubtful whether his father knew him
at first. He had asked for him once or twice. He knew the
Queen quite near the last when he seems to have gradually become
unconscious. The Prince of Wales' behaviour seems to have been
all that was perfect. He rushed into his mother's arms and
assured her that the object of his life would be to assist her. The
poor little Princess Alice, too, appears to have been perfect in
her conduct and desire to support her mother. Throughout his
illness the Prince had a very bad opinion of himself and thought
he should die. The Queen did not believe it, and was only told
on Friday of his great danger. After his death she wanted to kiss
his forehead, but the doctors interposed, and she submitted, saying that she would do as she was bid. They feared his illness,
which had turned to Typhus, might be infectious. Poor thing,
she prostrated herself upon his clothes and kissed them. They
have sent to stop the Princess Royal, if she had not left Berlin,
and to prevent her coming as now it is too late and she is not
well, and quite unfit to travel.''

''I could hear nothing about the Princess Royal,'' writes
Clarendon to the Duchess of Manchester the next day, ''but I
am afraid it will be the misery of her life not to have seen her
father before he died. He thought ill of himself throughout, and
the whole of the last week felt sure he would not recover. It is
sad to think, but I fear it is true, that he had not the benefit of
the best medical aid. Holland and Clark are not even average
old women, and nobody who is really ill would think of sending
for either of them. Jenner has had little practice and experience,
and they would have been all if Palmerston had not written a
letter of such fierce remonstrance that Watson was sent for. But
Watson (who is no specialist in fever cases) at once saw that he
came too late to do any good, and that the case had got too much
ahead to afford hope of recovery. . . . One cannot speak with
certainty; but it is horrible to think that such a life *may* have
been sacrificed to Sir J. Clark's selfish jealousy of every member
of his profession. . . . When I came back last night I found
that Miladi had written to you. It is a great vexation to forego
the pleasure of seeing you here [the Grove], but I am sure you
will think we are right not to have a large gay party within a
week of that poor man's funeral. I would rather be accused of

courtiership than that the Queen should for a moment think me ungrateful for all the kindness I have for so many years received from her and the Prince. . . . Palmerston,'' he adds, ''has been shocked by the event beyond what you have supposed possible, and is *very* far from well.''

On the 20th, Clarendon had the following communication from Sir George Lewis:

''We were told yesterday that the funeral would be on Monday morning (*i.e.*, December 23rd), that there would be a special train from Paddington by which you could doubtless come; that we were to wear, not uniforms, but plain black evening dress, with trousers and boots. Those who have orders are to wear them.''

And while Clarendon, the male members of the Royal family, and the great Officers of State were attending the last ceremony in St. George's: Victoria, utterly forlorn and desolate, utterly alone, looked out upon the dreary waters of the Solent through an Osborne window, and repeated to herself over and over again, '' I *will* do my duty; I will, I *will* do my duty.''

She remained shrouded at Osborne through January. She could not bear contact with the outside world at first, and she dreaded seeing her Ministers. Business was sent to her as usual by her own request, and while she was occupied with it she was calm and collected, but when it was finished she became again the picture of grief. Her health had not materially suffered. She ate and slept well, but had grown very thin; and she was dreadfully tired and obviously suffering from shock. ''It was sad,'' Kathy notes from the recital of an eyewitness, ''to see the Queen so weak—she who was always so strong and able to take so much exercise—that she seems hardly able to move one leg before the other.''

§ 2

At the end of January, Uncle Leopold of Belgium came over to be with her for a short time, and he at once realised that she must see Palmerston. Her feelings were very mixed. He had written her a truly understanding letter when the Prince had died, a letter that seemed to come straight from the heart. But there were so many associations, too many associations perhaps; and memories of the old bitter days, when she and Albert plotted his downfall, *would* keep coming back into her mind. But it was her duty to see him: Albert would certainly have wished it. And see him she would. She sighed and wept and composed herself for the interview. It was, as a matter of fact, painful—far more

painful than she could have imagined—but for a different reason.
What she and the Prince had utterly miscalculated in their whole
dealings with Palmerston was the fact that he was human,
intensely human. Perhaps that was his point; perhaps that was
his appeal to the nation. But since her relations with him had
been entirely political, and not very pleasant at that, she had
never got to know him as a person. But now he came to her as
one human being to another; and the spectacle of his genuine
grief for her unnerved her considerably, but at the same time
softened her towards him. He was very kind, genuinely moved,
and very forbearing, and talked in the most natural and fatherly
way about Bertie.

Immunised by this first contact with the official world, she felt
she might see others. She sent for Clarendon. He, too, would
be kind and forbearing. He had truly estimated the Prince's
worth; and with him, moreover, there would be no unpleasant
memories. He was not a member of the present Government;
but it might be easier to see the others after she had seen him.
She asked him to come down on February 3rd. Clarendon
thought it wise to see Palmerston before he went, and accordingly
had an interview with him as he passed through London.

"It was a good thought of his," writes Kathy, "and Lord
Palmerston was evidently pleased, and took it as a mark of confidence. He told Clarendon all that he had said to the Queen in
order that, if he thought proper, he might hold the same language.
It did not amount to much," she adds, "as he could not speak
of the Queen without tears in his eyes. He said it was appalling
to see how thin and worn she looked. Dr. Jenner," she continues, "the Queen's resident physician told Lord Palmerston
that the thinness rather increased; but that being out in the air
did her good and that Princess Alice, who slept in the same room
with her, said that she slept well. Lord Palmerston thinks that
any Government will have trouble from her adherence to Prince
Albert's opinions, of which she will constitute herself the sole
judge, but he is not much alarmed about that I conceive," says
Kathy, "because Prince Albert's opinions were very sound.
The serious misfortune Lord Palmerston sees looking ahead is
her unconquerable aversion to the Prince of Wales. He said to
the Queen all that he ventured to do on the subject, which was
not much, and without the least effect. He said that with
Clarendon's tact he might have a better chance, and he urged
him to try. But Clarendon thought he might not have an opportunity and felt, beforehand, that it must be useless, as from what
she said of their discordant dispositions and the manner in which
the poor boy's presence even irritated her, it is evidently a *parti
pris*. She wants him to marry but not till he is 22 (why, Lord
Palmerston did not know). Clarendon saw no traces of his recent
illness in Lord Palmerston, and he was in very good spirits about

his Ministerial stability; and said that local squabbles explained adverse elections.''

Clarendon arrived at Osborne at about seven o'clock in the evening of the day he had seen Palmerston, and was met on arriving by a note from Lady Ely, saying that Princess Alice wished to see him directly.

''She was everything,'' writes Kathy, ''that her letters led him to expect she would be, a good deal affected at first, but did not cry much. . . . All she said about her father was perfect; and in her anxiety about her mother there was a tenderness and judgment but, at the same time, an absence of blindness to defects, that were really wonderful for her age. Even Lady Caroline Barrington admits she had no idea she had so much character, or that there was so much in her.''

Clarendon dined with the household; and at 9.30 the Queen sent for him. The meeting was painful in the extreme, and the Queen broke down utterly; but at last she grew calmer and talked to him as a friend of her intentions and of her plans. She said she had so longed to see him, and the next day Princess Alice and King Leopold told Clarendon that his visit had given great pleasure to the Queen, particularly as he had not tried to console her, but had taken the line that all consolation was a mockery.

A sympathetic ear in that strained household was more than anyone could resist, and the next day Clarendon had scarcely a moment to himself. Directly after breakfast Sir James Clark asked to see him, and for nearly two hours poured out to him every detail of the Prince's last illness. He had hardly got back to his room when Princess Alice sent for him, and he stayed with her from ten-thirty to twelve o'clock. King Leopold then expressed a desire to see him, and Clarendon was with him till two o'clock. After luncheon he had three-quarters of an hour with Sir Charles Phipps. ''After which,'' says Kathy, ''he took a walk by himself and returned at four to write his letters, and had actually begun one to me, when the Prince of Wales came into his room, and was with him till half-past six, when the Queen sent for him again and kept him till eight-fifteen. After dinner the Prince of Wales asked him to come and smoke with him and kept him till it was time for bed. So,'' concludes Kathy, ''he has been pretty exclusively occupied by the folks at Osborne, royal and others, all of whom seemed to desire an *outpouring*.'' To all and sundry he seems to have preached tact, moderation and forbearance.

In his second interview with the Queen, Victoria showed moments of embarrassing emotion, and Clarendon comforted and calmed her as best he might. He talked to her much of the Prince of Wales and said more to her than others had dared to say on that subject. "Indeed," says Kathy, "King Leopold told him, when he reported what he had said, that he himself had not ventured to say as much to my good Victoria." To the Prince of Wales he gave much fatherly advice, leading him on to talk about himself, of his friends at Oxford and Cambridge, and trying to implant in his mind the ambition to be a leader amongst them, and to set a high standard of living and thinking; an example of excellence to which they would readily respond. It was a new idea to the Prince, and Clarendon saw that it had its effect upon him. There was no harm in him, Clarendon thought, "but he is weak, idle and *very* young for his age, just the character that wants encouraging and kind usage in order to be saved from hypocrisy. He is now quite honest," continues Kathy, quoting Clarendon, "but stands great risk of being driven to deceit, the arm of the weak against the strong, and, as Clarendon told the Queen, the people of England care much more to have an honest, trustworthy man than a genius on the throne. The going abroad now is the best thing he can do, Clarendon thinks, for things would only go from bad to worse if he remained at home, and one must hope that time and good advice, and the Prince of Wales' success in his travels may bring the Queen to reason about him. Clarendon found this situation worse than he expected. It was, he said, a positive monomania with her. She got quite excited while speaking of him, and said that it quite irritated her to see him in the room. I believe the poor boy knows of his mother's dislike of him, but seems to have the good taste not to speak of it."

Palmerston and John Russell came for a Council before Clarendon left, and Clarendon told Palmerston all that had passed. "He was more pleased and grateful," says Kathy, "than Clarendon ever remembers to have seen him, for the Viscount, he says, is not in general warm in his expressions. . . ." Clarendon returned to London with Lord Palmerston, who took him in his carriage from the train and again thanked him warmly.

§ 3

Another year dawned, and Clarendon, still out of office, enjoyed the tranquillity of the Grove, from the library of which he kept in close touch with what was going on by means of a voluminous correspondence, both sent and received.

Two commissions were offered him this year, both of which he readily accepted. One was to be a member of the triumvirate which was to decide upon a national memorial to the Prince.

The other two members of the Commission were Lord Derby and Sir Charles Eastlake, then President of the Royal Academy. And it is to be feared that these three gentlemen, aided and abetted by Mr. Gilbert Scott, are responsible for the Albert Memorial! *Autres temps autre goût.* The other task Clarendon was asked to perform was more congenial to him. It was to be chairman of a committee that had been formed to enquire into the state of public school education. The work was interesting, but as president he felt a certain diffidence.

"We have had before us all the biggest swells in science," he writes to the Duchess of Manchester, "Dr. Carpenter, Sir Charles Lyell, Faraday, Hooker, Owen and Max Müller. I don't know when I have been so interested as in hearing the opinion of these eminent men, each from his own point of view, upon the deplorable neglect of physical science, and natural history in our system of public education. The chief task of examining these giants fell upon me as President, and I never felt more shy, as of course I did not want to expose my ignorance more than was necessary. We are now going to have a very different batch of witnesses—viz., boys who have left school long enough to be able to judge whether their time was well-employed, and yet not long enough to have lost their school-boy impressions. Can't you fancy all this being very interesting?"

The Queen's state of mind was still giving much anxiety to those about her. Her health was good; but nothing could penetrate the depth of her grief and give her comfort. Her whole life seemed shattered, struck down in its prime by the calamity that had befallen her. She attended to business; but, not having the Prince's directing mind to arrange and co-ordinate all her papers, she became muddled and confused. It all seemed too much for her. She liked to see Clarendon; and that summer and spring he was at Osborne on more than one occasion. These visits placed him in an awkward position, since not being one of her Ministers she had in reality no occasion to see him. Palmerston understood the situation perfectly; but Clarendon was a little nervous of Russell's reaction to it. However, he gave no sign, and the Queen was at pains to explain to Clarendon—as she perhaps did to Russell—that she desired to see him as an intimate friend of her husband's.

In June he stayed at Windsor for two nights, and found the Queen, who had been to Balmoral, in much better health, but still thin and worn.

"She talked much about the Prince of Wales, and Clarendon was able to give her much wholesome advice about her treatment of him—how she ought to try to develop his mind by showing him correspondence and consulting him on matters of home and foreign policy, instead of treating him as a child."

On this occasion the Queen even complained to Clarendon of the Prince's appearance, and notably of his legs, which she thought so displeasing.

"Clarendon," writes Kathy, "was able to assure her that people did not agree with her in this, and thought his looks very pleasing, and that as regards his legs, if his character were admirable nobody would think of his legs, and that, besides, people always wore trousers!!"

After this she talked very intimately of herself. Thus Kathy proceeds with her journal:

'She told him that she had received a great deal of kindness and sympathy, but that the *only* person who had quite understood her feelings and put himself in imagination exactly in her situation and expressed what he thought she would feel was himself (Clarendon); that it was therefore unnecessary for her to detail what were her sentiments, but that he would understand them. But she felt that her mind was strained to the utmost, that she was obliged to make decisions on her own, that she had never had to do so before, that it had all been done for her, that she could not bear it, and that she was afraid of going mad. She said that the Prince used to read and arrange everything for her, to save her all trouble, to bring her things she merely had to sign, and explain them to her and tell her what to do about them, and that now she had to do all this herself; that she was determined not to give up; that she saw many people and did a good deal, but that her mind was strained to its limit.'

'When she and Clarendon talked about the possible change of Ministry, the scene in the House of Commons the other day, etc., and the evident attempt made on the part of the Derbyites to turn out the present Government, she said that she felt *that* would be what she could not stand, that she would throw everything up, that she knew that she would go mad, that three times at Balmoral she had thought she was going mad, and that all that a change of Ministry would entail upon her now would be more than her reason could stand; that if they wished to kill her—and most *thankful* to them she would be for that result—they would drive on a change of Government, but that it would kill her, and that through *madness*. She wished the Opposition to know this. Lord Derby she thought she could depend upon, but she knew the Prince's opinion of Disraeli. She wished Clarendon to let them know what the result to her would be of a change of Government now. Clarendon answered that he was not on intimate terms with any of the Opposition except Lord Derby, but that since they were both members of the Commission for the memorial to the Prince Consort, he often had opportunities of speaking to him, but he did not know what degree of influence Lord Derby possessed over the other principal members of the Opposition; that the Queen must know him (Clarendon) well enough to be aware that he never wished to interfere, but that of course he should be ready to do anything Her Majesty wished, but did she *really* wish that he should make such a communication to Lord Derby? To this the Queen replied that she did wish it, that she *particularly* wished it, that Clarendon was the *only* person to whom she could make such an avowal of the state of her mind, and that he was the *only* person who, from his peculiar circumstances, could make such a statement to Lord Derby.'

'Clarendon had only to express his readiness to comply with her wishes; and so eager was she upon the subject that when he was leaving her she said, "You will remember, Lord Clarendon, my message?" and she desired him to write to her and communicate the result.'

'Whilst talking of the state of her mind her eye and manner became excited, and Clarendon could see that any encouragement would put her into a highly nervous state. She tapped her forehead with her hand and said, "My reason, my reason."'

Curiously enough, Clarendon was meeting Lord Derby that night at dinner at the Skelmerdales'. After dinner he drew Derby aside and explained the situation to him. "Good Lord," said Derby, "I didn't know she cared so much for them [the present Government] as *that*." To which Clarendon replied that it had nothing whatever to do with liking or disliking any persons or Government, but had solely reference to herself, to her own present state of mind, and her inability to stand further pressure on it. It also, he explained, had reference only to the present Session; that another year things would have to take their course; but that a grave responsibility would rest on him (Lord Derby) if, having received this communication from the Queen about the state of her health, he allowed his party to bring on a crisis. Derby was surprised and alarmed, and considered it a most serious situation, as indeed it was.

"Lord Derby," writes Kathy, "then endeavoured to justify the proceedings of his party in the House of Commons the other night, and to blame Lord Palmerston for accepting as hostile an amendment which was not intended as such. To this Clarendon, firing up, said that he had not come there to talk politics with Lord Derby, but since Lord Derby had chosen to begin upon politics he must defend Lord Palmerston's course, and say that in his place he would have done exactly the same; and that it was evidently a party move, if not to turn out Lord Palmerston, at least to discredit the Government, and that he had taken it in a very spirited and proper way.''

So the sparks flew over the port, while Derby hummed and hawed and considered the matter in all its bearings. But the Queen's message went home, and for the rest of that Session no more attacks were made upon the Government, and Palmerston was left in undisputed mastery of the field.

That autumn the Queen met the Princess Alexandra of Denmark, and was charmed with her. The marriage between her and the Prince of Wales was arranged at this time. And so 1862 ended in gay parties and festivities at the Grove and a general excitement over the royal marriage.

CHAPTER XXVIII
THE SHADOW OF GERMAN EXPANSION

§ 1

IN 1863 Clarendon lost one of the closest and most intimate friends of his life—Sir George Cornewall Lewis, Theresa's husband. It was a great blow to him, for of late the two men had become very close in the association of public life. They corresponded frequently; they saw each other often; the relationship had come to mean more to each than the fortuitous fact of being brothers-in-law. At first sight there would seem to be very little similarity between the brothers-in-law; for Cornewall Lewis was austere and forbidding, while Clarendon was gay and forthcoming. But beneath Clarendon's suave and facile exterior there was, and always had been, an unexpressed doubt, a sub-conscious detachment from the intimate contact of life. To those who saw beneath the surface this gave him the appearance of cynicism and insincerity, and was the sort of thing that made Sir Henry Bulwer, who met him in Paris four years later, quote a *bon mot* of a Frenchwoman about Talleyrand: "I would give him my favours," she said, "but not my confidence." As a matter of fact, this was not the general feeling about Clarendon, for his quick and sympathetic manner gained for him a more than average share of this world's confidences. But an acute observer, as Henry Bulwer certainly was, saw beneath the exterior, and guessed that the suave and brilliant manner concealed a question mark within. Had Clarendon believed in life as, for instance, Palmerston believed in life, he must have pushed his political career to its conclusion, and when the supreme political office came within his grasp, as it did on two occasions, he would have closed his hand upon the prize without hesitation. His failure to do so is deeply symptomatic. The difference, perhaps, between Lewis and Clarendon was that Lewis was perfectly aware of his own detachment, whereas Clarendon was not.

To Theresa this loss was a deep affliction; for her guarded nature had found happiness in a man who took very little out of her emotionally, but was a perfect companion, an affectionate friend, who combined a complacent and unexacting domesticity with a distinguished public career.

Hardly had he been laid in his grave than news came that Kathy's mother, Lady Verulam, was dying. For half a century the aristocratic old lady had bullied and cajoled and commanded her numerous offspring, and for half a century they had one and all adored her. And now they all sat in the house in Grosvenor Square, Kathy included, waiting for the end. She had had a good life, she was satisfied with what she had done, and she died in an atmosphere of enormous complacency. A wicked family legend avers that towards the end she made as if to speak. Those about her bent eagerly forward to catch her last words. "Four daughters," she said. "Yes, Mamma? Yes, Mamma?" cried the family encouragingly. "Four Countesses," she said firmly, and died.

In the summer Clarendon went to Wiesbaden to take the waters. While he was there there took place at Frankfurt a conference of German Kings to discuss a project for reforming the Bund. Russell wrote to Clarendon and asked him to go to Frankfurt and pick up what political gossip he could. Accordingly, at much inconvenience and expense, he made the journey and attended the conference, and his letters to Russell of what was passing on the subject elicited from that candid Minister the slightly cynical remark that Clarendon's communications confirmed what he himself always maintained—namely, that a hundred spies could not ascertain as much as one English gentleman in whom Princes and Ministers believed that they could safely trust.

§ 2

And now Clarendon's period of tranquillity was over. Once more he was fated to take on the burden of office. In the spring of 1864 he re-entered the Government as Chancellor of the Duchy of Manchester. The Duke of Newcastle resigned the Colonial Office at this time, and Palmerston would have asked Clarendon to accept the post, but he was told by the Whigs that there was considerable grumbling over the fact that so many of the chief offices of State were held at the moment by peers, and that if the discontent in the Commons were to go so far as to embody itself in an adverse motion the said motion might be carried against Ministers. Palmerston, therefore, hesitated. He wanted Clarendon back, and all his colleagues in the Cabinet were with him in this; but in view of the report of the Whips he did not venture to offer him the now vacant Colonial Office. Accordingly, he proposed to move Cardwell, who was a commoner, into that post, and to offer Clarendon Cardwell's vacated post as Chancellor of the Duchy. He sent for Clarendon and explained matters. Clarendon demurred, allowed himself to be tempted, and finally accepted.

"If the Government were prospering, and sailing before the

wind,'' he wrote to Granville, '' I could not have brought myself
to say ' Yes.' But seeing breakers ahead I could not refuse an
oar in a boat with old friends.''

But in returning to the Government at this juncture, and not in
the capacity of Secretary of State for Foreign Affairs, he was not
free from the criticism of inconsistency, and *The Times*, which was
at the moment railing at the Government's foreign policy, took
the opportunity of sneering at this new political trick of bolstering
up the Government and gibing at Clarendon for accepting the
'' cushion of the Cabinet '' (as they described the Chancellorship
of the Duchy). His acceptance of the post, *The Times* averred,
proved beyond a doubt that he endorsed in full the present foreign
policy of the Government. This, of course, was not true, and the
gentlemen in Printing House Square knew that it was not true;
but it was as good a missile as any to fling at the Government and
might make some consciences uneasy at Westminster. It did.
Clarendon was furious with Palmerston for not having conciliated
Delane before his own appointment was made public. '' Palmerston,'' he wrote to Kathy on April 5th, '' was full of flattering
speeches at my joining, but I cut them pretty short.''

§ 3

Hardly had he become a member of the Government than he
was offered a job very much in the province of his capacities: that
of paving the way with the Emperor for the conference of Powers
which had already been convened to discuss the Danish-Schleswig-
Holstein situation. Clarendon accepted the task with a heavy
heart, having no faith at all that a solution would be arrived at
palatable to any of the Powers involved, and pretty certain, as he
averred, that '' we would be the only persons there not bent upon
defeating the objects for which they profess to meet.''

As to the Schleswig-Holstein question, when the complicated
thing first began to appear on the European theatre the year
before, Palmerston is reported to have raised a jovial head from
a despatch he was reading, and exclaimed: '' There are only three
people in Europe who ever understood the Schleswig-Holstein
question: the Prince Consort, a Danish statesman, and myself.
The Prince Consort is dead, the Danish statesman is mad, and as
for myself, I have forgotten all about it.'' Diplomatically we
stood thus in the matter:

By a treaty of 1852, Austria, Prussia, Great Britain, France,
Russia and Sweden—a formidable array of Powers—granted to
Denmark the possession of the Duchies Schleswig and Holstein.
Now the possession of Holstein meant access to the harbour of
Kiel, and long before 1862 Bismarck knew that he needed Holstein

for the realisation of United Germany. The sequence of events has a sinister and topical ring to it. By 1863 he had persuaded the Emperor of Austria that a grave injustice to a German-speaking people was being perpetrated by the Danes. A few judiciously inserted spokes in the smooth-running wheels of diplomacy, and several seemingly respectable causes for criticism of the Danish claims were made to appear. The whole of Europe saw the shadow of future events, and Palmerston chose this moment to take up one of those apparently gallant but unsubstantial positions which since the eighteenth century down to our own days have led such men as the Corsican patriots and Haile Selassie to take risks which they deemed covered by a British guarantee of support. "Anyone," Palmerston affirmed, "who attempted to interfere with the independence of Denmark would find that he had others besides Denmark to contend with." But when, shortly afterwards, a large Austro-Prussian army was actually found in possession of the Duchies, another sequence of events, which may not seem unfamiliar to us, occurred. The statesmen of Europe coalesced round a green table. It became immediately clear that France would not fight to defend the Treaty of 1852, nor, it appeared, was any other signatory to that treaty prepared to take the field, while Palmerston at home discovered that the Cabinet would not consent to send an English army to defend Denmark.

Clarendon was sent over to Paris a few days before the conference was due to meet. His task, it may be imagined, was not a pleasing one.

However, his reception in Paris surprised him. He was hailed by all and sundry as the *deus ex machina*, as the one person who really understood European problems, as the one Englishman who could really comprehend the French mentality, even as the one person in the world who could manage the Emperor. All this made him open his eyes very wide. Political memories are short; he had been out of things for over five years, and he really never imagined that he had established such a reputation in the few weeks he had spent at the peace conference five years before. "I find myself a personage," he writes to Kathy, "and can only hope that I behave as such, and that five years more pleasantly spent at the Grove do not make me appear rustic." The Cowleys gave a great political party for him at the Embassy, at which he met everybody who was anybody. "The compliments," he writes, "were too absurd, and almost offensive in their exaggeration. My return to the Government was of European importance—the salvation of the Alliance with France—the means of bringing the Emperor to a true view of his own interests—and bosh of that sort without end."

He had long conversations with Persigny, Fould, Rouher and

Walewski, all very satisfactory as regards the Alliance and the continuance of peaceful relations with France, but of very little account in respect to the Danish question. Finally, he saw the Emperor himself, who was most warm in his *accueil*, and said he was delighted to have this opportunity of frankly stating his views on a number of subjects to an *ancien ami*.

On Denmark he took exactly the view which Clarendon had told John Russell he would take as early as January, when the Clarendons had been fellow-guests with Russell at Strawberry Hill. And Clarendon could not budge the Emperor from his determination to do nothing in the matter of the treaty. He did, however, manage to make him abandon his idea of a plebiscite for the Duchies, and the visit was fruitful in other ways. "I think my explanations about the congress, and our reception of Garibaldi were satisfactory to him," he writes. "But both were necessary," he adds ominously.

The conference was a failure, as he foretold it would be, and for the reasons he gave. France was determined to do nothing. And Bismarck was determined so to set the conference by the ears through his Prussian representatives that nothing could or would be effected by it. And this he managed to do. But Clarendon's part in the conference was not an enviable one. With England it had been a case of barking and not biting.

Russell and Palmerston had barked loudly and persistently at Germany for the past eight months. And when Germany bared her teeth and showed she meant business, the British dogs trotted unconcernedly off in the opposite direction. It was for Clarendon at the conference and Russell at the Foreign Office to show the reason why. They did; but, as was to be expected, not in a manner likely under the circumstances to redound greatly to the honour of Britain. Arguing that the treaty obligation of 1852 was *joint*, and not *joint and several*, we backed out of the affairs of Denmark and left her to her fate. That her fate entailed the loss of both the Duchies and of Lanenberg as well did not gild the pill or lessen (in this instance, at any rate) the truth of Derby's censure in the Lords:

"Thanks to the noble Earl (Russell) and his colleagues," he said, "we have at this moment not a single friend in Europe; and this great England, which never gave a promise without the intention of performing, which never threatened without the full determination of striking, which never made a demand without being prepared to enforce it, is now in such a position that its menaces are disregarded, its magniloquent language is ridiculed, and its remonstrances are treated with contemptuous indifference."

Feeling ran high in England, not only for our diplomatic humiliation, but also for the fact that Denmark and all that concerned it had suddenly come much to the fore in England owing to the immense popularity of the Princess of Wales. There is no doubt that the Government lost ground over the event, as votes of censure in both Houses plainly showed. In the Lords Ministers were actually defeated by nine votes. But around Disraeli's motion in the Commons Gladstone was able to weave so rich and sonorous a cloak of oratory that in the end the Government scraped through. It was as well, perhaps, that Parliament was prorogued at this time and that the long relaxing summer months were to intervene before it met again. During that time most of the Liberals who had been shocked at their chief's behaviour had come to realise that, after all, a war had been averted, and anyway the only alternative to Palmerston was Derby and his henchman Disraeli.

CHAPTER XXIX

DEATH OF PALMERSTON

§ 1

IN the middle of all these political happenings which we have just related, and at the height of the London season of that year (1864), an event took place very intimate and personal to the Clarendons, an event which hardly took them by surprise because they had seen it coming, and for which, since the happiness of their eldest daughter was involved, they had nothing but the sincerest thankfulness. Constance became engaged to Lord Derby's second son, Freddy Stanley. The Clarendons had seen much of him of late and had got to know and to respect him. He had been with them everywhere that season, and on Monday, May 2nd, Kathy notes in her diary:

"I and the girls went to Lady Howard's ball where the *dénouement*, the happy *dénouement*, of our love affair took place. Blessed be a most merciful Providence for the prospects of happiness for my darling child. . . . Very thankful, and very happy."

She writes next day:

"The more I see of Freddy Stanley, the more I like him; and Constance is radiant with happiness. F. Stanley came first; then Clarendon by appointment to see the Prince of Wales. Then Clarendon and I went to the Drawing Room where we were overwhelmed with congratulations. . . . Freddy took Constance off in the morning to see Lord and Lady Derby, who received her *à bras ouverts*."

It was characteristic of the age that on both sides all political animosities were laid aside in genuine pleasure at the event. Constance was marrying the son of Clarendon's bitterest political opponent, a man who had attacked him repeatedly in and out of Parliament. But when they met at the House of Lords on the afternoon after Constance's engagement there was nothing but smiles and handshakes, the mutual congratulations of two genuinely delighted and very human old gentlemen at the happiness of their offspring who were about to marry each other.

The wedding took place at St. Paul's, Knightsbridge, on May 31st, and was a very brilliant affair:

"Our darling Constance's wedding day," writes the truly Victorian Kathy under that date, "a day of great agitation, but of great happiness, for we have great confidence under a merciful Providence in her prospects. Freddy is excellent and charming: seems *so* attached to her, and the worldly concerns are sufficiently comfortable to make us easy, though the settlements are by no means brilliant. The marriage was an excessively pretty one— in St. Paul's, Knightsbridge, and Freddy's battalion lined the Church at their own desire—at least their being there was an entirely voluntary act, and it was settled with Mr. Liddell, the Clergyman, that as they were in great numbers they would look well, lining the Church, and a very pretty effect it had. (They all seem, too, so fond of Freddy.) Constance looked lovely as a bride, dear darling, she behaved so well."

There was a reception afterwards at Grosvenor Crescent, from which the young couple departed. And that night the others went to the opera, but Kathy remained at home. "I preferred," she said, "to occupy myself about my dear Constance, and packing up all her jewels to go after her to-morrow."

In the late summer the Clarendons, taking Emily (now the only unmarried daughter left to them), went abroad for an extensive tour, visiting Venice (with which we are told Emily was "perfectly enraptured") and Trieste and Verona and Milan, where they dined with Granville "the polite," who was also making a tour in Italy at the time. The winter passed pleasantly enough. "We made some visits: had some company. Had a little dance in January, 1865. Neither the F. Stanleys, nor the Skelmies could, however, be at it; but Emily did the honours beautifully as only young lady at the Grove. We went to London before Easter this year, as Clarendon was in Office."

§ 2

The spring and summer of 1865 passed uneventfully enough. Palmerston's position was unassailable. The country loved him, believed in him, respected him. In the Lords Derby might threaten and deplore; in the Commons Disraeli might bring all the barbs of his invective to bear on that venerable figure. It was no use at all. "Pam" was the common-sense Englishman who stood no nonsense from anybody. He might make mistakes (but who didn't?); he might at moments be injudicious (but who isn't?); and anyhow he had a marvellous gift of getting out of scrapes. He was the darling of the people, the typical English country gentleman: firm in his decisions and fair in his dealings. There was nobody like him. Moreover, he seemed perennial and immortal—now in his eighty-first year, and apparently still hale and hearty. The Septennial Parliament of 1859 was drawing to a close, only one more year to go, and Palmerston decided not to wait that year, but to demand a fresh mandate from the country after the session in July. July, therefore, was given over to elections, the result of which was a foregone conclusion. The Government was returned with a smashing majority, and Palmerston seemed stronger than ever. In August, Clarendon went, as he now often did in the summer, to Wiesbaden. In September he was back again at the Grove. And then in October it happened—the unforeseen, the incredible thing—Palmerston died.

England couldn't believe it, wouldn't believe it, was totally unprepared for it. So used were people to his continued presence at the head of affairs, so used were they to his blithe figure seen everywhere in London, to the wide top-hat and the tight frock-coat, to the explosive laugh and the expansive gestures, that they failed to perceive—even those who knew him best—that he was old, that he was very old indeed, and that for the past year the jaunty manner, the Palmerstonian optimism was only assumed under the pressure of a conscious effort. He was not very well that summer, though it was difficult to say what was the matter with him. Visitors to Brocket who had not seen him for some months felt that this time he had lost ground. But he played up bravely; pottered about in the sun; was interested in everything when Em's eye was upon him, and still wrote to his colleagues, Clarendon included. And then early in October he caught a chill and became seriously ill at once. Yet at first it seemed that he would get the better of it, and a bulletin was issued which gave every hope of recovery. But the heart that had begun beating in 1785 was tired—tired to exhaustion. It rallied and sank; rallied again, and finally, on the morning of October 18th, it ceased.

And with it ceased something brave and unaccountable and nonchalant in the annals of English public life. "The last candle of the eighteenth century was out," says Mr. Guedalla. Perhaps it was that. Never again were the affairs of England to be handled with that ease and naturalness—one had almost said "grace"—which the veteran statesman who had served his apprenticeship under Castlereagh, Canning and Pitt brought to bear upon them. Not often again would England feel the impress upon her affairs of a personality at once to be loved, to be feared, to be respected. Mistakes he had made, but they were of the human order. Overbearing he had been, but mostly to foreigners and in the cause of England! With something raffish and of another age about him, he swung life at his wrist with the ease of a tasselled cane. And if, in his case, life included the governance of England, what of that? What was there to make a fuss about? It was all in the day's work. So passed something gallant and undefeated from the English stage. England was never to see his like again.

"Eheu," wrote Gladstone. "Death has laid low the most towering antlers in all the forest."

It was a great blow to Clarendon. Not only had he lost his chief, but an intimate friend as well. All the old suspicions had been cleared up and forgotten years before. For the past decade there was no one of his colleagues in whom Palmerston put more trust, or in whom he more often confided than Clarendon. At one period he communicated with him almost daily. "I have been at pains to count those (letters) written to Clarendon in Palmerston's own hand during a single year"—1857—writes Sir Herbert Maxwell. "They number three hundred and ten, ranging over the whole field of politics, foreign and domestic, diverging not infrequently into personal matters. And Clarendon on his side could never forget that it was Palmerston who gave him his first job: who picked him out, an obscure civil servant, lost in the wilds of the Customs Office, and sent him, as full-blown Minister, to Spain. And yet there was consolation for him in the circumstance of his death.

"He died," he wrote to Granville some days later, "at the best moment for himself, in the plenitude of his political and intellectual power, just after the triumph awarded him by the country at the elections, without suffering, or change of habits, or loss of consciousness, plucky and *Palmerston* to the last moment. He held a great bundle of sticks together: they are now unbound, and there is no one to tie them up again."

Victoria was not so moved.

". . . Poor Lord Palmerston, alias Pilgerstein," she wrote to Uncle Leopold. "It is very *striking*, and is another link with the past—the happy past—which is gone, and in many ways he is a great loss. He had many valuable qualities, though many bad ones, and we had God knows! terrible trouble with him about Foreign Affairs. Still, as Prime Minister, he managed affairs at home well, and behaved to me well. But I never liked him; or could ever the least respect him, nor could I forget his conduct, on certain occasions, to my Angel. He was very vindictive, and *personal* feelings influenced his political acts very much. Still he is a loss. . . ."

He was buried in Westminster Abbey on October 27th, Clarendon being one of the pall-bearers.

That year the penalty of old age took its toll, for hardly more than a week elapsed when Clarendon was summoned to the bedside of his sister, Theresa Lewis. She had been ailing all that summer, but in the autumn the disease from which she was suffering took a sudden turn for the worse. On November 7th Clarendon was summoned to Oxford, where she lay.

"She was so shrunk and changed," he wrote next day to Lady Salisbury, "that I should hardly have known her, and her weakness was such that even with my ear close to her lips I could scarcely distinguish what her whisper was intended to convey. My brother left Oxford at 12 to-day, and says that it was then but a question of hours, and that all would be over by this evening. Alas! Alas! You can have no idea how I loved her, and what a blank her death will create in my existence—for as long as it lasts."

CHAPTER XXX
THE NEW DISPENSATION

§ 1

NO one was more alive to the change that Palmerston's death involved than Gladstone himself. It is true to say that he had an immense admiration for the late Prime Minister, and that the news of his death was a great shock. At the same time we find him eager enough for the future—his future, as it was so largely to be. Before the Queen had so much as sent for Lord Russell, Gladstone had written the following to him:

"MY DEAR LORD RUSSELL,
    "I have received to-night by telegraph the appalling news of Lord Palmerston's decease.
    "None of us, I suppose, were prepared for this event in the sense of having communicated as to what should follow.
    "The Queen must take the first step, but I cannot feel uncertain as to what it will be.
    "Your former place as her Minister, your powers, experience, services and renown, do not leave room for doubt that you will be sent for.
    "Your hands will be entirely free. You are pledged probably to no one, certainly not to me.
    "*But any Government now to be formed cannot be wholly a continuation; it must be in some degree a new commencement.*"

The italics are ours, and speak for themselves. He concludes this strange epistle by informing the aged Russell that he is more than ready to carry on in the new Government in exactly the same capacity as he served in the old—namely, as Chancellor of the Exchequer.

The Queen, as was to be expected, did send for Russell; and Russell, who by going to the Lords two years before had thought that he had virtually retired from active politics, found himself once more Prime Minister. Rather sadly he realised that he would have it all his own way now. Of course, there was Gladstone. But it was not unlikely that he and Gladstone would see eye to eye in these days. And may not this perhaps have been an unconscious source of irritation to the aged peer?

As a result of the new dispensation it was necessary to make a few changes in the disposition of the Cabinet. One of the first of these affected Clarendon, as Russell at once asked him to cede

331

the Duchy of Lancaster and to go to his old post at the Foreign
Office. Very reluctantly he acquiesced. For years out of office,
and then a year of office without the burden and responsibility of
a public department, had disaccustomed Clarendon to the toil
involved in the conduct of a department like the Foreign Office.
And although he had always a conscience with regard to foreign
affairs, and felt bound, always, to accept the Foreign Office when
offered to him, he approached his task this time with a marked
absence of zeal.

He was growing old; the gout troubled him considerably; his
mind was not as fresh and active as it used to be. He found it
increasingly hard to delegate work to other people. Routine
fussed him; he was over-conscientious.

"I despise myself for not being able to imitate my predecessor's
example [Russell]," he writes to Lady Salisbury, "but I cannot.
I have not his enviable nature. I cannot leave papers un-
answered and people unseen because they bore me; and I am
just as great a fool now as I was seven years ago."

But the affairs of Europe and England's place in them were,
and continued to be, his passionate preoccupation; and, as it
happened, and as he very well knew, it was a far from uneventful
moment in the history of Europe. New forces were at work;
new strains and stresses were being felt; a new orientation was
taking place. The sun of the second Empire was lowering in
the west. Men's eyes looked eastward and northward to beyond
the Rhine, where a strange new life was making itself felt.

Clarendon was uneasy at the look of things. Aware of his
own experience of European affairs, which was equal—if not
greater than any in England at the time, he was well content to
be called at this juncture to take over the conduct of Foreign
Affairs. Moreover, he was not displeased at serving under
Russell. The two were friends of long standing now. And
Clarendon always felt a degree of loyalty towards Russell from as
far back as the old viceregal days in Ireland. They had worked
on many occasions together towards common ends; and although
there had been sometimes a coolness between them, and sometimes almost a rupture, Clarendon never harboured *rancune*.
And besides, in the end, everyone always forgave Johnny. His
conduct might appear to be almost a stab in the back, his ways
uncertain always, and always unpredictable; but in the end he
invariably produced a cause of justification, some mysterious
reason, unlike anybody else's, for what he did; and though one
might condemn his conduct, one was generally forced to believe
that his motives were pure.

The waters appeared to close over the abyss that Lord Palmerston's death had made, and up to Christmas of that year the colleagues settled amicably enough to their business.

"I have never assisted at Cabinets more entirely harmonious than those held since Earl John has put his little hand to the helm."

So wrote Clarendon to Lady Salisbury in the same letter as that quoted above. But there were not lacking omens and signs of coming events. The situation in the Whig party was big with fate. Everybody saw it, and everybody pretended not to see it. For the party was pledged to Reform, and with Palmerston dead, and Russell and Gladstone unbridled at last, what might the future not bring?

§ 2

The Queen opened Parliament in person on February 6th, 1866, "the first time," said Kathy, "since her widowhood." She continues:

"She has had all sorts of vagaries about it, but it ended in her appearing in a black silk gown with her widow's cap, and a small sort of crown at the back of her head."

The Royal Speech, which was read from the Throne by the Lord Chancellor, made ominous reference to the subject of Parliamentary Reform, and both sides realised with something of a shudder that this odious question hung round their necks like a millstone, for the Tories were just as much pledged to Reform as the Whigs. Had they not recently fallen on a Reform Bill of their own? They could hardly resist legislation from the Whigs on a subject which they themselves had initiated. Naturally, there were enthusiasts for Reform on both sides. But the moderates, the large bulk of the rank and file of both parties, were apathetic, if not hostile. And certainly there was no enthusiasm outside Parliament. Bright expended all the pearls of his oratory in vain upon provincial audiences. He told incurious artisans that they were one and all struggling towards a great constitutional end; that history would remember them always as privates in that great army that went forward to constitutional victory.

"It is a great and noble purpose that we have set ourselves to achieve," he would cry, "but it is a purpose that cannot fail if we are but true to it, and to ourselves."

It sounded very nice. It was mildly flattering. Mildly they cheered, and then went back to work (which after all was the business of life), and forgot all about Mr. Bright and his fine

phrases. The country at this point of affairs would not catch
fire over the question of the vote. Later—a very few months
later—it was different. But then the question had become a bone
of parliamentary contention, whipped up in the press, and embodied in parliamentary figures, Russell, Derby, Disraeli—a very
different affair. But at the beginning of 1866, and on its own
merit, there was no burning interest in the franchise outside the
walls of Westminster.

"The question of Parliamentary Reform," writes Professor
Marriott, "was, in the 'fifties and 'sixties of last century, almost
entirely academic. It was raised by the *a priori* speculations
of philosophic liberalism, rather than by democratic demand.
The machine was, by general consent, working well. Its legislative products, though sparse in quantity, were carefully conceived, and have, for the most part, stood the test of experience."*

But the pundits in Parliament were adamant for Reform: not
only such adjustment of the franchise as would meet the needs
of the increasing urban populations, but a philosophic recon-
sideration of the whole basis of the franchise. Reform was intel-
lectually in the air. Reform there must be. And so in these
years England was forced on to her fate.

The long-expected Bill was introduced by Gladstone on
March 12th. It dealt only with the franchise, and was com-
mended by the House as a simple, even modest, measure. It was
proposed to reduce the borough franchise from £10 to £7, and
the country franchise to £14; to enfranchise "lodgers," com-
pound householders, and depositors in savings banks who had
£50 continuously to their credit over a period of two years. It
all seemed innocent enough, but careful statisticians estimated
that it would add four hundred thousand new voters to the
franchise.

Opposition to it came, in the first place, not so much from the
Tory benches, as from the heart of the Whig party itself. There
was a large and not unimportant section of the Liberals that was
resolutely set against any further tampering with the constitutional aspect of election to Parliament. Of these, Robert Lowe,
whose influence in the House of Commons through this year and
the next was remarkable, constituted himself the head. From
the midst of the Whig benches he rose again and again to attack
the Bill, on principle and detail. With him was Horsman, who
also carried weight, and between them they built up, in the heart
of the Whig party, a considerable and dangerous opposition to
the passage of the Bill. Lowe was an eloquent speaker, something of a scholar, and no mean politician. He had also this in

---

* *England Since Waterloo*, by Marriott.

his favour, he was passionately convinced. His opposition to Reform in the Parliament of 1866 and 1867 was no party trick, no move in a political game. It was dictated by a veritable horror: the honest and whole-hearted revulsion of his nature from what he considered would be the effects of a dangerously extended franchise. At moments his conviction rendered him positively prophetic. And certainly the force of it shook the House.

Round Lowe and Horsman gathered the disaffected members of the party, who, like them, feared the extension of the franchise. Bright, the enthusiast of the other side, passionate advocate of Reform, thundered daily at this group, pouring forth the vials of his sarcasm upon its members, and nicknaming them the "Adullamites"—"Broken men who rallied round David in the cave of Adullam." And by this name they were from now on known in the House.

Gladstone, nettled and alarmed by this snake in the bosom of the party, proceeded cumbrously with the Bill. In debate after debate he unfolded its implications and expounded its clauses; and as often as Gladstone extolled its principles, as often did Lowe rise to denounce them. At the second reading he made a speech the peroration of which long remained famous.

"Uncoerced by any external force," he cried, "not borne down by any internal calamity, but in the full plethora of our wealth, and in the surfeit of our too exuberant prosperity, with our own rash and inconsiderate hands, we are about to pluck down on our heads the venerable temple of our liberty and our glory."*

The Opposition gathered strength, the "cave" overflowed. On an amendment of Lord Grosvenor on April 27th, the Government were saved by only five votes. Grosvenor had asked the House to refuse to proceed with the Bill until the Government had laid before it their scheme of redistribution. Although the amendment was lost, and there was therefore no obligation on the Government to do so, they did now lay before the House their scheme for redistribution. It proved a modest enough measure. But by now the temper of the House was up; the Opposition in the ascendant. Despite the efforts of Russell and Gladstone in favour of the Bill, there was little real driving force behind it in Parliament, and none outside. By the time it reached the Committee stage it was in a highly dangerous position, and on June 18th Lord Dunkellin, one of the "cave," dealt it its death-blow on an amendment to substitute a rating for a rental qualification for the borough franchise. The Government were defeated by eleven votes.

* *Annual Register.*

In consequence of this defeat the Ministry tendered their resignation to the Queen, but not without considerable discussion and Cabinet dissent. The problem was, should they resign, or dissolve and go to the country, or endeavour to re-establish themselves by a vote of confidence? The Cabinet were hopelessly divided on the subject and Russell uncertain how to act. Clarendon hotly opposed resignation, both on party grounds and on grounds of sheer expediency. He remonstrated with Russell both by letter and by word of mouth in the Cabinet to this effect. Russell was irresolute, but in the end veered towards resignation. On June 25th the Cabinet decided in favour of resignation. Clarendon renewed his remonstrances.

"The decision of to-day," he writes to Russell the same evening, "causes me such distress of mind that I cannot help asking you to consider whether some form of resolution cannot be found that will command a majority, and, at the same time, satisfy, I will not say the honour of the Government, but the exigencies of Gladstone; and they are distinct things," he adds drily.

The Queen saw the situation in the same light as Clarendon, and perhaps for the same reasons. She wrote angrily to Russell:

"In the present state of Europe," she said, "and the apathy which Lord Russell admits to exist in the Country on the subject of Reform, the Queen cannot think it consistent with the Duty which Ministers owe to herself and the Country that they should abandon their posts in consequence of their defeat on a matter of detail (not of principle) in a question which never can be settled unless all sides are prepared to make concessions."

Russell admitted the force of the Queen's argument. But then he had Gladstone to deal with. And Gladstone was very much on his high horse at the moment. His eloquence had carried most of the Cabinet with him. Russell had no alternative. He persisted in his resignation, and on June 26th the Queen sent for Lord Derby.

CHAPTER XXXI
OUR WORLD IN THE MAKING

§ I

SO much attention had been riveted upon Home Affairs in the course of the early months of 1866 that what had taken place on the Continent, and what was actually still in process of taking place, had to a large extent escaped the notice of even the most reasonable men. That the balance of power in Europe was being materially threatened by a new and equivocal force; that the Napoleonic régime and all the delicate threads attached to it was visibly declining; that the power of Austria was threatened with instant annihilation—these problems, and all the implications involved by them, seemed to have been passed over by a nation intent upon its own internal problems and difficulties.

But Clarendon was fully alive to the situation on the Continent. And so, for that matter, was the Queen. And in different degrees their opposition to the hasty resignation of the Whig Government was dictated by the same motives. Russell and Gladstone seemed to be, both of them, criminally unaware that they were deserting their posts in the midst of a first-class Continental crisis. On the very day on which Russell tendered his resignation to the Queen, Prussia declared war on Austria and the German Bund. Central Europe was threatened with profound convulsion.

The campaign that followed, as short and decisive as von Moltke's brilliantly reorganised army could make it, proved the culmination of the first stage of Bismarck's programme for Prussia. Through all the tortuous complications of the Schleswig-Holstein affair, and the campaign that ensued—by which, be it said, he had blinded the world from believing that the acquisition of the harbour of Kiel was the sole object in view—Bismarck had never for one moment averted his eyes from the real, the secret, the hidden motive of his ambition for Prussia—the shattering of the Hapsburg power; the breaking up of the old German Confederation of States that hung loosely to the Hapsburg rule; the formation of a new Bund, this time bound by fear and necessity to the chariot wheel of Prussia. This was the first, the necessary first stage of an even larger programme. And this, striking exactly at the moment when everything was technically ready, he now, with his henchman von Moltke, proceeded to effect.

22

Everything was thought out—the nature and extent of the campaign by von Moltke, the political reactions in Europe by Bismarck himself. He was a consummate diplomatist, and since human values, in face of the bigness of his political visions, had no significance for him at all, he could stand detached from the personalities of politics and watch their reactions with the dispassionate interest of a scientist inspecting a colony of germs. This gave him a knowledge and power over men which few other statesmen in Europe possessed at the time. A man like Napoleon III was as a flute in his hands; he could play what tune he liked upon him. In the campaign that he was planning for Prussia it was necessary to secure the rigid neutrality of France. What more easy than to meet Napoleon casually at Biarritz in the autumn of 1865; to hint of coming events; to dangle before the imperial eyes a not too definite bait of "compensation" (a most useful word in diplomacy); to talk glibly, and not too specifically, of Luxemburg; and even, but this a little banteringly and only to whet the royal appetite, of Belgium itself?

And now in June, 1866, all was ready. At a word from Bismarck the German legions were launched to the assault. Six weeks afterwards, at Sadowa, the Hapsburg lay quivering in the dust under the heel of Prussia. That huge, cumbrous, but convenient and necessary thing, the great Austrian Empire in Europe, was shattered; its ascendancy over; its place taken by an equivocal, upstart nation—a nation without history or tradition, without a past and with nothing but a present. Prussia emerged from the conflict, sprang fully armed and parthenogenic, like some terrible distorted Athene, into the arena of world politics, and the re-orientation of Europe began.

§ 2

Small wonder that with these events impending (events which were still hidden from the view of most Englishmen) Clarendon should have implored Russell not to resign. But Russell was obdurate; and Derby, sensing that some first-class crisis was about to take place, begged Clarendon to remain on at the Foreign Office, where his name inspired confidence. It was a sincere offer, and the Queen supported it. But those who made it must have been poor psychologists if they believed that Clarendon would accept the post. Loyalty to friends and colleagues was a cardinal point in his creed of political honour. His usefulness ceased, so he thought, when his friends went out of office. He took only a few hours in which to make up his mind, for his letter declining Derby's offer bears the same date as Derby's letter to him suggesting the plan. Acquainted with the incident, Russell

was drily grateful for Clarendon's loyalty and sourly critical
of the new Government, in which Lord Stanley held the post of
Secretary for Foreign Affairs.

Released once more from office the Clarendons spent the late
autumn and winter of that year in Rome, whither also for re-
laxation and relief quite a number of the late Cabinet had fled.
The Gladstones, the Cardwells, the Duke of Argyll, the Clarendons all met in the Eternal City, and the fevered antics of Gladstone on holiday were the constant amusement of the others.

"Italian art, archæology, and literature, are Gladstone's sole
occupation," writes Clarendon to Lady Salisbury. "Every
morning at eight he lectures his wife and daughters upon Dante,
and requires them to pause and give the root of every word. He
runs about all day to shops and galleries, and only last night told
me that he hadn't time for the reading-room, and had not seen
an English paper for three or four days. . . ."

Three of the ex-Ministers had private audiences with the Pope,
and Abraham Hayward wrote to Lord Halifax that, on Manning's
report, the Pope was "charmed with Lord Clarendon," "disappointed with Gladstone," and "bored with the Duke of Argyll."
This was amusingly confirmed by Gladstone, who in later years
used always to quote with glee what the epigrammatic Leo said:

"I like, but do not understand, Mr. Gladstone. Mr. Cardwell I understand but do not like. I both like and understand
Lord Clarendon; the Duke of Argyll I neither understand nor
like."

They were all back again in the spring to assist at what proved
one of the most momentous sessions that Westminster had ever
witnessed. For now it was the Tories' turn to introduce a
Reform Bill. And the Bill that they framed, its nature and
extent, the manner in which Gladstone seized hold of its clauses
one by one, pulverising the safeguards by which the Tories had
sought to stem the full tide of manhood suffrage; the titanic
struggle that ensued between two personalities, Gladstone and
Disraeli; the wild prognostications of disaster on both sides;
Disraeli's passionate belief in a democratic future for England;
and old Derby's fearful phrase, forced out of him by the sheer
magnitude of the change, the famous "It's a leap in the dark"—
all these together make the first six months of 1867 one of the
most dramatic periods in the whole annals of Parliament. The
ultimate decision in England as to whether there should be a
group of people who *ruled* and a mass that were *ruled,* or whether
the mass itself should rule and the group in Parliament should

be simply its servants—this was the ultimate issue. The Reform
Bill of 1867 raised questions of principle which were fundamental,
and which were felt to be so at the time. It was far more important, it was far more revolutionary than the Act of 1832,
which in comparison to it seems a mere readjustment of the
mechanical gear of Parliament.

The measure which Disraeli introduced in 1867 in its final
form not only added nearly a million voters to the register but
established the principle of eligibility upon which every further
Act of franchise extension has been based. Given the Act of
1867, every subsequent Act was inevitable, right down to the
Act of recent years which practically gave an elective vote to
every breathing individual who was not an infant or mentally
deficient.

It was a tremendous tussle. Robert Lowe, like Cassandra,
stood upon the walls prophesying doom. John Bright, champion
of the people, poured out his oratory in defence of Gladstone's
amendments. Disraeli, sardonic and unperturbed, expounded
and defended the Bill in a series of brilliant orations, seeming to
bend to the will of the Opposition, but determined that his Bill
should become law. Gladstone himself, immensely verbose, immensely technical, pressed home his amendments *vi et armis*,
nervous at the magnitude of his undertaking and irritable at the
insubordination and disunion of his party behind him. The first
round of the contest ended just before the Easter recess, when one
of Gladstone's most cherished amendments was defeated, largely
by the instrumentality of a section of his own party, a radical
opposition which had lately formed and which was dubbed " The
Tea-room Party " by the House. It was an immense blow to his
personal prestige, and the great Liberal leader was incensed
beyond measure, even to the extent of seriously considering
abandoning the leadership of the party. It took half the Cabinet
and the protestations of half the country to pacify his injured
pride. However, it was pacified, and the resumption of affairs
after Easter found him in his place refreshed by the interlude and
eager for battle. From then onwards the Whigs had it all their
own way. It is impossible in the space to go into the legislative
details of this complicated measure. Suffice it to say that every
check, every safeguard with which Disraeli as a good Conservative had sought to hedge round the application by his startling
principles were assaulted and finally routed by Gladstone.

One by one the " counterpoises " went by the board; the
" dual vote " and the " lateral franchises " were abandoned.
The two years' qualifying residence was reduced to one; a
" lodger franchise " was inserted; the rating qualification for the
country franchise was reduced from £15 to £12; the voting paper

device was deleted. The Bill became a Bill for Household Suffrage *sans phrase*.

The debates in both Houses thundered on through the summer. But the end came at last. The Representation of the Peoples Bill received the Royal Assent on August 15th, 1867. In spite of all concessions, Disraeli had had his way. His Bill had become law. His party was still in power. Derby was alarmed at the extent of his own victory.

"Anyway, we've dished the Whigs," he remarked drily. But he was not sanguine. "It's a leap in the dark," he said.

Both parties were awed. Vernon Harcourt, a Whig himself, wrote to *The Times*, commenting on the suicide of the Tories. "It is not a party they have destroyed, it is a creed they have annihilated," he wrote.

James Lowther, a staunch Tory, was heard to remark that he really didn't know how he was going to face his constituents, "having refused a moderate measure from a good Christian and accepted an extreme one from a bad Jew." Lowe, who saw the future, implored all and sundry for immediate and extended forms of State education. "You must teach your masters their letters," he cried bitterly in the House.

But among all these gloomy prognostications Disraeli was jubilant.

"I, for my part," he said, "do not think the Country is in danger. I think England is safe in the race of men who inherit her: that she is safe in something much more precious than her accumulated capital, her accumulated experience. She is safe in her national character, in her fame, in the tradition of a thousand years, and in the glorious future which I believe awaits her."

Words, words, words. But do they measure the magnitude of the change effected by the Bill of 1867?

CHAPTER XXXII

LAST CALL TO OFFICE

§ 1

THE Bill, pregnant with implications for the future, itself closed the gates of the past and marked the end of a great parliamentary era and the beginning of a new. The giant figures that had controlled policy and Parliament in the past were growing old—too old to reach out into the future. Palmerston had gone, and his passing had opened the sluices. Such a Bill as the Reform Bill of 1867 could never have become law had he been alive at the time. Russell, the great reformer, the great Liberal, the ardent parliamentarian; Russell, now well stricken in years and impoverished in health, had, himself, retreated into private life, handing over the leadership of the Whig party to Gladstone. And now, after the Reform Bill of 1867, after his admitted "leap in the dark," Lord Derby—"the old 'un"—retired also, placing the party leadership in the highly equivocal hands of Disraeli.

A generation of statesmen was failing and a generation was rising—a generation brilliant but different, inspired by new standards and principles, faced with new problems. Modern parliamentary history really begins with the retirement of Russell and Derby and the accession of Gladstone and Disraeli. And in this new orientation of things Clarendon had indeed no part. His politics were all of the past, and his principles were inspired by the great figures of the past who had been his friends and his associates. We picture him at this time—or, rather, in 1868— an aristocratic old figure, tall but shrunken, failing a little in health; gay and irritable by turns as the gout approached or receded, but courteous and charming as ever; completely absorbed in foreign affairs and quite unaware that the old political summer was over, and that in a Cabinet of Cardwells and Goschens and Gladstones he would be a picturesque survival, a solitary bloom left over from more spacious days. A rising generation had already relegated him to the past. Wilfrid Scawen Blunt, who met him about this time, refers to him as "a white, sleek little old gentleman with an agreeable old-fashioned manner."

§ 2

In the spring of 1868, Emily became engaged to Odo Russell, a brother of the Duke of Bedford, the Clarendons being in Rome,

where Russell was Minister. They remained in Rome that year
till half-way through May, as Emily refused to be married till her
sisters Constance and Alice could come out and be with her for
the event, and both those "inconvenient girls," as Clarendon
calls them on this occasion, " mean to be confined in April." The
marriage duly took place, and the later summer found Clarendon
in Germany again, where he renewed his acquaintance with the
King and Queen of Prussia. He did not like the look of things
there. He liked it still less after a conversation with von Moltke.
This strange, unassuming man—" something between a notary
and a professor, and no more like a soldier than I am "—he found
quite ready to talk, and to talk frankly, though his modesty was
such that if left to himself he remained silent.

A little careful handling, however, and the spring of the doll
was released. The figure talked in the approved German manner,
said all it had to say and then stopped. What it said surprised
Clarendon a good deal. It said, for instance, quite blandly, and
beaming through spectacles, that if they had known that the
French could only bring 140,000 men into the field in 1866 they
would have finished matters off *at once and for good in a very
different fashion*. Ominous words; for since Sadowa was about
as complete a victory as any general in the field could very well
wish for, it left unpleasant conjectures as to what von Moltke and
Bismarck really wanted. Could it be the *complete* subjugation of
Germany? The Northern States were already toeing the line.
Did these two Prussians seek to place the Southern Confederation
beneath the heel of their country as well? And was their ignorance of French military resources and their uncertainty of French
neutrality the sole hindrances to that end? Clarendon was
alarmed, so alarmed that he deflected his return to England so as
to pass through Paris and to have minatory talks both with the
Emperor and with Lord Lyons, the astute British Minister, who
had lately been appointed to Paris.

For over fifteen years now Napoleon had been, with qualifications, supreme arbiter of European affairs. He had posed as the
mediator—almost the dictator—of European polity, and before
him the great autocracies of Russia and Austria had sunk back
into comparative insignificance. France was the power that
counted. Napoleon posed as the Emperor, the benign and well-
intentioned Emperor, of more than France. On the whole he
played the part successfully, and of course he could not have
played it at all without the connivance of Great Britain. Europe
had become accustomed to this attitude of France, and indulged
Napoleon in his antics. Round France and the Second Empire
had gathered all the threads of diplomacy for more than a decade.
For many reasons it was convenient that this should be so.

But now a nation had arisen, forged by battle into a formidable unity, a nation whose claim to a voice in the world's affairs was based on *force majeure*, on bayonets and bombs and 500,000 marching men. Behind those men, directing their course, was one of the astutest politicians that Europe had ever seen. The full extent of Bismarck's machinations was, of course, still hidden from the world. But what the world did realise, and realise at once after Sadowa, was that a nation had come into being, a new force in the destinies of Europe, which, by its very existence, apart from its intentions, challenged the supremacy of France in Europe.

Napoleon was fully alive to the situation. Clarendon found him restless and dispirited, superstitiously feeling that his star was set, and not sure of the reason why. He welcomed Clarendon warmly, and was keenly interested in his accounts of the conversations he had had in Germany. He professed his pacific intentions towards Germany, but warned Clarendon that he could not hold the army or the people back in the event of a direct provocation being given. He was disquieted and alarmed. Already the latent antagonism of France for this upstart rival had been expressed by angry shouts in the camp at Chalons that summer. Napoleon implored Clarendon to prevail upon the British Government to intervene and to devise a method by which France and Prussia could withdraw with honour on both sides from their present hostile and dangerous attitude. Napoleon had nothing himself to suggest, but his belief in "conferences" and the power of the British Government to prevent war was unrivalled, and he had great confidence in Clarendon's skill to avert dangerous eventualities, even though he might not be in office.

Clarendon returned to England at the end of October in an uneasy state of mind, and at once laid all the facts, and his own comments upon them, unreservedly before Lord Stanley. Stanley was inclined to derive more reassurance from the pacific protestations of Germany than Clarendon thought warrantable. And there for the moment the matter rested. Out of office he could do no more.

§ 3

However, there were not lacking signs that the Tory Government was cracking up. In the spring of 1868 came the elections; and it is ironical to consider that the first-fruits of the "leap in the dark" was a smashing victory—*not* for the Tories, who after all passed the prodigious Reform Bill, which gave so many new classes the vote—but for the other side, the Whigs, who either opposed it or sought to make it into something quite different from what it was.

What would happen now? wondered Clarendon. Would the

Queen send for Russell, or would she send for Gladstone straight away? It was said that Russell had retired from public life. The little "Pembroke Lodger," they said, was a hermit now, interested only in family affairs and the preparation of his literary papers for the Press. One feels that this speculation of Clarendon's about Russell was dictated by something more than the fact that his own plans depended to a certain extent upon what Russell would do. One feels that that glance over the shoulder towards Pembroke Lodge was a glance into the past, a wistful glance that held, too, something of a hope in it, a hope that the little man, his own old political chief and associate of so many years' standing, would come forth from his tent armed once more for the fray.

There is no doubt that Clarendon himself felt old and ill and disinclined for office at this juncture. Kathy, indeed, was anxious that he should take a complete rest and spend the winter, as before, in Rome. There was talk of their taking a "nurse" out with them if they went, so it is clear that his health was giving cause for anxiety. Moreover, that sincere admirer of his, the Queen of Holland, writes to him repeatedly at this juncture, disadvising his taking office. But he himself was anxious about the foreign situation. He felt he could still be of use in that quarter, still do something at the Foreign Office—were he offered the post—to mitigate the tension between Prussia and France; and he knew that if it were offered him he would accept it.

And then, on December 3rd, came the telegram which Clarendon had been partly dreading. It was from Gladstone, asking Clarendon to go and see him. So Clarendon repaired to Carlton Gardens determined to give Gladstone every opportunity of *not* having him in the Government if he saw that that was Gladstone's real wish, but determined also to accept office if Gladstone pressed him to do so and desired to have him at the Foreign Office. Gladstone he found as fresh as a schoolboy, having travelled all the way from Chester to Windsor at the Queen's urgent summons. (There was no talk of Russell, it appeared; the Queen had sent to Harwarden without so much as a glance towards Pembroke Lodge.) And now Gladstone made his views perfectly clear to Clarendon. He definitely implored him to take the Foreign Office in the Administration he was forming, and exerted all his efforts to persuade Clarendon to do so. Clarendon, on his part, gave the Prime Minister-to-be every occasion to back gracefully out of the offer. He said he was an " old stager," that " new blood " should be tried, or alternatively suggested Lord Granville, the Duke of Argyll. But Gladstone would have none of them for the Foreign Office, and when Clarendon saw that he was in earnest he relented.

But there was one circumstance in regard to Clarendon's taking the post at this juncture of which he was not aware, of which he was never aware, and which, had he known it, would have made it quite impossible for him to have accepted the post—any post— in the Government. It was a curious circumstance, and those whom it concerned were completely unprepared for it. It was a direct objection to Clarendon for the post of Foreign Secretary, and it came—from the Queen, of all people. . . .

As short a time as a week before Clarendon's interview with Gladstone in Carlton Gardens, Victoria had commanded it to be intimated to the latter that she would not, at any costs, have Clarendon as Foreign Secretary. When reasoned with, she replied that he was the only one of her Ministers who had ever been impertinent to her. The occasion of his so-called impertinence could never be ascertained from her. But she appeared to be adamant, and adduced other and equally groundless reasons for her aversion. He was too intimate with the Queen of Holland. He was unfitted for the post on public grounds, because of his opinions against German unity, "which she considered so right and necessary," and other such-like arguments. She had been, it appears, quite childish on the subject, and Charles Grey, her private secretary, and Lord Halifax had had a rough time with her.

"I told Charles," writes Lord Halifax in his diary, "that he should point out to the Queen that Lord Russell had made Clarendon Foreign Secretary, and that Lord Derby had offered the post to him; so that, in the opinion of both leaders, he was the best man for the post."

But it was of no use. She would not have Clarendon as Foreign Secretary. She would have no objection to him in another capacity—as President of the Council, for instance. She would prefer Granville as Foreign Secretary; or it might be well to bring Lord Lyons home, in which case Clarendon could go to Paris as Ambassador. But to have him at the Foreign Office, a position which more than any other position in the Cabinet brings a Minister in close and frequent touch with the Sovereign, no, she would not. She wanted Mr. Gladstone clearly to understand her views. And poor Charles Grey had to go off and break the news to Gladstone.

Now what caused Victoria to turn suddenly and violently in her mind against the very Minister who had stood so often and for so many years her friend at need, to whom she had turned to consult privately on her difficulties; who himself had known and respected Albert, to whom they had both turned in moments of strain and stress; whom of all her Ministers she had sent for as

PLATE 8.—THE EARL OF CLARENDON, K.G.

Statue at the foot of the Foreign Office staircase.

soon as she decently could after Albert's death, and who had never been anything but her loyal and devoted subject, it is difficult to say. Most probably she feared his views on the subject of German unity, and shrank from having a Foreign Secretary about her who sought in any way to counteract the influence that Albert's beloved country was coming to have in European affairs.

That the reasons she gave for her objection had no basis in reality is proved by the ease with which they were surmounted, and the fact that in her subsequent dealings with Clarendon as Foreign Secretary not the smallest hint of her former resentment ever appeared. The whole thing seemed effaced from her mind, and certainly Clarendon never had a suspicion that she had ever felt thus towards him. His desire for office was lukewarm enough; he was always personally diffident; and if he had had the smallest inkling that he was not *persona grata* to his Sovereign he would certainly have never dreamed of accepting the post.

By what alchemy Gladstone was able to spirit away the Queen's objections it is not known. But that they *were* completely spirited away before his interview with Clarendon in Carlton Terrace seems evident from the urgency with which he pleaded with Clarendon to accept the post. Had he any doubts as to Clarendon's reception by the Queen, he could not have held such language to him, fresh as he was from a talk with her.

And the secret was certainly well kept. For Clarendon had not the slightest suspicion of all that had passed. On December 10th we find him writing to Lady Salisbury:

"The Queen was just in her old form, and resumed the usual talk just as if it had not enjoyed (so far as I am concerned) a two and a half years' interruption. She seemed mightily pleased at the way in which we stand respecting the Conference, and hoped the Prince of Wales would read my *excellent* letter to the King of Greece. '*En voilà du sucre.*'"

And so the middle days of December saw Clarendon in his old room at Whitehall, with Mr. Hammond respectfully laying despatches upon his table, and the red boxes streaming in as before.

CHAPTER XXXIII
WORKING FOR PEACE

§ 1

EUROPEAN affairs were ominously tranquil. A conference was in progress, but not a very important one, and no unfortunate questions appeared likely to arise out of it. All seemed well. Our relations with the United States were strained owing to the eternally protracted negotiations with regard to the Alabama claims. It was a highly technical dispute on a matter of international law, and although angry recriminations were bandied from one side of the ocean to the other, it was very difficult to believe that in the end the situation would result in war. Clarendon worked endlessly and patiently on at the files with Mr. Reverdy-Johnson, the American Ambassador; and just as these two had concluded a treaty to submit the claims of both sides to arbitration, and were congratulating themselves and each other upon the happy issue, the Government of America played its well-known trick of repudiating the work of the man on the spot, proclaiming that arbitration was derogatory to the honour of the United States, and declaring the treaty that Johnson had concluded with Clarendon to be null and void. Whereupon the endless negotiations had to begin all over again on a new footing.

But though these and other such negotiations confronted Clarendon, the remoter but far more important question of Franco-Prussian relations was never far from his mind. And it so happened that an incident now occurred which indirectly had a bearing on those relations, which served to aggravate the ill-feeling already smouldering in both countries. The spring of 1869 was spent largely in negotiations—successful in the end—directed to divert a rupture over this incident.

The affair was trivial in its origin. A French and a Belgian railway company, whose lines adjoined, desired to amalgamate. The Belgian Cabinet, sensing a beginning of "peaceful penetration" on the part of France, passed a Bill which forbade concessions to foreign railway companies taking place without the authorisation of the Government. France, which was in a highly excitable condition, took fire; the Emperor rattled his sabre; a wave of ill-feeling swept over the country; and the English Press declared that Napoleon was creeping stealthily into Belgium by the back door. The Queen, always the instinctive mouthpiece of British opinion, gave her views on our obligations towards Belgium.

"The Queen," runs a memorandum of hers to Clarendon, ". . . has invariably expressed the strongest opinion that England was bound, not only by the obligations of Treaties, but by interests of vital importance to herself, to maintain the integrity and independence as well as the neutrality of Belgium; and that the best security for these essential objects would be found in the knowledge that any proceedings which seemed to threaten their violation would bring England at once into the field. The Queen did not mean that any official communication should be made on the subject, but that the habitual language of our Ministers at Berlin and Paris should be such as to leave no doubt as to the determination of England."

Clarendon was anxious, for he knew that any circumstance which severed Great Britain from France would play straight into the hands of Bismarck.

Prussia was not frightened of France. She guessed that France had nothing that could equal the efficiency of the new German fighting machine, either as to its organisation or its equipment. But behind France stood England. And at the helm of foreign affairs in England stood one of the most experienced diplomatists in Europe, and moreover one who Bismarck had now reason to known was fully alive to the hideous danger to France that the existence of this new Germany army constituted. And France, blind to everything but her own immediate *panache*, was playing Germany's game. Clarendon implored Lord Lyons to use the greatest discretion with all sides in Paris—not that he had not the highest confidence in Lord Lyons as a diplomatist, but that he considered the situation very grave.

The Emperor was on his high horse, and Clarendon feared that war with Germany might be the ultimate result of this quarrel with Belgium. The idea that France should embark upon such an undertaking, deprived by her own unwarrantable behaviour of British sympathy, was a cause of great distress to him. He sent a despatch to the Emperor himself exhorting forbearance. The reply, full of assurances of "good faith" and "eternal friendship," far from reassured Clarendon, who more than ever suspected the Emperor's motives, while the blindness of the French to the German menace astounded and provoked him.

"The policy of the French Government is perfectly understood at Berlin," he writes to Lord Lyons at this time, "where the leading object of Bismarck is to detach us from France. We might to-morrow, if we pleased, enter into a coalition with Prussia against France for the protection of Belgian independence, which is a European, and not exclusively French, question; but we will do nothing of the kind so long as there is a hope that France will act with common honesty. . . .

" I send you rather a curious despatch from Loftus. Bismarck's ways are inscrutable, and he is never to be relied on, but he had a union with us against France in his head ever since the Belgian business began, for Bernstorff, who never speaks without instructions, has said on more than one occasion to Gladstone and to me, that though Prussia would not undertake to defend Belgium singlehanded, as that country concerned England more nearly than Prussia, yet that we had but to say the word and we should soon come to terms. I treated it, as did Gladstone, rather as a *façon de parler*, and a ruse to detach us from France, which is Bismarck's main object, as I did not choose that Bernstorff should have to report the slightest encouragement to the suggestion, but it *may* come to that after all."

Meanwhile Prussia was behaving with exemplary restraint. Bismarck was far too great a diplomatist to show any excitement over the Belgian affair. Besides dropping a few hints in political circles, he stood superbly aloof. The time was not ripe; the curtain must not rise yet on the drama that he had prepared. The stage was set: the pulleys were ready; the back-cloths in position to rise and descend; the men to work them in their places. Only the bell from the auditorium—that little thin pencil of sound that should tell him that the audience, too, was ready—*that* had not struck yet. His eye was on the indicator. He watched Napoleon, and he watched Clarendon. And as he smoked eternally his curled meerschaum pipe, no one—except perhaps von Moltke— could say what was passing behind that strange, inscrutable countenance.

But all was not well with France. For eighteen years Napoleon had governed that country by the free exercise of his own personal will. His successful antics upon the stage of Europe, his great reputation, his more or less brilliant campaigns had so impressed his faithful subjects that they had been content thus to be ruled by him. But his star was no longer in the ascendant. Opposition had been growing, actual opposition to his dynasty, as well as theoretic Liberal and Socialist opposition to his position as an absolute monarch. France, fickle always to her forms of government, was becoming restless and ill at ease with this one. Change was coming; change was in the air.

Clarendon, whose insight into French politics was knowledgeable and profound, made a prophetic statement to Lyons that summer: " I have an instinct that they will drift into a Republic before another year is over," he wrote on August 31st, 1869. The Republic was actually proclaimed at Paris on September 4th,

1870. But Clarendon was not alive to have the melancholy satisfaction of seeing his prophecy fulfilled.

And now, in the early days of the year, there opened the last phase in that drama of suspense that was straining the sinews of France and Germany to breaking point. On the surface all seemed calm, all seemed for the best. But behind the politicians the nations were beginning to take fire. All the old racial and sociological rivalries between the Latin and Nordic peoples began to smoulder and burn in the heart of each nation, till they sprang into flame, in those last fateful July days, with the cries, "à Berlin" and "nach Paris."

History has proved that with Prussia the whole process was planned and deliberate.

"It must be confessed," reflected Bismarck to Treitschke, "that our linen was not always of the cleanest."

And thought with France the causes which led to the war cannot be said to have been fabricated, still, the challenge of Germany—when it came—coincided with a national restlessness, and found a ready response in the desire for change on a grand scale.

§ 2

Both nations, for different reasons, were pushed inevitably towards the destiny that awaited them. But in January, 1870, there appeared still to be time, still a possibility, that the course of events could be stayed; and the new French Government—faced by the necessity of imposing enormous and unpopular taxes for the continued maintenance of an army sufficient to cope with Prussia in the event of war—approached Clarendon delicately on the subject of Continental armaments.

"I had a long talk with La Valette to-day about disarmament," Clarendon writes to Lord Lyons on January 26th. "It is no new subject to me," he continues, "but one which I have long had at heart, although it presents serious difficulties on account of the King of Prussia's obstinacy. He does not meditate, or desire, war—far from it. But his army is his idol, and he won't make himself an iconoclast. Not so the Crown Prince, with whom I discussed the subject at great length a year ago. Our relations with Prussia are very friendly, and perhaps we are in as good a position as any other Power to make an attempt to bell the cat; and Count Daru may be sure that I will do all I can to meet his views, but I am sure that he will agree that some tact and *ménagement* are necessary."

Four days later the new Prime Minister, Ollivier, himself called upon Lord Lyons and further emphasised the necessity to France of Prussian disarmament.   He was very grateful for Clarendon's promise to use his good offices impartially and confidentially in Berlin; and he impressed Lord Lyons with the fact that he would not let the matter drop, but was anxious to go very insistently and thoroughly into the whole question.   Such negotiations as Clarendon could undertake must be—as Clarendon pointed out— of a purely confidential nature, and such as would compromise neither France nor Great Britain.   With this Ollivier was in entire agreement.   And upon his own responsibility, and without the knowledge of the Cabinet, Clarendon set about the delicate task which had been imposed upon him by France.   It was, as he said, a question he had very much at heart himself, the importance of which for the well-being of Europe was too obvious to labour.   But he had very little hope for the success of his efforts.   The Prussian army was the crowning glory of the old King of Prussia, and it was unlikely that he would consent to have it tampered with at the bidding of France.   However, Clarendon was determined to open the question with Bismarck at the first opportunity.

This occurred sooner than he expected; for only a few days after Clarendon's letter to Lyons, Count Bernstorff came to the Foreign Office with a despatch from Bismarck in which allusion was made to the friendly interest which Lord Clarendon had always shown in the welfare of Prussia, with other complimentary phrases to the same effect.   This gave Clarendon his text for a sermon on the question of armaments in Europe.   He replied to the despatch in a Memorandum which Lord Augustus Loftus was instructed to present confidentially and in person to Bismarck. The memorandum runs as follows:

" FOREIGN OFFICE,
" *February 2nd*, 1870.

" A few days ago Count Bernstorff read to me a despatch from Count Bismarck concerning the German Confederation, which contained some allusions to myself that gave me particular satisfaction, as a proof that Count Bismarck recognised the sincerity of my interest in the welfare and greatness of Germany.

"If I am not mistaken in this hope, he will not think that I abuse the confidence he seems disposed to place in me by asking him privately through you to consider a subject that I have long had at heart; and in making this request, it is, I am sure, unnecessary for me to disclaim any intention to interfere in the internal affairs of Prussia—such an intention would be alike presumptuous and useless.

" But it is in the general interest of Europe, of peace, and of humanity, that I desire to invite the attention of Count Bismarck to the enormous standing armies that now afflict Europe by constituting a state of things that is neither peace nor war, but

which is so destructive of confidence that men almost desire war
with all its horrors in order to arrive at some certainty of peace
—a state of things which withdraws millions of hands from pro-
ductive industry and heavily taxes the people to their own injury,
and renders them discontented with their rulers. It is a state of
things, in short, that no thoughtful man can contemplate without
sorrow and alarm; for this system is cruel, it is out of harmony
with the civilization of our age, and it is pregnant with danger.

"To modify this system would be a glorious work; it is one
that Prussia, better than any other Power, might undertake. She
would not only earn for herself the gratitude of Europe, but give
a great proof of her morality and power; it would be a fitting
complement of the military successes she has achieved.

"I know full well the difficulties that would beset such a
course of policy. I know how great and deserved is the King's
parental feeling and affection for his army; that he would view
its reduction with pain, and that he might not think it safe to
diminish its numerical force; but His Majesty is wise and foreseeing, and his moral courage is always equal to the measures
he believes to be right; and should Count Bismarck think it not
inconsistent with his duty to recommend a partial disarmament
to the King, I cannot but consider that the moment is a singularly
propitious one for the purpose.

"The great standing army of France would, of course, come
first under the consideration of the King, but France has been
never more peacefully disposed than at the present time, under
a responsible Government which cannot make war 'for an idea,'
because it represents a nation that is determined to maintain
peace so long as there is no just cause for war, and because the
Emperor entirely shares the feelings of his people. I know that
the present Government of France will seek for popularity and
power in a peaceful policy and in economy, notwithstanding the
vast and increasing wealth of the country, and the almost proverbial indifference of the people to taxation.

"There would consequently, I am convinced, be no opposition
on the part of the French Government to a reduction of the army
pari passu with Prussia. For reasons, however, quite intelligible,
neither Government may choose to take the initiative in such a
proposal; but if I had authority to do so, I do not doubt that the
Queen would allow me to sound the ground at Paris, in a manner
entirely confidential, that should in no way compromise either
Government, whatever might be the result of the suggestion.

"Pray read this letter to Count Bismarck with the sincere
expression of my esteem."

The innocence of this document measures the extent to which
Bismarck had masked his purpose. Nobody in Europe suspected
that ever since Sadowa the Prussian army had been reserved for
the destruction of France; that Bismarck and von Moltke were
only biding their time—waiting for the supreme opportunity to

"go in and win." But in justice to Clarendon and to the French
politicals, who were honestly seeking disarmament for its own
sake and for the welfare of the peace of the nations concerned, it
must be said that the kind of calculated cold-blooded murder
that Bismarck was contemplating was new to the politics of
Europe. They did not suspect it, because they had never experienced it. Craft, chicanery, double-crossing, all the normal
ills which diplomacy is heir to, these they were perfectly conver-
sant with. But the amorality of the Prussian scheme, the gigantic
cynicism and contempt for human values which enabled two men
to contemplate the wanton ruin of an Empire, their neighbour and
till now their friend, for the sake of national aggrandisement and
aggrandisement only; this, it must be confessed, had very rarely
been met with in Europe since the dark ages.

Lord Augustus Loftus dutifully presented Clarendon's document to Count Bismarck, and an interesting conversation ensued.
Bismarck was quick enough to see that, although he might leave
an unfavourable impression on the British Ambassador's mind,
the report of the conversation in London and Paris must not be
such that every door upon the disarmament question seemed
slammed to—and by Germany. He temporised. The question,
bristling with difficulties, must appear postponed. He laughed
at Loftus.

"You," he said, "live in a happy island, and have not to
fear an invasion. We are surrounded by three great Empires
with armies as large as our own, any two of whom might coalesce
against us."

What guarantee could be given for the maintenance of peace and
the security against danger? The whole question was very difficult. Look at the situation as it was last spring, he said. France
was in a highly aggressive mood. Even England did not know
what she would do next. This danger occurred only ten months
ago, and who can say that it may not occur again?

And then—and this was really his trump card—he sheltered
behind the King. It was well known in Europe that the Prussian
Army was the glory and delight of its King. Bismarck played
this for all it was worth.

"He said that he did not even dare to mention the subject of
your letter to the King," writes the crestfallen ambassador,
"much less show it to His Majesty. He would get into a fury
and immediately think that England was trying to weaken
Prussia at the expense of France. . . .

"I left your letter marked 'Confidential' in Bismarck's hands,
as I thought it essential that he should reflect upon the powerful
arguments it contains. . . .

"It is evident to me that there is not the smallest chance of inducing the King to listen to a reduction of his army, and I must fear that any proposals to him of this nature would only make him suspicious and distrustful of England."

But such a letter as Clarendon's required an official reply; and in the middle of February it came. It was a lengthy document, and characterised so as to allay suspicion and postpone the issue.

In the first paragraph Bismarck analysed Clarendon's plea for disarmament, and the latter's belief that the present was (owing to the pacific attitude of the French Government) an auspicious moment for launching such a project. Subsequently he expressed the view that every European State desired to see peace established and confidence maintained. Moreover, there was also, he averred, a practical side to this laudable desire for peace. "No German Government," he protested, "would wish to impose upon its people the maintenance of an army in excess of that proportion for which the requirements of its safety imperatively called." Then in words which echo curiously to-day he qualifies his acceptance of the principle of disarmament in these terms:

"We must reserve to ourselves the right of making a careful estimate of the relative positions of the Parties most deeply interested in the matter, and of judging whether the concessions which we ourselves might be expected to make stand in a fair and just proportion to those which it would be in the power of other nations to make."

Then follows the well-worn argument of Germany's geographic position—surrounded by rearming nations with no frontier assured. "Ringed round with bayonets" was the phrase used forty-four years later to describe a similar situation. Under these circumstances, the memorandum concluded, Clarendon must understand that Germany needed a bigger army than any other nation. Her position was unique. Could not the British Foreign Minister accept the view that so far from provoking war, Prussia's arms were a guarantee of peace?

When Count Daru heard the result of Clarendon's first effort he decided that France should set the example by reducing her own armaments as a show of good faith. But he implored Clarendon to continue negotiations in Berlin and to keep him informed on the results.

Clarendon wrote another memorandum, which he instructed Lord Augustus Loftus to read to Bismarck.

In this document he first drew attention to England's impartial rôle in any negotiation concerning disarmament, for it was obvious, he said, that England herself would never become a military power on the Continental scale, yet the peace, progress and prosperity of the Continent were her deep concern. He then declared his belief that the independence and honour of Prussia were essentially beneficial to Europe, but he questioned whether it were true that they were menaced. Could it honestly be said that Russia, Austria or France had evil intentions with regard to Prussia? Russia was well-known to be wholly engaged in Eastern expansion. Austria, dilapidated and disorganised, could not be considered dangerous. France, it was true, had 400,000 men under arms, whereas Prussia had only 300,000; but then the garrison of the French colonies and of certain important towns accounted for 100,000 French soldiers. When this was taken into consideration, it appeared that the striking weapon of both countries was equal. The forces of the great Continental Powers bore a certain proportion to each other; if by a common agreement each were to reduce its army by a certain number of men, the same proportion would be maintained, whilst the heavy burden would be alleviated.

France, he maintained, had already given proof of goodwill by reducing her annual conscription figures by one-tenth. This reduction might have been greater had Prussia shown any willingness to follow her lead. If Prussia did not alter her attitude, hers "must be the responsibility not only of maintaining so large a force herself, but of compelling other countries reluctantly to do the same."

Lord Augustus Loftus read this letter aloud to Bismarck, who made only two comments. In the first place, he thought that Clarendon had overestimated the number of French troops used to garrison the colonies. In the second place, he felt that France's pacific intentions arose largely from her Constitutional Government, which, as he pointed out, had only been in power for three months, and might be overthrown at any moment. In the discussion that followed between Lord Augustus and Bismarck on the text of the memorandum, Bismarck suggested that Clarendon, in his calculations, had excluded the possibility of an alliance between Austria and France. He further complained of the tone of the French Press and of the suspicious behaviour of the Danes.

Lord Augustus was left with the impression that, whilst wishing to appear not adverse to disarmament, Prussia had every intention of hedging the question round with so many conditions that no solution would be able to be found to it. Bismarck ended on a satirical note warning Lord Augustus that "care would have to be taken that the question of disarmament should not become one of contention, which might be followed perhaps by war." He promised to show Clarendon's memorandum to the King and let the British Minister know of its effect upon him in due course.

But Bismarck was sure of his ground. Not only was he certain
that the King would view the political aspect of disarmament in
an unfavourable light, but he knew further that any disarmament
sufficient to meet the proposals which were being made would
necessitate a repeal of legislative acts concerning the army, and
thereby imply a change in the whole Prussian military system,
which of course was not to be thought of. He had no fear of
showing Clarendon's memorandum to the King. He did so; and
" Most Gracious " was not at all pleased. He viewed the proposal as entirely inspired by French policy, and considered that
there was no regard for the safety of Prussia in the whole scheme.
Bismarck summoned Lord Augustus Loftus to an interview, and
broke the substance of the King's views none too gently to him.
In a tone of banter he again stressed the fact that England was an
island and not subject to these complicated considerations of self-
defence—except, of course, in regard to her Navy. When asked
by the astute old statesman to consider what reply England would
make to a suggestion that she should curtail her naval armaments,
the British Ambassador replied rather weakly that after all we
had just sold an ironclad to Prussia and were in negotiation to sell
others too—a retort which was received with the irreverent merriment it deserved.

" I saw," wrote the crestfallen Minister, " that it was useless to
pursue the question further."

Clarendon realised that the game was up. He wrote to Lord
Lyons in Paris instructing him to inform the French Ministers
that at the moment no useful purpose could be served in continuing the negotiations in Berlin. It was essential not to aggravate Prussia on the subject of armaments. Nothing further, he
thought, could be done until the French estimates came to be
discussed the following year, when, if it were shown that France
had set the example herself by considerably reducing her own
armaments, the matter might again be broached in Berlin. At
present he felt that the question should be allowed to drop.

§ 3

Looking at the problem in the light of after-events, two points
become clear. The first is the complete divergence of opinion
between France and Germany as to what constituted " aggression " in the particular case between them. France considered
that the absorption of any of the States of the Southern Confederation by Prussia would be an act of aggression—every whit as
much an act of aggression as if France herself absorbed them.
Prussia quite honestly considered that what happened within the

borders of Germany concerned nobody in Europe but the German people. Prussia knew that the Confederation of the South with the North was only a matter of time. She would not pledge herself not to work for it by every means in her power.

The second point that emerges from these negotiations is this: that Bismarck was only temporising. He had not the slightest intention of disarming or delimiting the Prussian effectives. To use Lord Newton's words, "It was the fixed and inexorable determination of Bismarck to force a conflict upon France whenever the favourable opportunity should arise."*

It is almost impossible for us, who know so well what followed after, to put ourselves mentally back into a Europe that did not suspect Bismarck's purposes. But as I have emphasised above, that kind of ruthlessness, the complete indifference to political morality that Bismarck's attitude implies, was something new in Europe. Nobody suspected it because nobody was on the lookout for it. Dangerous situations might arise between two countries and be dealt with by diplomacy—or war. But the kind of deliberate destruction which Bismarck was planning for France, first twisting her by crooked diplomacy into a position wherein she must fight for her honour against odds known to himself and von Moltke to be final and overwhelming—this was conduct strange to the custom and comity of the European family, and Foreign Secretaries may be pardoned for not suspecting the presence of this vile and un-Christian thing, even when it was festering in their very midst.

Clarendon, though he was very anxious over the situation between France and Prussia, did not gauge the full measure of Bismarck's policy. Nor certainly did the French Foreign Secretary, Count Daru. His suggestion that France should reduce her recruits by 10,000 men must have made Bismarck smile, as also Clarendon's homilies upon the beauties and benefits of peace. And yet Bismarck feared Clarendon; the latter, he knew, was fully aware that Prussia was up to something; he was a great force for peace in Europe, and he carried great weight. England was always an uncertain factor in European crises. And England was friends with Napoleon and with France. A Whig Government was in office, and the Liberals in England entertained chimerical ideals concerning war and peace, right and wrong, and such-like inconvenient notions. They were not realists in the modern sense. Was it coincidence or was it of set purpose that the bomb of the Hohenzollern candidature was not thrown till a fortnight after Lord Clarendon's death?

A year or so afterwards, when Clarendon's daughter, Lady Odo Russell, afterwards Lady Ampthill, was Ambassadress in Berlin,

* *Lord Lyons*, by Lord Newton.

she went with her husband to a party, where as it happened she sat next to Bismarck at dinner. It was their first meeting, and he turned to her quizzically:

"Never in my life, dear lady," he said, "was I more glad to hear of anything than I was to hear of your father's death."

The Ambassadress bridled, whereupon the old man patted her hand.

"Ach," he said, "you must not take it like that. What I mean is, that if your father had lived, he would have prevented the War."

Was it a pretty speech to a woman, or was it the sober truth? Bismarck was not much given to making pretty speeches. And it is a matter of history that he had waited till Clarendon was out of the way to cry, "Havoc."

The negotiations which Clarendon had conducted broke down in March. He did not revert again to the subject with Bismarck. But for the moment the sky seemed clear, and Prussia for the next three months was careful to give no sign of offence to France. It was the lull before the storm.

CHAPTER XXXIV

THE END

§ 1

IT had been a harassing year for Clarendon, quite apart from the onus of these negotiations. As we have seen, he was by no means well. Since 1867 his constitution, so robust and resilient of old, had shown signs of wear and tear. He suffered now from frequent attacks of gout, from which he did not recover as quickly as formerly. His spirits, however, were as good as ever, as was his interest in foreign politics. But home politics had been strenuous and fatiguing since his return to office, and the Cabinet had already on one occasion been nearly broken up. Gladstone came to power with the fixed determination to deal with Ireland. He declared sententiously that the "three branches of the Upas tree were the Church, the Land and Education." And he proceeded to deal with all three of them. In the session of 1869 he laid his axe to the Church by introducing a sweeping and highly controversial Disestablishment Bill, which he piloted thunderously through Parliament in the spring and summer. It came before the Lords in June, and Clarendon spoke in favour of it, citing his own experience in Ireland, and maintaining that in the light of it he considered the Bill was both just and necessary. It was not a very telling speech, but his friends appeared pleased. Socially he was seen everywhere that season, tall, bent, looking a little frail and withered and grey, but still *gaillard*. His laugh, that slow, protracted chuckle that exploded at length into a long, ringing cachinnation, was still heard in the salons and drawing-rooms of London, and it still had its effect. Everybody was charmed by the presence of Lord Clarendon. He still delighted in society, and he and Kathy were inveterate diners-out.

In the summer of 1869 he decided to give a Ball at the Foreign Office. But when he discovered that 4,000 people were the fewest that had a right to be asked on such an occasion, even *his* social talents quailed before such an undertaking, and he gave two big evening parties instead.

August and a part of September saw him at Wiesbaden again, with half an eye cocked upon European affairs while he sipped his waters and took his baths. Russian politics were a little uncertain, and, though he was on holiday—well, there was no reason why he should not have a talk with the powers that be.

". . . I have done my Gortchakoff," he writes to Lady Salisbury on September 7th, "having met him at Heidelberg as a place equi-distant between here and Baden. The Conference lasted three and a half hours; and we agreed that it *must* lead to a right good understanding between the Lion and the Bear . . . perhaps, however, the crafty man was only practising upon my youth and innocence."

Clarendon was back in time to grapple with Gladstone's Irish Land Act, which that indefatigable reformer began to expound in the autumn Cabinets. As early as May, Gladstone was preparing the framework of his second great Irish measure, and Granville, getting an inkling of its scope, warned him " the question may break us up." It very nearly did. Clarendon was hotly opposed to it; so were the Duke of Argyll, Lowe and Cardwell. These four wrangled incessantly with Gladstone at all the Cabinets held on the subject.

" Cabinet—chiefly on Ireland, and stiff," notes the Prime Minister laconically in his diary on November 3rd.

But the great Liberal statesman pursued the even tenor of his way undeterred by the protests of his lieutenants. He was, of course, by far the most remarkable personality in the Cabinet. His eloquence and erudition, his persuasive optimism, coupled with the extraordinary power he had of investing any measure his ingenuity might devise with an overwhelming sense of necessity, finally wore the opposition down, and the Cabinet presented a united front to the world by the time Gladstone came to introduce the Bill in the House. No resignations occurred.

§ 2

The months passed. Christmas came, and there were festivities at the Grove. Clarendon was a grandfather many times over by now, and he was never so happy as when his daughters and their progeny were all gathered together under his own hospitable roof. He would sit in his chair by the fire, watching with delight the antics of the younger generation. His eyes would sparkle and his laugh would ring out. And then when the scene fatigued him he would rise and wander off to his library to read, to write his letters and to smoke his endless cigarettes.

February was a bad month. It was dark and chill and foggy, and most of the Cabinet were ill.

The Duke of Argyll writes in his diary, February 8th:

" Called on Gladstone at 11—, found him seedy, and heard of the illness of Bright, Clarendon and Granville."

The same evening he received the following from Granville:

"MY DEAR ARGYLL,

"It is impossible to be too much alarmed at the state of health of the most eminent of the Cabinet. Poor Bright is gone, as far as this session is concerned. Clarendon was only saved from gout in the stomach by strong stimulants to his feet. Gladstone told Bessborough yesterday that he was sometimes alarmed for his own head. Cardwell at the last Cabinet sat close in to the fire, looking as if he wished to cut his throat, which was probably only the beginning of an influenza.

"I cannot say how sorry I am about Bright.

"Yours,

"G.

"(with head and throat stuffed with cold.)"*

The turn of the year was having its effect on all and sundry. But the spring came; the trees burgeoned in the parks; and the warm sun rehabilitated most. Clarendon, temporarily recovered, plied in his carriage between Grosvenor Crescent and Downing Street; the red boxes streamed in as usual, and still Mr. Hammond, with careful selection, laid the papers and letters on his great desk at the Foreign Office. He was able to cross Whitehall on foot, and he was often seen in his place in the House of Lords in the early summer. But in June his old enemy came to grips with him for the last time.

He was in the House, though slightly ailing, on the 24th; and he transacted business as late as the evening of the 25th. But that night he was assailed by a violent attack of gout. They applied stimulants to his feet, but from the first the family realised that his condition was grave. His colour was strange; he looked withered and shrivelled. They sent for Hyde, and he came. All next day the family watched and waited. But they had not long to wait. The twenty-seventh dawned. The sun was already bright upon the window-panes, and the jingle of carts floated heedlessly in from the direction of Belgrave Square, when, shortly after six o'clock, the watchers by the bedside realised that the change had come. Clarendon was dead, and death had overtaken him in the midst of his activities. On the coverlet, beside the still figure on the bed, lay two red boxes, which had been sent round the night before by the dutiful Mr. Hammond, and which Clarendon had insisted upon having by him for inspection later.

His death took the political world by surprise. Gladstone was shocked. The entry in his diary is laconic, but shows the extent of his liking and appreciation of Clarendon:

* Diary of the Duke of Argyll.

"An irreparable colleague, a statesman of many gifts, a most lovable and genial man," he wrote;

while John Russell at Pembroke Lodge was filing a letter he had received as late as the 25th, and writing on the envelope with careful accuracy:

"Lord Clarendon died on June 27th at six o'clock in the morning."

Deep and sincere feeling was shown in the House of Lords that night. Lord Granville rose to make an obituary speech. He spoke, as *The Times* said, under deep emotion.

". . . Your Lordships are aware," he said, "of the loss which the Sovereign, the people, and the family and friends of Lord Clarendon have this day sustained. I had known him from a boy; he was one of my dearest and most intimate friends, and I had an opportunity in political life, and as political colleague, of observing his singular ability, his great sagacity, his long experience, the moderation of his views, and those brilliant conversational powers which were almost exclusively used for the purposes of conciliation, and which gave such personal weight, not only with his own countrymen, but with all the Sovereigns of Europe with whom he came in contact; with their political Ministers, and with all the diplomatic representatives of the whole civilized world. (Cheers.)
"I believe there is no member of this House who has so many warmly attached friends as Lord Clarendon had. I am quite sure that he had no enemy here, and I believe there are very few of your Lordships who had not feelings of personal friendship towards him." (Cheers.)

After giving reasons why he considered that the business of the House should not be postponed on account of their loss, he concludes:

"I feel that the great man whom we have lost, dying under the weight of affairs, in the very act of trying to arrange a matter necessary with regard to civilization in Europe; he who, though he enjoyed life socially and domestically, as much as anybody I ever knew, would postpone everything to public business and duty to his country, would himself have preferred that we should not adopt an unusual course, whatever our feelings may be." (Cheers.)

Derby, who spoke next, also showed signs of great emotion:

". . . To the Members of this House, and not to us only, but I may venture to say to all the upper class of this country, Lord Clarendon set the example of a life of indefatigable industry passed in the service of the State. He has died in harness. Never again shall we hear those conversational powers in which counsels of the maturest wisdom were conveyed in language at once so simple, so unaffected, and so convincing. His memory will long flourish in our hearts, and even in these days of rapid change, England will not lightly forget a character so remarkable, and a career so brilliant.''

Lord Cowley rose to add his tribute to the memory of his friend. But after vainly endeavouring to articulate a sentence or two his emotion overcame him, and he resumed his seat amid the sympathetic murmurs of the House. Lord Westbury, who was down to introduce a highly controversial motion that night, agreed to postpone it. And in a somewhat chastened mood the House proceeded to a discussion of the Irish Land Act, which was before it at the time. *The Times* noted a distinct abatement in the acrimonious nature of the debate as compared with two nights earlier. It was as if Lord Clarendon's unseen but con- ciliatory presence was felt as a restraining influence in their lord- ships' deliberations. *The Times* mourned the departed Secretary of State in a long obituary of two columns (which was mostly a compendium of the facts of his life and career), and in a leading article which discussed his attributes and qualities. Already he was placed in an earlier category of statesmen, and a sharp contrast drawn between that category and a certain new tribe of poli- ticians faintly discernible since the Act of 1869, and destined, though *The Times* could hardly foresee this, to be the bane of later Parliamentary life in England: that race of political men— themselves the outcome of competitive examinations—whose policy is based on statistics and whose outlook is prescribed by Committees.

Far away in Germany Bismarck smiled. On the whole, all things were working for the best. At home, Granville succeeded Clarendon at the Foreign Office, where Mr. Hammond observed that never in the whole course of his experience could he remem- ber so tranquil a moment in the course of foreign affairs. This unfortunate statement was made on July 5th. Two hours later the news of the Hohenzollern candidature burst like a bomb upon an unsuspecting world. By the 15th, France and Prussia were at war.

BIBLIOGRAPHY

Clarendon Papers :

(a) Documents and Papers in the possession of the present Earl of Clarendon.

(b) Documents and Papers in the possession of the author—including the correspondence of the Fourth Countess of Clarendon.

Diaries of the First Earl of Verulam in the possession of the present Earl of Verulam.

Journal of the Fourth Countess of Clarendon (incomplete) in the possession of the author.

Foreign Office Despatches, now at the Record Office.

Life and Letters of the Fourth Earl of Clarendon. Sir Herbert Maxwell, Bart. (2 vols.)

Life of Lord John Russell. Spencer Walpole. (2 vols.)

The Later Correspondence of Lord John Russell, 1840-1878. Edited by G. P. Gooch.

Life of H. J. Temple, Viscount Palmerston, with selections from his diaries and correspondence, by Bulwer Lytton. Edited Hon. E. Ashley. (2 vols.)

Palmerston, by Philip Guedalla.

Memoirs of William, Second Viscount Melbourne, by William Torrens.

Lord Melbourne, by Henry Dunckley.

Life of Wellington, by Sir Herbert Maxwell, Bart. (2 vols.)

Lord Melbourne, by Bertram Newman.

Autobiography and Memories of the Eighth Duke of Argyll. Edited by Dowager Duchess of Argyll. (1906.)

The Duke, by Philip Guedalla.

Viscount Stratford de Redcliffe, by Baroness Burghclere.

The Life of George, Fourth Earl of Aberdeen, K.G., by Lady Frances Balfour.

Life of Granville George Leveson-Gower, Second Earl of Granville, K.G., 1815-1891. Hon. F. Leveson-Gower.

Lord Lyons, by Lord Newton.

Diary and Correspondence of the First Lord Cowley, by the Hon. F. A. Wellesley.

Journals, Charles Greville.

The First Lady Wharncliffe and her Family, by Lord Stuart Wortley.

Memoirs and Memories, by Theresa Earle.

Letters of Dorothea, Princess Lieven, during her residence in London, 1812-1834. Edited by L. G. Robinson.

The Unpublished Diaries and Political Sketches of Princess Lieven. Edited by L. G. Robinson.

Recollections of Lady Georgiana Peel.

Letters of Harriet, Countess of Granville. Edited by the Hon. F. Leveson-Gower. (2 vols.)

In Whig Society, by Mabell, Countess of Airlie.

Lady Palmerston and her Times, by Mabell, Countess of Airlie. (2 vols.)

The Earl of Beaconsfield, by Murray.

Life of Benjamin Disraeli, by Monypenny.

Gladstone, by John Morley.

Gladstone and Palmerston, by Philip Guedalla.

Talleyrand, by Duff-Cooper.

Metternich, by Algernon Cecil.

Letters of Emily Eden. Edited by Miss Dickinson.

A Great Lady's Friendships, by Baroness Burghclere.

Memoirs of Colonel Gronow. (2 vols.)

Queen Victoria, by Lytton Strachey.

Queen Victoria and Her Ministers, by Marriot.

Life of the Prince Consort, by Martin.

Letters of Queen Victoria.

Albert the Good, by Hector Bolitho.

Phases of the " Thirties," by Toynbee.

Political History of England, 1837-1901, by Sidney Low.

History of the English People, by Greene.

Annals of Our Times, 1837-1871.

The Political Progress of a Century, by MacKnight.

Guide to English History, by Cory.

The Paris Embassy during the Second Empire. Edited by Hon. F. A. Wellesley.

The Paris Embassy, 1800-1914.

The Second Empire, by Philip Guedalla.

Pamphlets on the Corn Laws. British Museum.

Pamphlets on the Great Reform Bill. British Museum.

Edinburgh Review, 1851. (January and April.)

Quarterly Review, 1856.

Eighty-five Years of Irish History, by Daunt. (2 vols.)

Recollections of Troubled Times in Irish History, by O'Sullivan.

Irish Memories, by O'Brien.

History of Ireland, 1798-1924, by the Right Hon. Sir James O'Connor. (2 vols.)

Ireland under English Rule, by Emmet. (2 vols.)

A Hundred Years of Irish History, by O'Brien.

An Irish Gentleman, by O'Moore.

Viceroys of Ireland, by O'Mahoney.

A Century of Spain and Portugal.

The War of Succession in Portugal and Spain, by Bolant.

A Queen at Bay, by D'Aubergne.

INDEX

INDEX
